PIRATE CLUB
BRAINWASH ESCAPE VICTIMS

Pirate Club

Brainwash Escape
VOLUME ONE Victims

Pirate Club: Brainwash Escape Victims, [Nov. 2005]. Published by SLG Publishing, P.O. Box 26427, San Jose, CA 85159-6427. Pirate Club is tm and c 2005 Derek Hunter, all rights reserved. no part of this publication may be reproduced without the permission of Derek Hunter and SLG Publishing, except for purposes of review. For a free catalog, call 1-800-866-8929 or visit our website at www.slavelabor.com. Printed in Canada.

art & story by:

derek hunter.

script assists:
elias pate & bryan young.

dedicated to:
rachel kay hunter

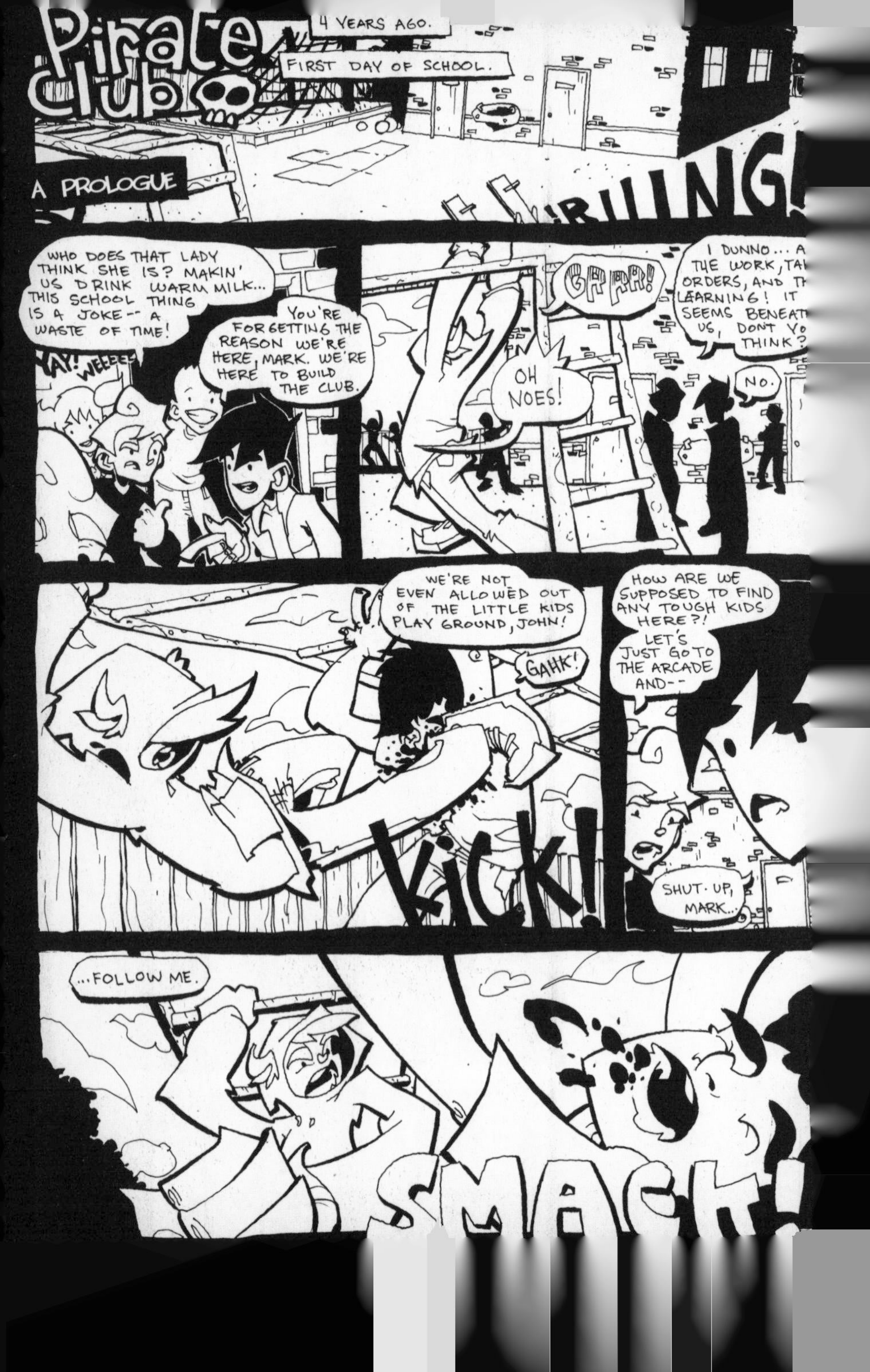
Pirate Club
A PROLOGUE
4 YEARS AGO.
FIRST DAY OF SCHOOL.
RIIIING!
WHO DOES THAT LADY THINK SHE IS? MAKIN' US DRINK WARM MILK... THIS SCHOOL THING IS A JOKE -- A WASTE OF TIME!
YAY! WEEEE!
YOU'RE FORGETTING THE REASON WE'RE HERE, MARK. WE'RE HERE TO BUILD THE CLUB.
GRRR!
OH NOES!
NO.
WE'RE NOT EVEN ALLOWED OUT OF THE LITTLE KIDS PLAY GROUND, JOHN!
GAHK!
KICK!
HOW ARE WE SUPPOSED TO FIND ANY TOUGH KIDS HERE?! LET'S JUST GO TO THE ARCADE AND--
SHUT UP, MARK...
...FOLLOW ME.
SMASH!

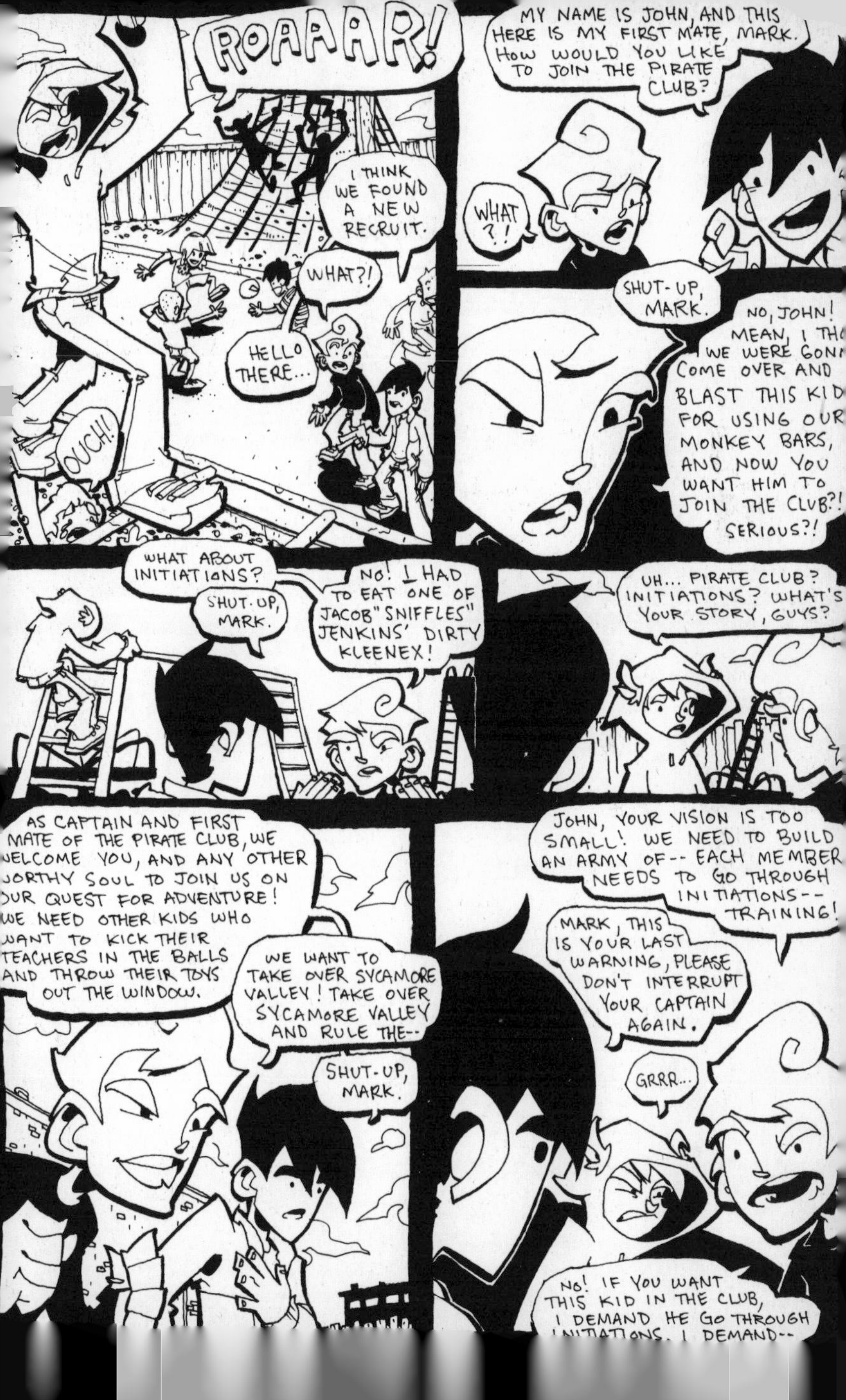
ROAAAR!
I THINK WE FOUND A NEW RECRUIT.
WHAT?!
HELLO THERE...
OUCH!
MY NAME IS JOHN, AND THIS HERE IS MY FIRST MATE, MARK. HOW WOULD YOU LIKE TO JOIN THE PIRATE CLUB?
WHAT?!
SHUT-UP, MARK.
NO, JOHN! MEAN, I THO WE WERE GONN COME OVER AND BLAST THIS KID FOR USING OUR MONKEY BARS, AND NOW YOU WANT HIM TO JOIN THE CLUB?! SERIOUS?!
WHAT ABOUT INITIATIONS?
SHUT-UP, MARK.
NO! I HAD TO EAT ONE OF JACOB "SNIFFLES" JENKINS' DIRTY KLEENEX!
UH... PIRATE CLUB? INITIATIONS? WHAT'S YOUR STORY, GUYS?
AS CAPTAIN AND FIRST MATE OF THE PIRATE CLUB, WE WELCOME YOU, AND ANY OTHER WORTHY SOUL TO JOIN US ON OUR QUEST FOR ADVENTURE! WE NEED OTHER KIDS WHO WANT TO KICK THEIR TEACHERS IN THE BALLS AND THROW THEIR TOYS OUT THE WINDOW.
WE WANT TO TAKE OVER SYCAMORE VALLEY! TAKE OVER SYCAMORE VALLEY AND RULE THE--
SHUT-UP, MARK.
JOHN, YOUR VISION IS TOO SMALL! WE NEED TO BUILD AN ARMY OF-- EACH MEMBER NEEDS TO GO THROUGH INITIATIONS-- TRAINING!
MARK, THIS IS YOUR LAST WARNING, PLEASE DON'T INTERRUPT YOUR CAPTAIN AGAIN.
GRRR...
NO! IF YOU WANT THIS KID IN THE CLUB, I DEMAND HE GO THROUGH INITIATIONS. I DEMAND--

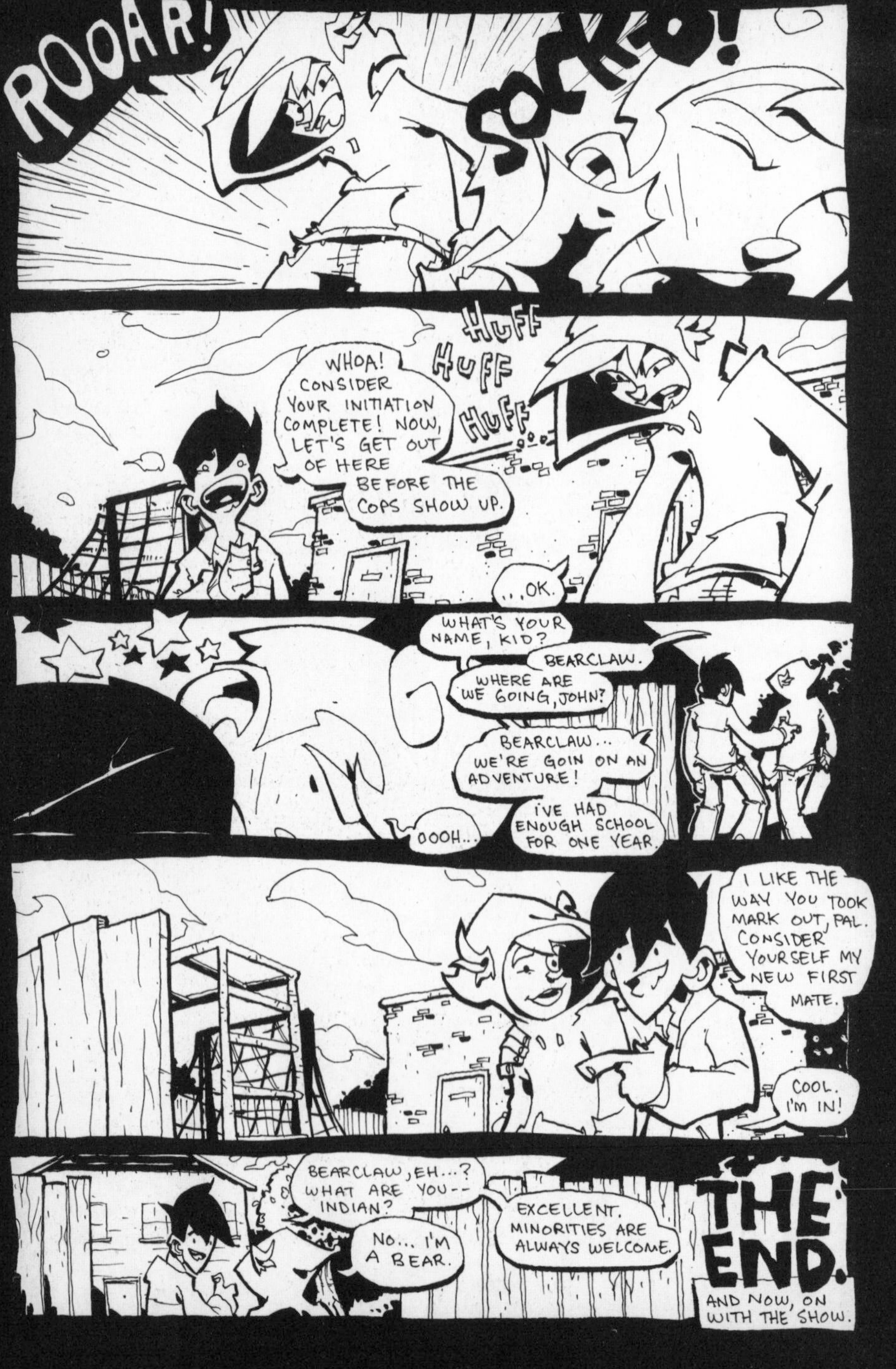
ROOAR!
SOCKO!
WHOA! CONSIDER YOUR INITIATION COMPLETE! NOW, LET'S GET OUT OF HERE BEFORE THE COPS SHOW UP.
HUFF HUFF HUFF
...OK.
WHAT'S YOUR NAME, KID?
BEARCLAW.
WHERE ARE WE GOING, JOHN?
BEARCLAW... WE'RE GOIN ON AN ADVENTURE!
I'VE HAD ENOUGH SCHOOL FOR ONE YEAR.
OOOH...
I LIKE THE WAY YOU TOOK MARK OUT, PAL. CONSIDER YOURSELF MY NEW FIRST MATE.
COOL. I'M IN!
BEARCLAW, EH...? WHAT ARE YOU-- INDIAN?
NO... I'M A BEAR.
EXCELLENT. MINORITIES ARE ALWAYS WELCOME.
THE END.
AND NOW, ON WITH THE SHOW.

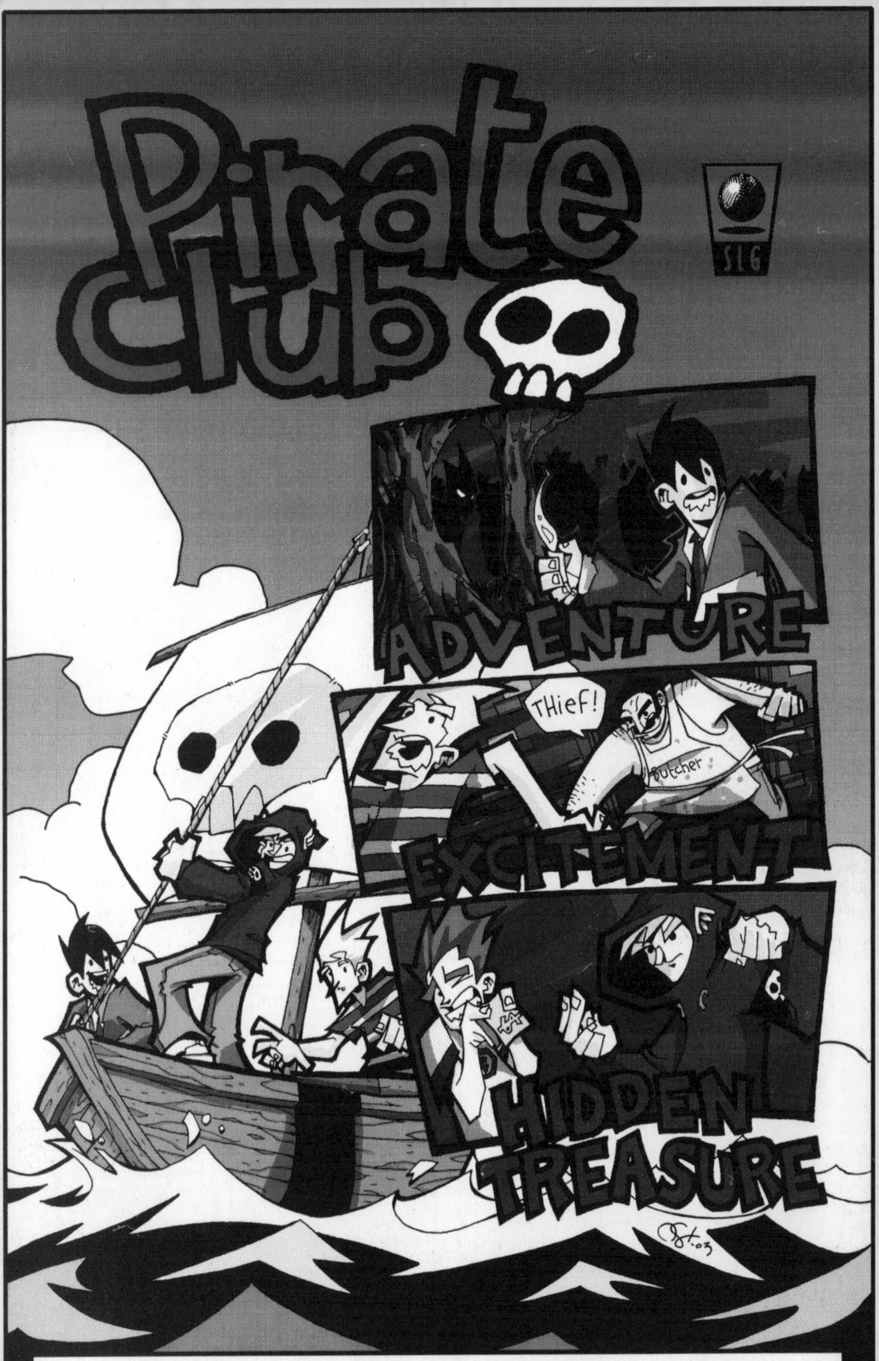
Pirate club
SLG
ADVENTURE
THief!
Butcher
EXCITEMENT
HIDDEN TREASURE

CHAPTER 1

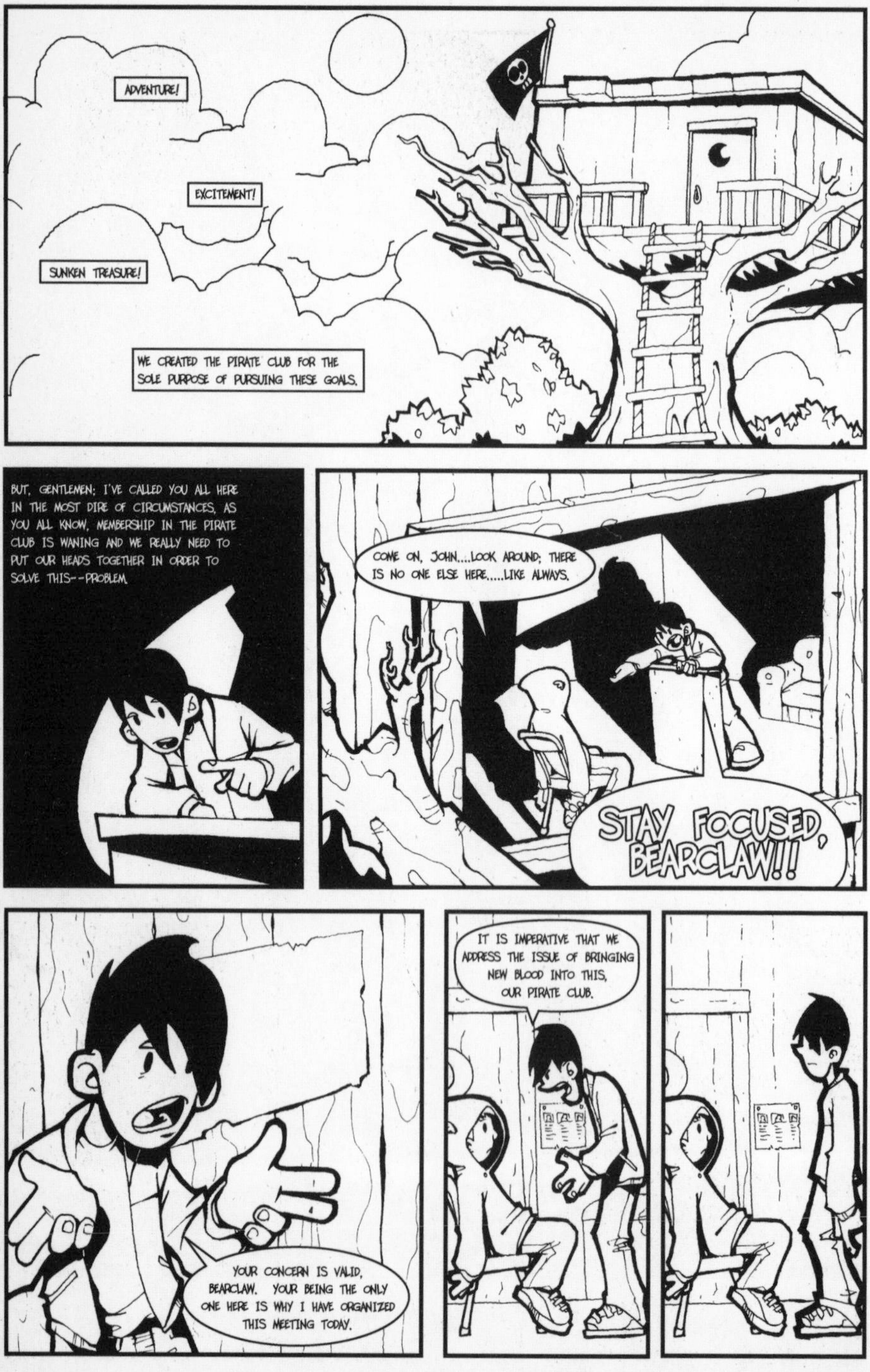
ADVENTURE!
EXCITEMENT!
SUNKEN TREASURE!
WE CREATED THE PIRATE CLUB FOR THE SOLE PURPOSE OF PURSUING THESE GOALS.
BUT, GENTLEMEN; I'VE CALLED YOU ALL HERE IN THE MOST DIRE OF CIRCUMSTANCES. AS YOU ALL KNOW, MEMBERSHIP IN THE PIRATE CLUB IS WANING AND WE REALLY NEED TO PUT OUR HEADS TOGETHER IN ORDER TO SOLVE THIS--PROBLEM.
COME ON, JOHN....LOOK AROUND; THERE IS NO ONE ELSE HERE.....LIKE ALWAYS.
STAY FOCUSED, BEARCLAW!!
YOUR CONCERN IS VALID, BEARCLAW. YOUR BEING THE ONLY ONE HERE IS WHY I HAVE ORGANIZED THIS MEETING TODAY.
IT IS IMPERATIVE THAT WE ADDRESS THE ISSUE OF BRINGING NEW BLOOD INTO THIS, OUR PIRATE CLUB.

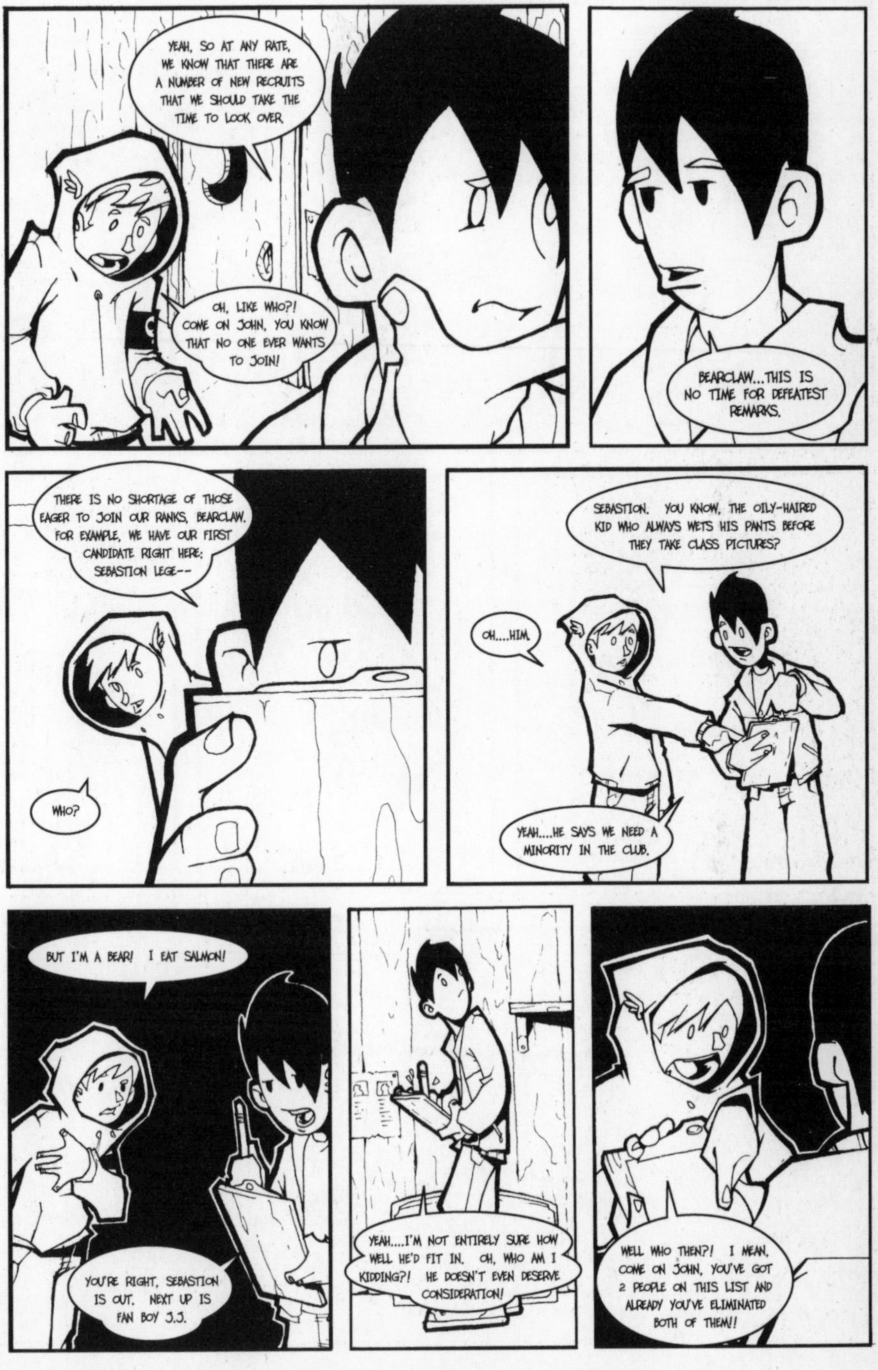
YEAH, SO AT ANY RATE, WE KNOW THAT THERE ARE A NUMBER OF NEW RECRUITS THAT WE SHOULD TAKE THE TIME TO LOOK OVER.
OH, LIKE WHO?! COME ON JOHN, YOU KNOW THAT NO ONE EVER WANTS TO JOIN!
BEARCLAW...THIS IS NO TIME FOR DEFEATEST REMARKS.
THERE IS NO SHORTAGE OF THOSE EAGER TO JOIN OUR RANKS, BEARCLAW. FOR EXAMPLE, WE HAVE OUR FIRST CANDIDATE RIGHT HERE: SEBASTION LEGE--
WHO?
SEBASTION. YOU KNOW, THE OILY-HAIRED KID WHO ALWAYS WETS HIS PANTS BEFORE THEY TAKE CLASS PICTURES?
OH....HIM.
YEAH....HE SAYS WE NEED A MINORITY IN THE CLUB.
BUT I'M A BEAR! I EAT SALMON!
YOU'RE RIGHT, SEBASTION IS OUT. NEXT UP IS FAN BOY J.J.
YEAH....I'M NOT ENTIRELY SURE HOW WELL HE'D FIT IN. OH, WHO AM I KIDDING?! HE DOESN'T EVEN DESERVE CONSIDERATION!
WELL WHO THEN?! I MEAN, COME ON JOHN, YOU'VE GOT 2 PEOPLE ON THIS LIST AND ALREADY YOU'VE ELIMINATED BOTH OF THEM!!

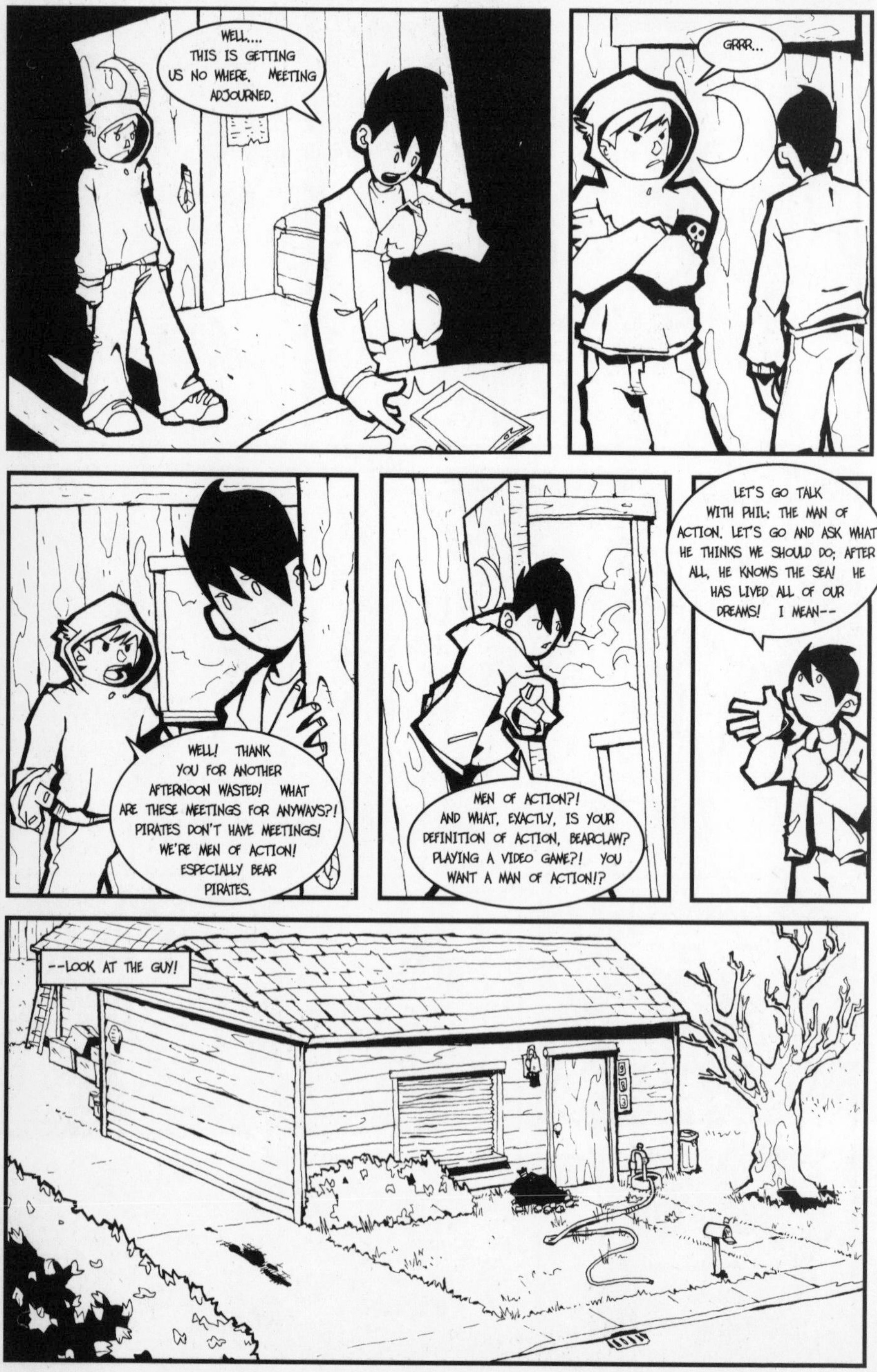
WELL....
THIS IS GETTING
US NO WHERE. MEETING
ADJOURNED.
GRRR...
WELL! THANK YOU FOR ANOTHER AFTERNOON WASTED! WHAT ARE THESE MEETINGS FOR ANYWAYS?! PIRATES DON'T HAVE MEETINGS! WE'RE MEN OF ACTION! ESPECIALLY BEAR PIRATES.
MEN OF ACTION?! AND WHAT, EXACTLY, IS YOUR DEFINITION OF ACTION, BEARCLAW? PLAYING A VIDEO GAME?! YOU WANT A MAN OF ACTION!?
LET'S GO TALK WITH PHIL: THE MAN OF ACTION. LET'S GO AND ASK WHAT HE THINKS WE SHOULD DO; AFTER ALL, HE KNOWS THE SEA! HE HAS LIVED ALL OF OUR DREAMS! I MEAN--
--LOOK AT THE GUY!

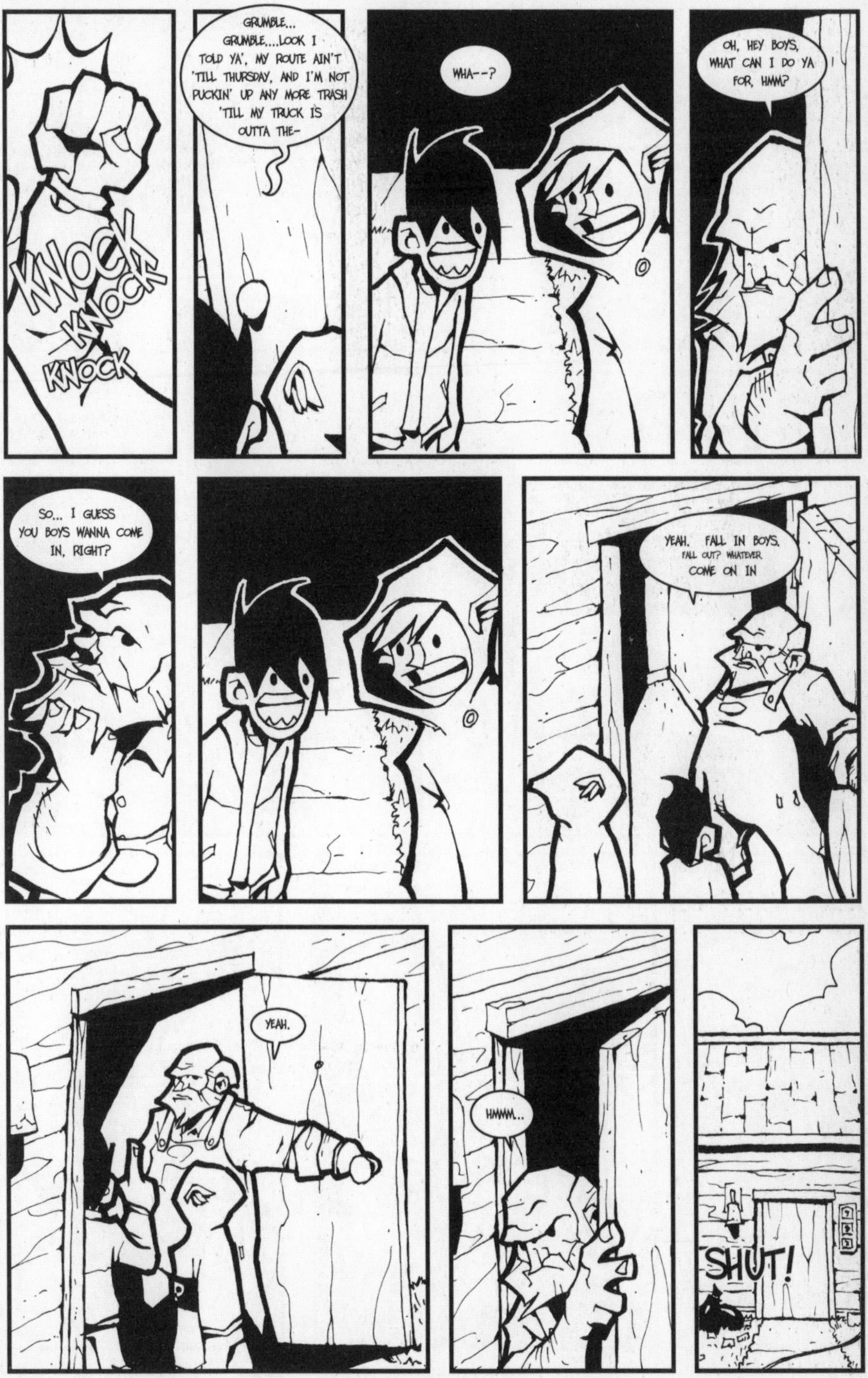

KNOCK
KNOCK
KNOCK
GRUMBLE... GRUMBLE....LOOK I TOLD YA', MY ROUTE AIN'T 'TILL THURSDAY, AND I'M NOT PUCKIN' UP ANY MORE TRASH 'TILL MY TRUCK IS OUTTA THE-
WHA--?
OH, HEY BOYS, WHAT CAN I DO YA FOR, HMM?
SO... I GUESS YOU BOYS WANNA COME IN, RIGHT?
YEAH. FALL IN BOYS. FALL OUT? WHATEVER COME ON IN
YEAH.
HMMM...
SHUT!

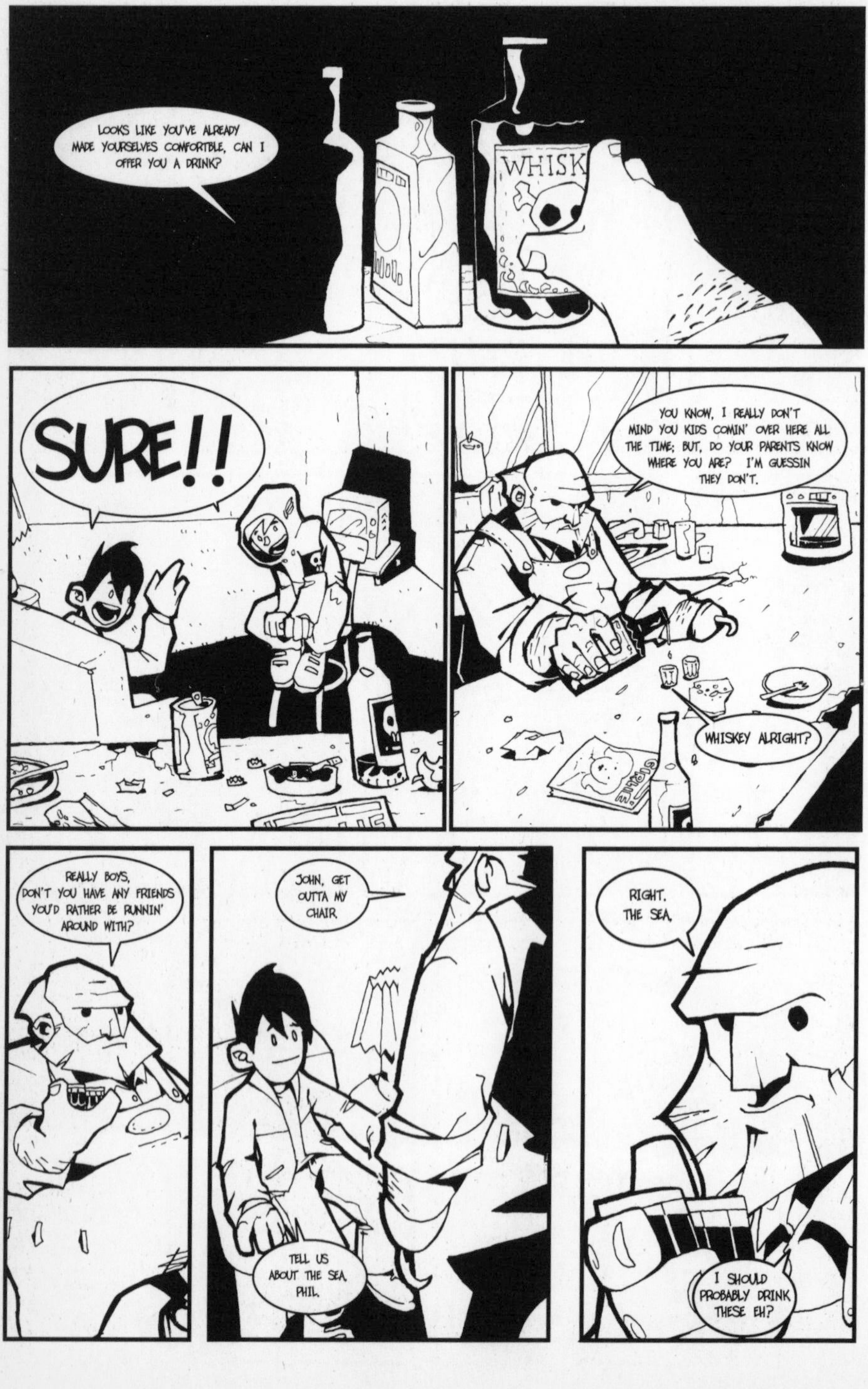
LOOKS LIKE YOU'VE ALREADY MADE YOURSELVES COMFORTBLE, CAN I OFFER YOU A DRINK?
WHISK
SURE!!
YOU KNOW, I REALLY DON'T MIND YOU KIDS COMIN' OVER HERE ALL THE TIME; BUT, DO YOUR PARENTS KNOW WHERE YOU ARE? I'M GUESSIN THEY DON'T.
WHISKEY ALRIGHT?
REALLY BOYS, DON'T YOU HAVE ANY FRIENDS YOU'D RATHER BE RUNNIN' AROUND WITH?
JOHN, GET OUTTA MY CHAIR
TELL US ABOUT THE SEA, PHIL.
RIGHT. THE SEA.
I SHOULD PROBABLY DRINK THESE EH?

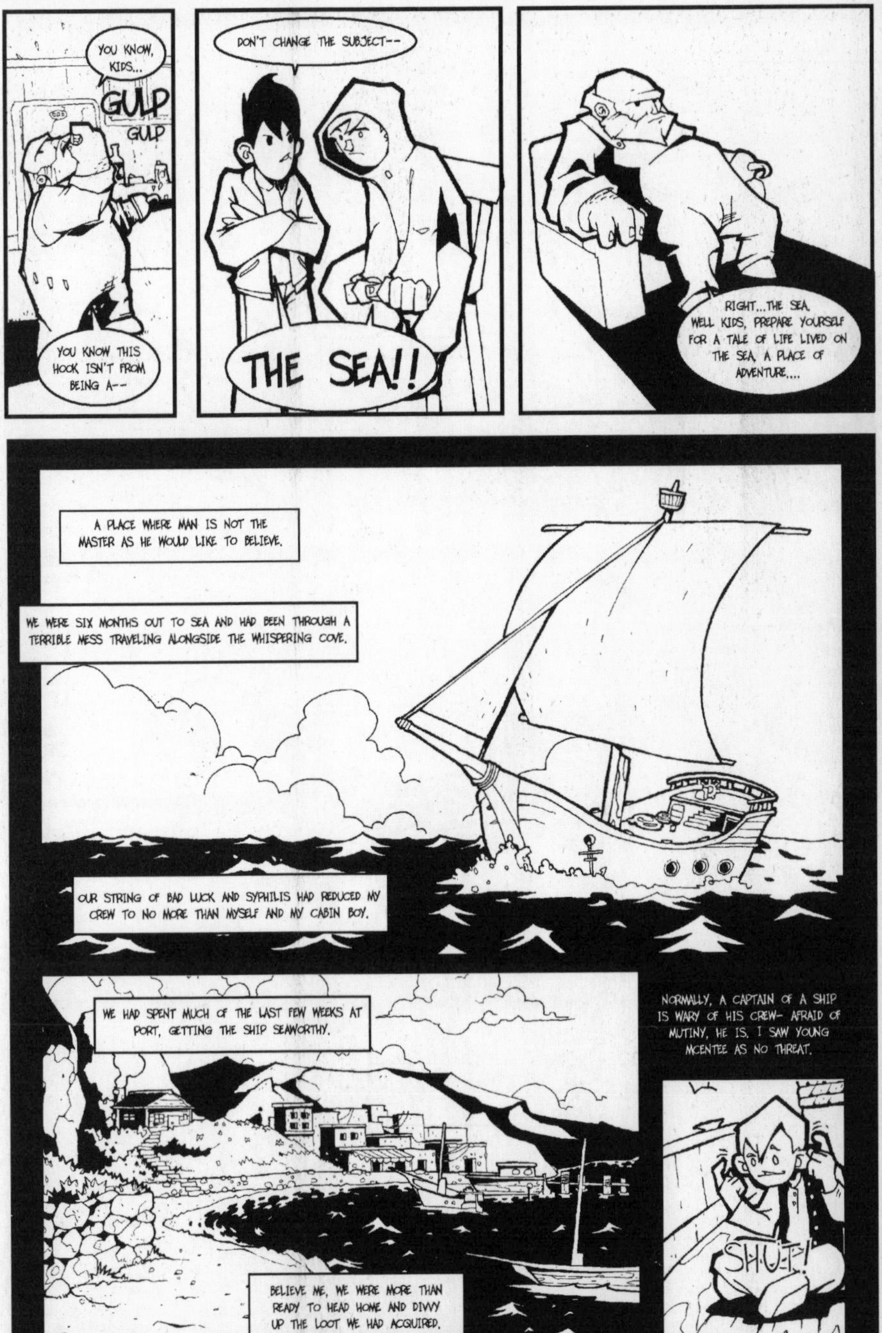

YOU KNOW, KIDS...
GULP
GULP
YOU KNOW THIS HOOK ISN'T FROM BEING A--
DON'T CHANGE THE SUBJECT--
THE SEA!!
RIGHT...THE SEA. WELL KIDS, PREPARE YOURSELF FOR A TALE OF LIFE LIVED ON THE SEA, A PLACE OF ADVENTURE....
A PLACE WHERE MAN IS NOT THE MASTER AS HE WOULD LIKE TO BELIEVE.
WE WERE SIX MONTHS OUT TO SEA AND HAD BEEN THROUGH A TERRIBLE MESS TRAVELING ALONGSIDE THE WHISPERING COVE.
OUR STRING OF BAD LUCK AND SYPHILIS HAD REDUCED MY CREW TO NO MORE THAN MYSELF AND MY CABIN BOY.
WE HAD SPENT MUCH OF THE LAST FEW WEEKS AT PORT, GETTING THE SHIP SEAWORTHY.
BELIEVE ME, WE WERE MORE THAN READY TO HEAD HOME AND DIVVY UP THE LOOT WE HAD ACQUIRED.
NORMALLY, A CAPTAIN OF A SHIP IS WARY OF HIS CREW- AFRAID OF MUTINY, HE IS. I SAW YOUNG MCENTEE AS NO THREAT.
SHUT!

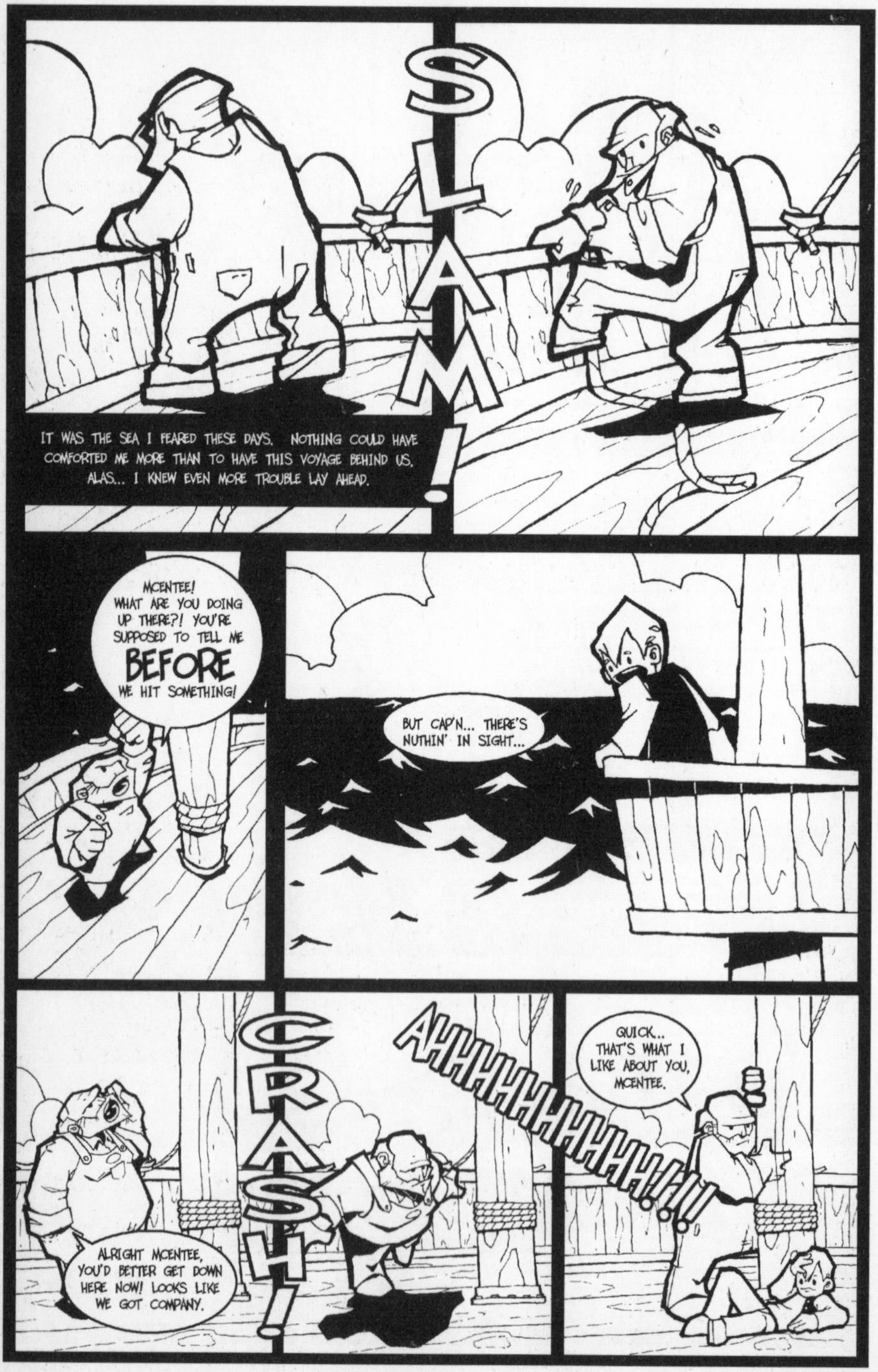
SLAM!
IT WAS THE SEA I FEARED THESE DAYS. NOTHING COULD HAVE COMFORTED ME MORE THAN TO HAVE THIS VOYAGE BEHIND US. ALAS... I KNEW EVEN MORE TROUBLE LAY AHEAD.
MCENTEE! WHAT ARE YOU DOING UP THERE?! YOU'RE SUPPOSED TO TELL ME BEFORE WE HIT SOMETHING!
BUT CAP'N... THERE'S NUTHIN' IN SIGHT...
ALRIGHT MCENTEE, YOU'D BETTER GET DOWN HERE NOW! LOOKS LIKE WE GOT COMPANY.
CRASH!
AHHHHHHHHHHHHHH!!!!!
QUICK... THAT'S WHAT I LIKE ABOUT YOU, MCENTEE.

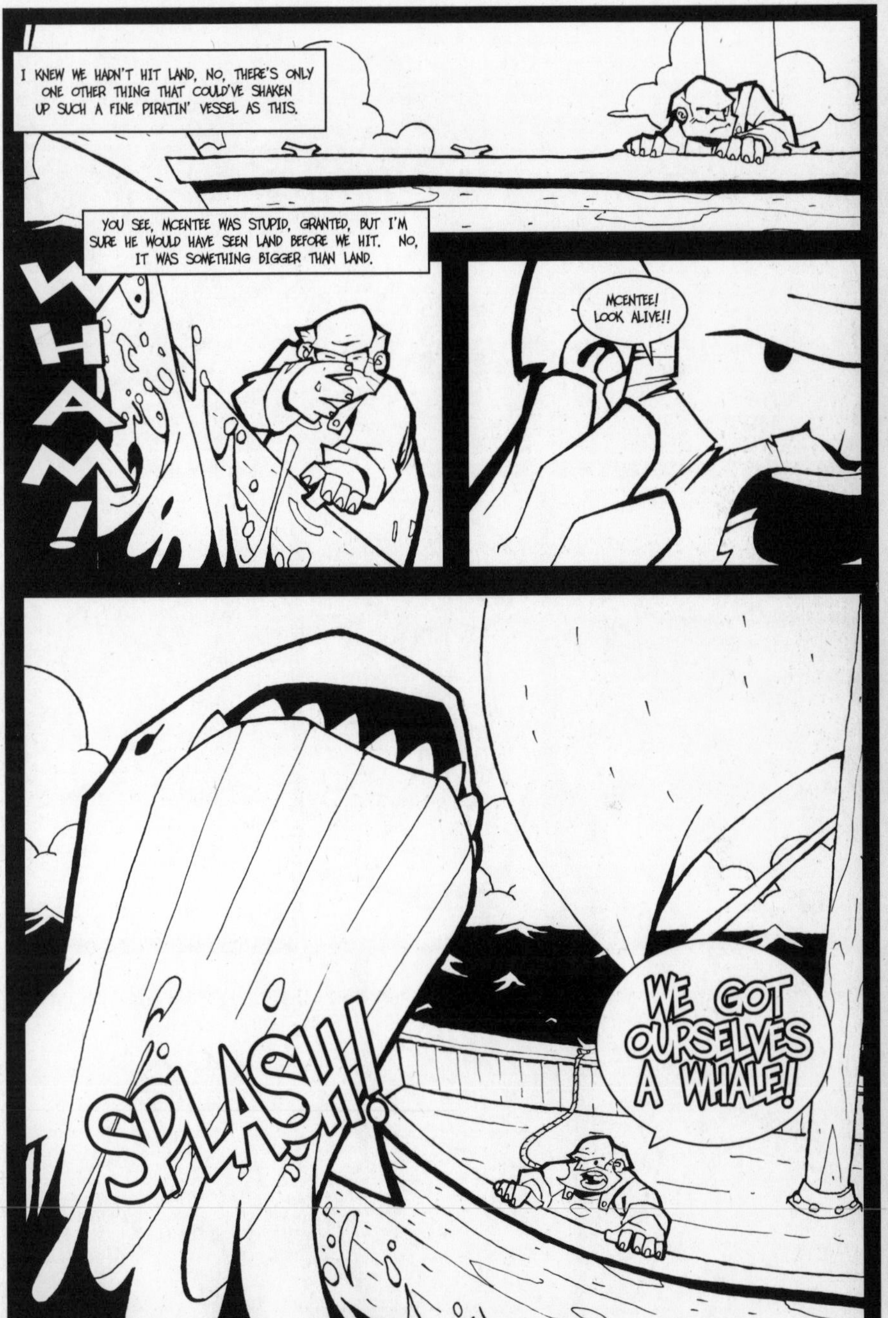
I KNEW WE HADN'T HIT LAND, NO, THERE'S ONLY ONE OTHER THING THAT COULD'VE SHAKEN UP SUCH A FINE PIRATIN' VESSEL AS THIS.
YOU SEE, MCENTEE WAS STUPID, GRANTED, BUT I'M SURE HE WOULD HAVE SEEN LAND BEFORE WE HIT. NO, IT WAS SOMETHING BIGGER THAN LAND.
WHAM!
MCENTEE! LOOK ALIVE!!
SPLASH!
WE GOT OURSELVES A WHALE!

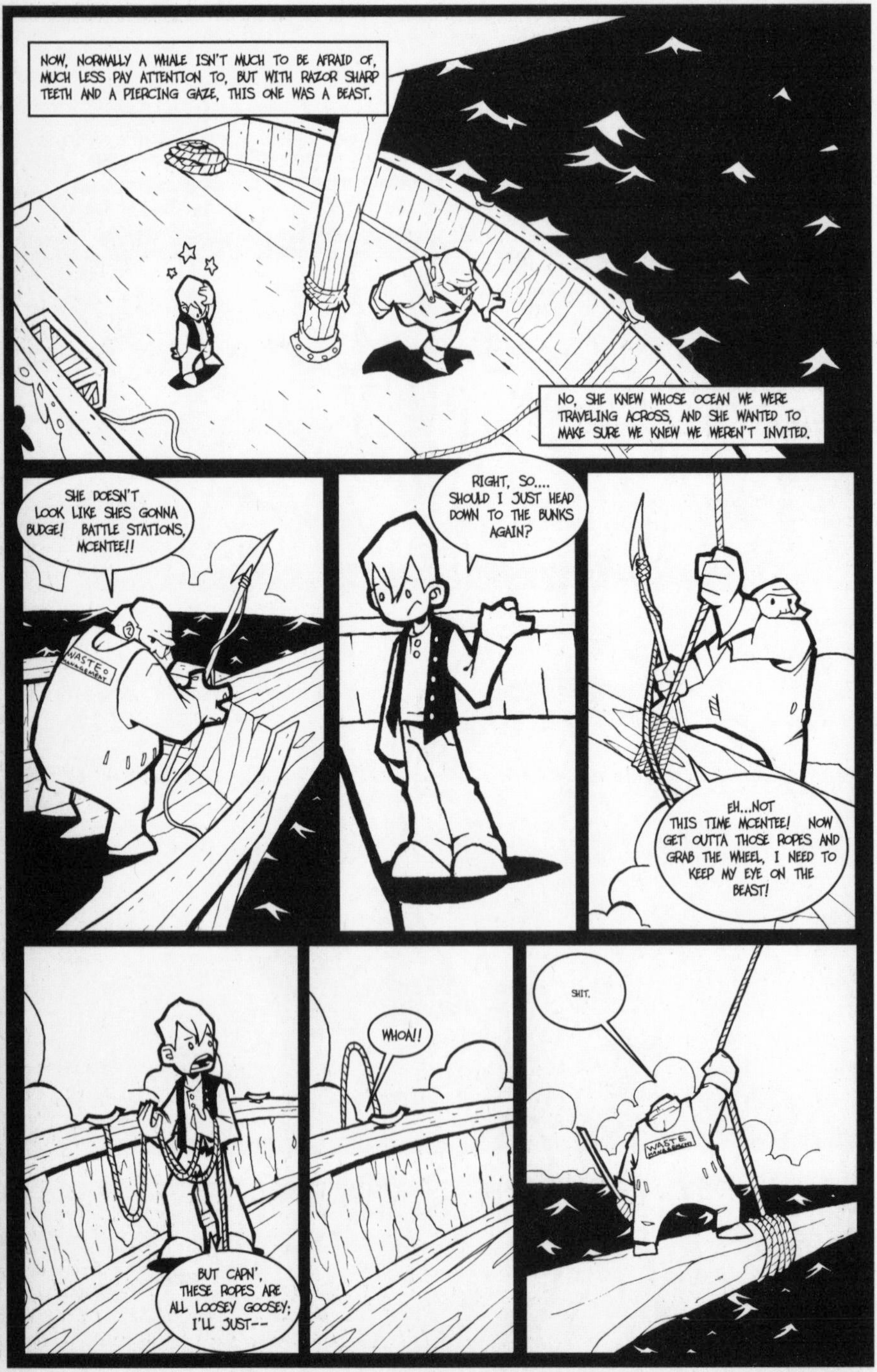
NOW, NORMALLY A WHALE ISN'T MUCH TO BE AFRAID OF, MUCH LESS PAY ATTENTION TO, BUT WITH RAZOR SHARP TEETH AND A PIERCING GAZE, THIS ONE WAS A BEAST.
NO, SHE KNEW WHOSE OCEAN WE WERE TRAVELING ACROSS, AND SHE WANTED TO MAKE SURE WE KNEW WE WEREN'T INVITED.
SHE DOESN'T LOOK LIKE SHES GONNA BUDGE! BATTLE STATIONS, MCENTEE!!
WASTE MANAGEMENT
RIGHT, SO.... SHOULD I JUST HEAD DOWN TO THE BUNKS AGAIN?
EH...NOT THIS TIME MCENTEE! NOW GET OUTTA THOSE ROPES AND GRAB THE WHEEL, I NEED TO KEEP MY EYE ON THE BEAST!
BUT CAPN', THESE ROPES ARE ALL LOOSEY GOOSEY; I'LL JUST--
WHOA!!
SHIT.
WASTE

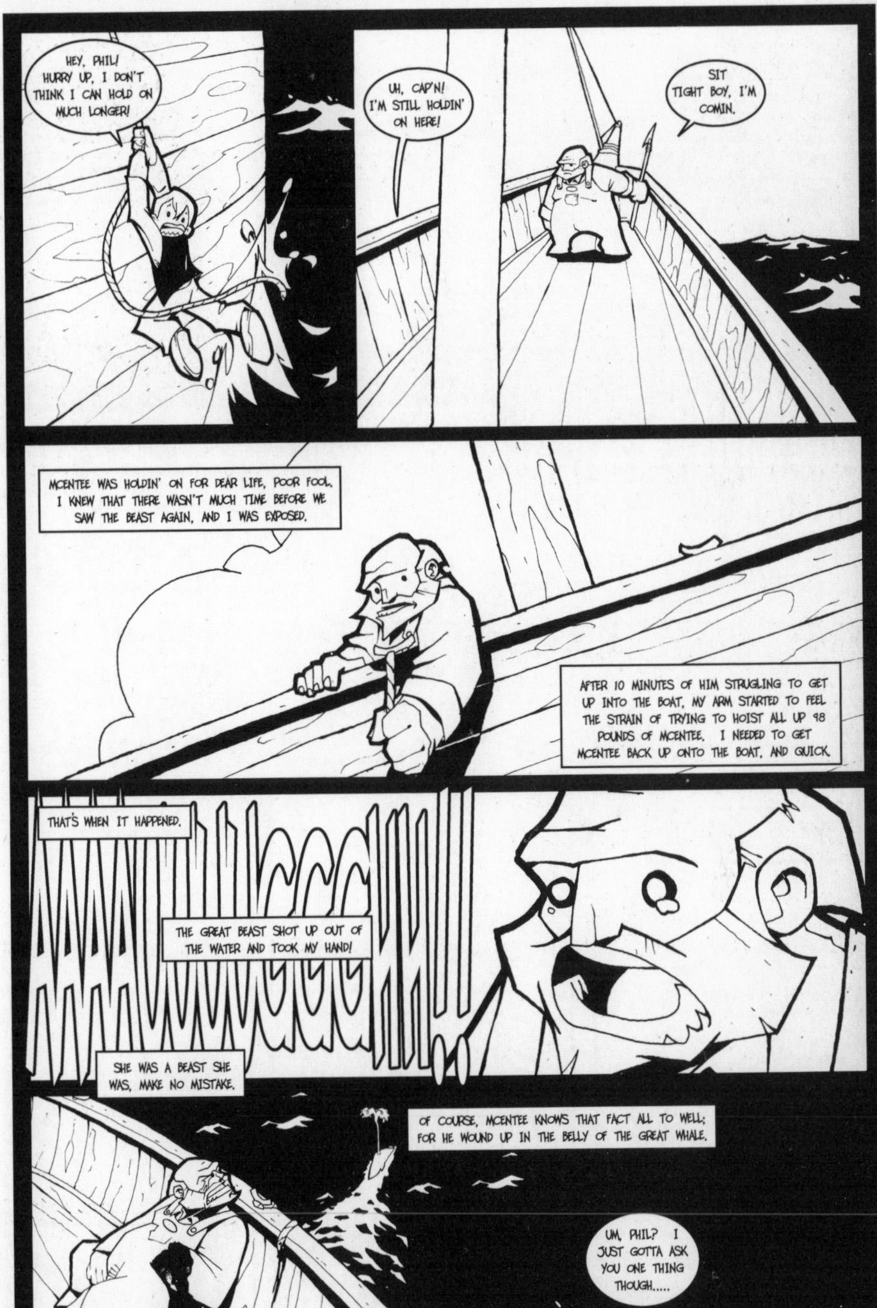

HEY, PHIL! HURRY UP, I DON'T THINK I CAN HOLD ON MUCH LONGER!
UH, CAP'N! I'M STILL HOLDIN' ON HERE!
SIT TIGHT BOY, I'M COMIN.
MCENTEE WAS HOLDIN' ON FOR DEAR LIFE, POOR FOOL. I KNEW THAT THERE WASN'T MUCH TIME BEFORE WE SAW THE BEAST AGAIN, AND I WAS EXPOSED.
AFTER 10 MINUTES OF HIM STRUGLING TO GET UP INTO THE BOAT, MY ARM STARTED TO FEEL THE STRAIN OF TRYING TO HOIST ALL UP 98 POUNDS OF MCENTEE. I NEEDED TO GET MCENTEE BACK UP ONTO THE BOAT, AND QUICK.
THAT'S WHEN IT HAPPENED.
AAAAUUUUGGGGHHH!!
THE GREAT BEAST SHOT UP OUT OF THE WATER AND TOOK MY HAND!
SHE WAS A BEAST SHE WAS, MAKE NO MISTAKE.
OF COURSE, MCENTEE KNOWS THAT FACT ALL TO WELL; FOR HE WOUND UP IN THE BELLY OF THE GREAT WHALE.
UM, PHIL? I JUST GOTTA ASK YOU ONE THING THOUGH.....

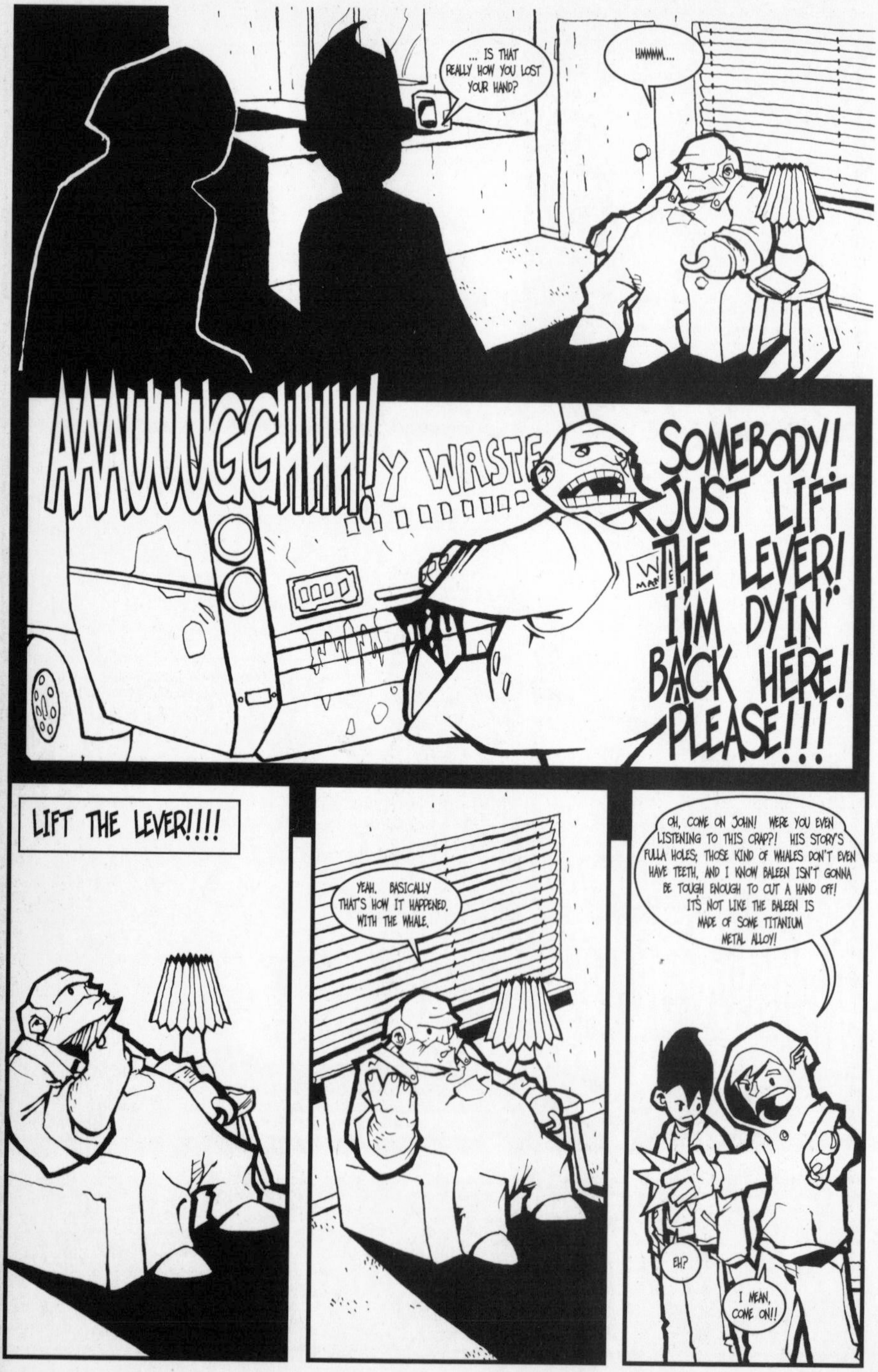

... IS THAT REALLY HOW YOU LOST YOUR HAND?
HMMMM...
AAAUUUGGHHH!
Y WASTE
SOMEBODY! JUST LIFT THE LEVER! I'M DYIN' BACK HERE! PLEASE!!!
LIFT THE LEVER!!!!
YEAH. BASICALLY THAT'S HOW IT HAPPENED. WITH THE WHALE.
OH, COME ON JOHN! WERE YOU EVEN LISTENING TO THIS CRAP?! HIS STORY'S FULLA HOLES; THOSE KIND OF WHALES DON'T EVEN HAVE TEETH, AND I KNOW BALEEN ISN'T GONNA BE TOUGH ENOUGH TO CUT A HAND OFF! IT'S NOT LIKE THE BALEEN IS MADE OF SOME TITANIUM METAL ALLOY!
EH?
I MEAN, COME ON!!

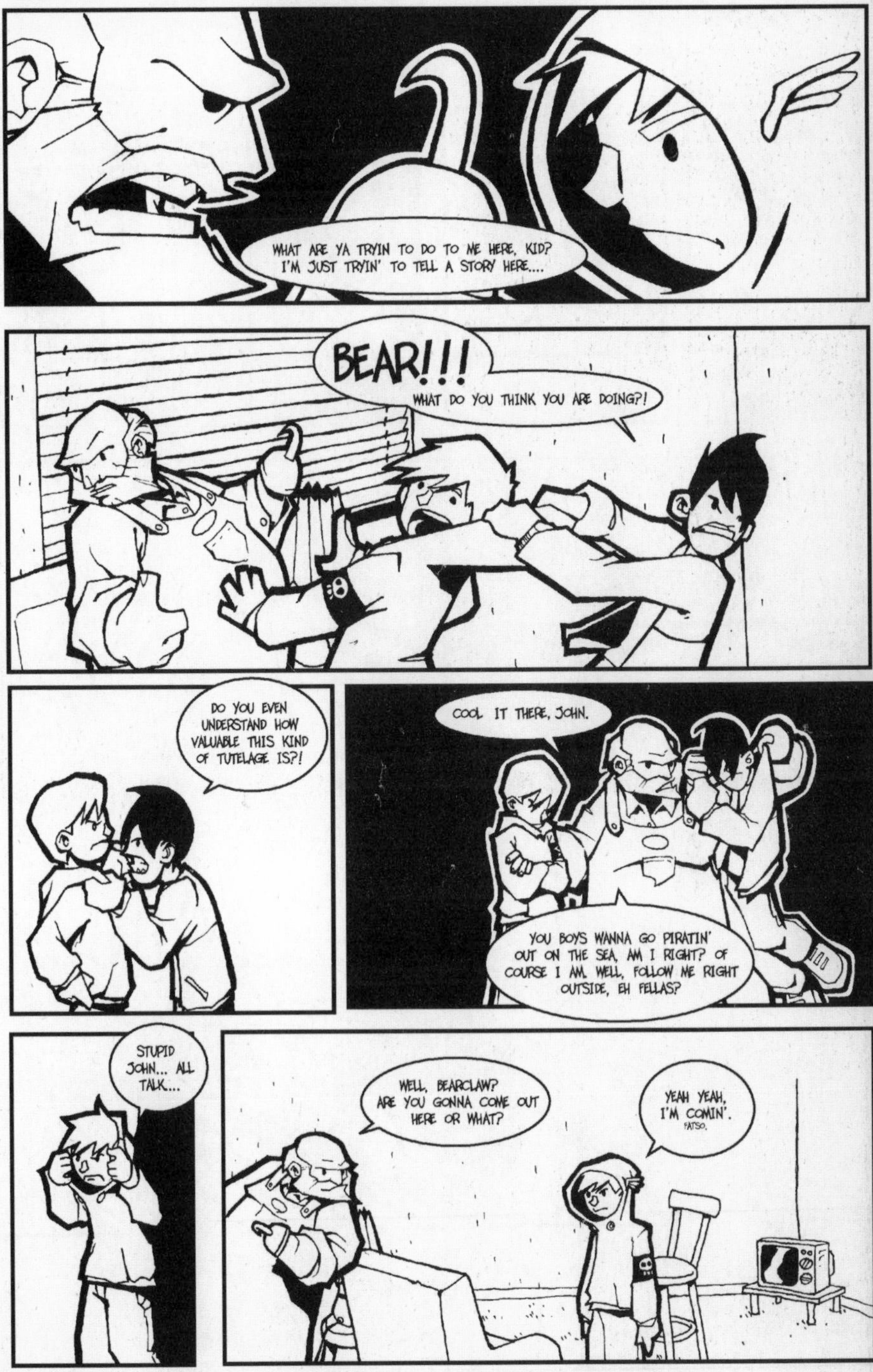
WHAT ARE YA TRYIN TO DO TO ME HERE, KID? I'M JUST TRYIN' TO TELL A STORY HERE....
BEAR!!!
WHAT DO YOU THINK YOU ARE DOING?!
DO YOU EVEN UNDERSTAND HOW VALUABLE THIS KIND OF TUTELAGE IS?!
COOL IT THERE, JOHN.
YOU BOYS WANNA GO PIRATIN' OUT ON THE SEA, AM I RIGHT? OF COURSE I AM. WELL, FOLLOW ME RIGHT OUTSIDE, EH FELLAS?
STUPID JOHN... ALL TALK...
WELL, BEARCLAW? ARE YOU GONNA COME OUT HERE OR WHAT?
YEAH YEAH, I'M COMIN'.
FATSO.

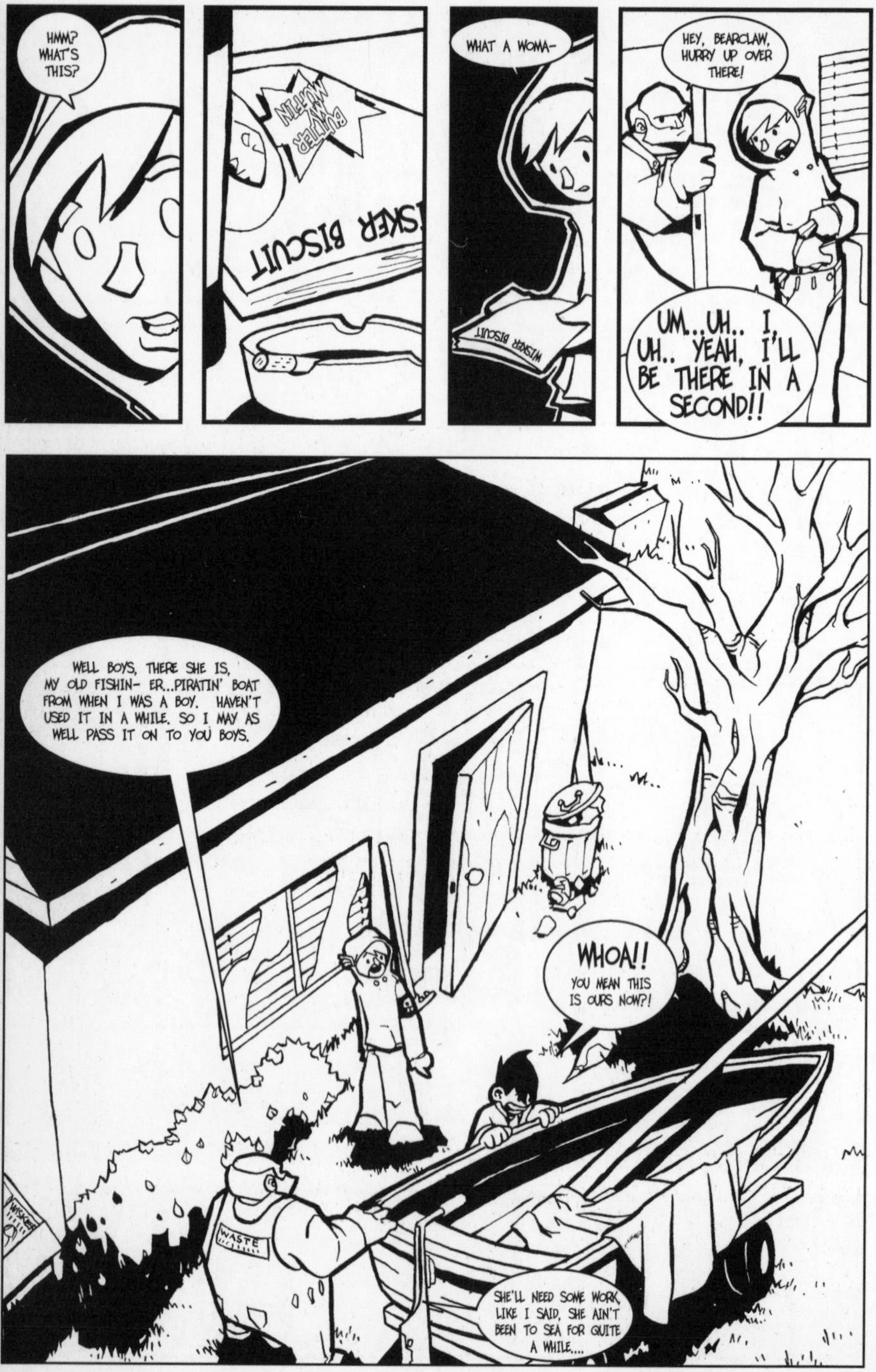
HMM? WHAT'S THIS?
BUTTER MY MUFFIN
WISKER BISCUIT
WHAT A WOMA-
WISKER BISCUIT
HEY, BEARCLAW, HURRY UP OVER THERE!
UM...UH.. I, UH.. YEAH, I'LL BE THERE IN A SECOND!!
WELL BOYS, THERE SHE IS, MY OLD FISHIN- ER...PIRATIN' BOAT FROM WHEN I WAS A BOY. HAVEN'T USED IT IN A WHILE. SO I MAY AS WELL PASS IT ON TO YOU BOYS.
WHOA!! YOU MEAN THIS IS OURS NOW?!
WASTE
SHE'LL NEED SOME WORK, LIKE I SAID, SHE AIN'T BEEN TO SEA FOR QUITE A WHILE....

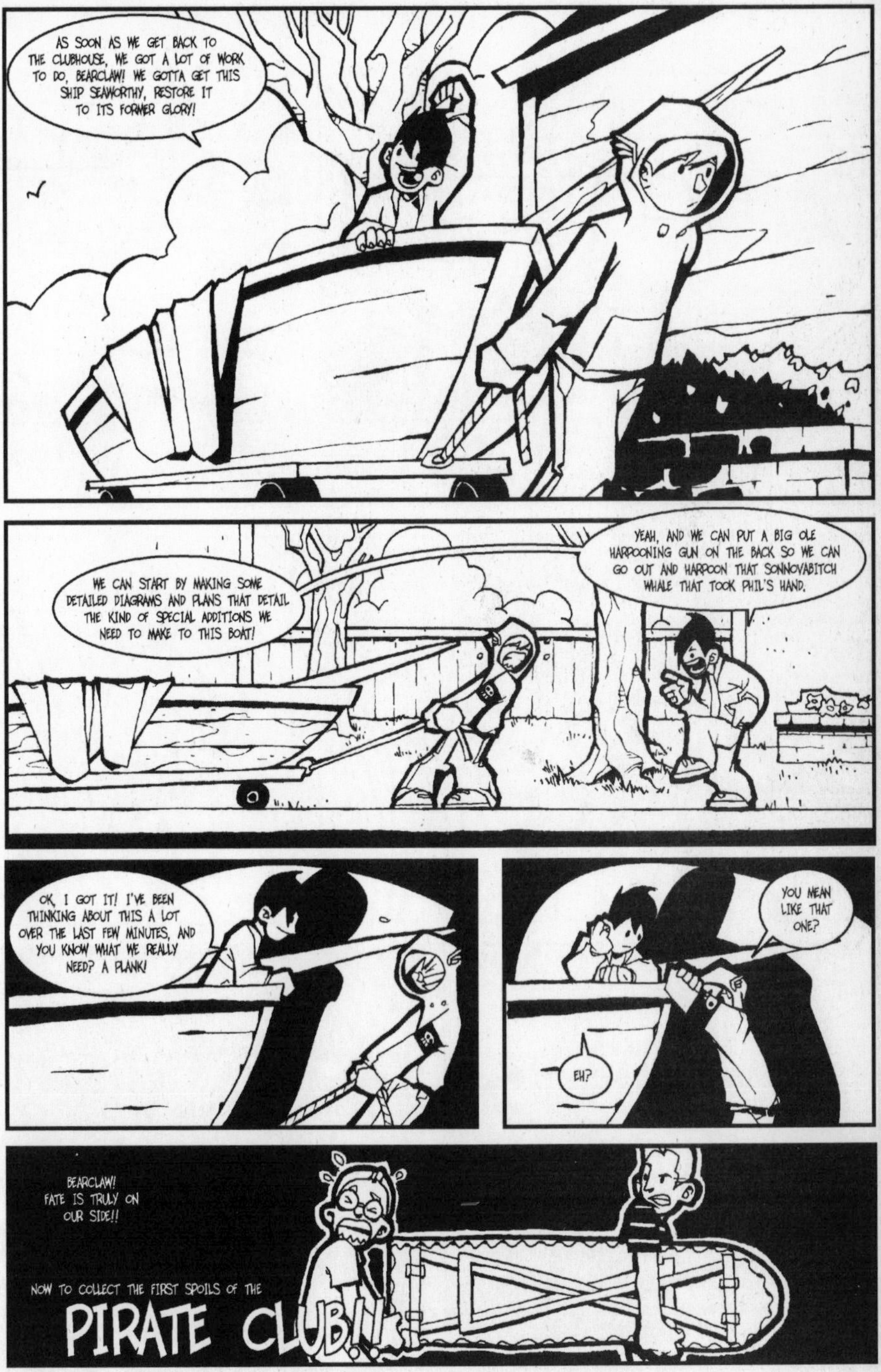
AS SOON AS WE GET BACK TO THE CLUBHOUSE, WE GOT A LOT OF WORK TO DO, BEARCLAW! WE GOTTA GET THIS SHIP SEAWORTHY, RESTORE IT TO ITS FORMER GLORY!
WE CAN START BY MAKING SOME DETAILED DIAGRAMS AND PLANS THAT DETAIL THE KIND OF SPECIAL ADDITIONS WE NEED TO MAKE TO THIS BOAT!
YEAH, AND WE CAN PUT A BIG OLE HARPOONING GUN ON THE BACK SO WE CAN GO OUT AND HARPOON THAT SONNOVABITCH WHALE THAT TOOK PHIL'S HAND.
OK, I GOT IT! I'VE BEEN THINKING ABOUT THIS A LOT OVER THE LAST FEW MINUTES, AND YOU KNOW WHAT WE REALLY NEED? A PLANK!
YOU MEAN LIKE THAT ONE?
EH?
BEARCLAW! FATE IS TRULY ON OUR SIDE!!
NOW TO COLLECT THE FIRST SPOILS OF THE
PIRATE CLUB!!

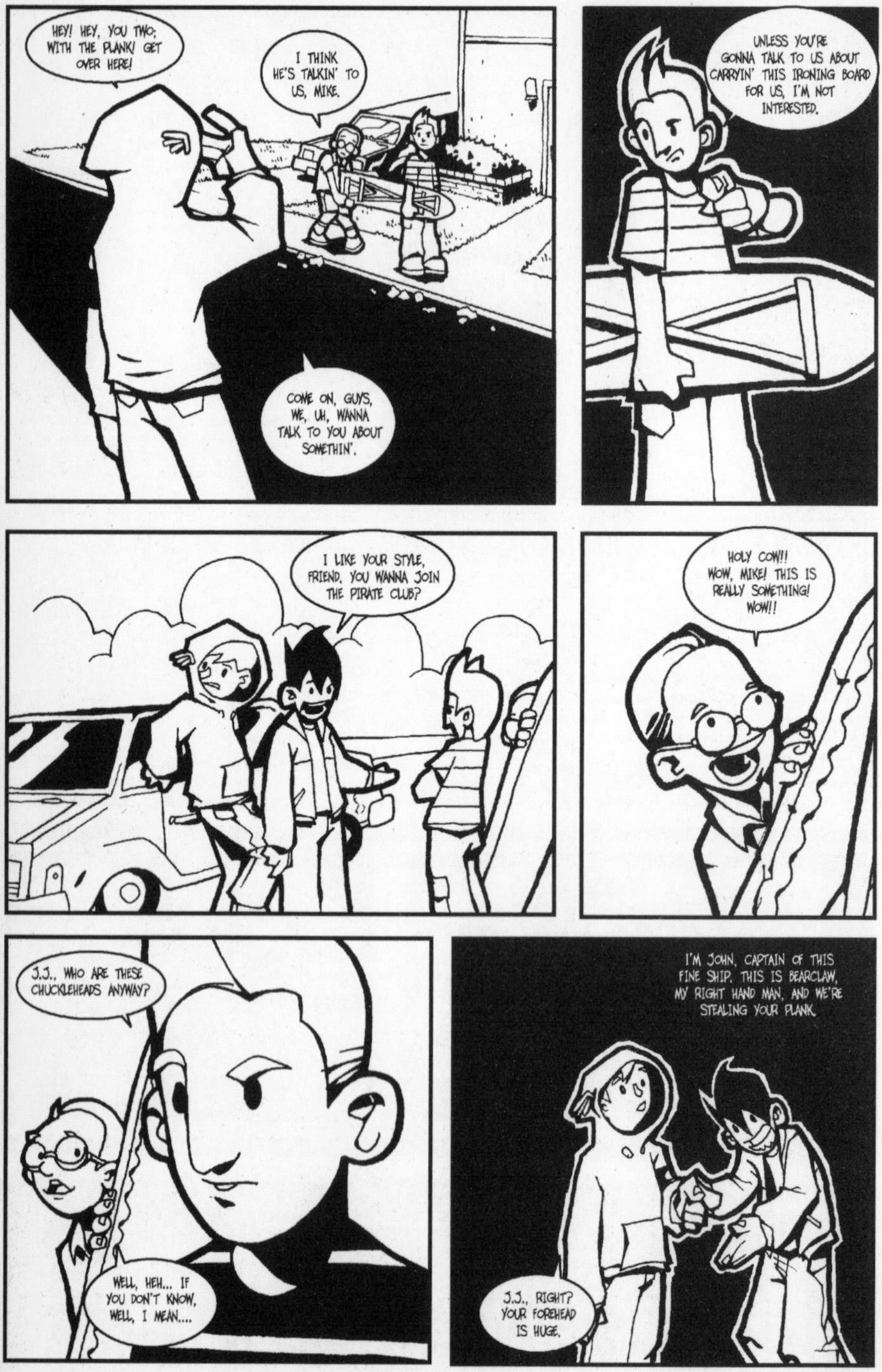
HEY! HEY, YOU TWO; WITH THE PLANK! GET OVER HERE!
I THINK HE'S TALKIN' TO US, MIKE.
COME ON, GUYS, WE, UH, WANNA TALK TO YOU ABOUT SOMETHIN'.
UNLESS YOU'RE GONNA TALK TO US ABOUT CARRYIN' THIS IRONING BOARD FOR US, I'M NOT INTERESTED.
I LIKE YOUR STYLE, FRIEND. YOU WANNA JOIN THE PIRATE CLUB?
HOLY COW!! WOW, MIKE! THIS IS REALLY SOMETHING! WOW!!
J.J., WHO ARE THESE CHUCKLEHEADS ANYWAY?
WELL, HEH... IF YOU DON'T KNOW, WELL, I MEAN....
I'M JOHN, CAPTAIN OF THIS FINE SHIP. THIS IS BEARCLAW, MY RIGHT HAND MAN, AND WE'RE STEALING YOUR PLANK.
J.J., RIGHT? YOUR FOREHEAD IS HUGE.

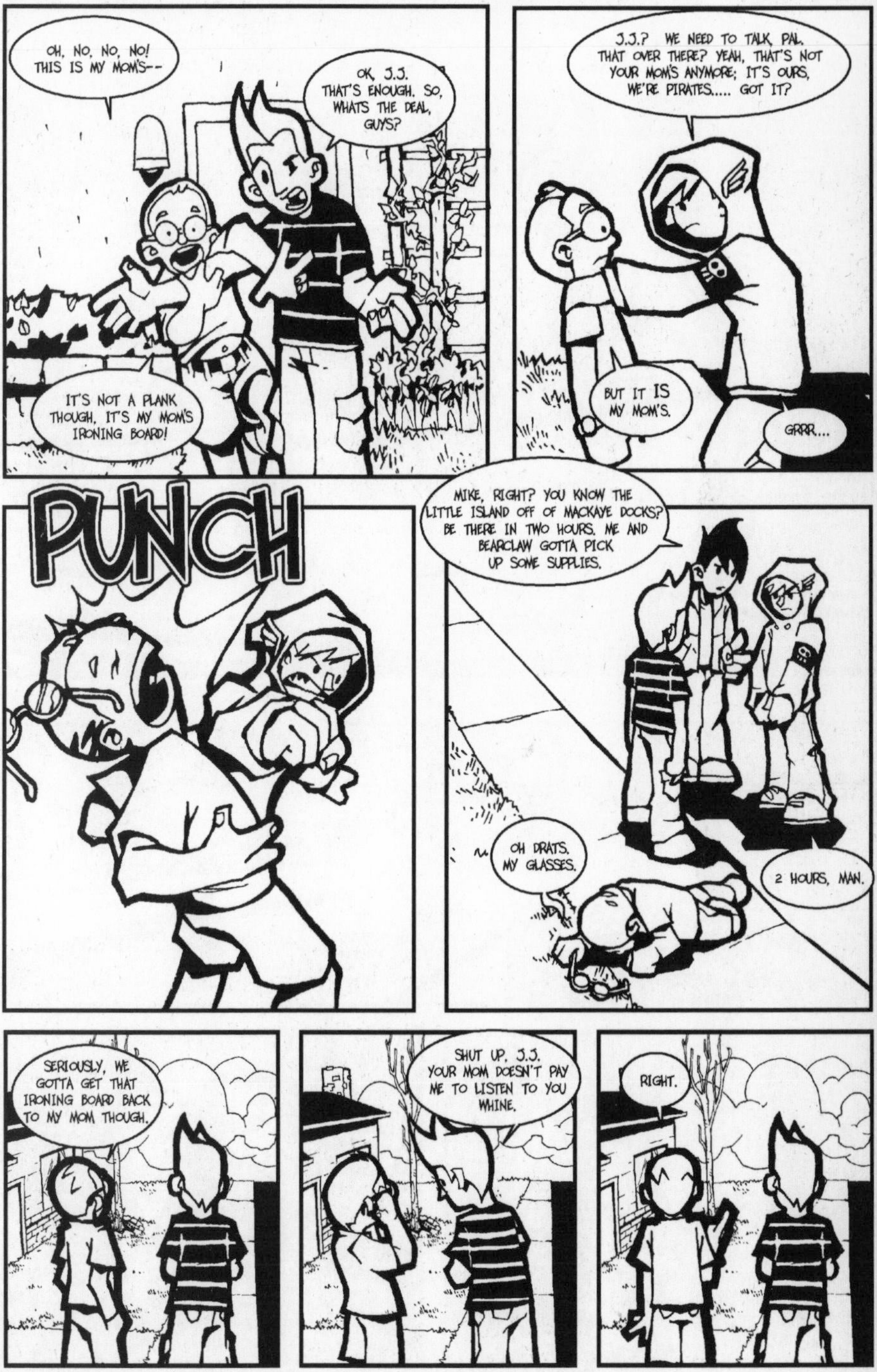
OH, NO, NO, NO!
THIS IS MY MOM'S--
OK, J.J.
THAT'S ENOUGH. SO,
WHATS THE DEAL,
GUYS?
IT'S NOT A PLANK
THOUGH. IT'S MY MOM'S
IRONING BOARD!
J.J.? WE NEED TO TALK, PAL.
THAT OVER THERE? YEAH, THAT'S NOT
YOUR MOM'S ANYMORE; IT'S OURS,
WE'RE PIRATES..... GOT IT?
BUT IT IS
MY MOM'S.
GRRR...
PUNCH
MIKE, RIGHT? YOU KNOW THE
LITTLE ISLAND OFF OF MACKAYE DOCKS?
BE THERE IN TWO HOURS. ME AND
BEARCLAW GOTTA PICK
UP SOME SUPPLIES.
OH DRATS.
MY GLASSES.
2 HOURS, MAN.
SERIOUSLY, WE
GOTTA GET THAT
IRONING BOARD BACK
TO MY MOM THOUGH.
SHUT UP, J.J.
YOUR MOM DOESN'T PAY
ME TO LISTEN TO YOU
WHINE.
RIGHT.

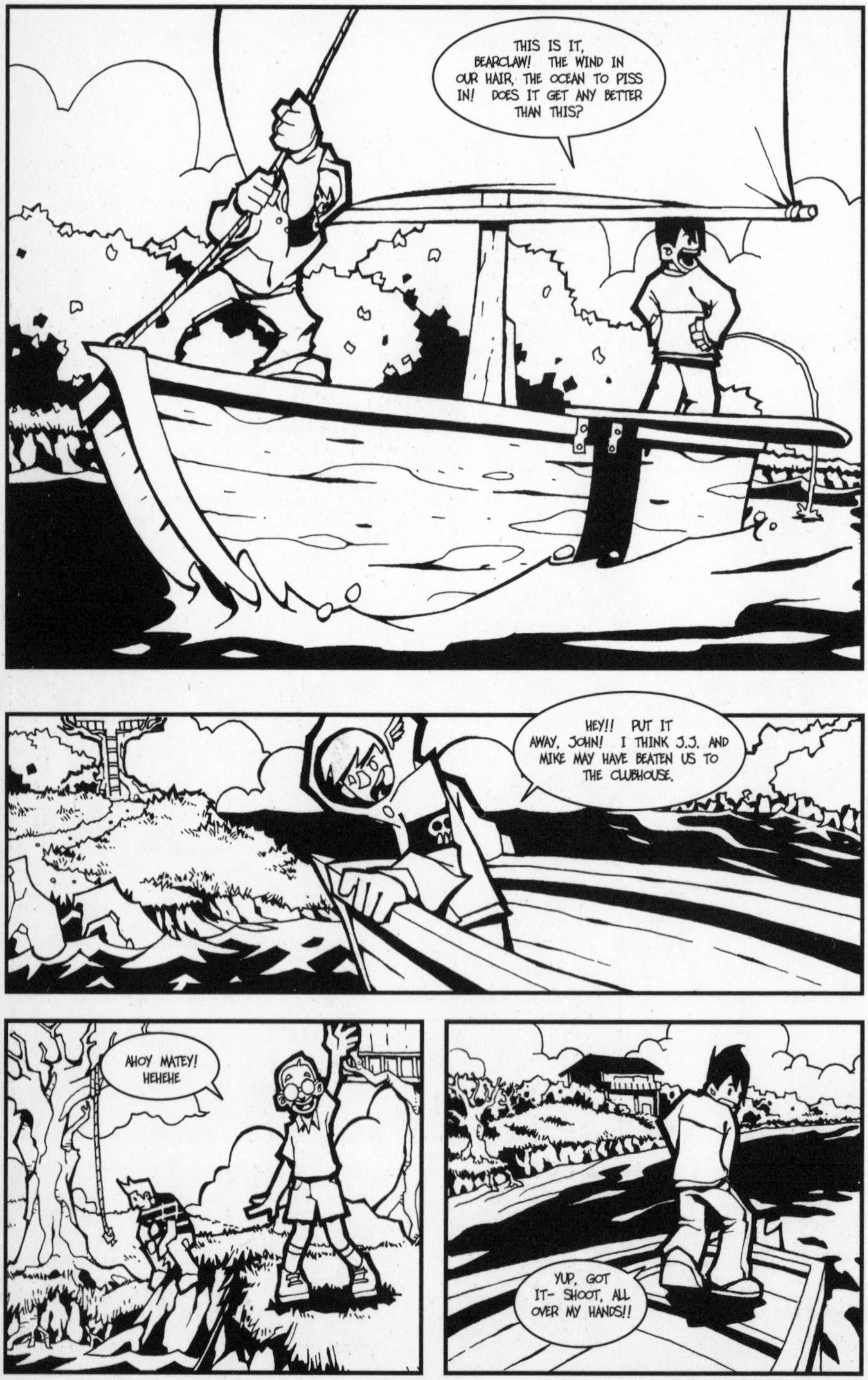
THIS IS IT, BEARCLAW! THE WIND IN OUR HAIR, THE OCEAN TO PISS IN! DOES IT GET ANY BETTER THAN THIS?
HEY!! PUT IT AWAY, JOHN! I THINK J.J. AND MIKE MAY HAVE BEATEN US TO THE CLUBHOUSE.
AHOY MATEY! HEHEHE
YUP, GOT IT- SHOOT, ALL OVER MY HANDS!!

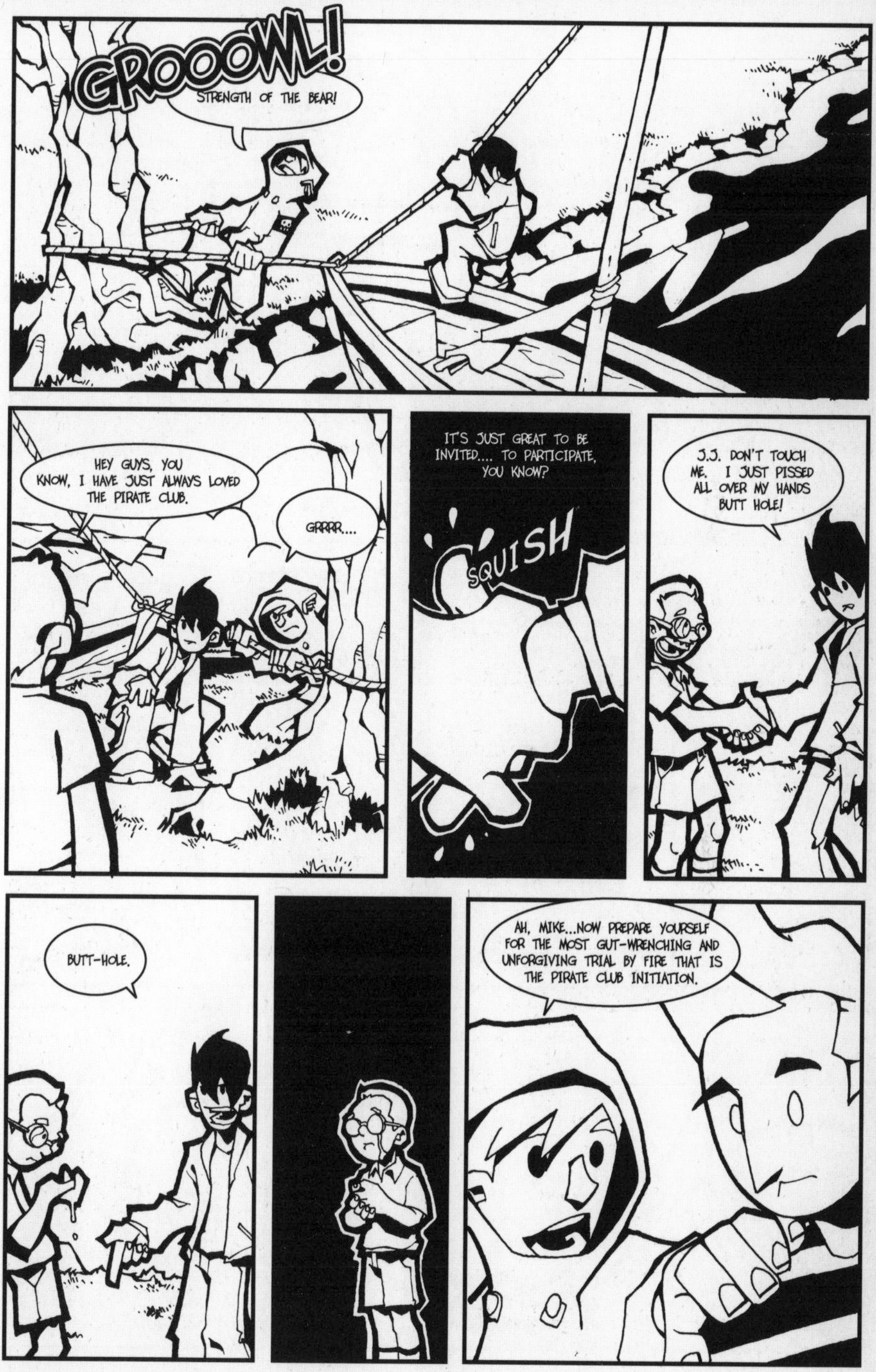
GROOOWL!
STRENGTH OF THE BEAR!
HEY GUYS, YOU KNOW, I HAVE JUST ALWAYS LOVED THE PIRATE CLUB.
GRRRR....
IT'S JUST GREAT TO BE INVITED.... TO PARTICIPATE, YOU KNOW?
SQUISH
J.J. DON'T TOUCH ME. I JUST PISSED ALL OVER MY HANDS BUTT HOLE!
BUTT-HOLE.
AH, MIKE...NOW PREPARE YOURSELF FOR THE MOST GUT-WRENCHING AND UNFORGIVING TRIAL BY FIRE THAT IS THE PIRATE CLUB INITIATION.

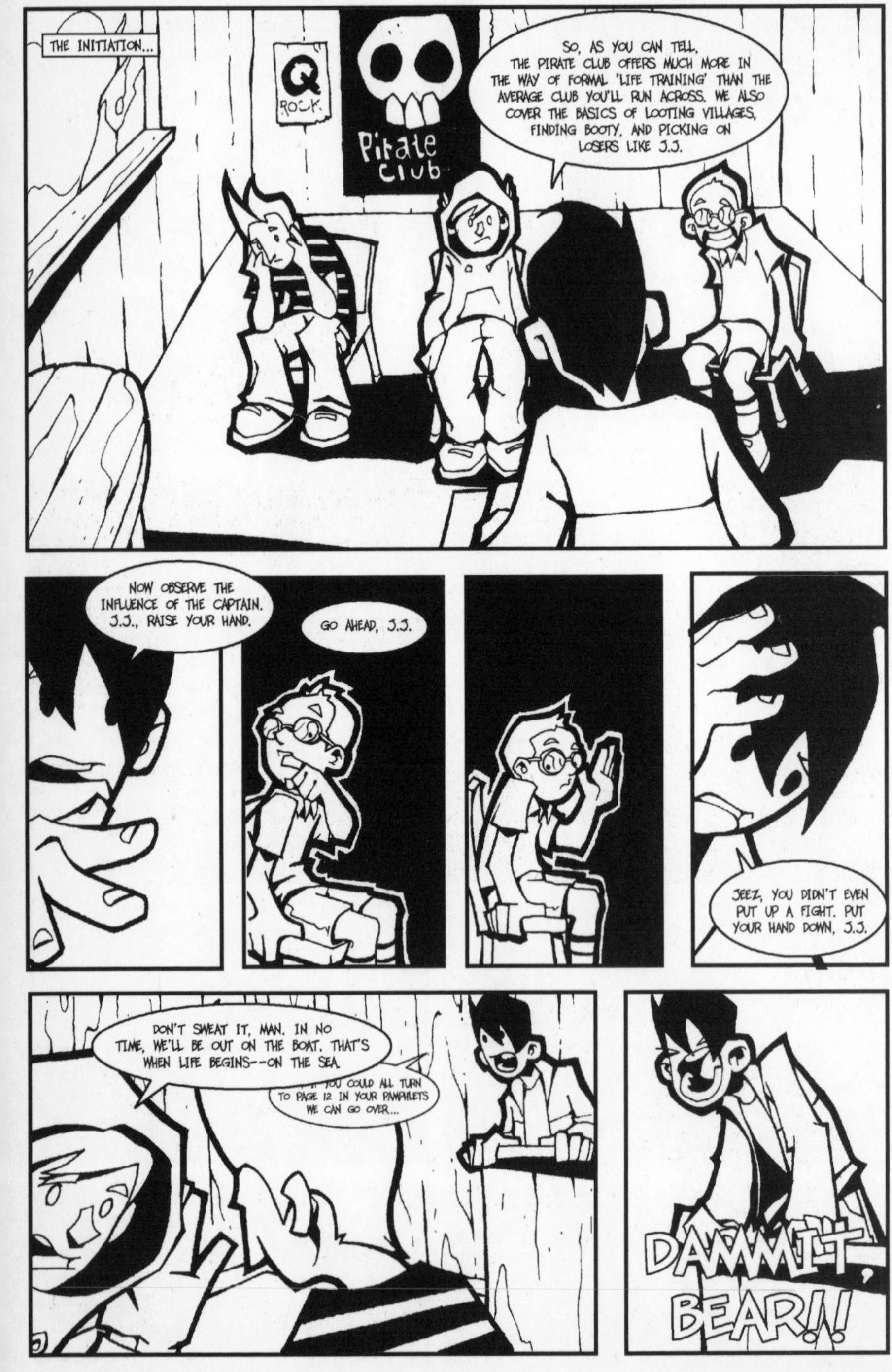
THE INITIATION...
Q ROCK
Pirate club
SO, AS YOU CAN TELL, THE PIRATE CLUB OFFERS MUCH MORE IN THE WAY OF FORMAL 'LIFE TRAINING' THAN THE AVERAGE CLUB YOU'LL RUN ACROSS. WE ALSO COVER THE BASICS OF LOOTING VILLAGES, FINDING BOOTY, AND PICKING ON LOSERS LIKE J.J.
NOW OBSERVE THE INFLUENCE OF THE CAPTAIN. J.J., RAISE YOUR HAND.
GO AHEAD, J.J.
JEEZ, YOU DIDN'T EVEN PUT UP A FIGHT. PUT YOUR HAND DOWN, J.J.
DON'T SWEAT IT, MAN. IN NO TIME, WE'LL BE OUT ON THE BOAT. THAT'S WHEN LIFE BEGINS--ON THE SEA.
...IF YOU COULD ALL TURN TO PAGE 12 IN YOUR PAMPHLETS WE CAN GO OVER...
DAMMIT, BEAR!!

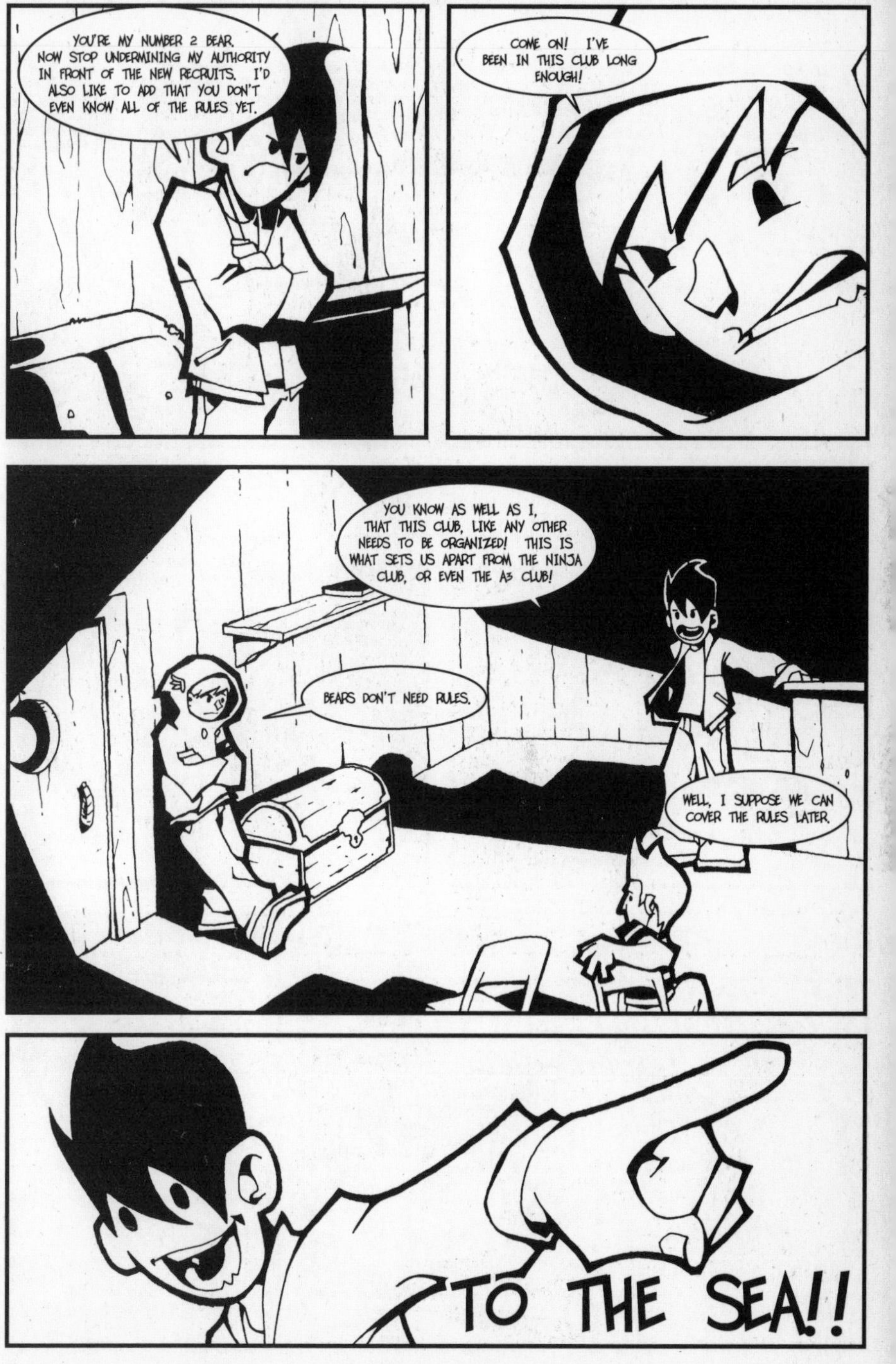

YOU'RE MY NUMBER 2 BEAR. NOW STOP UNDERMINING MY AUTHORITY IN FRONT OF THE NEW RECRUITS. I'D ALSO LIKE TO ADD THAT YOU DON'T EVEN KNOW ALL OF THE RULES YET.
COME ON! I'VE BEEN IN THIS CLUB LONG ENOUGH!
YOU KNOW AS WELL AS I, THAT THIS CLUB, LIKE ANY OTHER NEEDS TO BE ORGANIZED! THIS IS WHAT SETS US APART FROM THE NINJA CLUB, OR EVEN THE A3 CLUB!
BEARS DON'T NEED RULES.
WELL, I SUPPOSE WE CAN COVER THE RULES LATER.
TO THE SEA!!

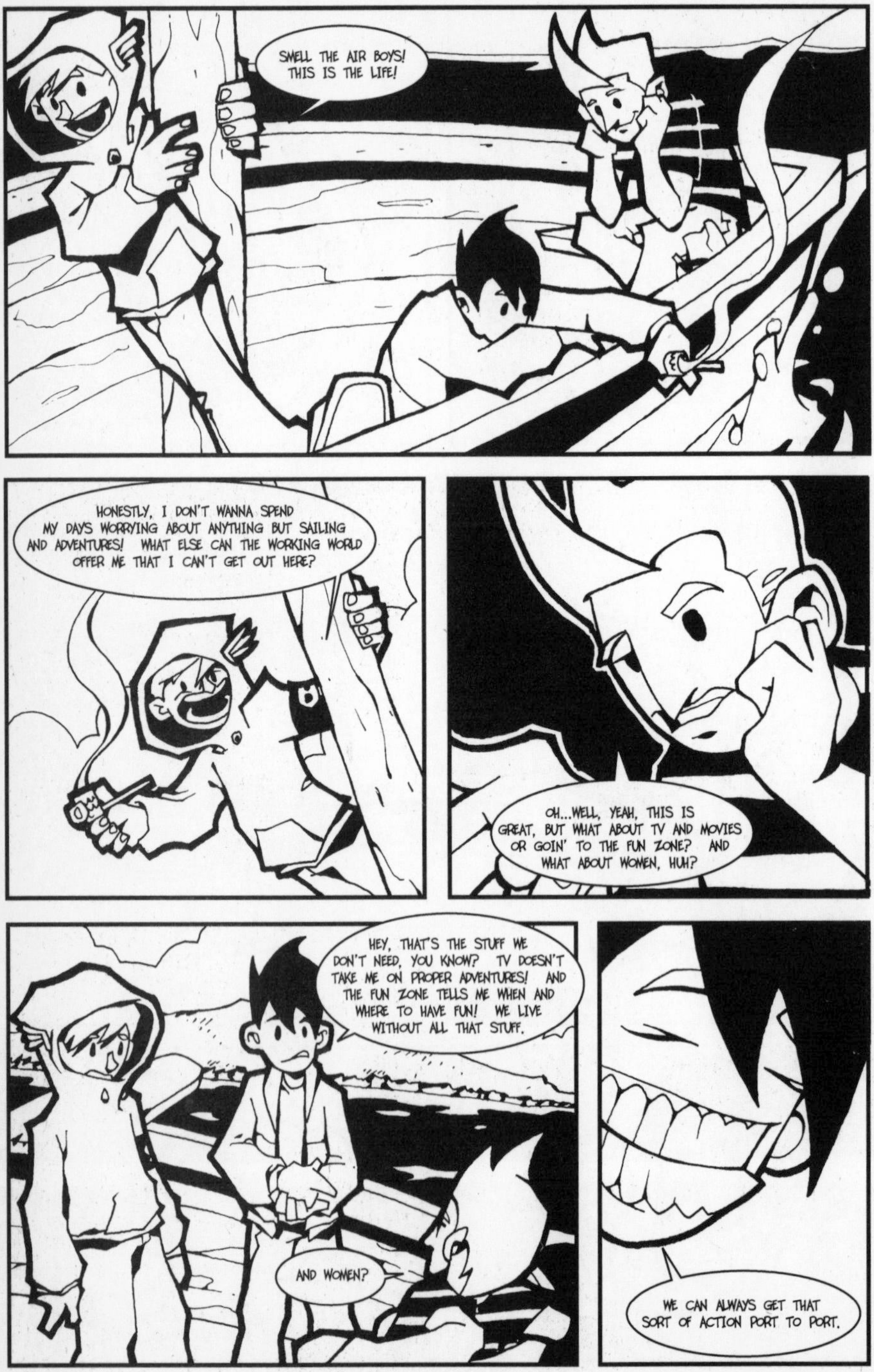
SMELL THE AIR BOYS! THIS IS THE LIFE!
HONESTLY, I DON'T WANNA SPEND MY DAYS WORRYING ABOUT ANYTHING BUT SAILING AND ADVENTURES! WHAT ELSE CAN THE WORKING WORLD OFFER ME THAT I CAN'T GET OUT HERE?
OH...WELL, YEAH, THIS IS GREAT, BUT WHAT ABOUT TV AND MOVIES OR GOIN' TO THE FUN ZONE? AND WHAT ABOUT WOMEN, HUH?
HEY, THAT'S THE STUFF WE DON'T NEED, YOU KNOW? TV DOESN'T TAKE ME ON PROPER ADVENTURES! AND THE FUN ZONE TELLS ME WHEN AND WHERE TO HAVE FUN! WE LIVE WITHOUT ALL THAT STUFF.
AND WOMEN?
WE CAN ALWAYS GET THAT SORT OF ACTION PORT TO PORT.

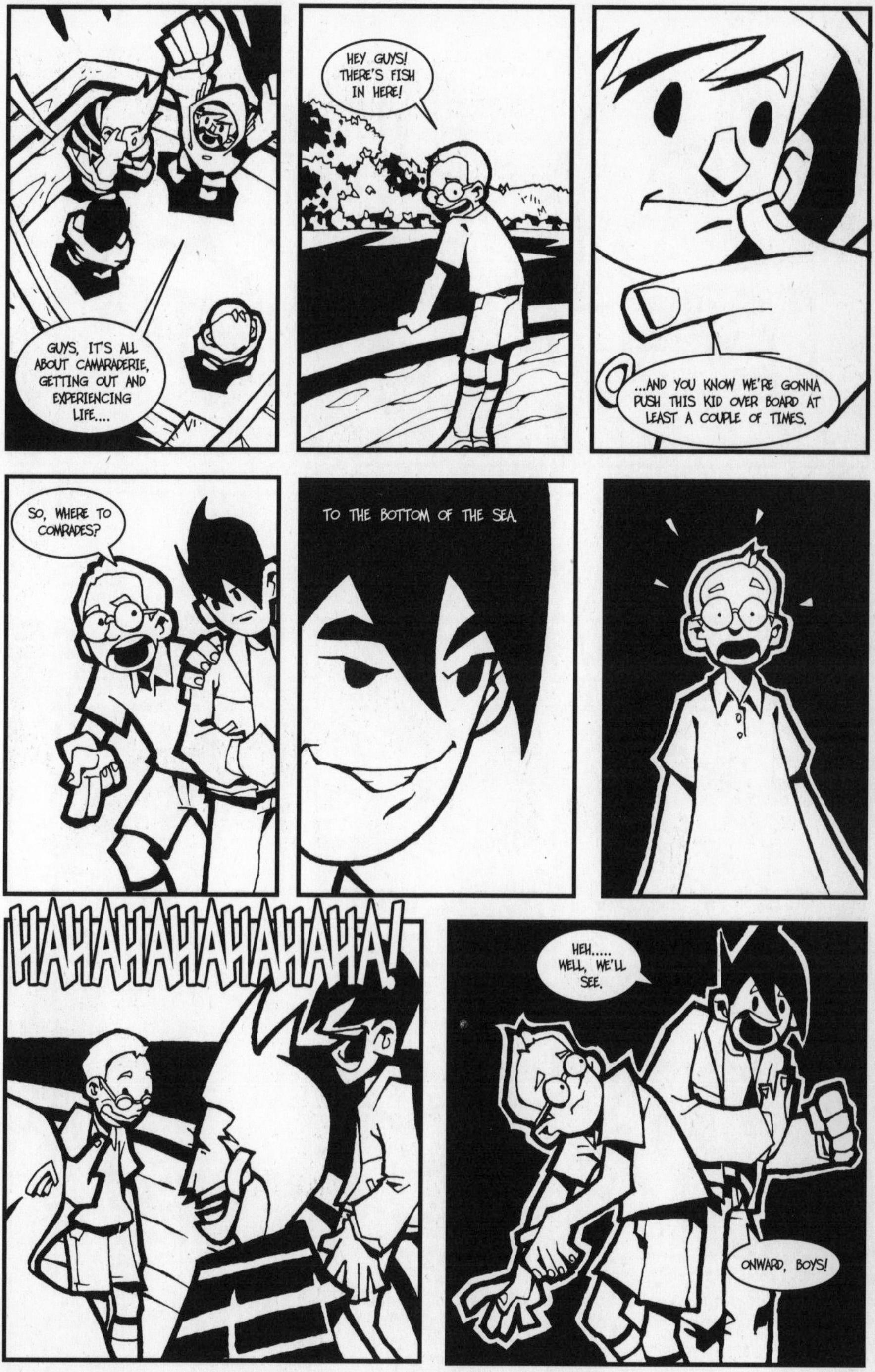
GUYS, IT'S ALL ABOUT CAMARADERIE, GETTING OUT AND EXPERIENCING LIFE....
HEY GUYS! THERE'S FISH IN HERE!
...AND YOU KNOW WE'RE GONNA PUSH THIS KID OVER BOARD AT LEAST A COUPLE OF TIMES.
SO, WHERE TO COMRADES?
TO THE BOTTOM OF THE SEA.
HAHAHAHAHAHAHAHA!
HEH..... WELL, WE'LL SEE.
ONWARD, BOYS!

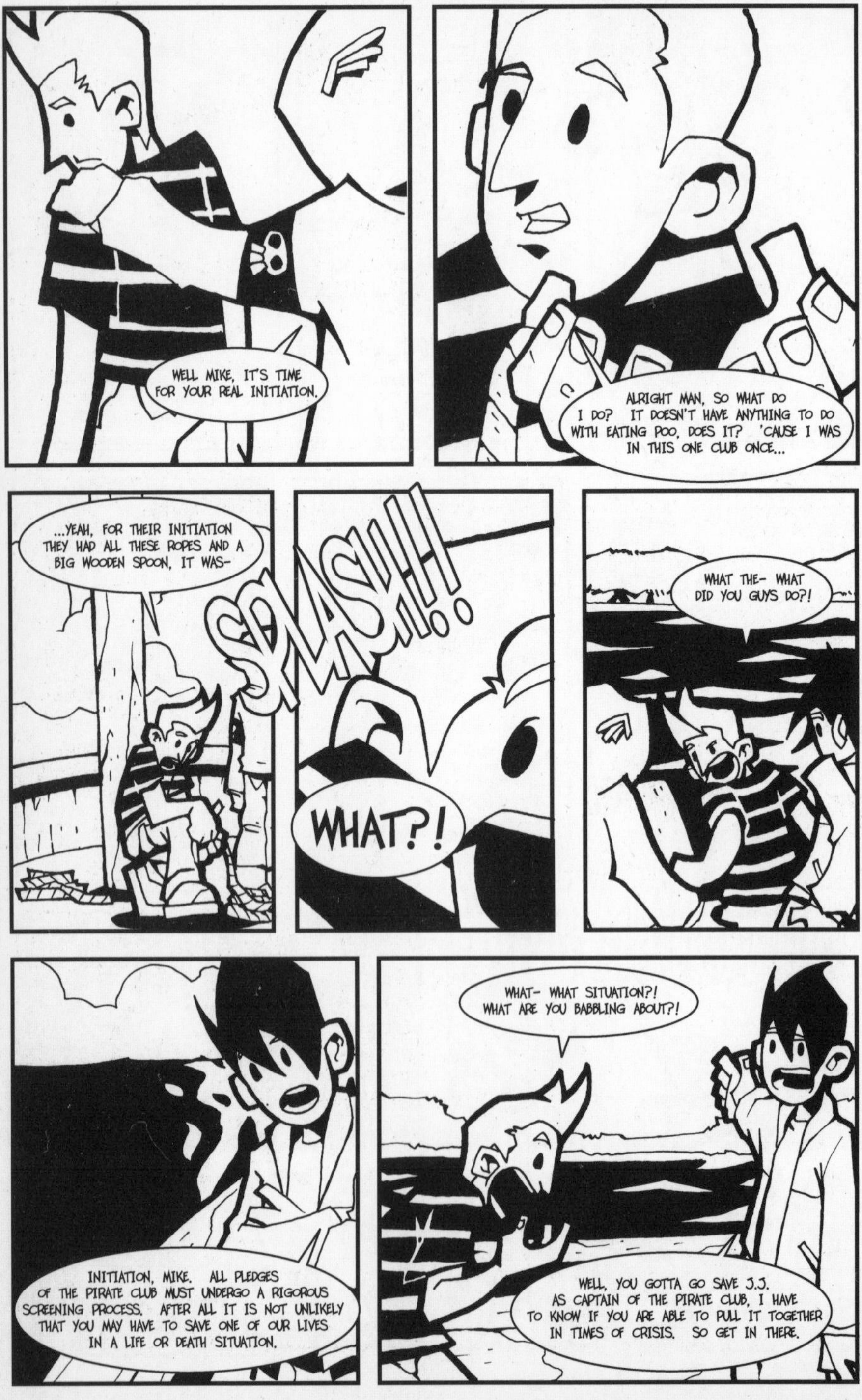
WELL MIKE, IT'S TIME FOR YOUR REAL INITIATION.
ALRIGHT MAN, SO WHAT DO I DO? IT DOESN'T HAVE ANYTHING TO DO WITH EATING POO, DOES IT? 'CAUSE I WAS IN THIS ONE CLUB ONCE...
...YEAH, FOR THEIR INITIATION THEY HAD ALL THESE ROPES AND A BIG WOODEN SPOON, IT WAS-
SPLASH!!
WHAT?!
WHAT THE- WHAT DID YOU GUYS DO?!
INITIATION, MIKE. ALL PLEDGES OF THE PIRATE CLUB MUST UNDERGO A RIGOROUS SCREENING PROCESS. AFTER ALL IT IS NOT UNLIKELY THAT YOU MAY HAVE TO SAVE ONE OF OUR LIVES IN A LIFE OR DEATH SITUATION.
WHAT- WHAT SITUATION?! WHAT ARE YOU BABBLING ABOUT?!
WELL, YOU GOTTA GO SAVE J.J. AS CAPTAIN OF THE PIRATE CLUB, I HAVE TO KNOW IF YOU ARE ABLE TO PULL IT TOGETHER IN TIMES OF CRISIS. SO GET IN THERE.

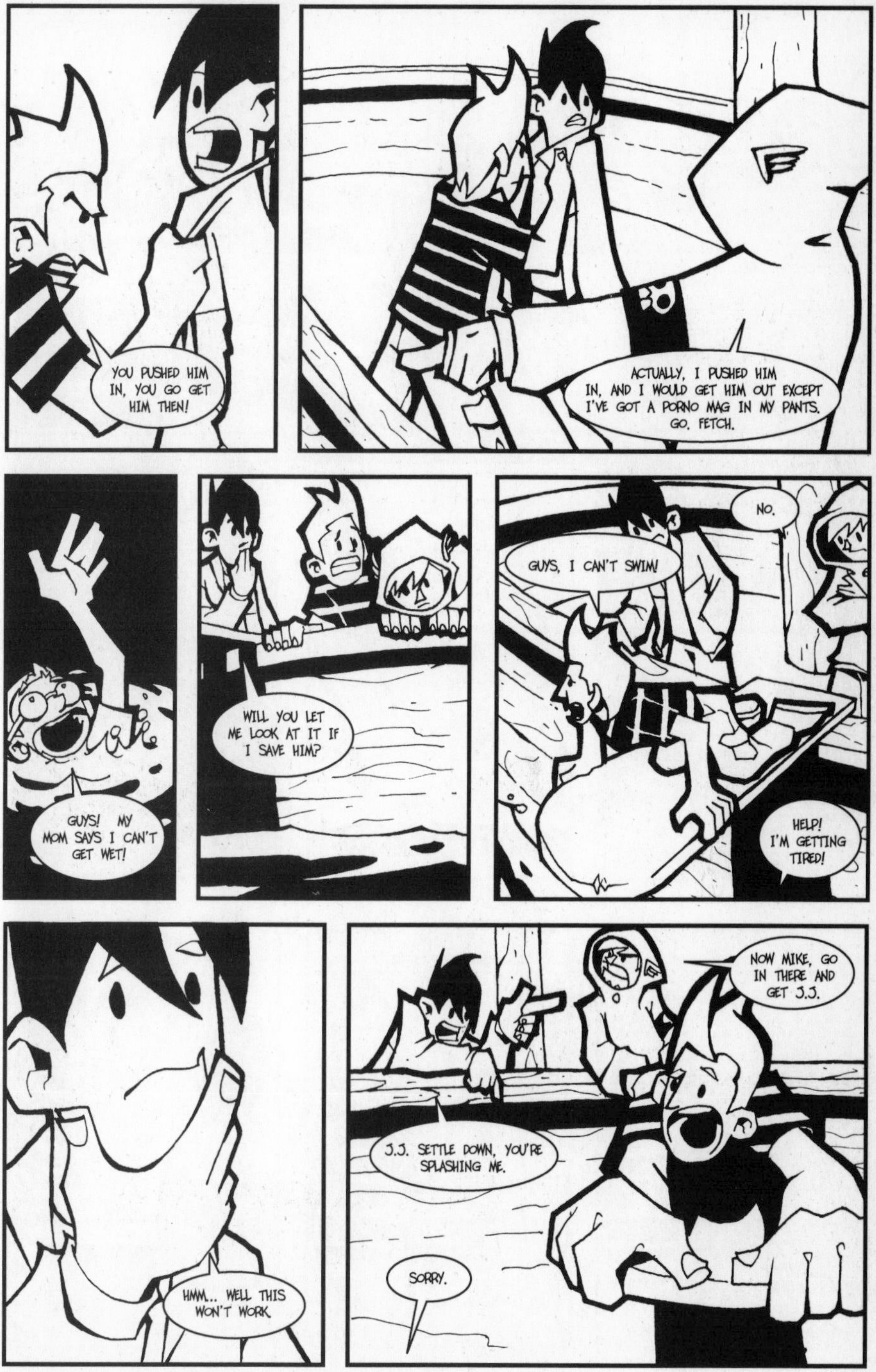

YOU PUSHED HIM IN, YOU GO GET HIM THEN!
ACTUALLY, I PUSHED HIM IN, AND I WOULD GET HIM OUT EXCEPT I'VE GOT A PORNO MAG IN MY PANTS. GO. FETCH.
GUYS! MY MOM SAYS I CAN'T GET WET!
WILL YOU LET ME LOOK AT IT IF I SAVE HIM?
NO.
GUYS, I CAN'T SWIM!
HELP! I'M GETTING TIRED!
HMM... WELL THIS WON'T WORK.
NOW MIKE, GO IN THERE AND GET J.J.
J.J. SETTLE DOWN, YOU'RE SPLASHING ME.
SORRY.

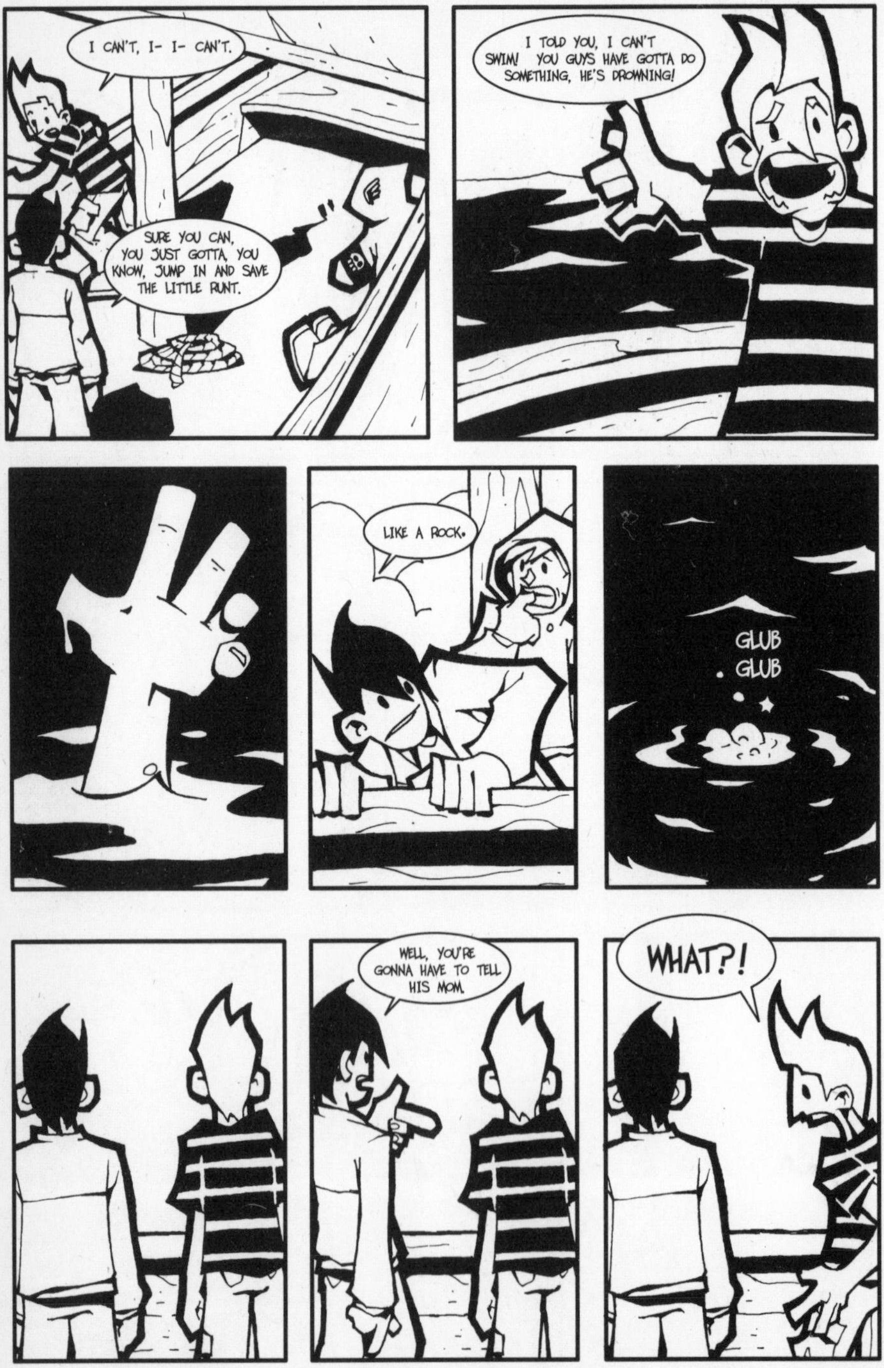
I CAN'T, I- I- CAN'T.
SURE YOU CAN, YOU JUST GOTTA, YOU KNOW, JUMP IN AND SAVE THE LITTLE RUNT.
I TOLD YOU, I CAN'T SWIM! YOU GUYS HAVE GOTTA DO SOMETHING, HE'S DROWNING!
LIKE A ROCK.
GLUB
GLUB
WELL, YOU'RE GONNA HAVE TO TELL HIS MOM.
WHAT?!

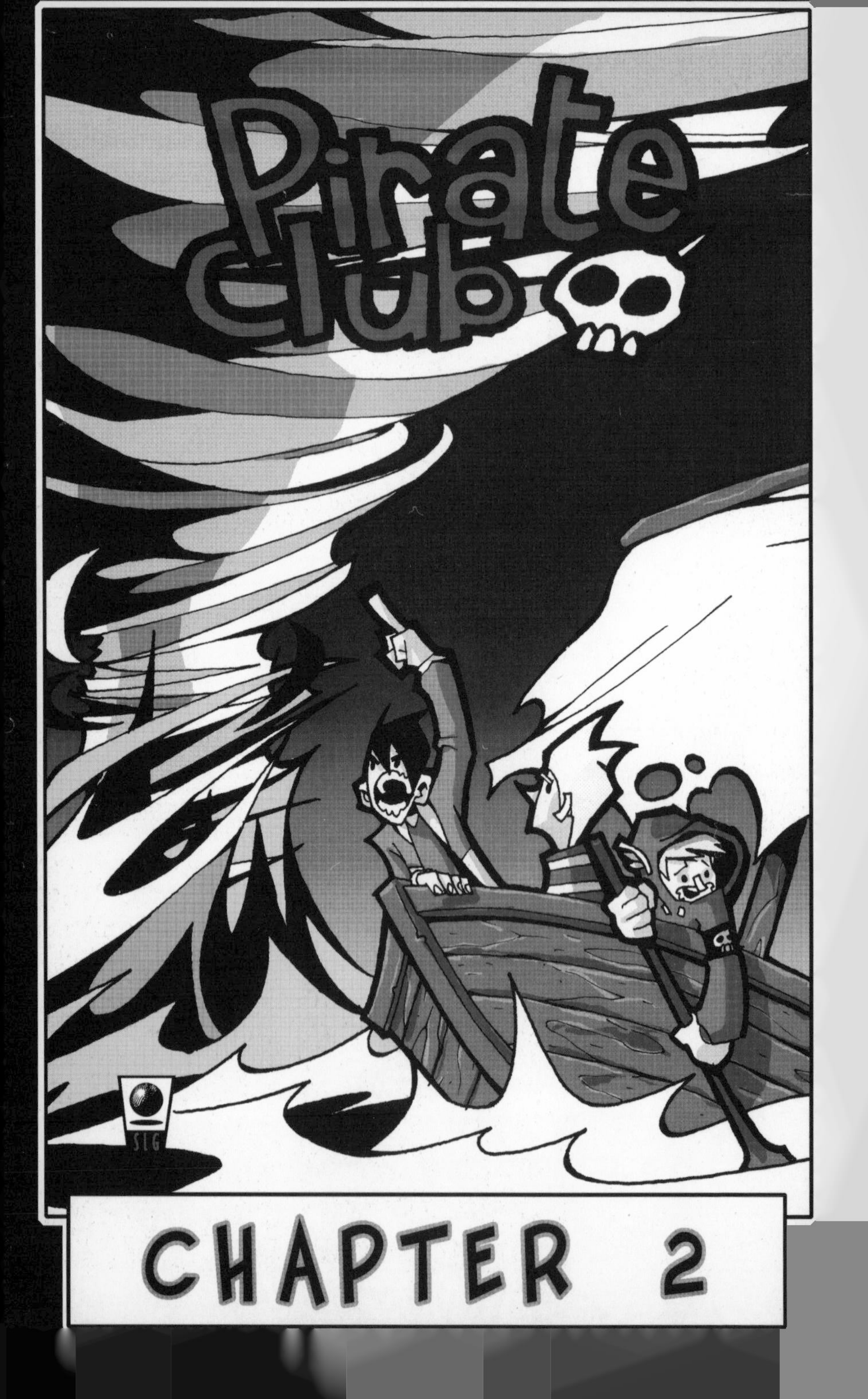
Pirate club
SLG

CHAPTER 2

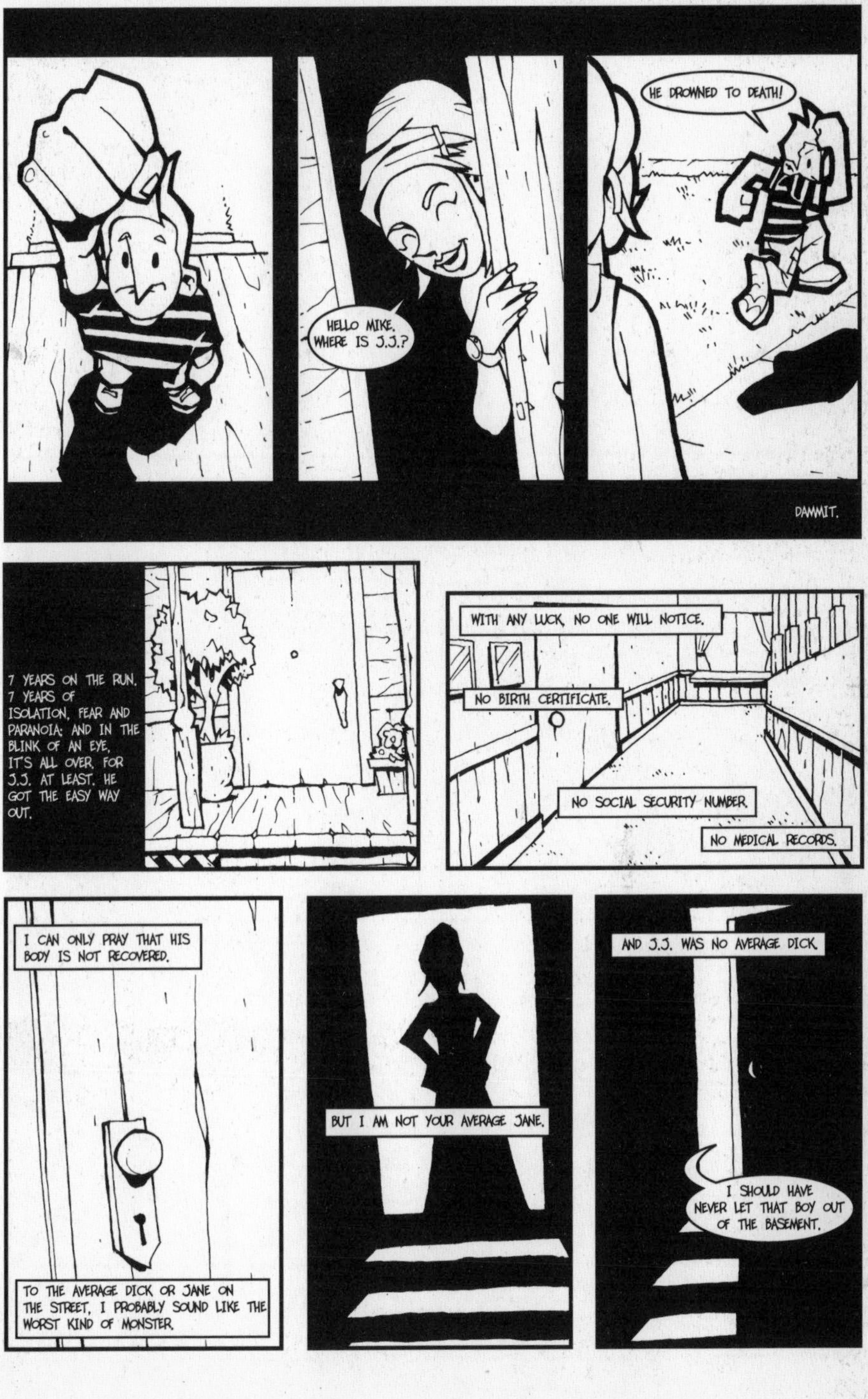
HELLO MIKE. WHERE IS J.J.?
HE DROWNED TO DEATH!
DAMMIT.
7 YEARS ON THE RUN. 7 YEARS OF ISOLATION, FEAR AND PARANOIA; AND IN THE BLINK OF AN EYE, IT'S ALL OVER. FOR J.J. AT LEAST. HE GOT THE EASY WAY OUT.
WITH ANY LUCK, NO ONE WILL NOTICE.
NO BIRTH CERTIFICATE.
NO SOCIAL SECURITY NUMBER.
NO MEDICAL RECORDS.
I CAN ONLY PRAY THAT HIS BODY IS NOT RECOVERED.
TO THE AVERAGE DICK OR JANE ON THE STREET, I PROBABLY SOUND LIKE THE WORST KIND OF MONSTER.
BUT I AM NOT YOUR AVERAGE JANE.
AND J.J. WAS NO AVERAGE DICK.
I SHOULD HAVE NEVER LET THAT BOY OUT OF THE BASEMENT.

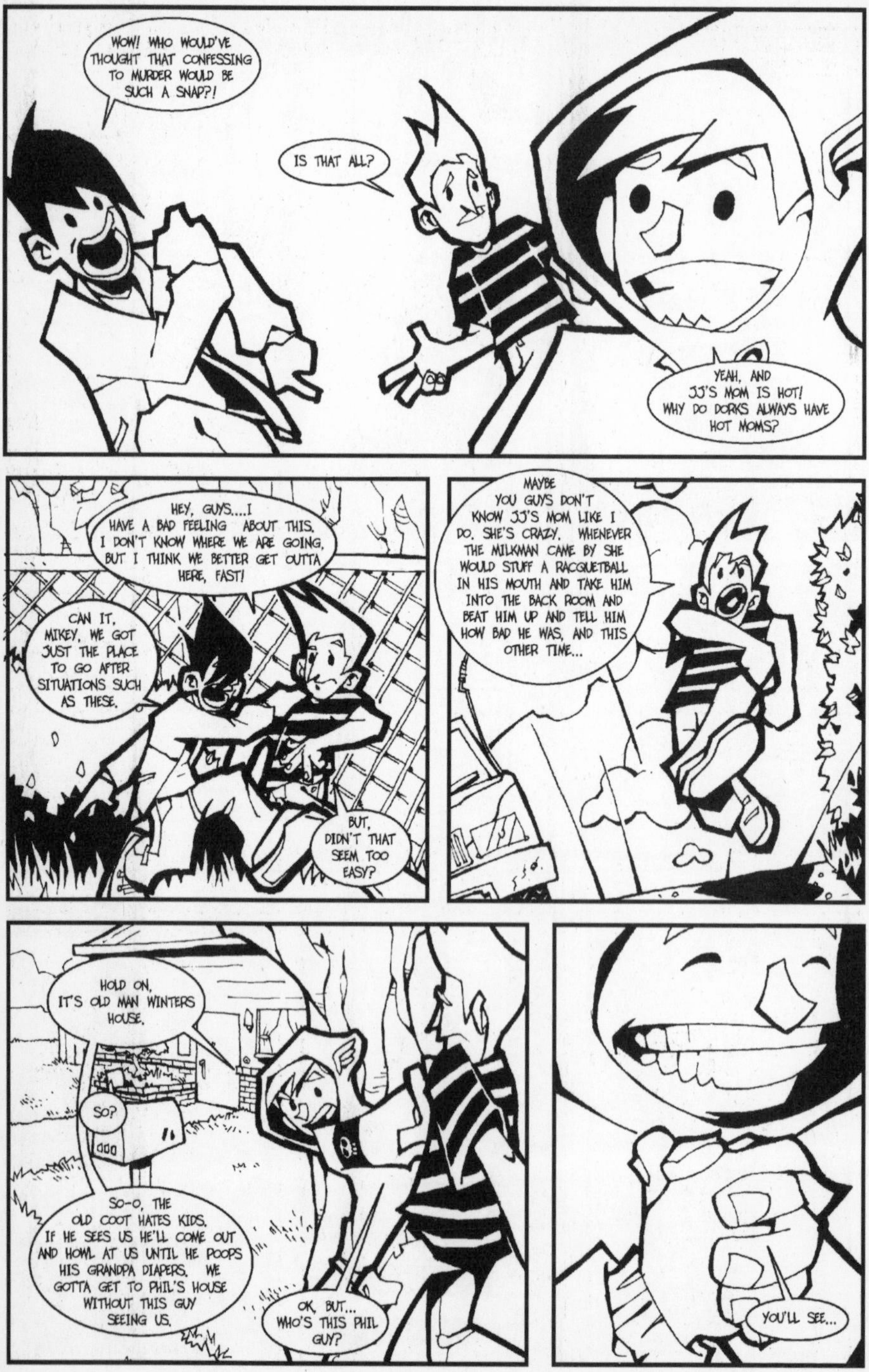

WOW! WHO WOULD'VE THOUGHT THAT CONFESSING TO MURDER WOULD BE SUCH A SNAP?!
IS THAT ALL?
YEAH, AND JJ'S MOM IS HOT! WHY DO DORKS ALWAYS HAVE HOT MOMS?
HEY, GUYS....I HAVE A BAD FEELING ABOUT THIS. I DON'T KNOW WHERE WE ARE GOING, BUT I THINK WE BETTER GET OUTTA HERE, FAST!
CAN IT, MIKEY, WE GOT JUST THE PLACE TO GO AFTER SITUATIONS SUCH AS THESE.
BUT, DIDN'T THAT SEEM TOO EASY?
MAYBE YOU GUYS DON'T KNOW JJ'S MOM LIKE I DO. SHE'S CRAZY. WHENEVER THE MILKMAN CAME BY SHE WOULD STUFF A RACQUETBALL IN HIS MOUTH AND TAKE HIM INTO THE BACK ROOM AND BEAT HIM UP AND TELL HIM HOW BAD HE WAS, AND THIS OTHER TIME...
HOLD ON, IT'S OLD MAN WINTERS HOUSE.
SO?
SO-O, THE OLD COOT HATES KIDS. IF HE SEES US HE'LL COME OUT AND HOWL AT US UNTIL HE POOPS HIS GRANDPA DIAPERS. WE GOTTA GET TO PHIL'S HOUSE WITHOUT THIS GUY SEEING US.
OK, BUT... WHO'S THIS PHIL GUY?
YOU'LL SEE...

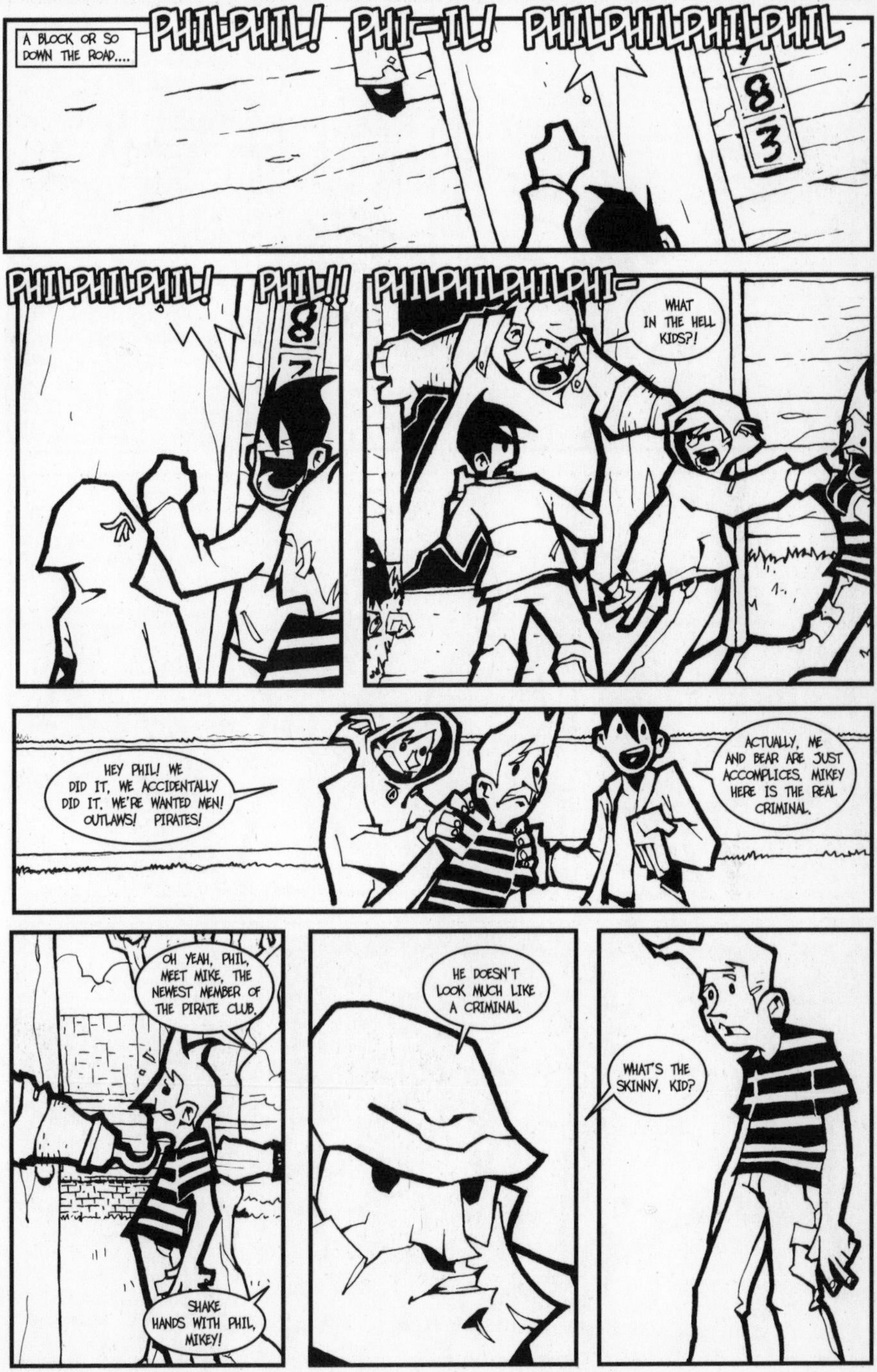
A BLOCK OR SO DOWN THE ROAD....
PHILPHIL! PHI-IL! PHILPHILPHILPHIL
PHILPHILPHIL! PHIL!! PHILPHILPHILPHI-
WHAT IN THE HELL KIDS?!
HEY PHIL! WE DID IT. WE ACCIDENTALLY DID IT. WE'RE WANTED MEN! OUTLAWS! PIRATES!
ACTUALLY, ME AND BEAR ARE JUST ACCOMPLICES. MIKEY HERE IS THE REAL CRIMINAL.
OH YEAH, PHIL, MEET MIKE, THE NEWEST MEMBER OF THE PIRATE CLUB.
SHAKE HANDS WITH PHIL, MIKEY!
HE DOESN'T LOOK MUCH LIKE A CRIMINAL.
WHAT'S THE SKINNY, KID?

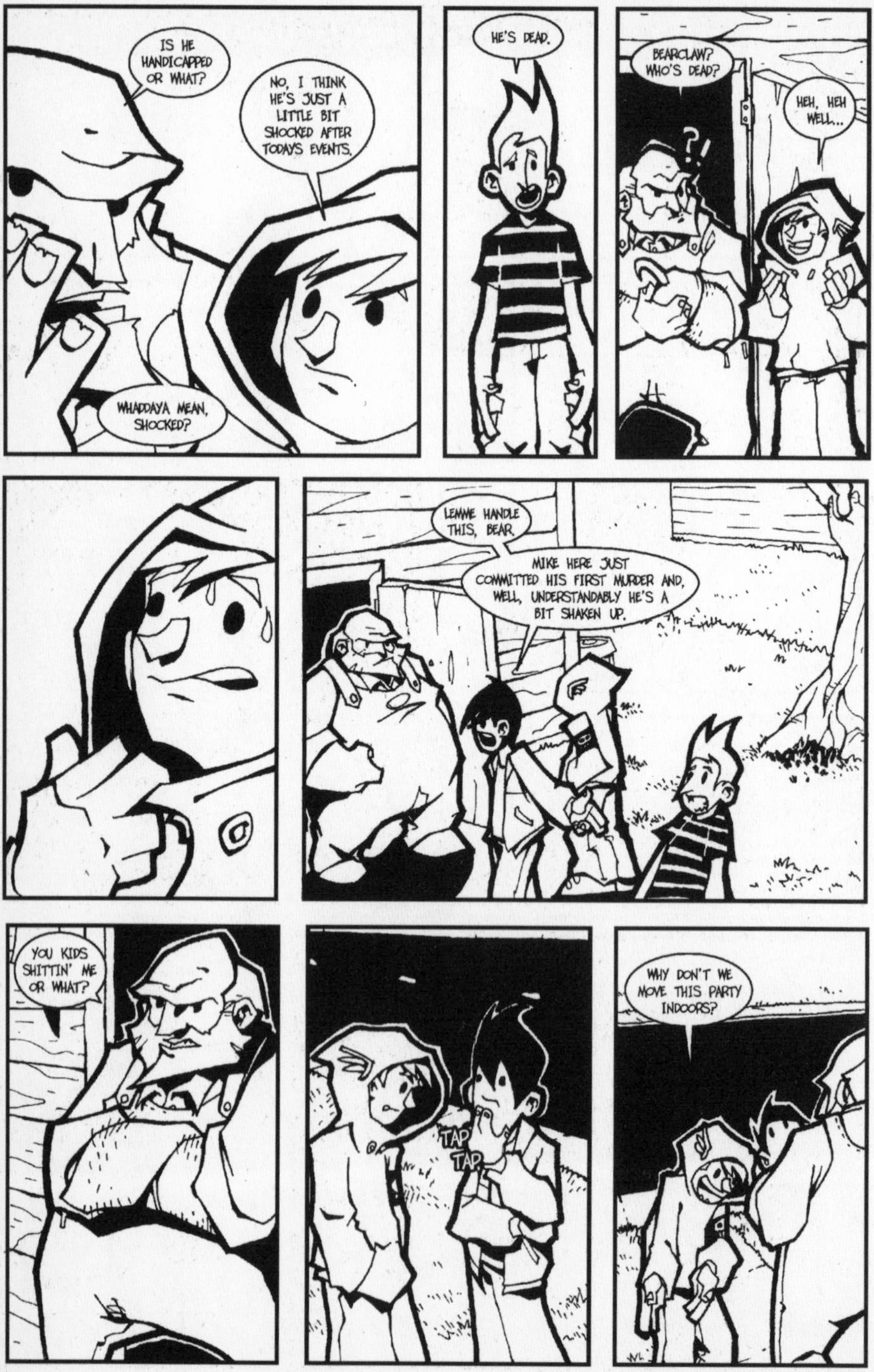
IS HE HANDICAPPED OR WHAT?
NO, I THINK HE'S JUST A LITTLE BIT SHOCKED AFTER TODAYS EVENTS.
WHADDAYA MEAN, SHOCKED?
HE'S DEAD.
BEARCLAW? WHO'S DEAD?
?!
HEH, HEH WELL...
LEMME HANDLE THIS, BEAR.
MIKE HERE JUST COMMITTED HIS FIRST MURDER AND, WELL, UNDERSTANDABLY HE'S A BIT SHAKEN UP.
YOU KIDS SHITTIN' ME OR WHAT?
TAP TAP
WHY DON'T WE MOVE THIS PARTY INDOORS?

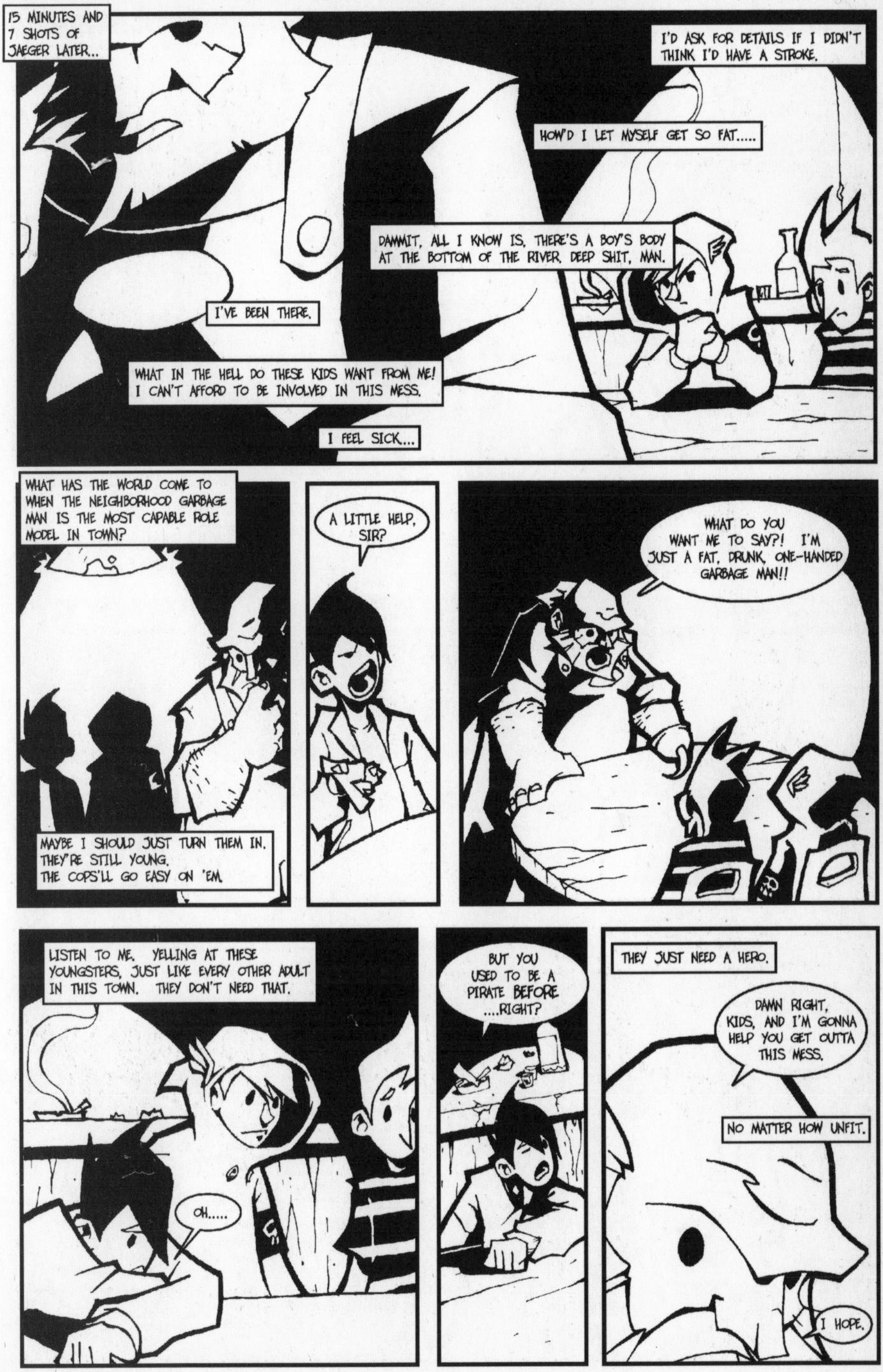
15 MINUTES AND 7 SHOTS OF JAEGER LATER...
I'D ASK FOR DETAILS IF I DIDN'T THINK I'D HAVE A STROKE.
HOW'D I LET MYSELF GET SO FAT.....
DAMMIT, ALL I KNOW IS, THERE'S A BOY'S BODY AT THE BOTTOM OF THE RIVER. DEEP SHIT, MAN.
I'VE BEEN THERE.
WHAT IN THE HELL DO THESE KIDS WANT FROM ME! I CAN'T AFFORD TO BE INVOLVED IN THIS MESS.
I FEEL SICK...
WHAT HAS THE WORLD COME TO WHEN THE NEIGHBORHOOD GARBAGE MAN IS THE MOST CAPABLE ROLE MODEL IN TOWN?
MAYBE I SHOULD JUST TURN THEM IN. THEY'RE STILL YOUNG. THE COPS'LL GO EASY ON 'EM.
A LITTLE HELP, SIR?
WHAT DO YOU WANT ME TO SAY?! I'M JUST A FAT, DRUNK, ONE-HANDED GARBAGE MAN!!
LISTEN TO ME. YELLING AT THESE YOUNGSTERS, JUST LIKE EVERY OTHER ADULT IN THIS TOWN. THEY DON'T NEED THAT.
OH.....
BUT YOU USED TO BE A PIRATE BEFORE ....RIGHT?
THEY JUST NEED A HERO.
DAMN RIGHT, KIDS, AND I'M GONNA HELP YOU GET OUTTA THIS MESS.
NO MATTER HOW UNFIT.
I HOPE.

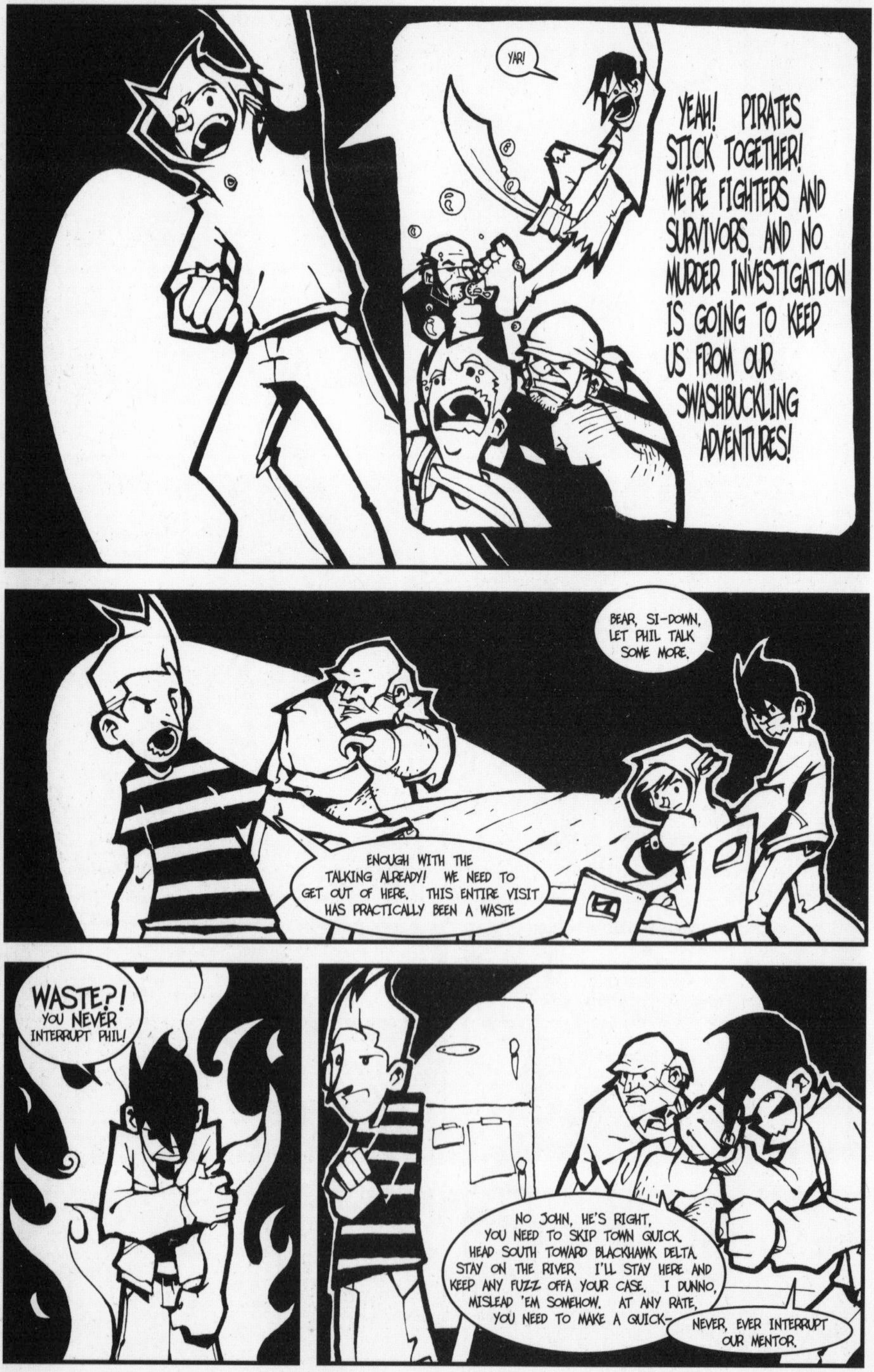
YAR!
YEAH! PIRATES STICK TOGETHER! WE'RE FIGHTERS AND SURVIVORS, AND NO MURDER INVESTIGATION IS GOING TO KEEP US FROM OUR SWASHBUCKLING ADVENTURES!
BEAR, SI-DOWN, LET PHIL TALK SOME MORE.
ENOUGH WITH THE TALKING ALREADY! WE NEED TO GET OUT OF HERE. THIS ENTIRE VISIT HAS PRACTICALLY BEEN A WASTE
WASTE?! YOU NEVER INTERRUPT PHIL!
NO JOHN, HE'S RIGHT, YOU NEED TO SKIP TOWN QUICK. HEAD SOUTH TOWARD BLACKHAWK DELTA. STAY ON THE RIVER. I'LL STAY HERE AND KEEP ANY FUZZ OFFA YOUR CASE. I DUNNO, MISLEAD 'EM SOMEHOW. AT ANY RATE, YOU NEED TO MAKE A QUICK-
NEVER, EVER INTERRUPT OUR MENTOR.

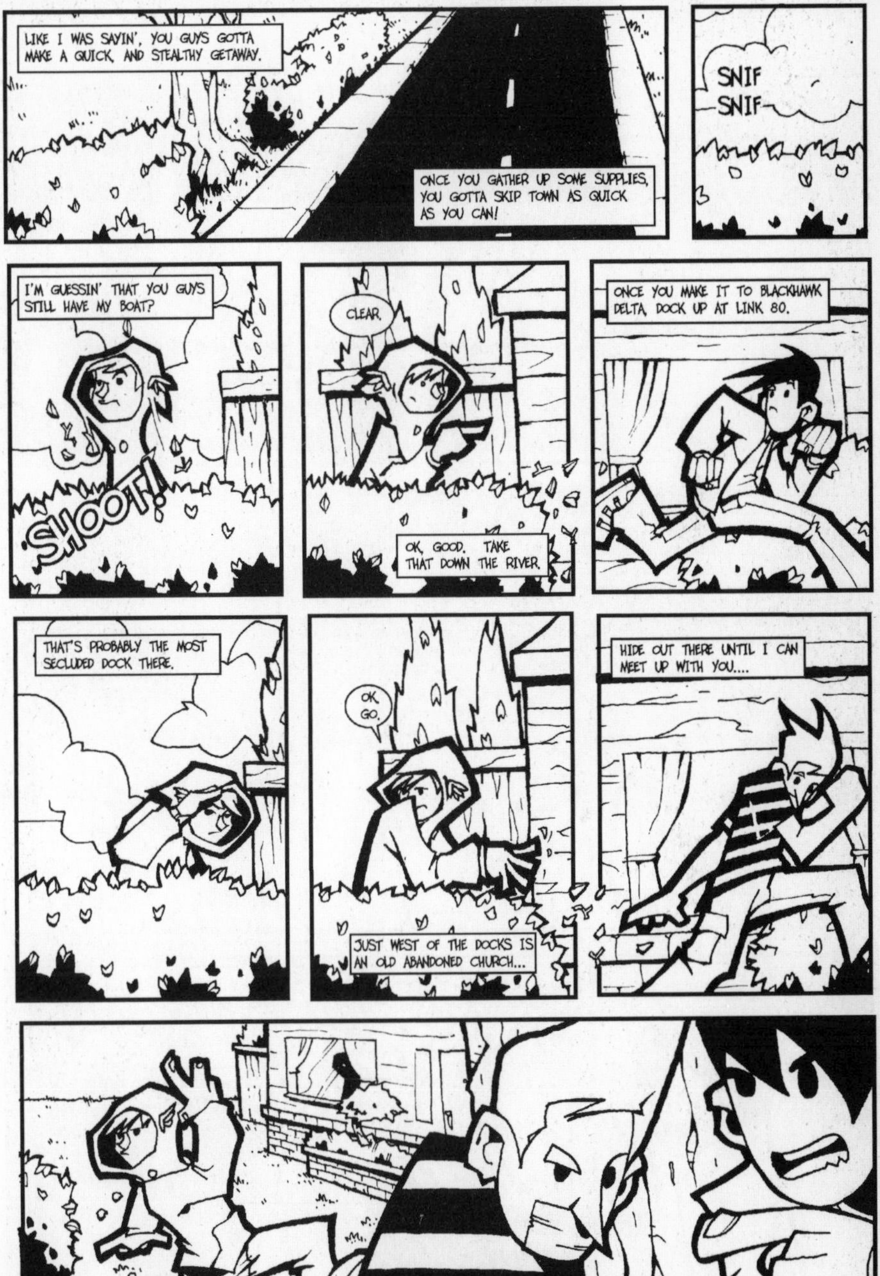
LIKE I WAS SAYIN', YOU GUYS GOTTA MAKE A QUICK, AND STEALTHY GETAWAY.
ONCE YOU GATHER UP SOME SUPPLIES, YOU GOTTA SKIP TOWN AS QUICK AS YOU CAN!
SNIF
SNIF
I'M GUESSIN' THAT YOU GUYS STILL HAVE MY BOAT?
SHOOT!
CLEAR.
OK, GOOD. TAKE THAT DOWN THE RIVER.
ONCE YOU MAKE IT TO BLACKHAWK DELTA, DOCK UP AT LINK 80.
THAT'S PROBABLY THE MOST SECLUDED DOCK THERE.
OK. GO.
JUST WEST OF THE DOCKS IS AN OLD ABANDONED CHURCH...
HIDE OUT THERE UNTIL I CAN MEET UP WITH YOU....
GOT IT? NOW GO GET SOME SUPPLIES AND BE ON YOUR WAY!
THAT'LL TEACH YOU TO INTERRUPT OUR MENTOR.

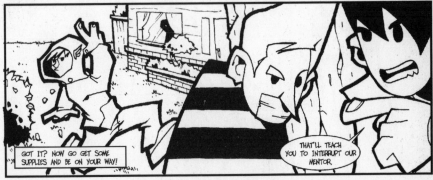

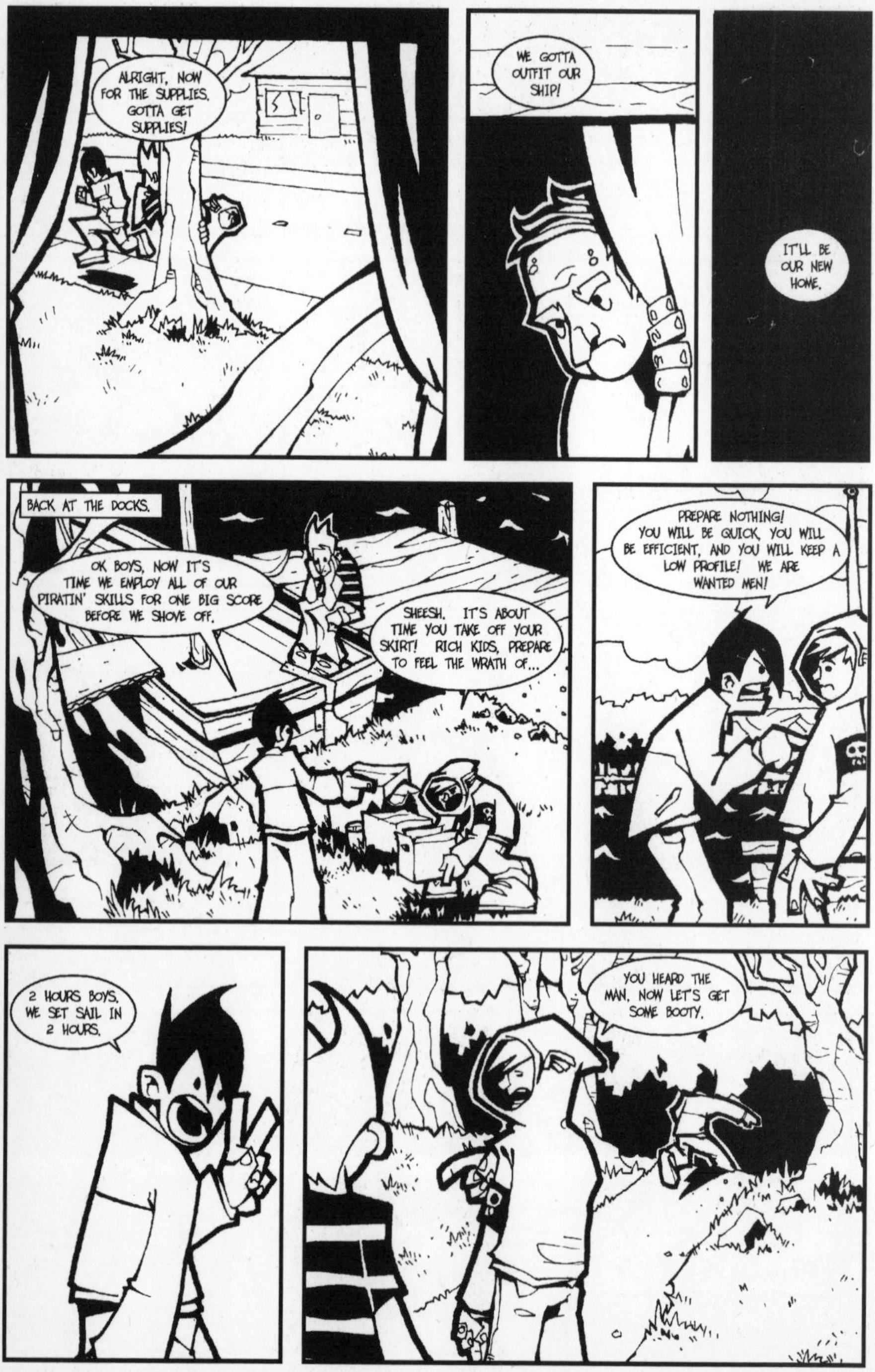
ALRIGHT, NOW FOR THE SUPPLIES. GOTTA GET SUPPLIES!
WE GOTTA OUTFIT OUR SHIP!
IT'LL BE OUR NEW HOME.
BACK AT THE DOCKS.
OK BOYS, NOW IT'S TIME WE EMPLOY ALL OF OUR PIRATIN' SKILLS FOR ONE BIG SCORE BEFORE WE SHOVE OFF.
SHEESH. IT'S ABOUT TIME YOU TAKE OFF YOUR SKIRT! RICH KIDS, PREPARE TO FEEL THE WRATH OF...
PREPARE NOTHING! YOU WILL BE QUICK, YOU WILL BE EFFICIENT, AND YOU WILL KEEP A LOW PROFILE! WE ARE WANTED MEN!
2 HOURS BOYS. WE SET SAIL IN 2 HOURS.
YOU HEARD THE MAN. NOW LET'S GET SOME BOOTY.

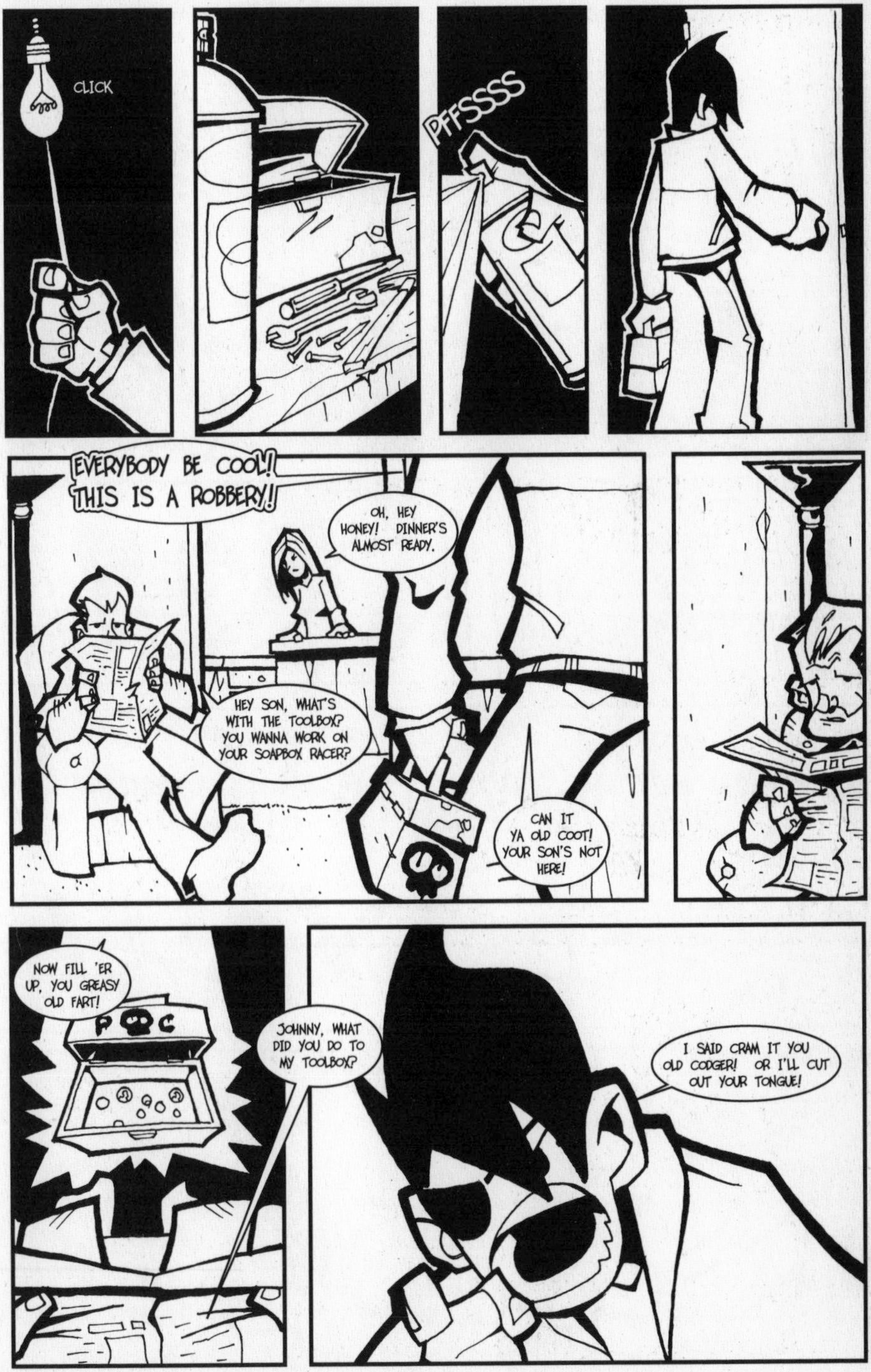
CLICK
PFFSSSS
EVERYBODY BE COOL! THIS IS A ROBBERY!
OH, HEY HONEY! DINNER'S ALMOST READY.
HEY SON, WHAT'S WITH THE TOOLBOX? YOU WANNA WORK ON YOUR SOAPBOX RACER?
CAN IT YA OLD COOT! YOUR SON'S NOT HERE!
NOW FILL 'ER UP, YOU GREASY OLD FART!
JOHNNY, WHAT DID YOU DO TO MY TOOLBOX?
I SAID CRAM IT YOU OLD CODGER! OR I'LL CUT OUT YOUR TONGUE!

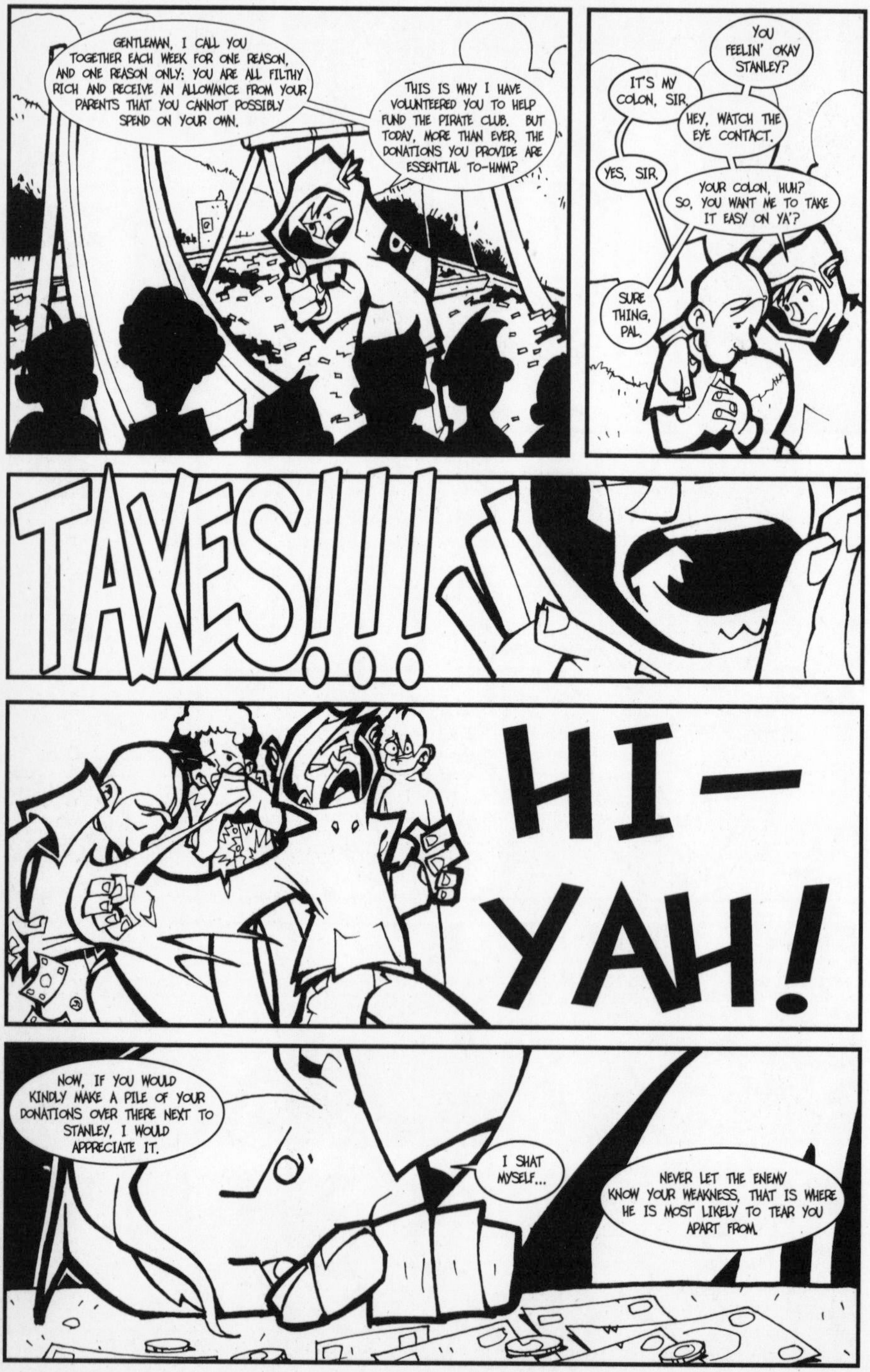
GENTLEMAN, I CALL YOU TOGETHER EACH WEEK FOR ONE REASON, AND ONE REASON ONLY: YOU ARE ALL FILTHY RICH AND RECEIVE AN ALLOWANCE FROM YOUR PARENTS THAT YOU CANNOT POSSIBLY SPEND ON YOUR OWN.
THIS IS WHY I HAVE VOLUNTEERED YOU TO HELP FUND THE PIRATE CLUB. BUT TODAY, MORE THAN EVER, THE DONATIONS YOU PROVIDE ARE ESSENTIAL TO-HMM?
YOU FEELIN' OKAY STANLEY?
IT'S MY COLON, SIR.
HEY, WATCH THE EYE CONTACT.
YES, SIR.
YOUR COLON, HUH? SO, YOU WANT ME TO TAKE IT EASY ON YA'?
SURE THING, PAL.
TAXES!!!
HI-YAH!
NOW, IF YOU WOULD KINDLY MAKE A PILE OF YOUR DONATIONS OVER THERE NEXT TO STANLEY, I WOULD APPRECIATE IT.
I SHAT MYSELF...
NEVER LET THE ENEMY KNOW YOUR WEAKNESS, THAT IS WHERE HE IS MOST LIKELY TO TEAR YOU APART FROM.

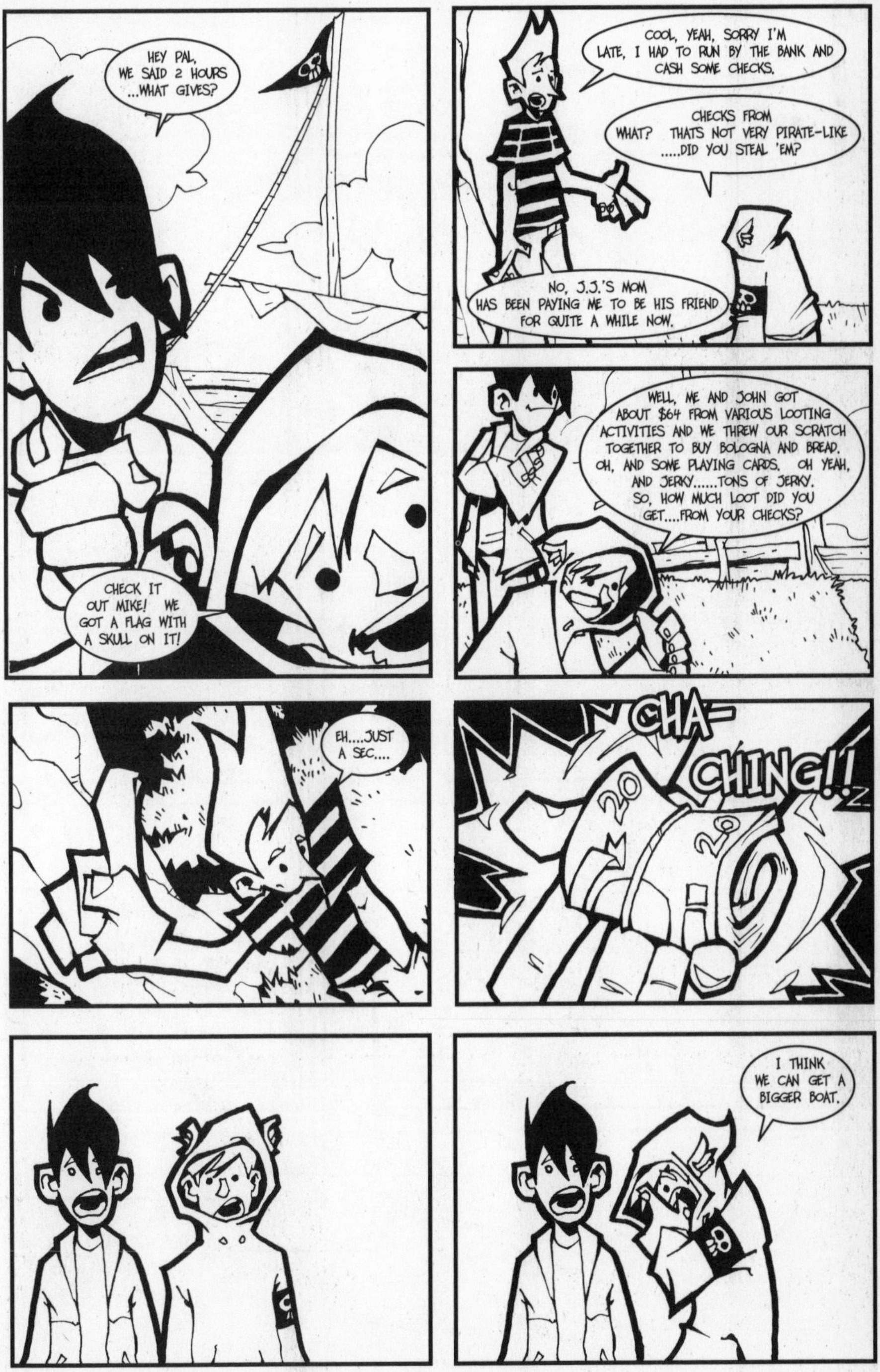

HEY PAL, WE SAID 2 HOURS ...WHAT GIVES?
CHECK IT OUT MIKE! WE GOT A FLAG WITH A SKULL ON IT!
COOL, YEAH, SORRY I'M LATE, I HAD TO RUN BY THE BANK AND CASH SOME CHECKS.
CHECKS FROM WHAT? THATS NOT VERY PIRATE-LIKE .....DID YOU STEAL 'EM?
NO, J.J.'S MOM HAS BEEN PAYING ME TO BE HIS FRIEND FOR QUITE A WHILE NOW.
WELL, ME AND JOHN GOT ABOUT $64 FROM VARIOUS LOOTING ACTIVITIES AND WE THREW OUR SCRATCH TOGETHER TO BUY BOLOGNA AND BREAD. OH, AND SOME PLAYING CARDS. OH YEAH, AND JERKY......TONS OF JERKY. SO, HOW MUCH LOOT DID YOU GET....FROM YOUR CHECKS?
EH....JUST A SEC....
CHA-CHING!!
I THINK WE CAN GET A BIGGER BOAT.

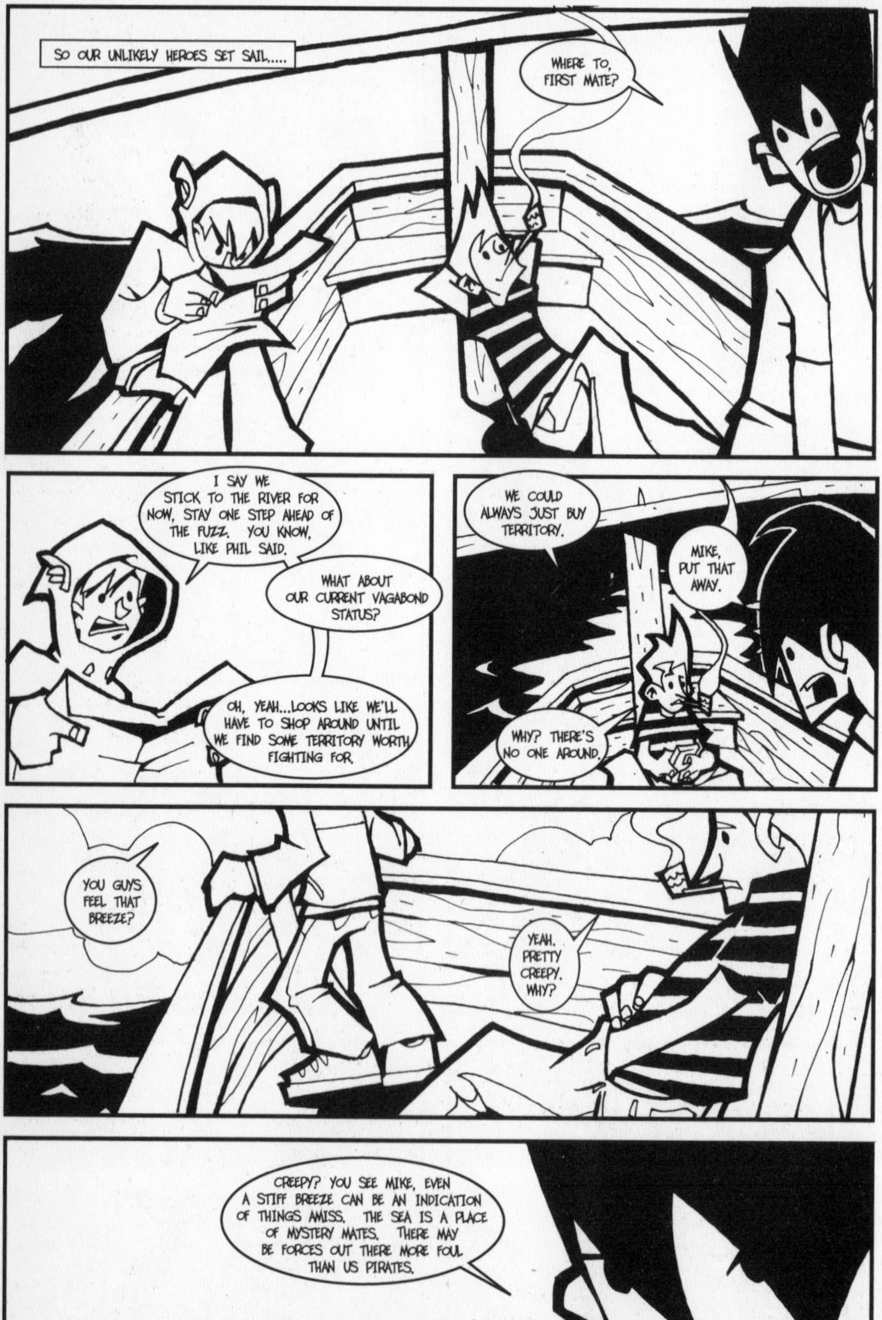
SO OUR UNLIKELY HEROES SET SAIL.....
WHERE TO, FIRST MATE?
I SAY WE STICK TO THE RIVER FOR NOW, STAY ONE STEP AHEAD OF THE FUZZ. YOU KNOW, LIKE PHIL SAID.
WHAT ABOUT OUR CURRENT VAGABOND STATUS?
OH, YEAH...LOOKS LIKE WE'LL HAVE TO SHOP AROUND UNTIL WE FIND SOME TERRITORY WORTH FIGHTING FOR.
WE COULD ALWAYS JUST BUY TERRITORY.
MIKE, PUT THAT AWAY.
WHY? THERE'S NO ONE AROUND.
YOU GUYS FEEL THAT BREEZE?
YEAH. PRETTY CREEPY. WHY?
CREEPY? YOU SEE MIKE, EVEN A STIFF BREEZE CAN BE AN INDICATION OF THINGS AMISS. THE SEA IS A PLACE OF MYSTERY MATES. THERE MAY BE FORCES OUT THERE MORE FOUL THAN US PIRATES.

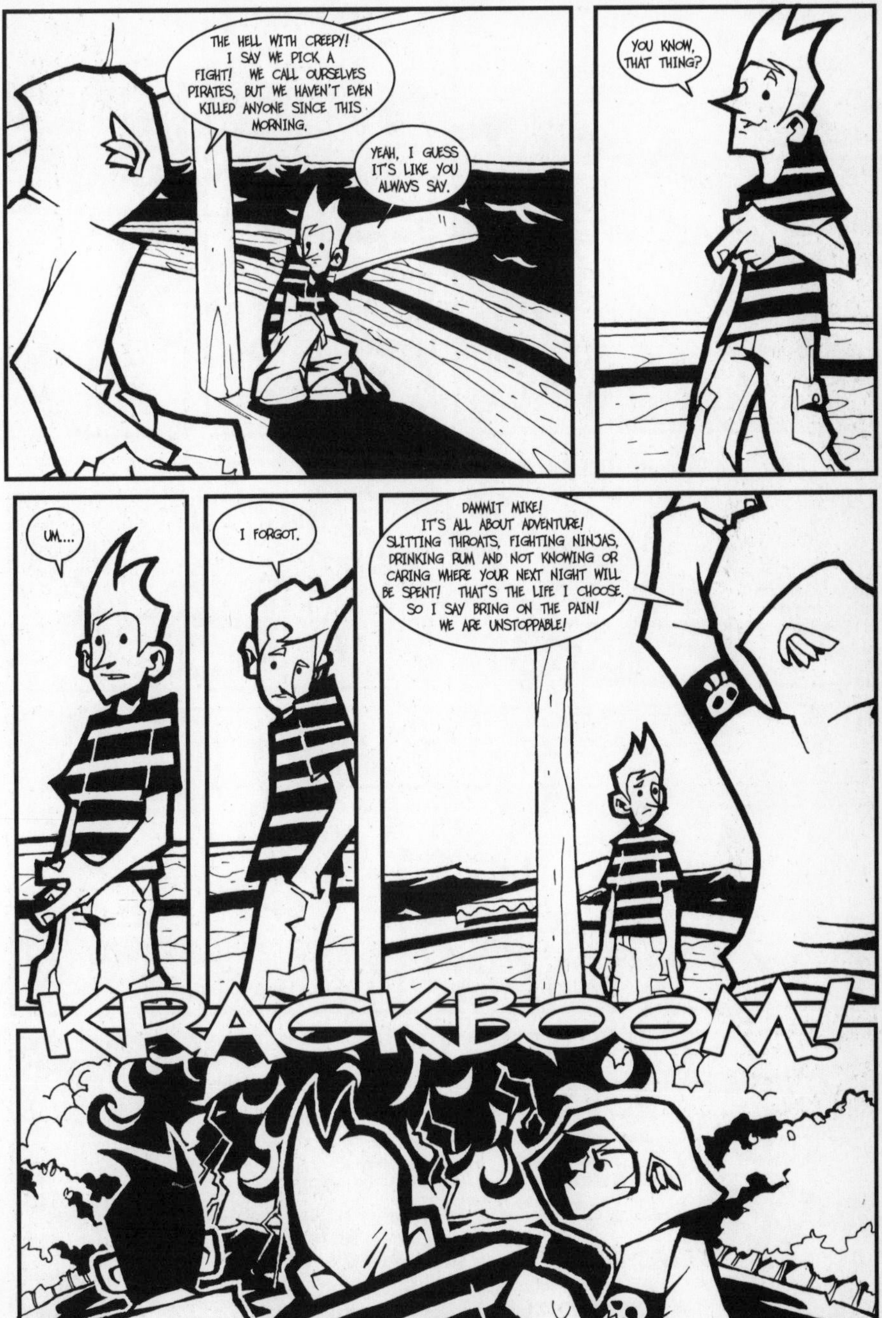
THE HELL WITH CREEPY! I SAY WE PICK A FIGHT! WE CALL OURSELVES PIRATES, BUT WE HAVEN'T EVEN KILLED ANYONE SINCE THIS MORNING.
YEAH, I GUESS IT'S LIKE YOU ALWAYS SAY.
YOU KNOW, THAT THING?
UM...
I FORGOT.
DAMMIT MIKE! IT'S ALL ABOUT ADVENTURE! SLITTING THROATS, FIGHTING NINJAS, DRINKING RUM AND NOT KNOWING OR CARING WHERE YOUR NEXT NIGHT WILL BE SPENT! THAT'S THE LIFE I CHOOSE. SO I SAY BRING ON THE PAIN! WE ARE UNSTOPPABLE!
KRACKBOOM!

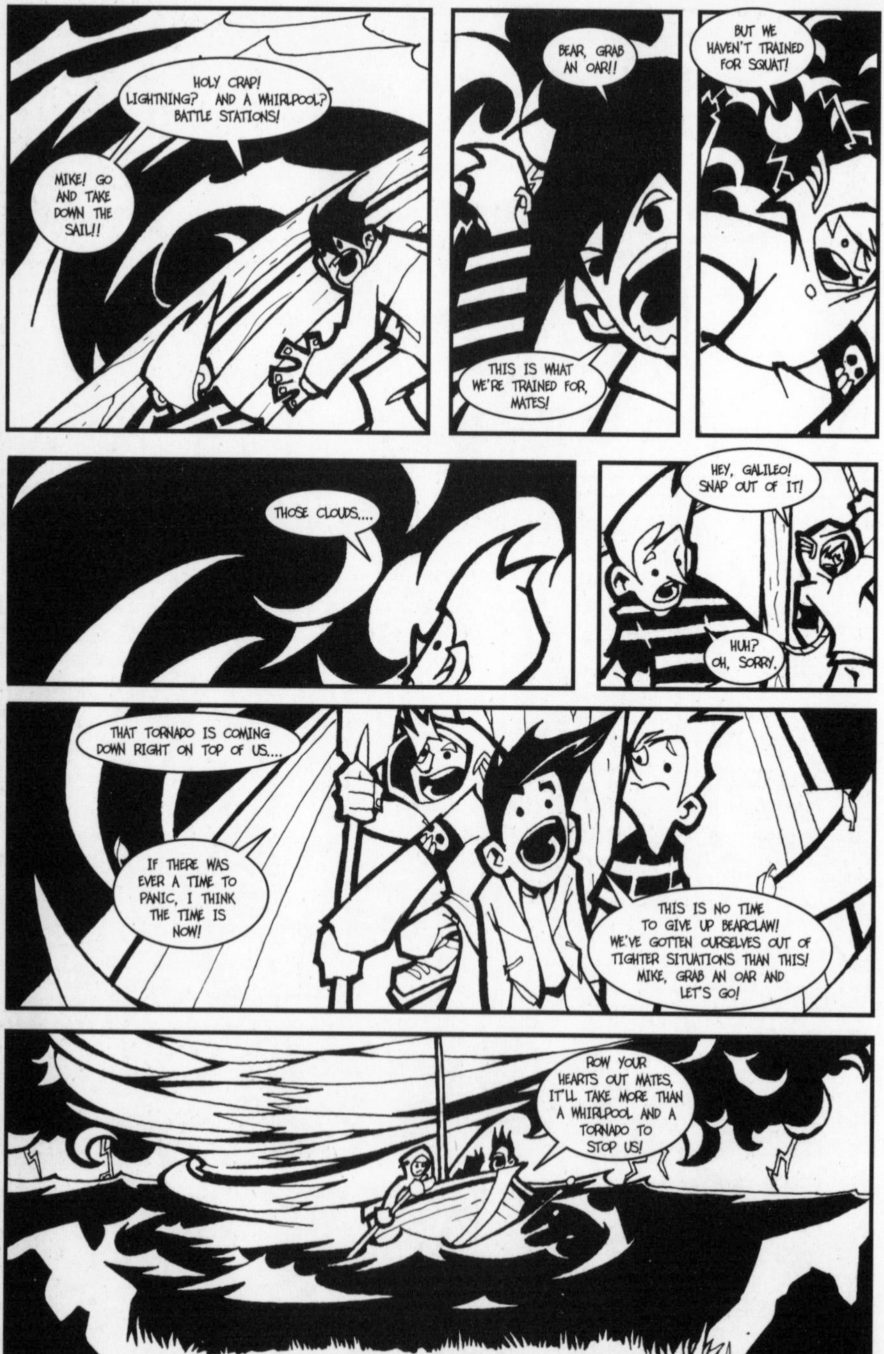
HOLY CRAP! LIGHTNING? AND A WHIRLPOOL? BATTLE STATIONS!
MIKE! GO AND TAKE DOWN THE SAIL!!
BEAR, GRAB AN OAR!!
THIS IS WHAT WE'RE TRAINED FOR, MATES!
BUT WE HAVEN'T TRAINED FOR SQUAT!
THOSE CLOUDS....
HEY, GALILEO! SNAP OUT OF IT!
HUH? OH, SORRY.
THAT TORNADO IS COMING DOWN RIGHT ON TOP OF US....
IF THERE WAS EVER A TIME TO PANIC, I THINK THE TIME IS NOW!
THIS IS NO TIME TO GIVE UP BEARCLAW! WE'VE GOTTEN OURSELVES OUT OF TIGHTER SITUATIONS THAN THIS! MIKE, GRAB AN OAR AND LET'S GO!
ROW YOUR HEARTS OUT MATES, IT'LL TAKE MORE THAN A WHIRLPOOL AND A TORNADO TO STOP US!

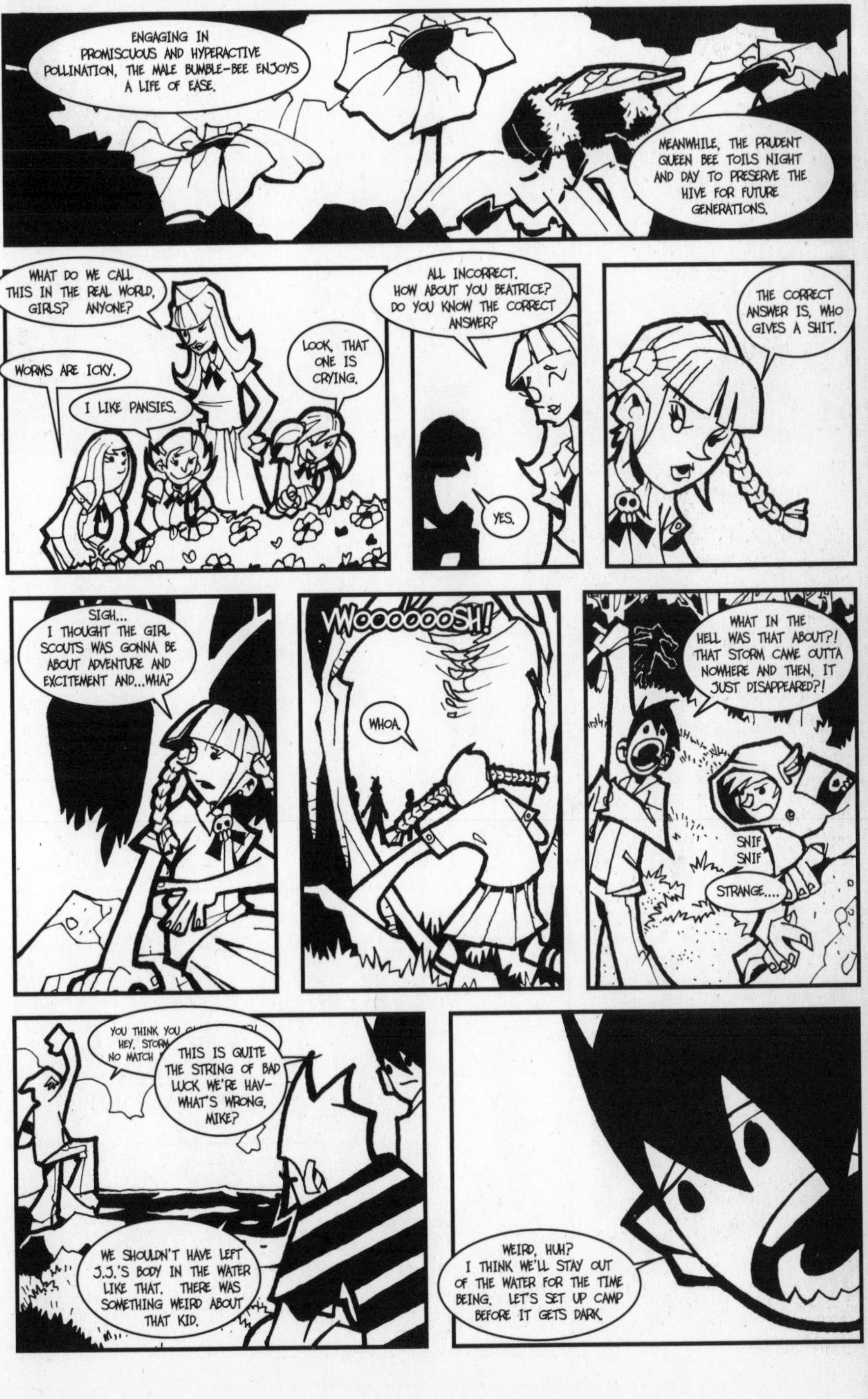
ENGAGING IN PROMISCUOUS AND HYPERACTIVE POLLINATION, THE MALE BUMBLE-BEE ENJOYS A LIFE OF EASE.
MEANWHILE, THE PRUDENT QUEEN BEE TOILS NIGHT AND DAY TO PRESERVE THE HIVE FOR FUTURE GENERATIONS.
WHAT DO WE CALL THIS IN THE REAL WORLD, GIRLS? ANYONE?
WORMS ARE ICKY.
I LIKE PANSIES.
LOOK, THAT ONE IS CRYING.
ALL INCORRECT. HOW ABOUT YOU BEATRICE? DO YOU KNOW THE CORRECT ANSWER?
YES.
THE CORRECT ANSWER IS, WHO GIVES A SHIT.
SIGH... I THOUGHT THE GIRL SCOUTS WAS GONNA BE ABOUT ADVENTURE AND EXCITEMENT AND...WHA?
VWOOOOOOSH!
WHOA.
WHAT IN THE HELL WAS THAT ABOUT?! THAT STORM CAME OUTTA NOWHERE AND THEN, IT JUST DISAPPEARED?!
SNIF SNIF
STRANGE....
YOU THINK YOU
HEY, STORM
NO MATCH
THIS IS QUITE THE STRING OF BAD LUCK WE'RE HAV- WHAT'S WRONG, MIKE?
WE SHOULDN'T HAVE LEFT J.J.'S BODY IN THE WATER LIKE THAT. THERE WAS SOMETHING WEIRD ABOUT THAT KID.
WEIRD, HUH? I THINK WE'LL STAY OUT OF THE WATER FOR THE TIME BEING. LET'S SET UP CAMP BEFORE IT GETS DARK.

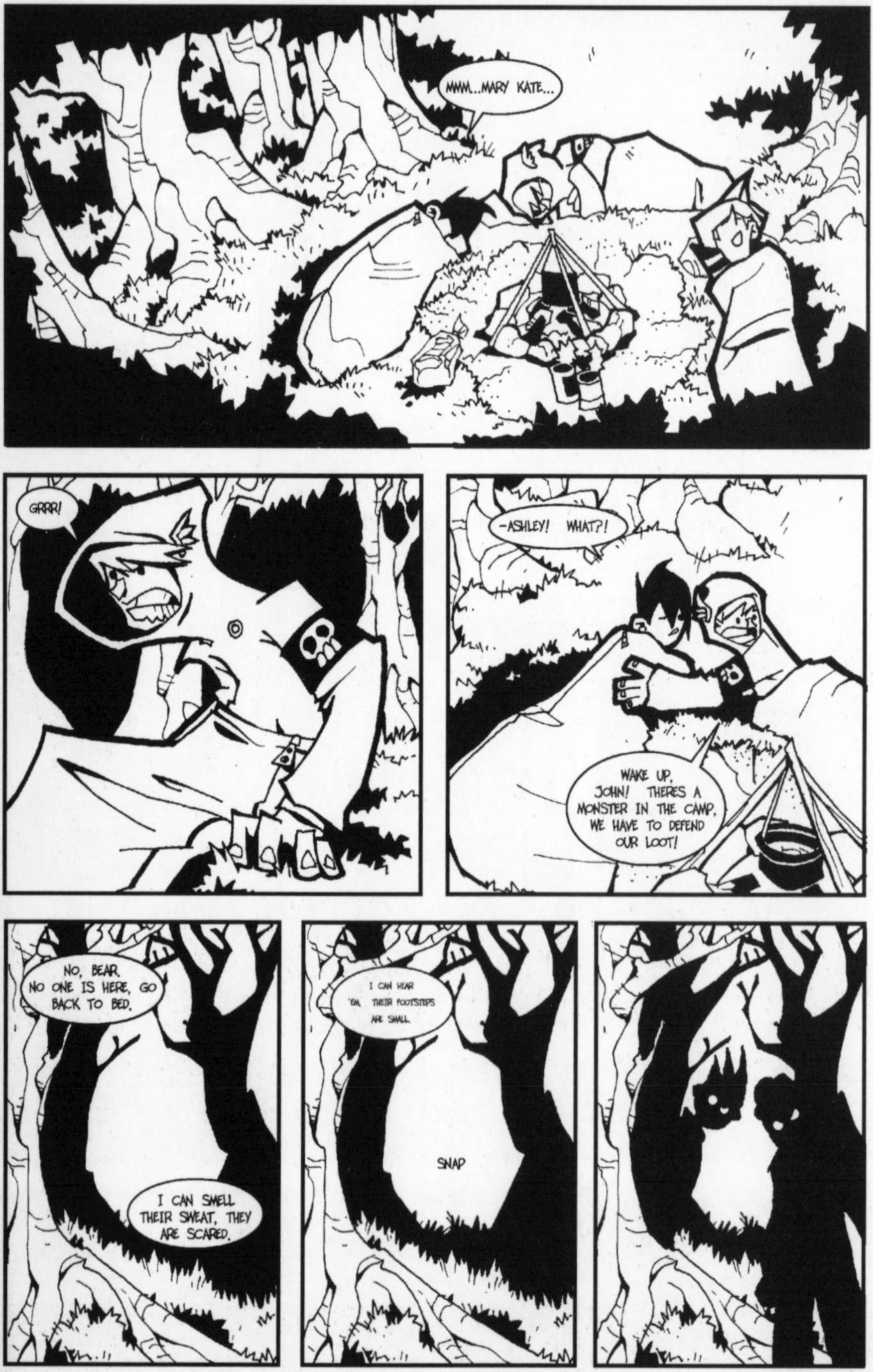

MMM...MARY KATE...
GRRR!
-ASHLEY! WHAT?!
WAKE UP, JOHN! THERES A MONSTER IN THE CAMP, WE HAVE TO DEFEND OUR LOOT!
NO, BEAR. NO ONE IS HERE, GO BACK TO BED.
I CAN SMELL THEIR SWEAT, THEY ARE SCARED.
I CAN HEAR 'EM. THEIR FOOTSTEPS ARE SMALL.
SNAP

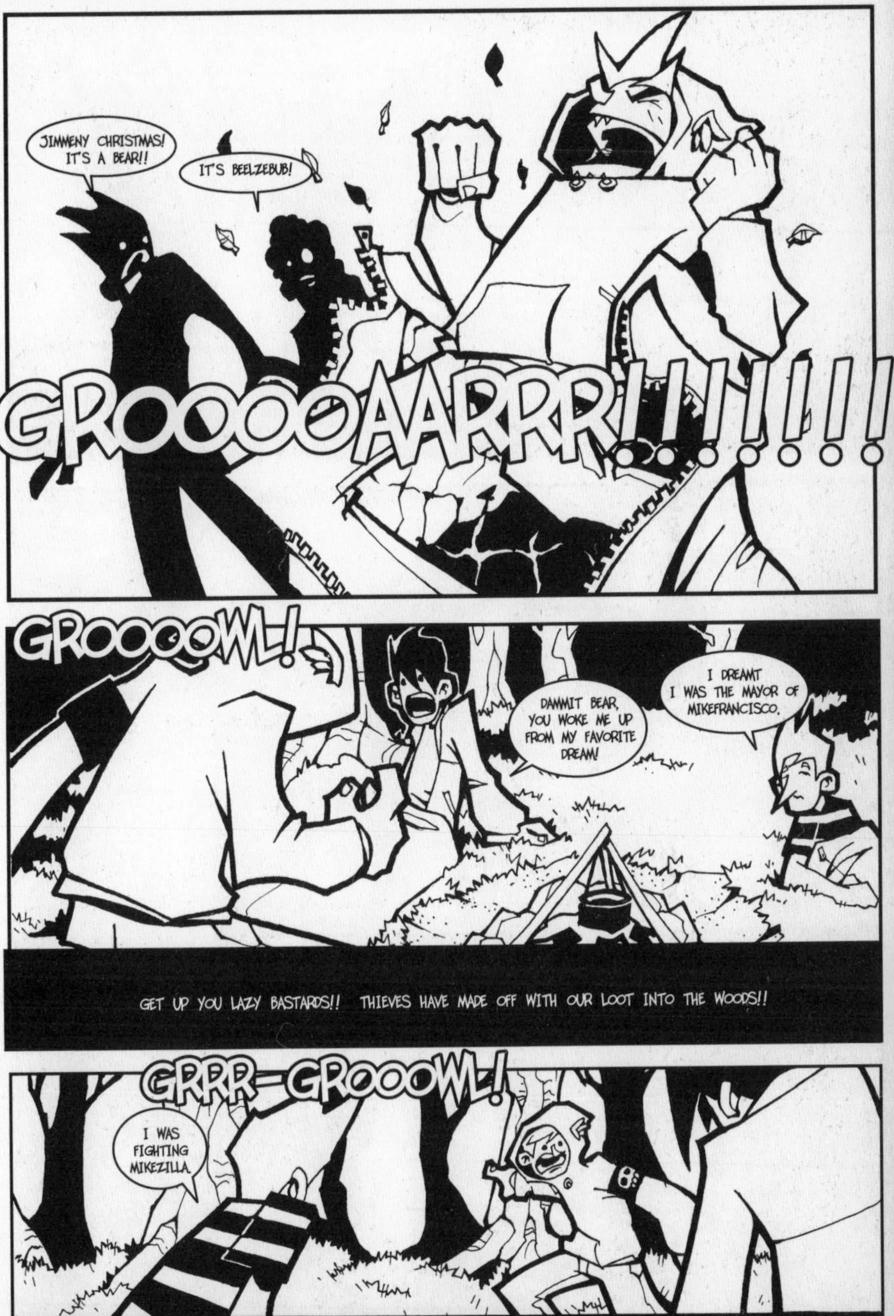

JIMMENY CHRISTMAS! IT'S A BEAR!!
IT'S BEELZEBUB!
GROOOOOAARRR!!!!!!!!
GROOOOOWL!
DAMMIT BEAR, YOU WOKE ME UP FROM MY FAVORITE DREAM!
I DREAMT I WAS THE MAYOR OF MIKEFRANCISCO.
GET UP YOU LAZY BASTARDS!! THIEVES HAVE MADE OFF WITH OUR LOOT INTO THE WOODS!!
GRRR-GROOOOWL!
I WAS FIGHTING MIKEZILLA.
QUICKLY MATES! SCREW NUTS AND BERRIES. TODAY WE TASTE MAN-FLESH!

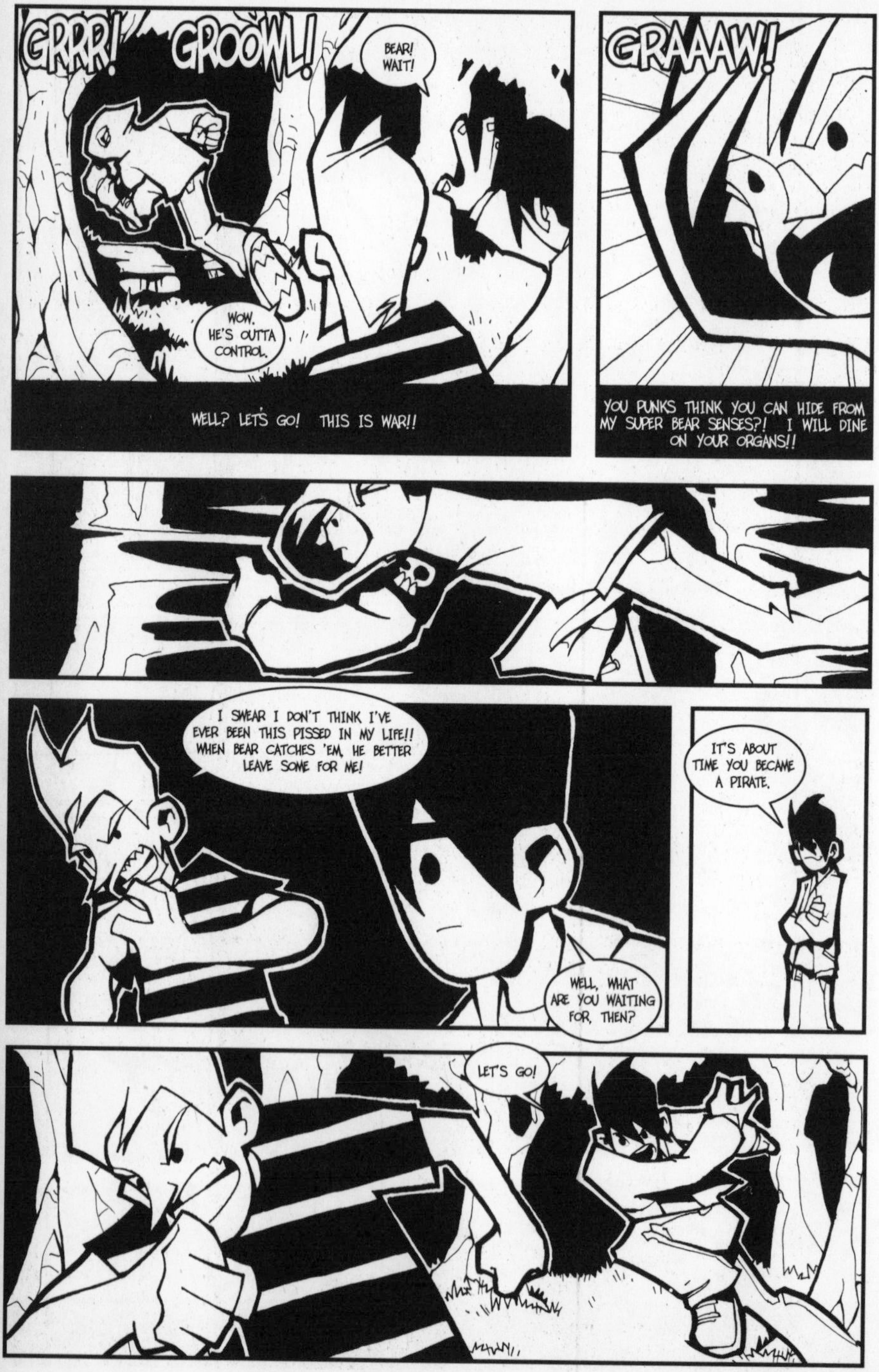
GRRR!
GROOWL!
BEAR! WAIT!
WOW. HE'S OUTTA CONTROL.
WELL? LET'S GO! THIS IS WAR!!
GRAAAW!
YOU PUNKS THINK YOU CAN HIDE FROM MY SUPER BEAR SENSES?! I WILL DINE ON YOUR ORGANS!!
I SWEAR I DON'T THINK I'VE EVER BEEN THIS PISSED IN MY LIFE!! WHEN BEAR CATCHES 'EM, HE BETTER LEAVE SOME FOR ME!
WELL, WHAT ARE YOU WAITING FOR, THEN?
IT'S ABOUT TIME YOU BECAME A PIRATE.
LET'S GO!

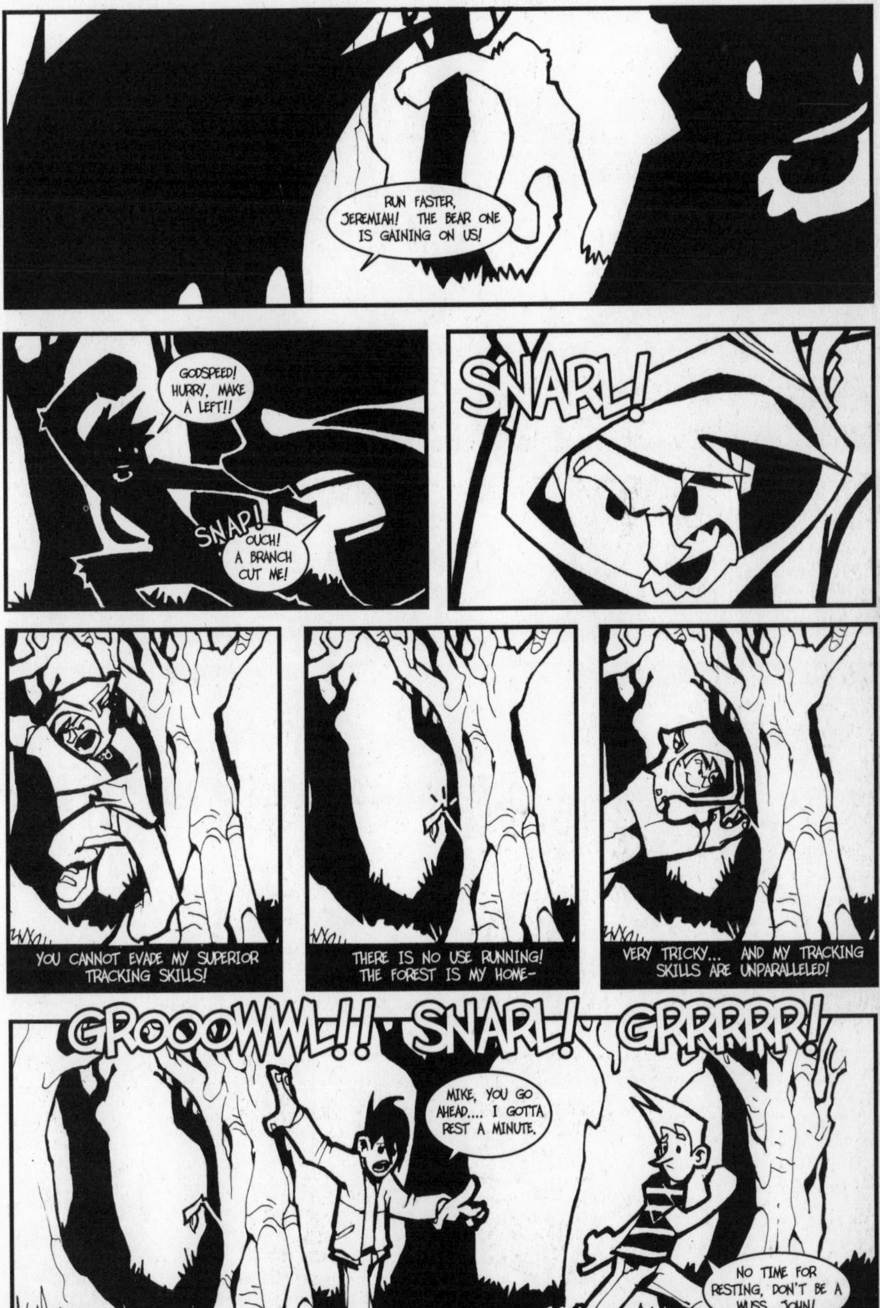
RUN FASTER, JEREMIAH! THE BEAR ONE IS GAINING ON US!
GODSPEED! HURRY, MAKE A LEFT!!
SNAP!
OUCH! A BRANCH CUT ME!
SNARL!
YOU CANNOT EVADE MY SUPERIOR TRACKING SKILLS!
THERE IS NO USE RUNNING! THE FOREST IS MY HOME-
VERY TRICKY... AND MY TRACKING SKILLS ARE UNPARALLELED!
GROOOWWL!! SNARL! GRRRRR!
MIKE, YOU GO AHEAD.... I GOTTA REST A MINUTE.
NO TIME FOR RESTING, DON'T BE A WUSS, JOHN!
ALRIGHT YOU LITTLE TURDS! YOU'RE TESTING MY PATIENCE! WHEN I CATCH YOU I'M GONNA RIP YOUR LUNGS OUT YOUR NOSTRILS!

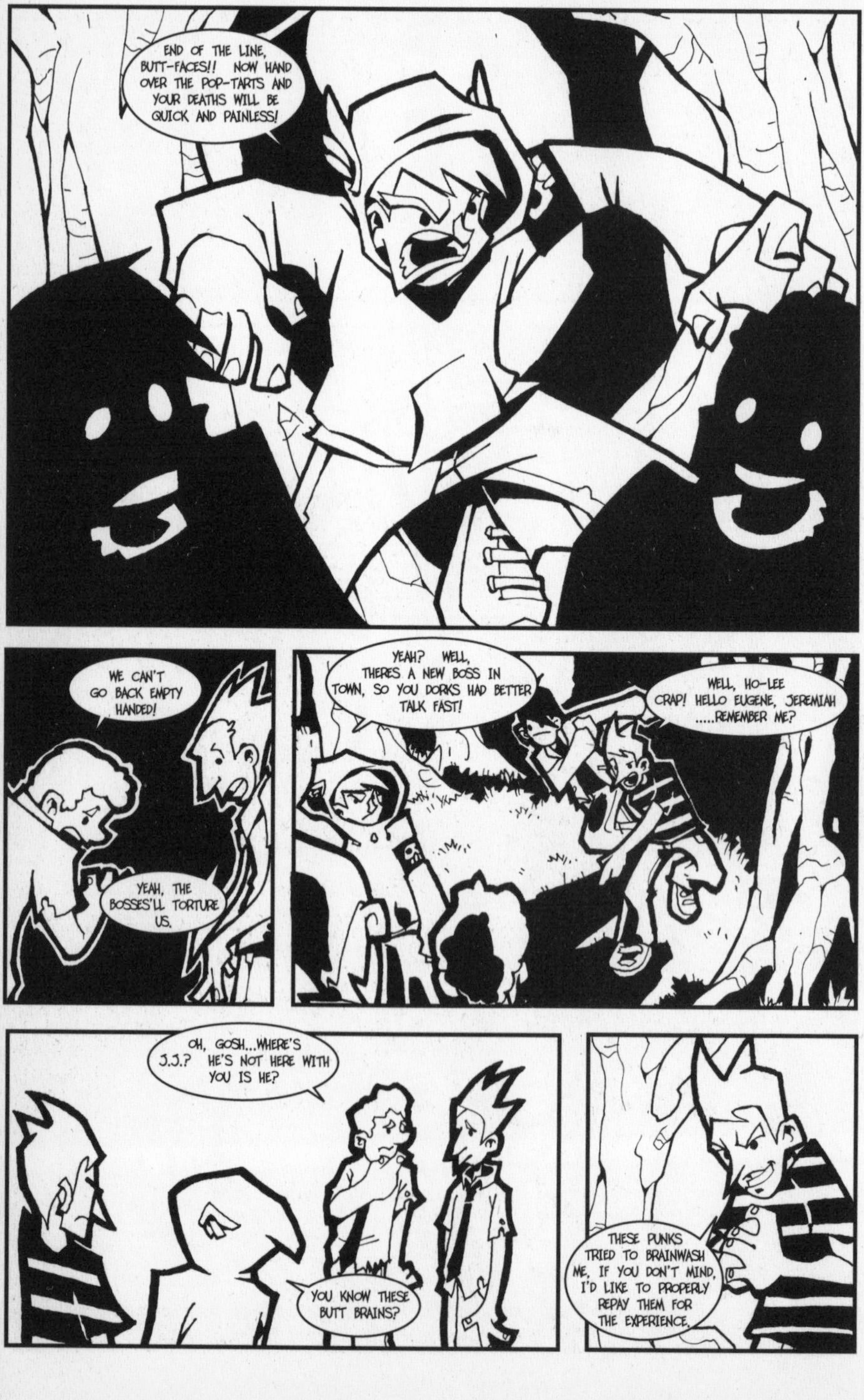
END OF THE LINE, BUTT-FACES!! NOW HAND OVER THE POP-TARTS AND YOUR DEATHS WILL BE QUICK AND PAINLESS!
WE CAN'T GO BACK EMPTY HANDED!
YEAH, THE BOSSES'LL TORTURE US.
YEAH? WELL, THERES A NEW BOSS IN TOWN, SO YOU DORKS HAD BETTER TALK FAST!
WELL, HO-LEE CRAP! HELLO EUGENE, JEREMIAH .....REMEMBER ME?
OH, GOSH...WHERE'S J.J.? HE'S NOT HERE WITH YOU IS HE?
YOU KNOW THESE BUTT BRAINS?
THESE PUNKS TRIED TO BRAINWASH ME, IF YOU DON'T MIND, I'D LIKE TO PROPERLY REPAY THEM FOR THE EXPERIENCE.

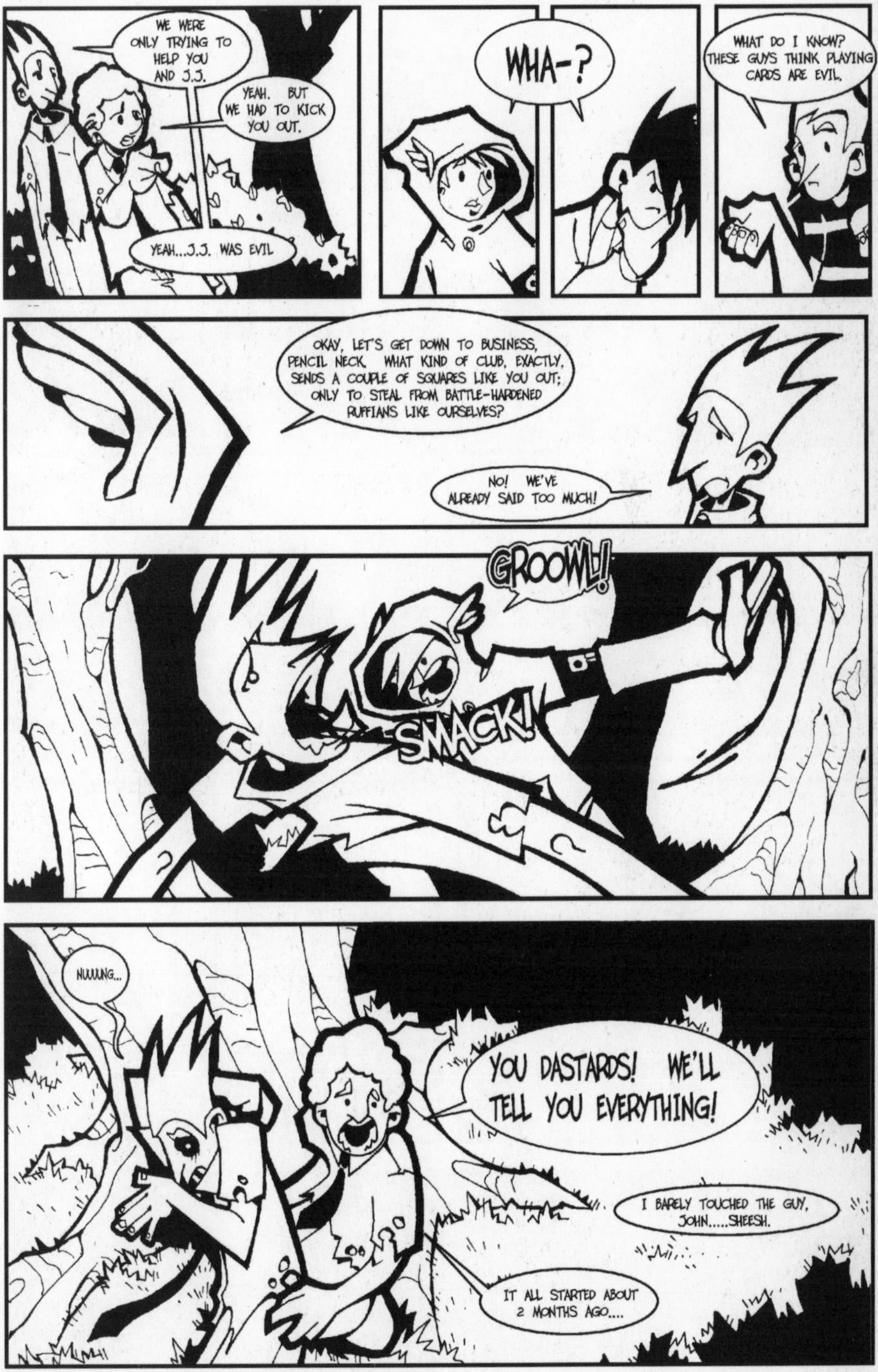

WE WERE ONLY TRYING TO HELP YOU AND J.J.
YEAH. BUT WE HAD TO KICK YOU OUT.
YEAH...J.J. WAS EVIL
WHA-?
WHAT DO I KNOW? THESE GUYS THINK PLAYING CARDS ARE EVIL.
OKAY, LET'S GET DOWN TO BUSINESS, PENCIL NECK. WHAT KIND OF CLUB, EXACTLY, SENDS A COUPLE OF SQUARES LIKE YOU OUT; ONLY TO STEAL FROM BATTLE-HARDENED RUFFIANS LIKE OURSELVES?
NO! WE'VE ALREADY SAID TOO MUCH!
GROOWL!
SMACK!
NUUUNG...
YOU DASTARDS! WE'LL TELL YOU EVERYTHING!
I BARELY TOUCHED THE GUY, JOHN.....SHEESH.
IT ALL STARTED ABOUT 2 MONTHS AGO....

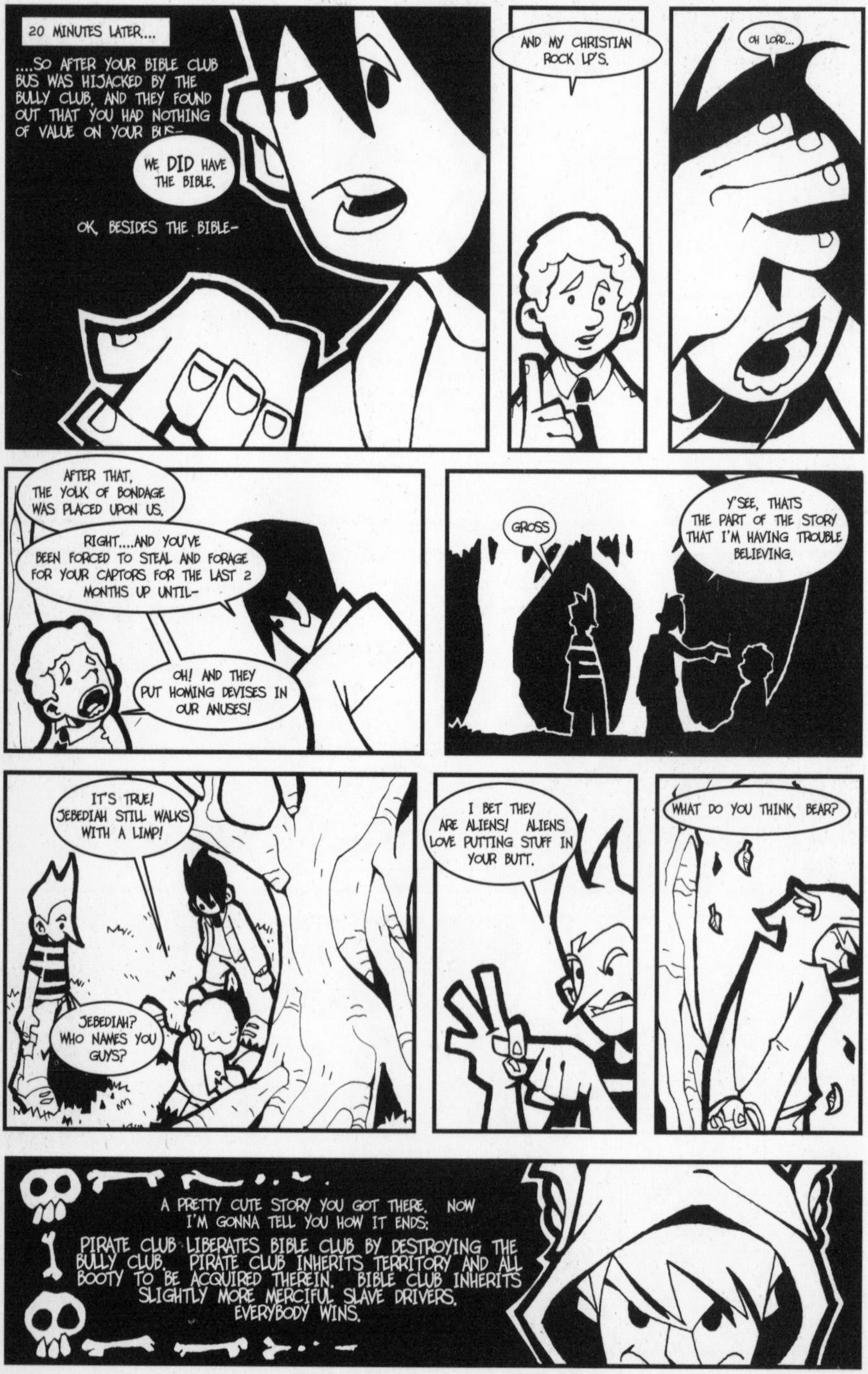
20 MINUTES LATER....
....SO AFTER YOUR BIBLE CLUB BUS WAS HIJACKED BY THE BULLY CLUB, AND THEY FOUND OUT THAT YOU HAD NOTHING OF VALUE ON YOUR BUS-
WE DID HAVE THE BIBLE.
OK, BESIDES THE BIBLE-
AND MY CHRISTIAN ROCK LP'S.
OH LORD...
AFTER THAT, THE YOLK OF BONDAGE WAS PLACED UPON US.
RIGHT....AND YOU'VE BEEN FORCED TO STEAL AND FORAGE FOR YOUR CAPTORS FOR THE LAST 2 MONTHS UP UNTIL-
OH! AND THEY PUT HOMING DEVISES IN OUR ANUSES!
GROSS
Y'SEE, THATS THE PART OF THE STORY THAT I'M HAVING TROUBLE BELIEVING.
IT'S TRUE! JEBEDIAH STILL WALKS WITH A LIMP!
JEBEDIAH? WHO NAMES YOU GUYS?
I BET THEY ARE ALIENS! ALIENS LOVE PUTTING STUFF IN YOUR BUTT.
WHAT DO YOU THINK, BEAR?
A PRETTY CUTE STORY YOU GOT THERE. NOW I'M GONNA TELL YOU HOW IT ENDS:
PIRATE CLUB LIBERATES BIBLE CLUB BY DESTROYING THE BULLY CLUB. PIRATE CLUB INHERITS TERRITORY AND ALL BOOTY TO BE ACQUIRED THEREIN. BIBLE CLUB INHERITS SLIGHTLY MORE MERCIFUL SLAVE DRIVERS. EVERYBODY WINS.

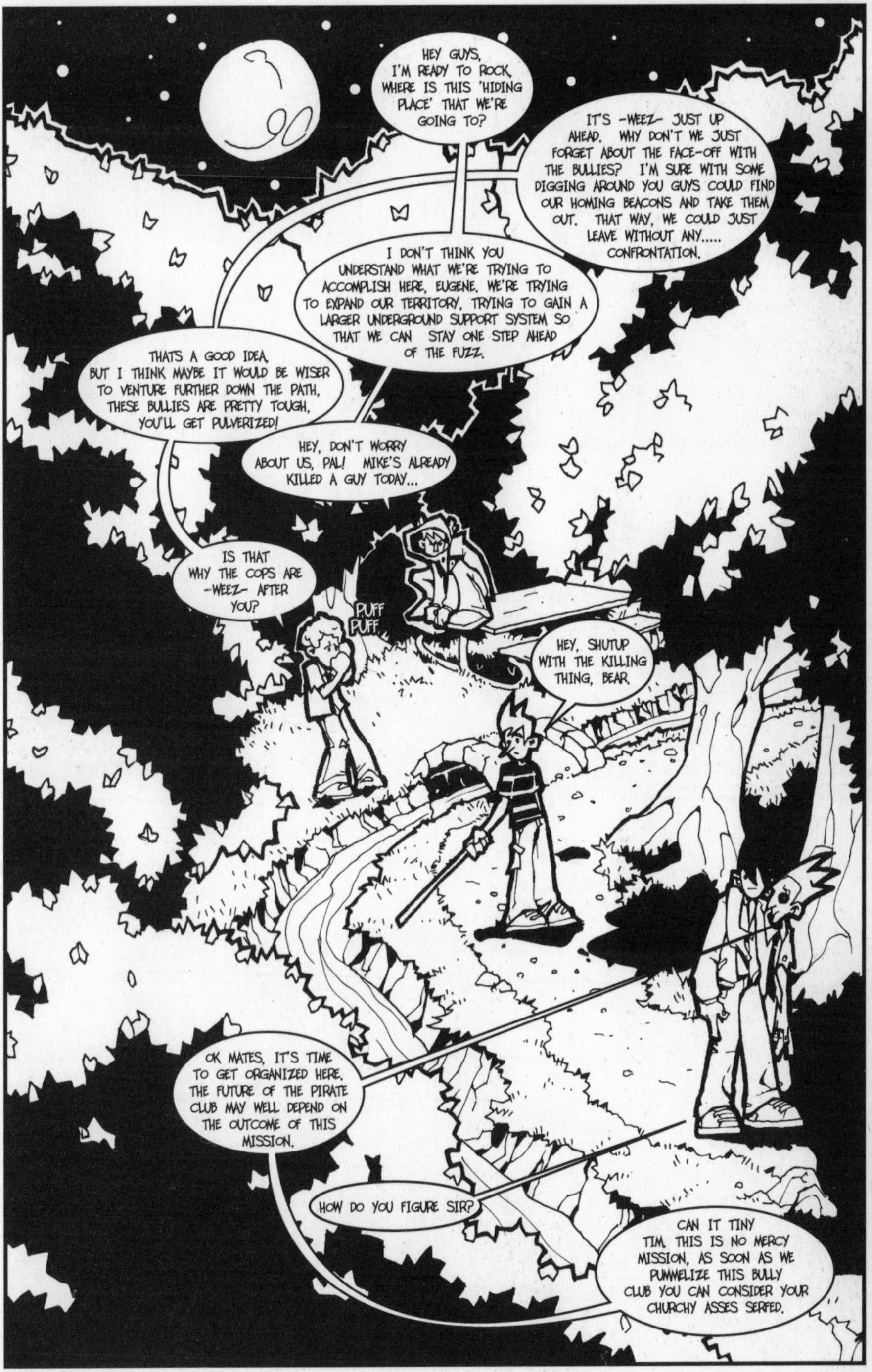

HEY GUYS, I'M READY TO ROCK, WHERE IS THIS 'HIDING PLACE' THAT WE'RE GOING TO?
IT'S -WEEZ- JUST UP AHEAD. WHY DON'T WE JUST FORGET ABOUT THE FACE-OFF WITH THE BULLIES? I'M SURE WITH SOME DIGGING AROUND YOU GUYS COULD FIND OUR HOMING BEACONS AND TAKE THEM OUT. THAT WAY, WE COULD JUST LEAVE WITHOUT ANY..... CONFRONTATION.
I DON'T THINK YOU UNDERSTAND WHAT WE'RE TRYING TO ACCOMPLISH HERE, EUGENE. WE'RE TRYING TO EXPAND OUR TERRITORY, TRYING TO GAIN A LARGER UNDERGROUND SUPPORT SYSTEM SO THAT WE CAN STAY ONE STEP AHEAD OF THE FUZZ.
THATS A GOOD IDEA, BUT I THINK MAYBE IT WOULD BE WISER TO VENTURE FURTHER DOWN THE PATH, THESE BULLIES ARE PRETTY TOUGH, YOU'LL GET PULVERIZED!
HEY, DON'T WORRY ABOUT US, PAL! MIKE'S ALREADY KILLED A GUY TODAY...
IS THAT WHY THE COPS ARE -WEEZ- AFTER YOU?
PUFF PUFF
HEY, SHUTUP WITH THE KILLING THING, BEAR.
OK MATES, IT'S TIME TO GET ORGANIZED HERE. THE FUTURE OF THE PIRATE CLUB MAY WELL DEPEND ON THE OUTCOME OF THIS MISSION.
HOW DO YOU FIGURE SIR?
CAN IT TINY TIM. THIS IS NO MERCY MISSION, AS SOON AS WE PUMMELIZE THIS BULLY CLUB YOU CAN CONSIDER YOUR CHURCHY ASSES SERFED.

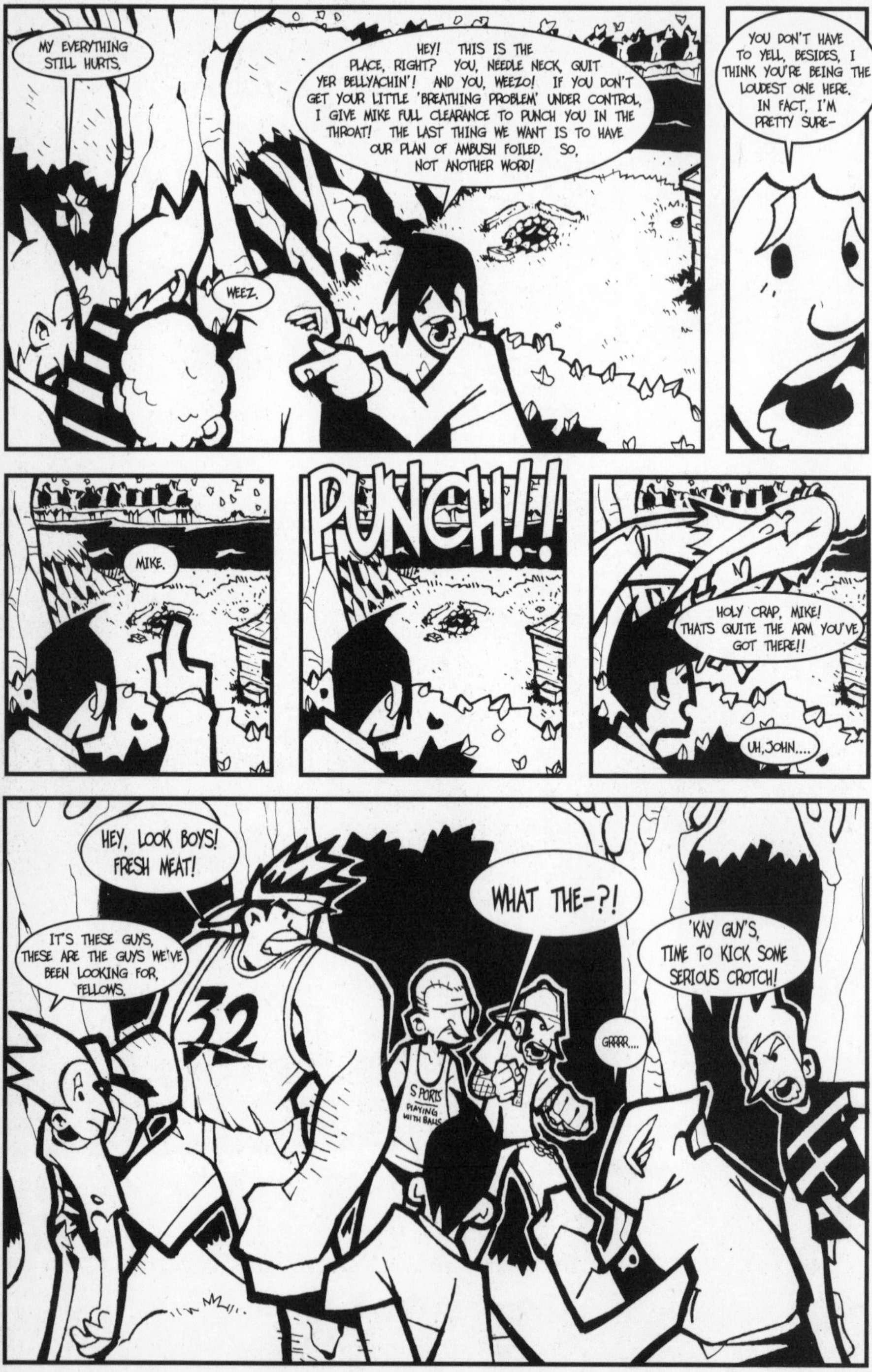
MY EVERYTHING STILL HURTS.
HEY! THIS IS THE PLACE, RIGHT? YOU, NEEDLE NECK, QUIT YER BELLYACHIN'! AND YOU, WEEZO! IF YOU DON'T GET YOUR LITTLE 'BREATHING PROBLEM' UNDER CONTROL, I GIVE MIKE FULL CLEARANCE TO PUNCH YOU IN THE THROAT! THE LAST THING WE WANT IS TO HAVE OUR PLAN OF AMBUSH FOILED. SO, NOT ANOTHER WORD!
WEEZ.
YOU DON'T HAVE TO YELL, BESIDES, I THINK YOU'RE BEING THE LOUDEST ONE HERE. IN FACT, I'M PRETTY SURE-
MIKE.
PUNCH!!
HOLY CRAP, MIKE! THATS QUITE THE ARM YOU'VE GOT THERE!!
UH, JOHN....
HEY, LOOK BOYS! FRESH MEAT!
IT'S THESE GUYS, THESE ARE THE GUYS WE'VE BEEN LOOKING FOR, FELLOWS.
WHAT THE-?!
'KAY GUY'S, TIME TO KICK SOME SERIOUS CROTCH!
GRRRR....
32
SPORTS PLAYING WITH BALLS

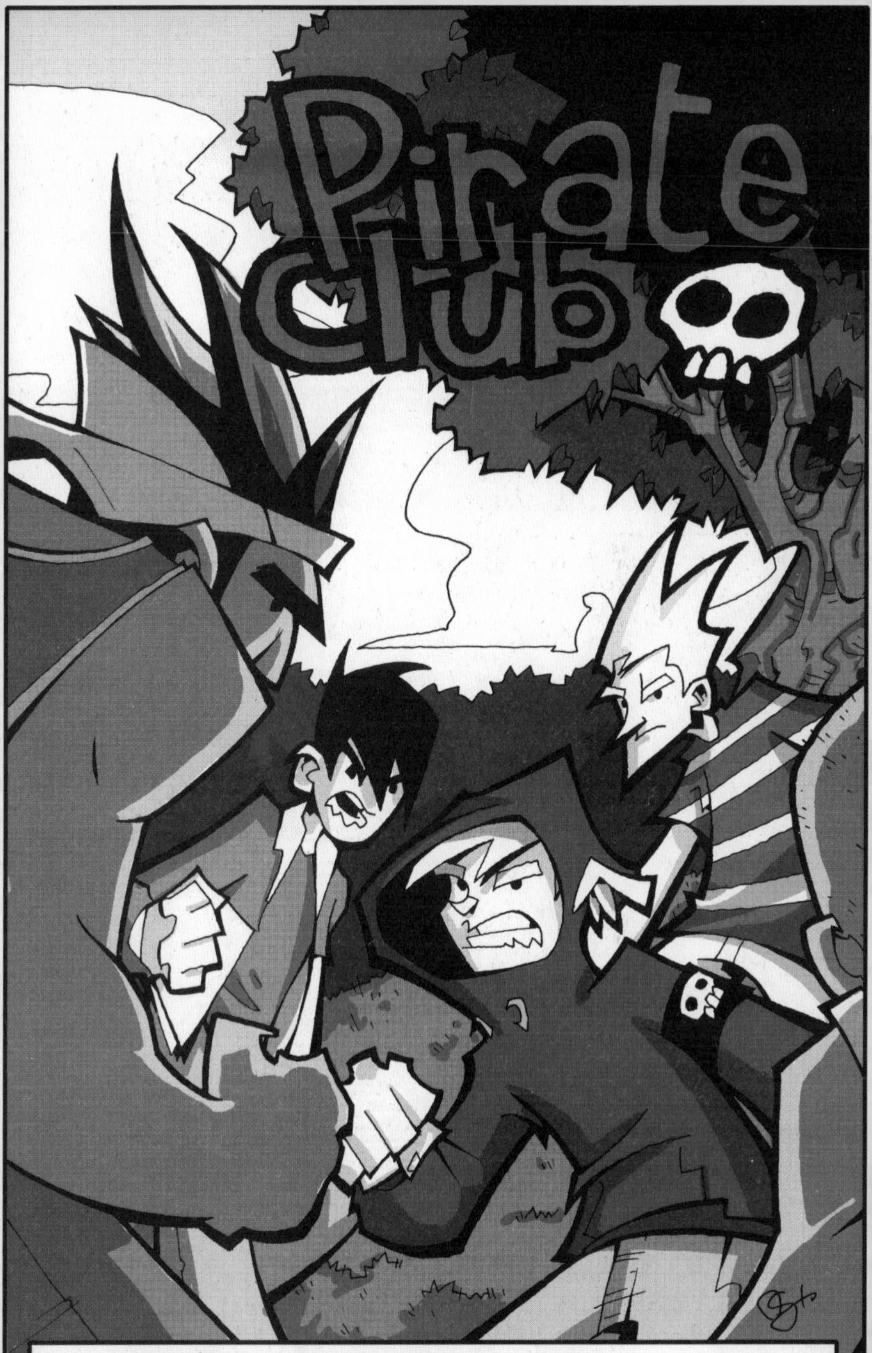
Pirate Club

CHAPTER 3

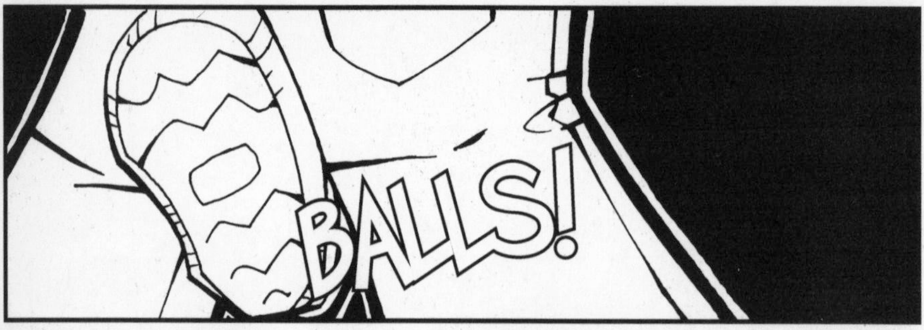
BALLS!

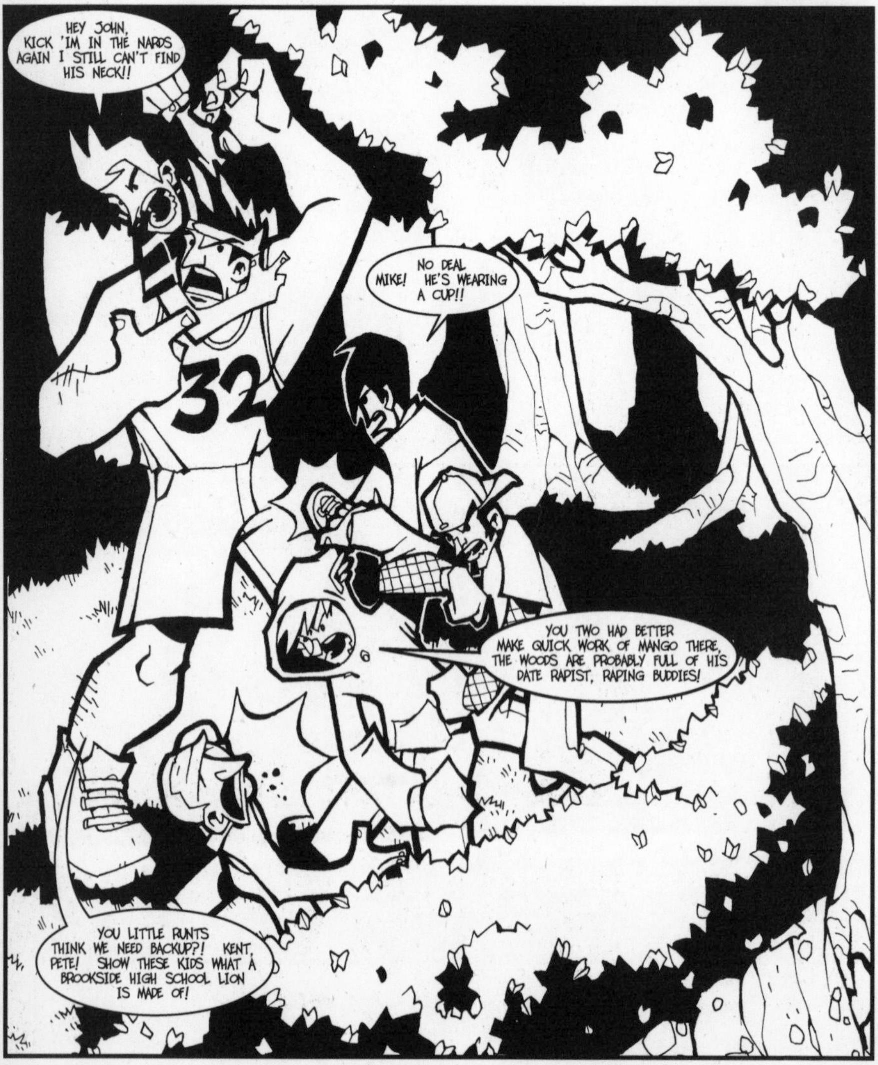
HEY JOHN, KICK 'IM IN THE NARDS AGAIN I STILL CAN'T FIND HIS NECK!!
NO DEAL MIKE! HE'S WEARING A CUP!!
YOU TWO HAD BETTER MAKE QUICK WORK OF MANGO THERE, THE WOODS ARE PROBABLY FULL OF HIS DATE RAPIST, RAPING BUDDIES!
YOU LITTLE RUNTS THINK WE NEED BACKUP?! KENT, PETE! SHOW THESE KIDS WHAT A BROOKSIDE HIGH SCHOOL LION IS MADE OF!
32

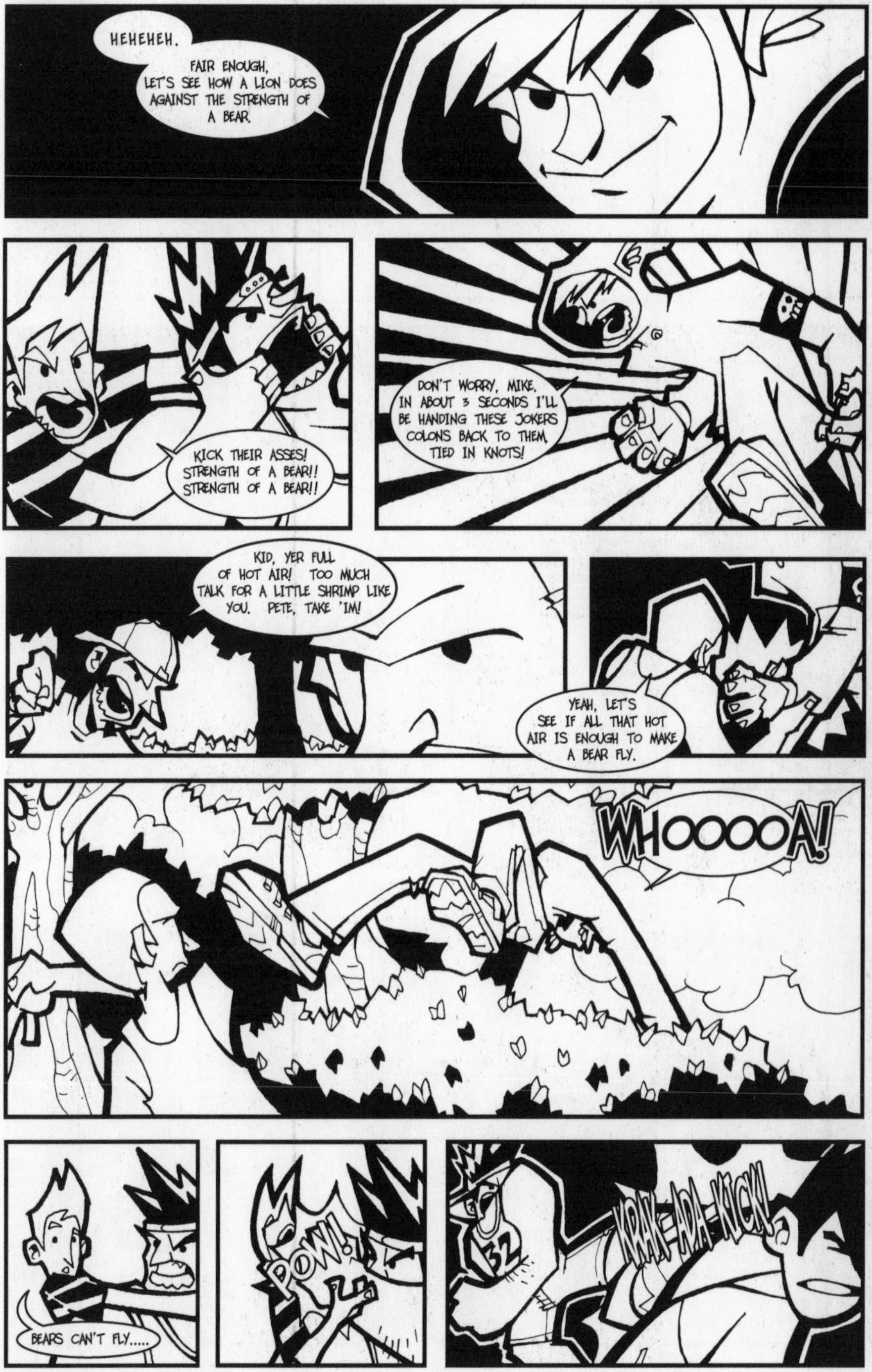
HEHEHEH.
FAIR ENOUGH, LET'S SEE HOW A LION DOES AGAINST THE STRENGTH OF A BEAR.
KICK THEIR ASSES! STRENGTH OF A BEAR!! STRENGTH OF A BEAR!!
DON'T WORRY, MIKE. IN ABOUT 3 SECONDS I'LL BE HANDING THESE JOKERS COLONS BACK TO THEM, TIED IN KNOTS!
KID, YER FULL OF HOT AIR! TOO MUCH TALK FOR A LITTLE SHRIMP LIKE YOU. PETE, TAKE 'IM!
YEAH, LET'S SEE IF ALL THAT HOT AIR IS ENOUGH TO MAKE A BEAR FLY.
WHOOOOA!
BEARS CAN'T FLY.....
POW!
KRAK-ADA-KICK!

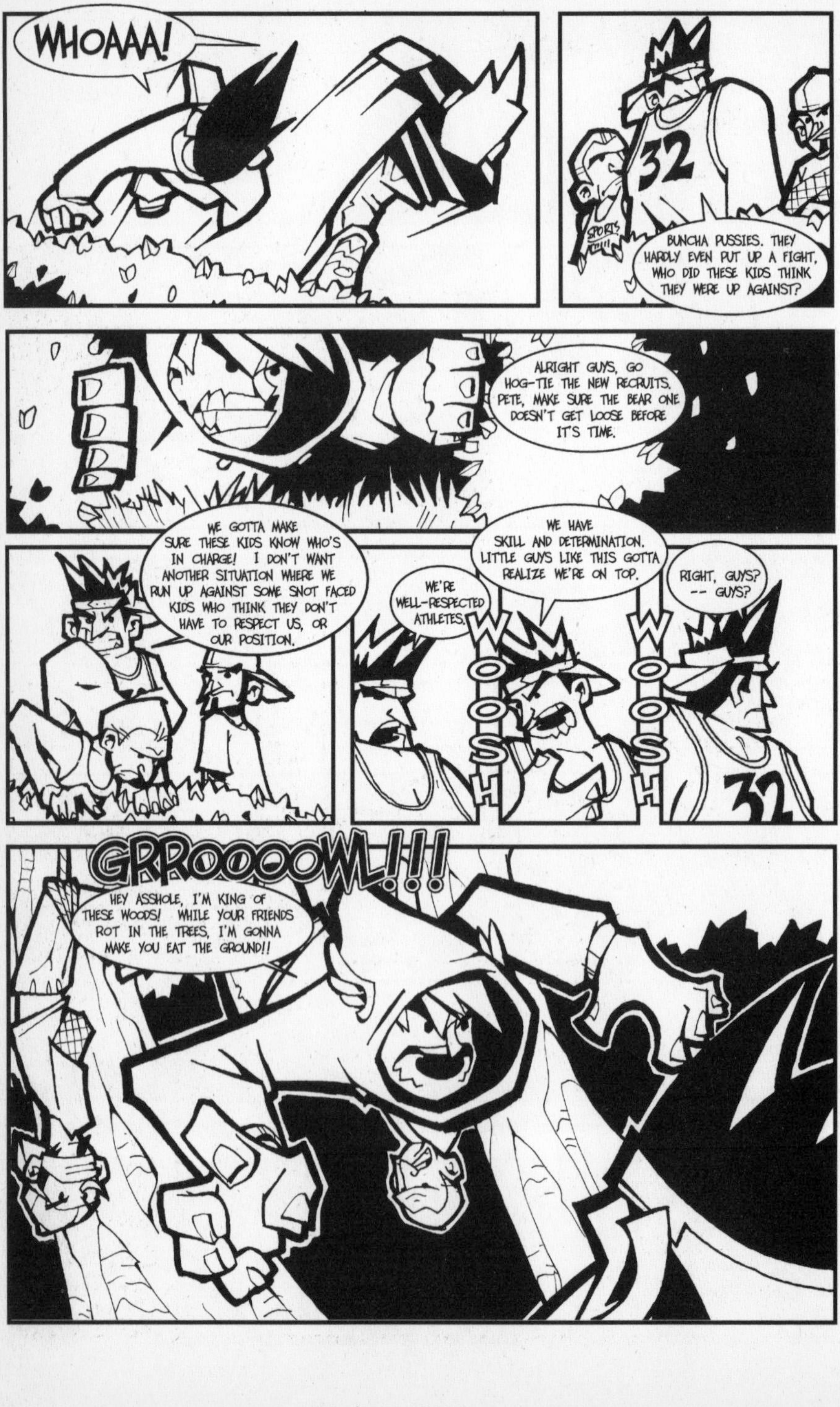
WHOAAA!
BUNCHA PUSSIES. THEY HARDLY EVEN PUT UP A FIGHT, WHO DID THESE KIDS THINK THEY WERE UP AGAINST?
ALRIGHT GUYS, GO HOG-TIE THE NEW RECRUITS. PETE, MAKE SURE THE BEAR ONE DOESN'T GET LOOSE BEFORE IT'S TIME.
WE GOTTA MAKE SURE THESE KIDS KNOW WHO'S IN CHARGE! I DON'T WANT ANOTHER SITUATION WHERE WE RUN UP AGAINST SOME SNOT FACED KIDS WHO THINK THEY DON'T HAVE TO RESPECT US, OR OUR POSITION.
WE'RE WELL-RESPECTED ATHLETES.
WOOSH
WE HAVE SKILL AND DETERMINATION. LITTLE GUYS LIKE THIS GOTTA REALIZE WE'RE ON TOP.
WOOSH
RIGHT, GUYS? -- GUYS?
GRROOOOOWL!!!
HEY ASSHOLE, I'M KING OF THESE WOODS! WHILE YOUR FRIENDS ROT IN THE TREES, I'M GONNA MAKE YOU EAT THE GROUND!!

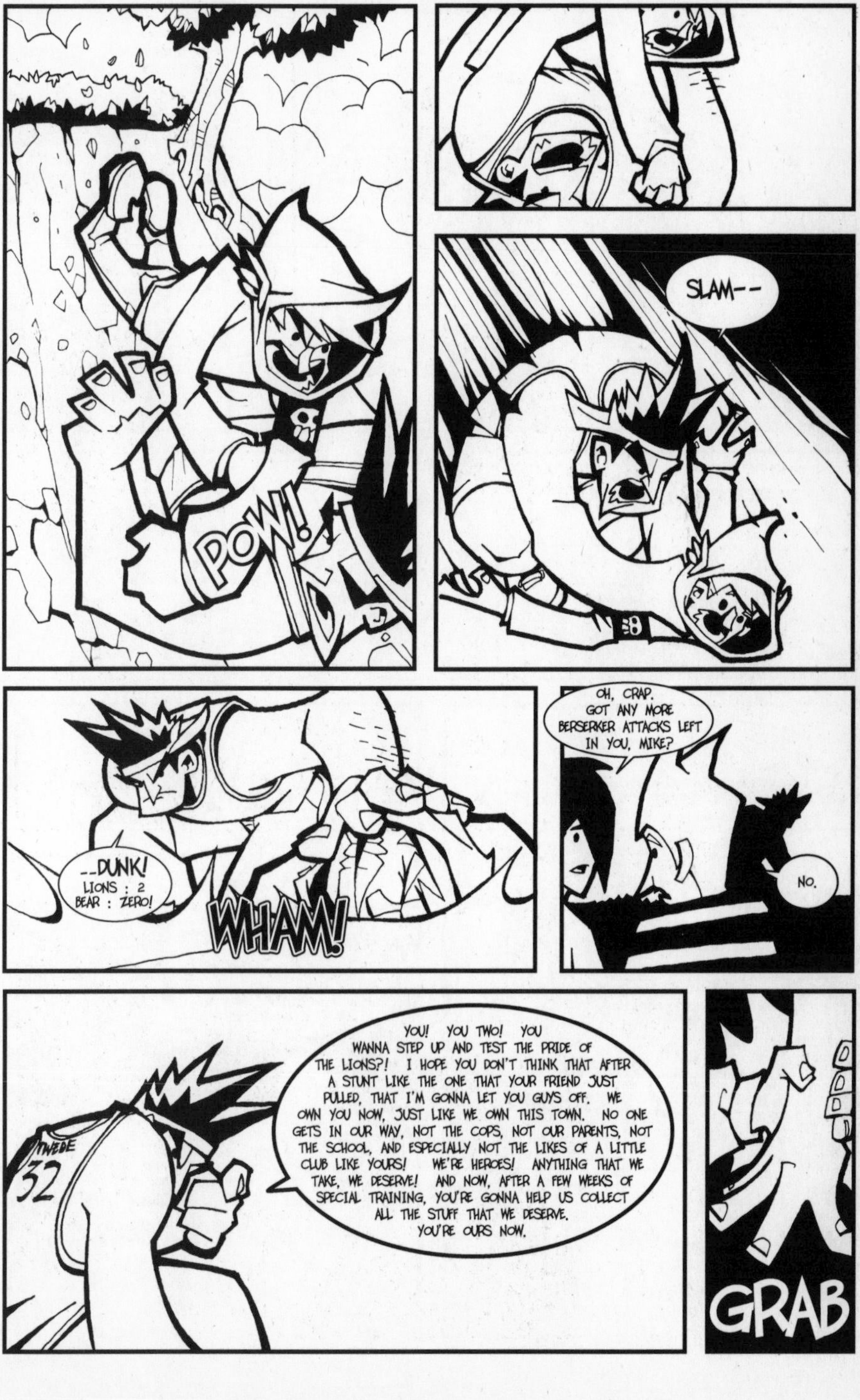
POW!
SLAM--
--DUNK!
LIONS : 2
BEAR : ZERO!
WHAM!
OH, CRAP. GOT ANY MORE BERSERKER ATTACKS LEFT IN YOU, MIKE?
NO.
TWEDE
32
YOU! YOU TWO! YOU WANNA STEP UP AND TEST THE PRIDE OF THE LIONS?! I HOPE YOU DON'T THINK THAT AFTER A STUNT LIKE THE ONE THAT YOUR FRIEND JUST PULLED, THAT I'M GONNA LET YOU GUYS OFF. WE OWN YOU NOW, JUST LIKE WE OWN THIS TOWN. NO ONE GETS IN OUR WAY, NOT THE COPS, NOT OUR PARENTS, NOT THE SCHOOL, AND ESPECIALLY NOT THE LIKES OF A LITTLE CLUB LIKE YOURS! WE'RE HEROES! ANYTHING THAT WE TAKE, WE DESERVE! AND NOW, AFTER A FEW WEEKS OF SPECIAL TRAINING, YOU'RE GONNA HELP US COLLECT ALL THE STUFF THAT WE DESERVE. YOU'RE OURS NOW.
GRAB

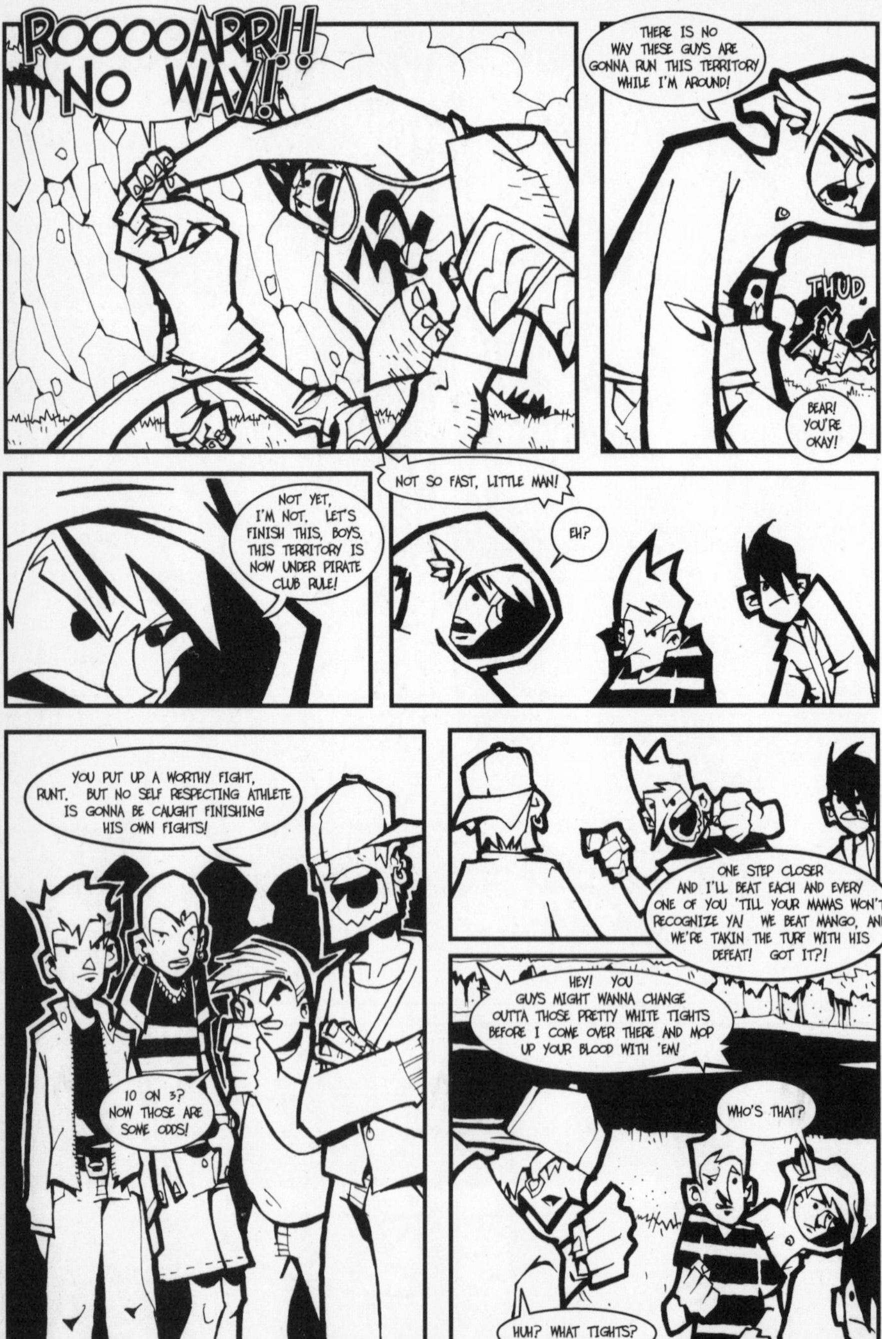
ROOOOARR!! NO WAY!
THERE IS NO WAY THESE GUYS ARE GONNA RUN THIS TERRITORY WHILE I'M AROUND!
THUD
BEAR! YOU'RE OKAY!
NOT YET, I'M NOT. LET'S FINISH THIS, BOYS. THIS TERRITORY IS NOW UNDER PIRATE CLUB RULE!
NOT SO FAST, LITTLE MAN!
EH?
YOU PUT UP A WORTHY FIGHT, RUNT. BUT NO SELF RESPECTING ATHLETE IS GONNA BE CAUGHT FINISHING HIS OWN FIGHTS!
10 ON 3? NOW THOSE ARE SOME ODDS!
ONE STEP CLOSER AND I'LL BEAT EACH AND EVERY ONE OF YOU 'TILL YOUR MAMAS WON'T RECOGNIZE YA! WE BEAT MANGO, AND WE'RE TAKIN THE TURF WITH HIS DEFEAT! GOT IT?!
HEY! YOU GUYS MIGHT WANNA CHANGE OUTTA THOSE PRETTY WHITE TIGHTS BEFORE I COME OVER THERE AND MOP UP YOUR BLOOD WITH 'EM!
WHO'S THAT?
HUH? WHAT TIGHTS?

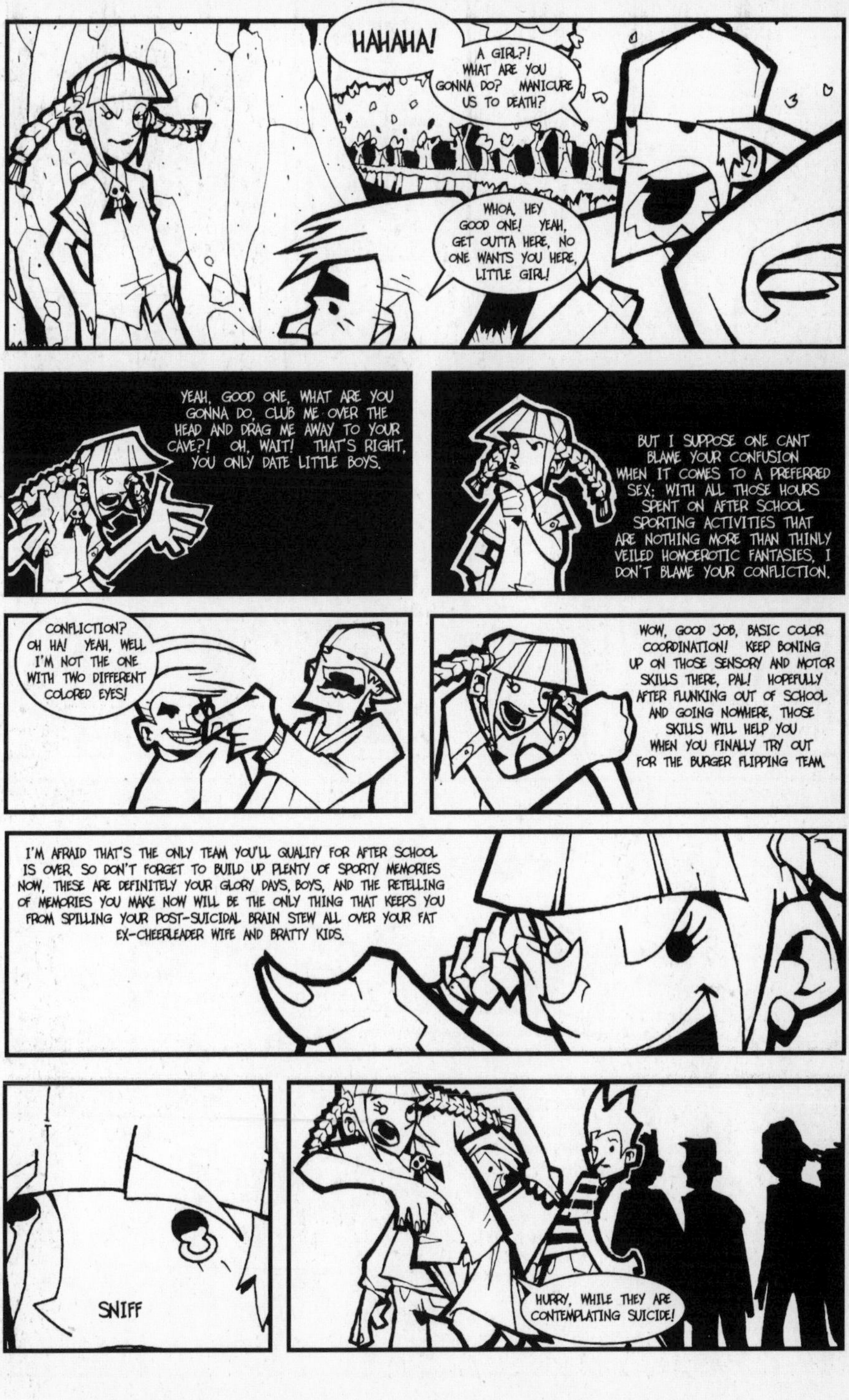
HAHAHA!
A GIRL?! WHAT ARE YOU GONNA DO? MANICURE US TO DEATH?
WHOA, HEY GOOD ONE! YEAH, GET OUTTA HERE, NO ONE WANTS YOU HERE, LITTLE GIRL!
YEAH, GOOD ONE, WHAT ARE YOU GONNA DO, CLUB ME OVER THE HEAD AND DRAG ME AWAY TO YOUR CAVE?! OH, WAIT! THAT'S RIGHT, YOU ONLY DATE LITTLE BOYS.
BUT I SUPPOSE ONE CANT BLAME YOUR CONFUSION WHEN IT COMES TO A PREFERRED SEX; WITH ALL THOSE HOURS SPENT ON AFTER SCHOOL SPORTING ACTIVITIES THAT ARE NOTHING MORE THAN THINLY VEILED HOMOEROTIC FANTASIES, I DON'T BLAME YOUR CONFLICTION.
CONFLICTION? OH HA! YEAH, WELL I'M NOT THE ONE WITH TWO DIFFERENT COLORED EYES!
WOW, GOOD JOB, BASIC COLOR COORDINATION! KEEP BONING UP ON THOSE SENSORY AND MOTOR SKILLS THERE, PAL! HOPEFULLY AFTER FLUNKING OUT OF SCHOOL AND GOING NOWHERE, THOSE SKILLS WILL HELP YOU WHEN YOU FINALLY TRY OUT FOR THE BURGER FLIPPING TEAM.
I'M AFRAID THAT'S THE ONLY TEAM YOU'LL QUALIFY FOR AFTER SCHOOL IS OVER. SO DON'T FORGET TO BUILD UP PLENTY OF SPORTY MEMORIES NOW, THESE ARE DEFINITELY YOUR GLORY DAYS, BOYS, AND THE RETELLING OF MEMORIES YOU MAKE NOW WILL BE THE ONLY THING THAT KEEPS YOU FROM SPILLING YOUR POST-SUICIDAL BRAIN STEW ALL OVER YOUR FAT EX-CHEERLEADER WIFE AND BRATTY KIDS.
SNIFF
HURRY, WHILE THEY ARE CONTEMPLATING SUICIDE!

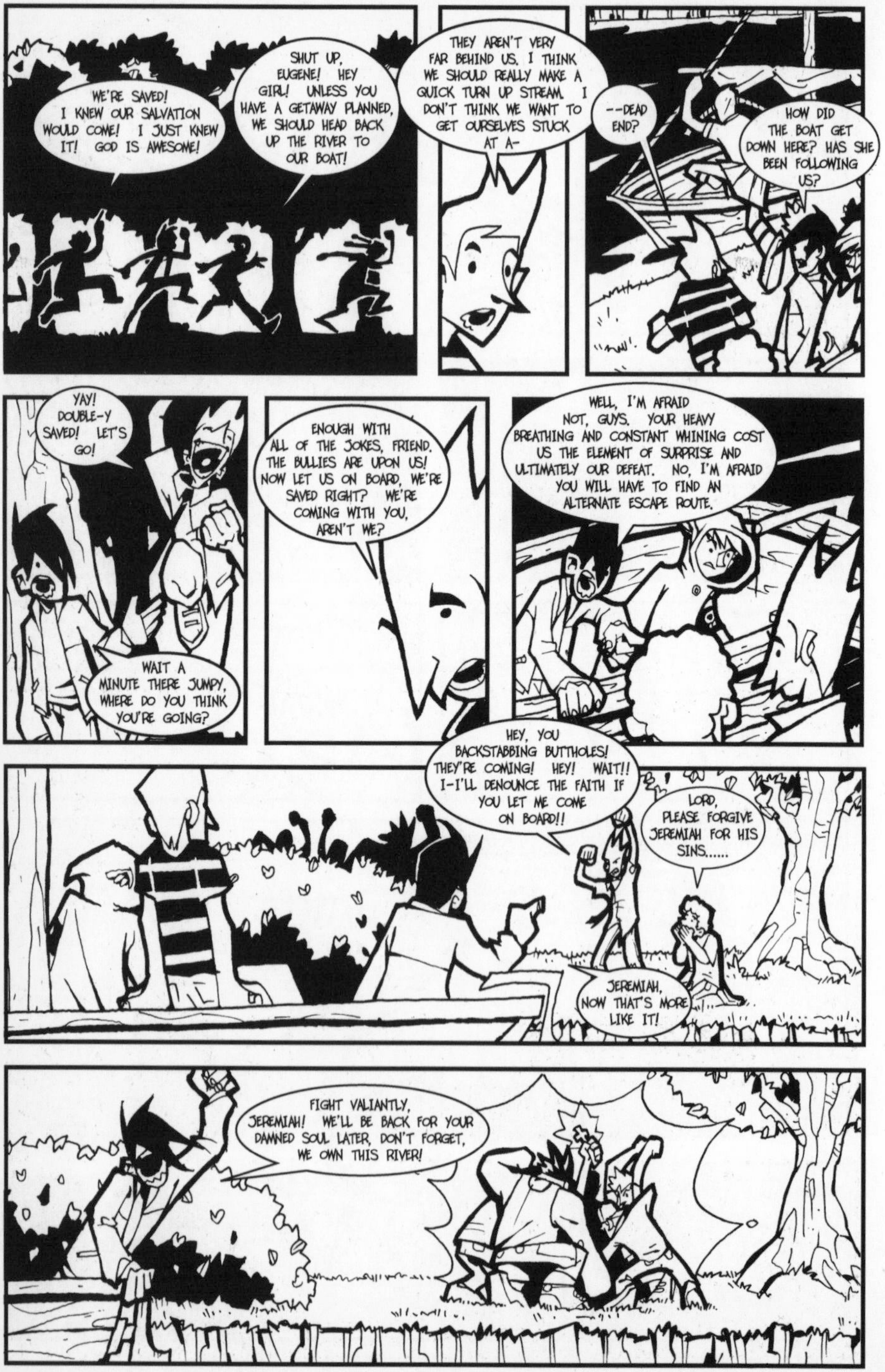

WE'RE SAVED! I KNEW OUR SALVATION WOULD COME! I JUST KNEW IT! GOD IS AWESOME!
SHUT UP, EUGENE! HEY GIRL! UNLESS YOU HAVE A GETAWAY PLANNED, WE SHOULD HEAD BACK UP THE RIVER TO OUR BOAT!
THEY AREN'T VERY FAR BEHIND US. I THINK WE SHOULD REALLY MAKE A QUICK TURN UP STREAM. I DON'T THINK WE WANT TO GET OURSELVES STUCK AT A-
--DEAD END?
HOW DID THE BOAT GET DOWN HERE? HAS SHE BEEN FOLLOWING US?
YAY! DOUBLE-Y SAVED! LET'S GO!
WAIT A MINUTE THERE JUMPY, WHERE DO YOU THINK YOU'RE GOING?
ENOUGH WITH ALL OF THE JOKES, FRIEND. THE BULLIES ARE UPON US! NOW LET US ON BOARD, WE'RE SAVED RIGHT? WE'RE COMING WITH YOU, AREN'T WE?
WELL, I'M AFRAID NOT, GUYS. YOUR HEAVY BREATHING AND CONSTANT WHINING COST US THE ELEMENT OF SURPRISE AND ULTIMATELY OUR DEFEAT. NO, I'M AFRAID YOU WILL HAVE TO FIND AN ALTERNATE ESCAPE ROUTE.
HEY, YOU BACKSTABBING BUTTHOLES! THEY'RE COMING! HEY! WAIT!! I-I'LL DENOUNCE THE FAITH IF YOU LET ME COME ON BOARD!!
LORD, PLEASE FORGIVE JEREMIAH FOR HIS SINS......
JEREMIAH, NOW THAT'S MORE LIKE IT!
FIGHT VALIANTLY, JEREMIAH! WE'LL BE BACK FOR YOUR DAMNED SOUL LATER, DON'T FORGET, WE OWN THIS RIVER!

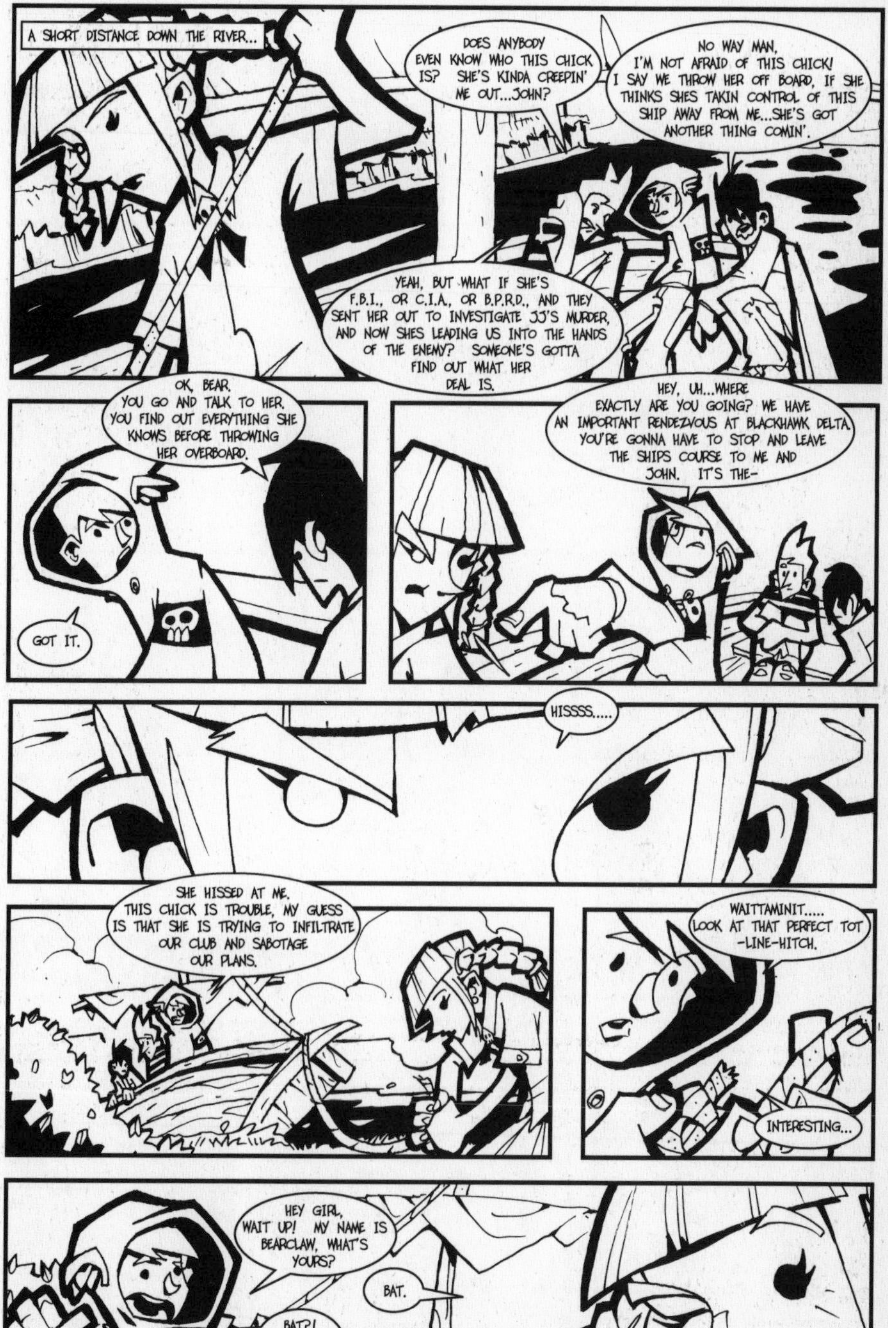

A SHORT DISTANCE DOWN THE RIVER...
DOES ANYBODY EVEN KNOW WHO THIS CHICK IS? SHE'S KINDA CREEPIN' ME OUT...JOHN?
NO WAY MAN, I'M NOT AFRAID OF THIS CHICK! I SAY WE THROW HER OFF BOARD, IF SHE THINKS SHES TAKIN CONTROL OF THIS SHIP AWAY FROM ME...SHE'S GOT ANOTHER THING COMIN'.
YEAH, BUT WHAT IF SHE'S F.B.I., OR C.I.A., OR B.P.R.D., AND THEY SENT HER OUT TO INVESTIGATE JJ'S MURDER, AND NOW SHES LEADING US INTO THE HANDS OF THE ENEMY? SOMEONE'S GOTTA FIND OUT WHAT HER DEAL IS.
OK, BEAR. YOU GO AND TALK TO HER. YOU FIND OUT EVERYTHING SHE KNOWS BEFORE THROWING HER OVERBOARD.
GOT IT.
HEY, UH...WHERE EXACTLY ARE YOU GOING? WE HAVE AN IMPORTANT RENDEZVOUS AT BLACKHAWK DELTA. YOU'RE GONNA HAVE TO STOP AND LEAVE THE SHIPS COURSE TO ME AND JOHN. IT'S THE-
HISSSS.....
SHE HISSED AT ME. THIS CHICK IS TROUBLE, MY GUESS IS THAT SHE IS TRYING TO INFILTRATE OUR CLUB AND SABOTAGE OUR PLANS.
WAITTAMINIT..... LOOK AT THAT PERFECT TOT -LINE-HITCH.
INTERESTING...
HEY GIRL, WAIT UP! MY NAME IS BEARCLAW, WHAT'S YOURS?
BAT.
BAT?! THAT'S RAD! BAT.

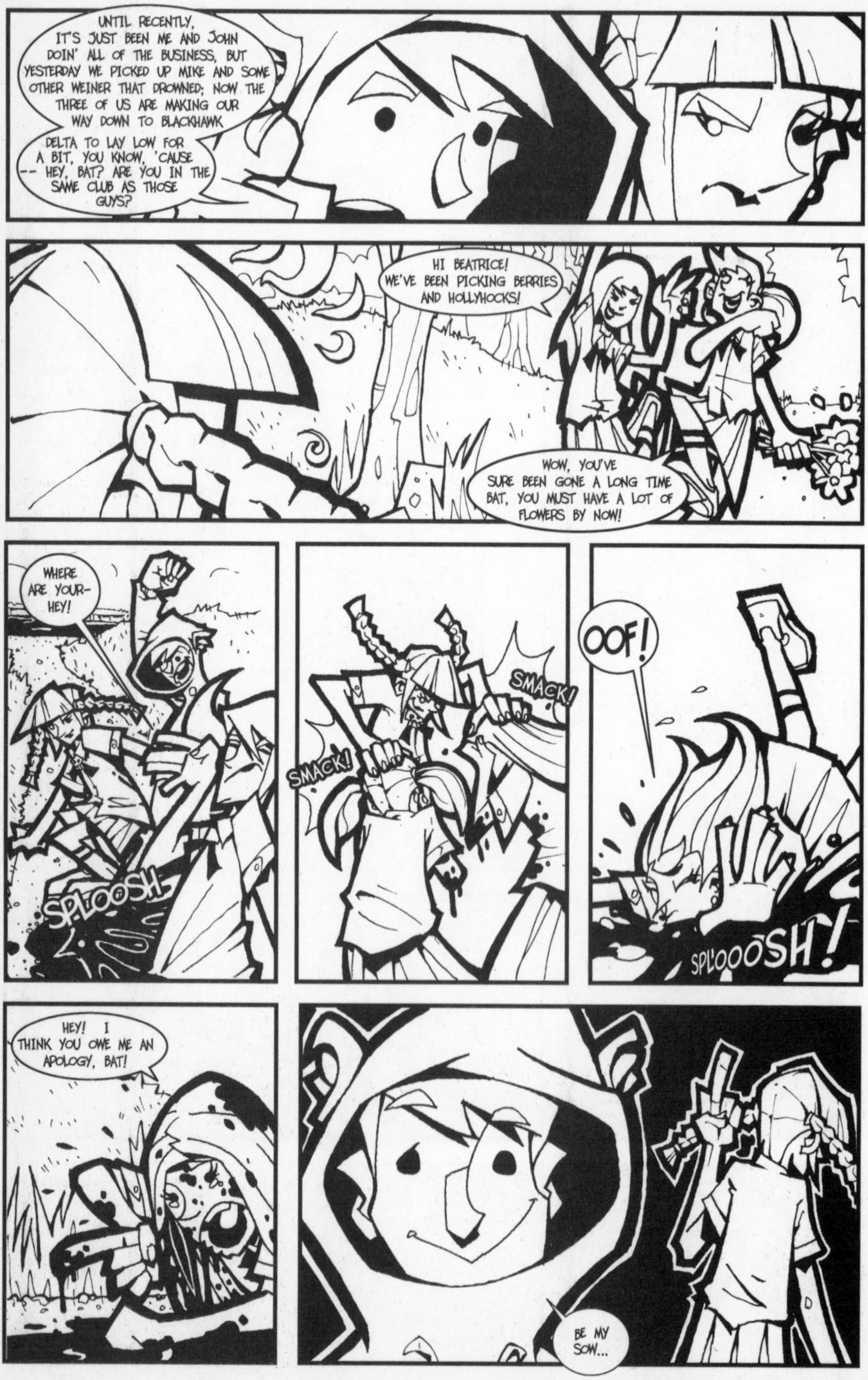
UNTIL RECENTLY, IT'S JUST BEEN ME AND JOHN DOIN' ALL OF THE BUSINESS, BUT YESTERDAY WE PICKED UP MIKE AND SOME OTHER WEINER THAT DROWNED; NOW THE THREE OF US ARE MAKING OUR WAY DOWN TO BLACKHAWK
DELTA TO LAY LOW FOR A BIT, YOU KNOW, 'CAUSE -- HEY, BAT? ARE YOU IN THE SAME CLUB AS THOSE GUYS?
HI BEATRICE! WE'VE BEEN PICKING BERRIES AND HOLLYHOCKS!
WOW, YOU'VE SURE BEEN GONE A LONG TIME BAT, YOU MUST HAVE A LOT OF FLOWERS BY NOW!
WHERE ARE YOUR- HEY!
SPLOOSH
SMACK!
SMACK!
OOF!
SPLOOOSH!
HEY! I THINK YOU OWE ME AN APOLOGY, BAT!
BE MY SOW...

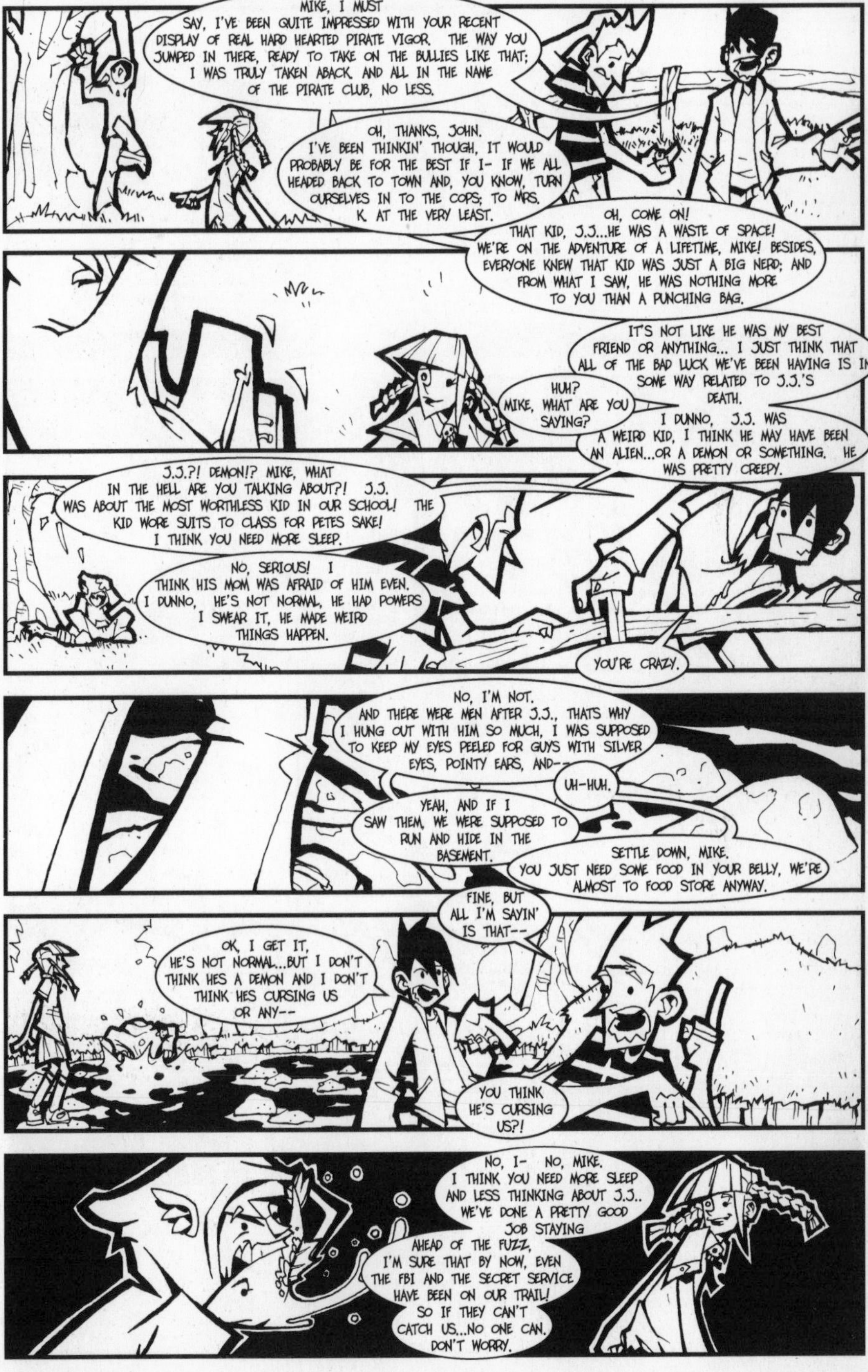
MIKE, I MUST SAY, I'VE BEEN QUITE IMPRESSED WITH YOUR RECENT DISPLAY OF REAL HARD HEARTED PIRATE VIGOR. THE WAY YOU JUMPED IN THERE, READY TO TAKE ON THE BULLIES LIKE THAT; I WAS TRULY TAKEN ABACK. AND ALL IN THE NAME OF THE PIRATE CLUB, NO LESS.
OH, THANKS, JOHN. I'VE BEEN THINKIN' THOUGH, IT WOULD PROBABLY BE FOR THE BEST IF I- IF WE ALL HEADED BACK TO TOWN AND, YOU KNOW, TURN OURSELVES IN TO THE COPS; TO MRS. K. AT THE VERY LEAST.
OH, COME ON! THAT KID, J.J...HE WAS A WASTE OF SPACE! WE'RE ON THE ADVENTURE OF A LIFETIME, MIKE! BESIDES, EVERYONE KNEW THAT KID WAS JUST A BIG NERD; AND FROM WHAT I SAW, HE WAS NOTHING MORE TO YOU THAN A PUNCHING BAG.
IT'S NOT LIKE HE WAS MY BEST FRIEND OR ANYTHING... I JUST THINK THAT ALL OF THE BAD LUCK WE'VE BEEN HAVING IS IN SOME WAY RELATED TO J.J.'S DEATH.
HUH? MIKE, WHAT ARE YOU SAYING?
I DUNNO, J.J. WAS A WEIRD KID, I THINK HE MAY HAVE BEEN AN ALIEN...OR A DEMON OR SOMETHING. HE WAS PRETTY CREEPY.
J.J.?! DEMON!? MIKE, WHAT IN THE HELL ARE YOU TALKING ABOUT?! J.J. WAS ABOUT THE MOST WORTHLESS KID IN OUR SCHOOL! THE KID WORE SUITS TO CLASS FOR PETES SAKE! I THINK YOU NEED MORE SLEEP.
NO, SERIOUS! I THINK HIS MOM WAS AFRAID OF HIM EVEN. I DUNNO, HE'S NOT NORMAL, HE HAD POWERS I SWEAR IT, HE MADE WEIRD THINGS HAPPEN.
YOU'RE CRAZY.
NO, I'M NOT. AND THERE WERE MEN AFTER J.J., THATS WHY I HUNG OUT WITH HIM SO MUCH, I WAS SUPPOSED TO KEEP MY EYES PEELED FOR GUYS WITH SILVER EYES, POINTY EARS, AND--
UH-HUH.
YEAH, AND IF I SAW THEM, WE WERE SUPPOSED TO RUN AND HIDE IN THE BASEMENT.
SETTLE DOWN, MIKE. YOU JUST NEED SOME FOOD IN YOUR BELLY, WE'RE ALMOST TO FOOD STORE ANYWAY.
FINE, BUT ALL I'M SAYIN' IS THAT--
OK, I GET IT, HE'S NOT NORMAL...BUT I DON'T THINK HES A DEMON AND I DON'T THINK HES CURSING US OR ANY--
YOU THINK HE'S CURSING US?!
NO, I- NO, MIKE. I THINK YOU NEED MORE SLEEP AND LESS THINKING ABOUT J.J.. WE'VE DONE A PRETTY GOOD JOB STAYING
AHEAD OF THE FUZZ, I'M SURE THAT BY NOW, EVEN THE FBI AND THE SECRET SERVICE HAVE BEEN ON OUR TRAIL! SO IF THEY CAN'T CATCH US...NO ONE CAN. DON'T WORRY.

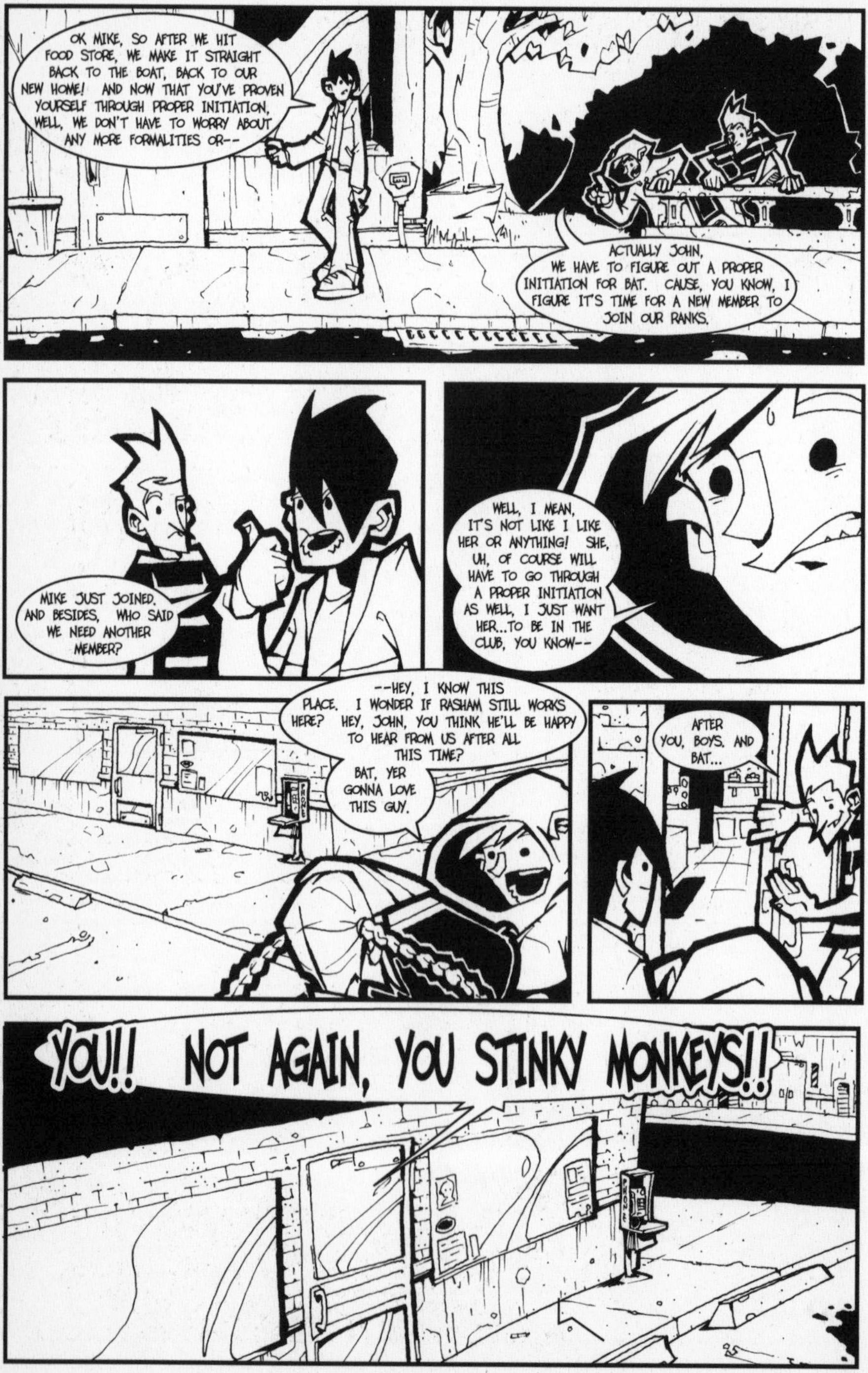
OK MIKE, SO AFTER WE HIT FOOD STORE, WE MAKE IT STRAIGHT BACK TO THE BOAT, BACK TO OUR NEW HOME! AND NOW THAT YOU'VE PROVEN YOURSELF THROUGH PROPER INITIATION, WELL, WE DON'T HAVE TO WORRY ABOUT ANY MORE FORMALITIES OR--
ACTUALLY JOHN, WE HAVE TO FIGURE OUT A PROPER INITIATION FOR BAT. CAUSE, YOU KNOW, I FIGURE IT'S TIME FOR A NEW MEMBER TO JOIN OUR RANKS.
MIKE JUST JOINED. AND BESIDES, WHO SAID WE NEED ANOTHER MEMBER?
WELL, I MEAN, IT'S NOT LIKE I LIKE HER OR ANYTHING! SHE, UH, OF COURSE WILL HAVE TO GO THROUGH A PROPER INITIATION AS WELL, I JUST WANT HER...TO BE IN THE CLUB, YOU KNOW--
--HEY, I KNOW THIS PLACE. I WONDER IF RASHAM STILL WORKS HERE? HEY, JOHN, YOU THINK HE'LL BE HAPPY TO HEAR FROM US AFTER ALL THIS TIME?
BAT, YER GONNA LOVE THIS GUY.
AFTER YOU, BOYS. AND BAT...
YOU!! NOT AGAIN, YOU STINKY MONKEYS!!

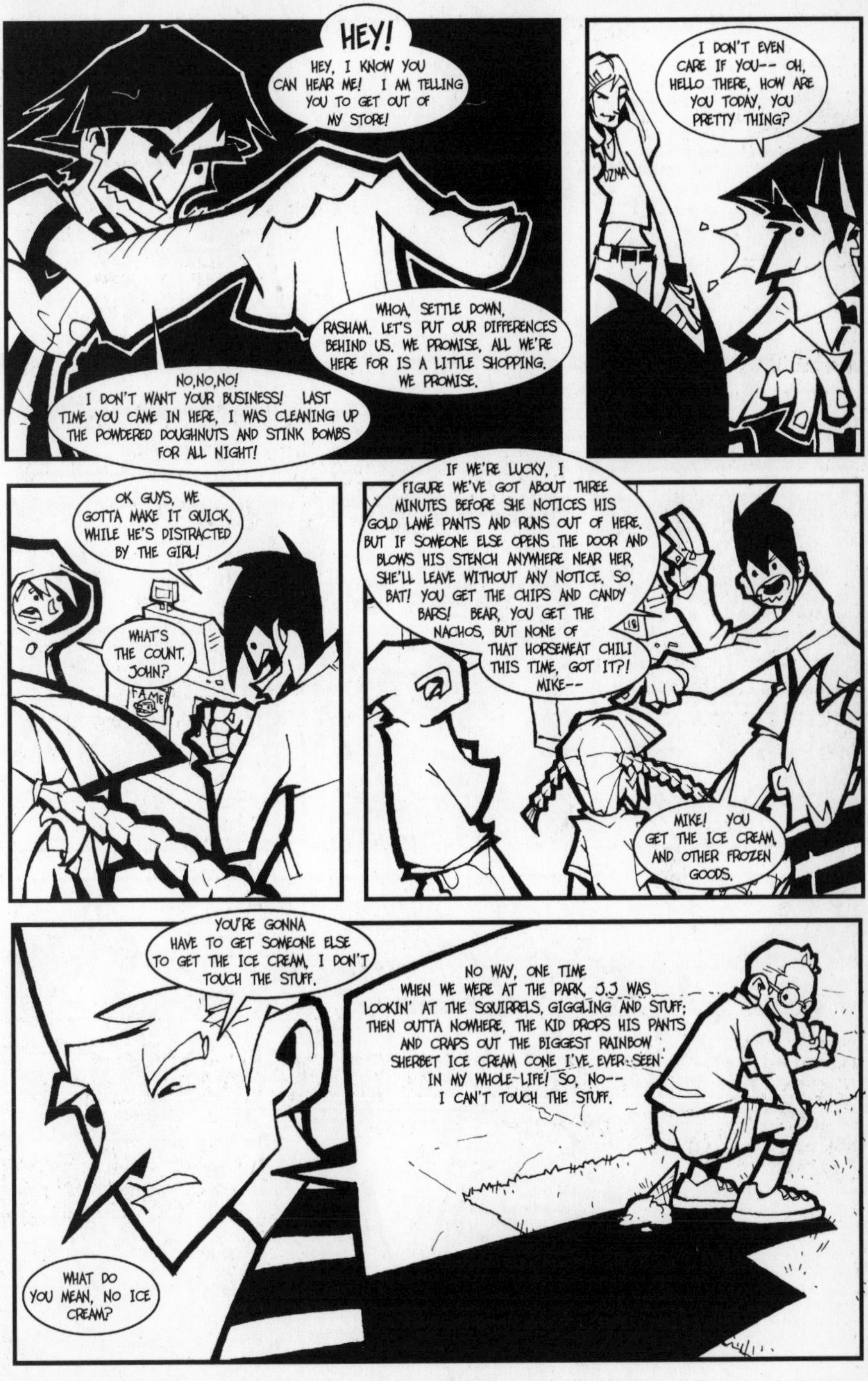
HEY!
HEY, I KNOW YOU CAN HEAR ME! I AM TELLING YOU TO GET OUT OF MY STORE!
WHOA, SETTLE DOWN, RASHAM. LET'S PUT OUR DIFFERENCES BEHIND US. WE PROMISE, ALL WE'RE HERE FOR IS A LITTLE SHOPPING. WE PROMISE.
NO,NO,NO! I DON'T WANT YOUR BUSINESS! LAST TIME YOU CAME IN HERE, I WAS CLEANING UP THE POWDERED DOUGHNUTS AND STINK BOMBS FOR ALL NIGHT!
I DON'T EVEN CARE IF YOU-- OH, HELLO THERE, HOW ARE YOU TODAY, YOU PRETTY THING?
OZMA
OK GUYS, WE GOTTA MAKE IT QUICK, WHILE HE'S DISTRACTED BY THE GIRL!
WHAT'S THE COUNT, JOHN?
FAME
IF WE'RE LUCKY, I FIGURE WE'VE GOT ABOUT THREE MINUTES BEFORE SHE NOTICES HIS GOLD LAMÉ PANTS AND RUNS OUT OF HERE. BUT IF SOMEONE ELSE OPENS THE DOOR AND BLOWS HIS STENCH ANYWHERE NEAR HER, SHE'LL LEAVE WITHOUT ANY NOTICE. SO, BAT! YOU GET THE CHIPS AND CANDY BARS! BEAR, YOU GET THE NACHOS, BUT NONE OF THAT HORSEMEAT CHILI THIS TIME, GOT IT?! MIKE--
MIKE! YOU GET THE ICE CREAM, AND OTHER FROZEN GOODS.
YOU'RE GONNA HAVE TO GET SOMEONE ELSE TO GET THE ICE CREAM, I DON'T TOUCH THE STUFF.
NO WAY, ONE TIME WHEN WE WERE AT THE PARK, J.J WAS LOOKIN' AT THE SQUIRRELS, GIGGLING AND STUFF; THEN OUTTA NOWHERE, THE KID DROPS HIS PANTS AND CRAPS OUT THE BIGGEST RAINBOW SHERBET ICE CREAM CONE I'VE EVER SEEN IN MY WHOLE LIFE! SO, NO-- I CAN'T TOUCH THE STUFF.
WHAT DO YOU MEAN, NO ICE CREAM?

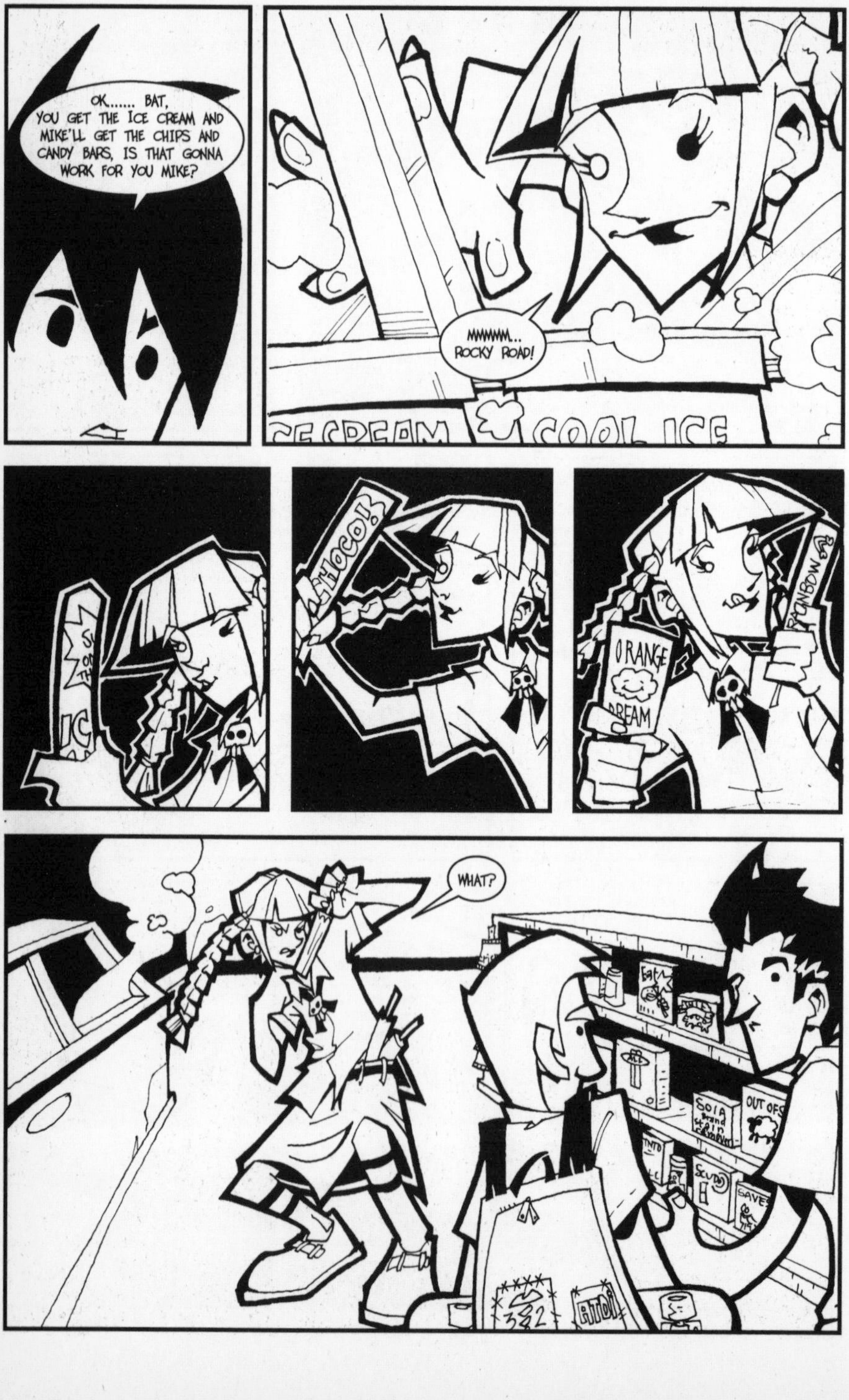
OK....... BAT, YOU GET THE ICE CREAM AND MIKE'LL GET THE CHIPS AND CANDY BARS, IS THAT GONNA WORK FOR YOU MIKE?
MMMMM... ROCKY ROAD!
COOL ICE
CHOCO
ORANGE DREAM
RAINBOW
WHAT?

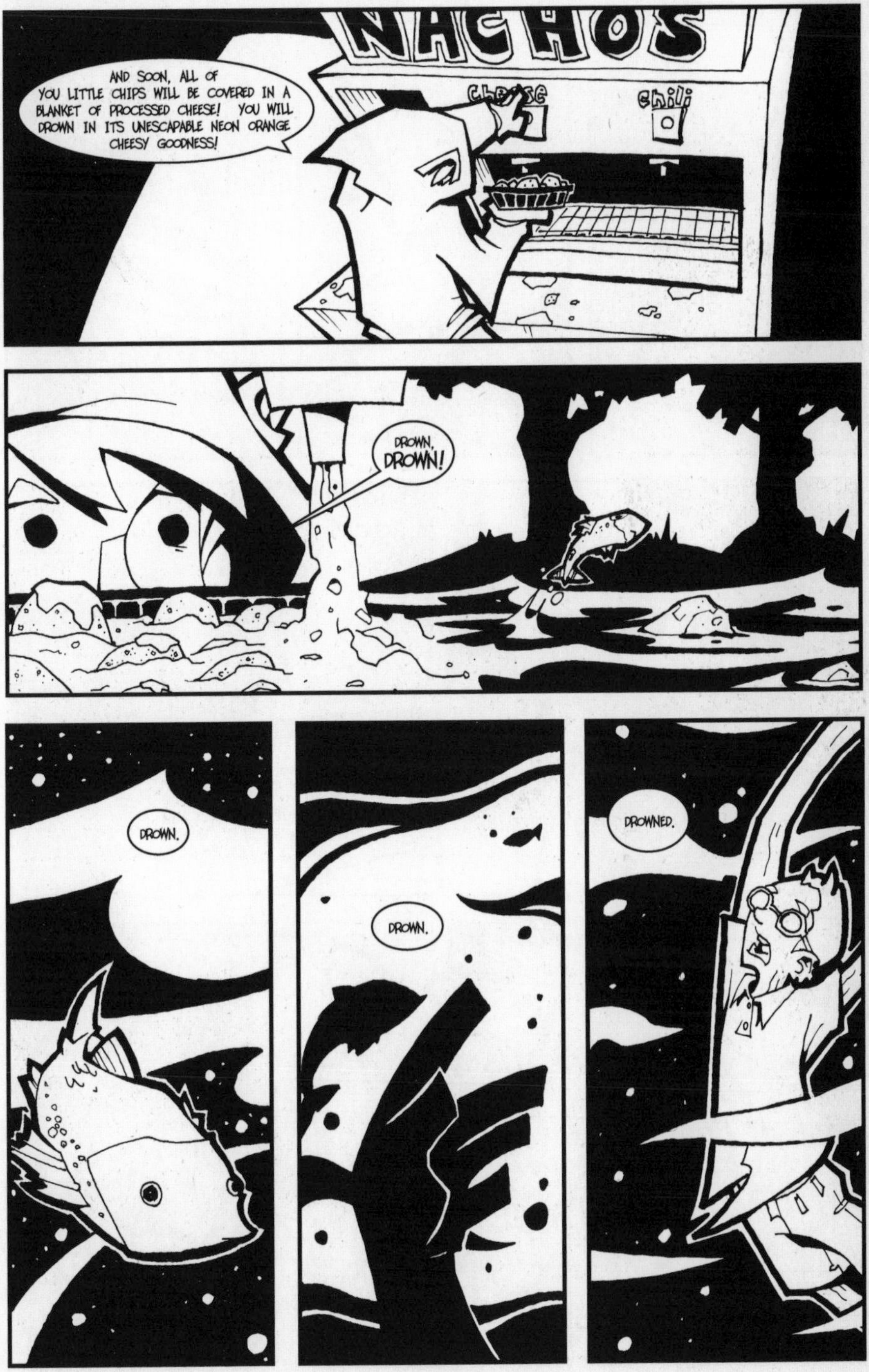
NACHOS
Cheese
Chili
AND SOON, ALL OF YOU LITTLE CHIPS WILL BE COVERED IN A BLANKET OF PROCESSED CHEESE! YOU WILL DROWN IN ITS UNESCAPABLE NEON ORANGE CHEESY GOODNESS!
DROWN, DROWN!
DROWN.
DROWN.
DROWNED.

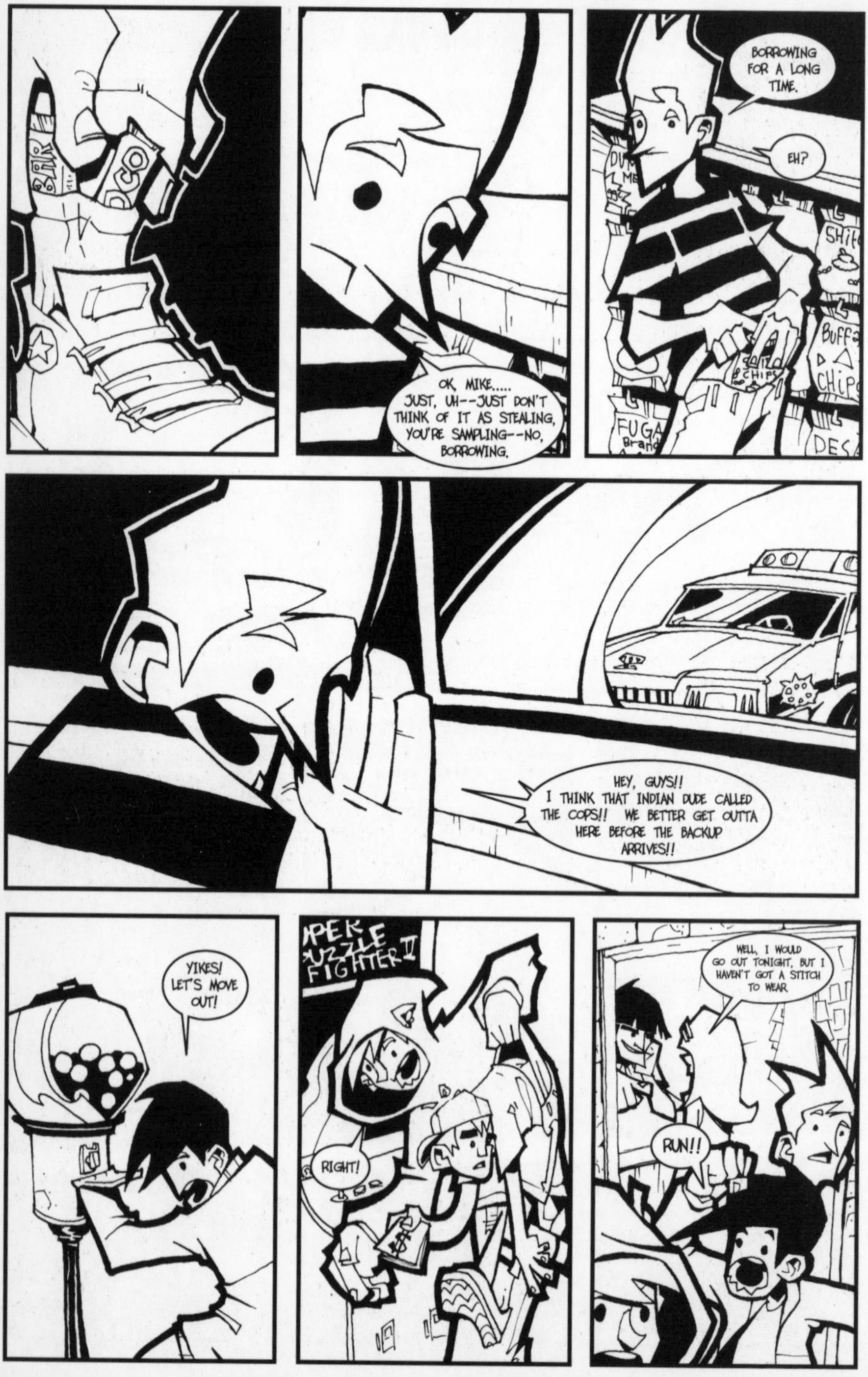
OK, MIKE.....
JUST, UH--JUST DON'T THINK OF IT AS STEALING, YOU'RE SAMPLING--NO, BORROWING.
BORROWING FOR A LONG TIME.
EH?
HEY, GUYS!! I THINK THAT INDIAN DUDE CALLED THE COPS!! WE BETTER GET OUTTA HERE BEFORE THE BACKUP ARRIVES!!
YIKES! LET'S MOVE OUT!
RIGHT!
WELL, I WOULD GO OUT TONIGHT, BUT I HAVEN'T GOT A STITCH TO WEAR
RUN!!

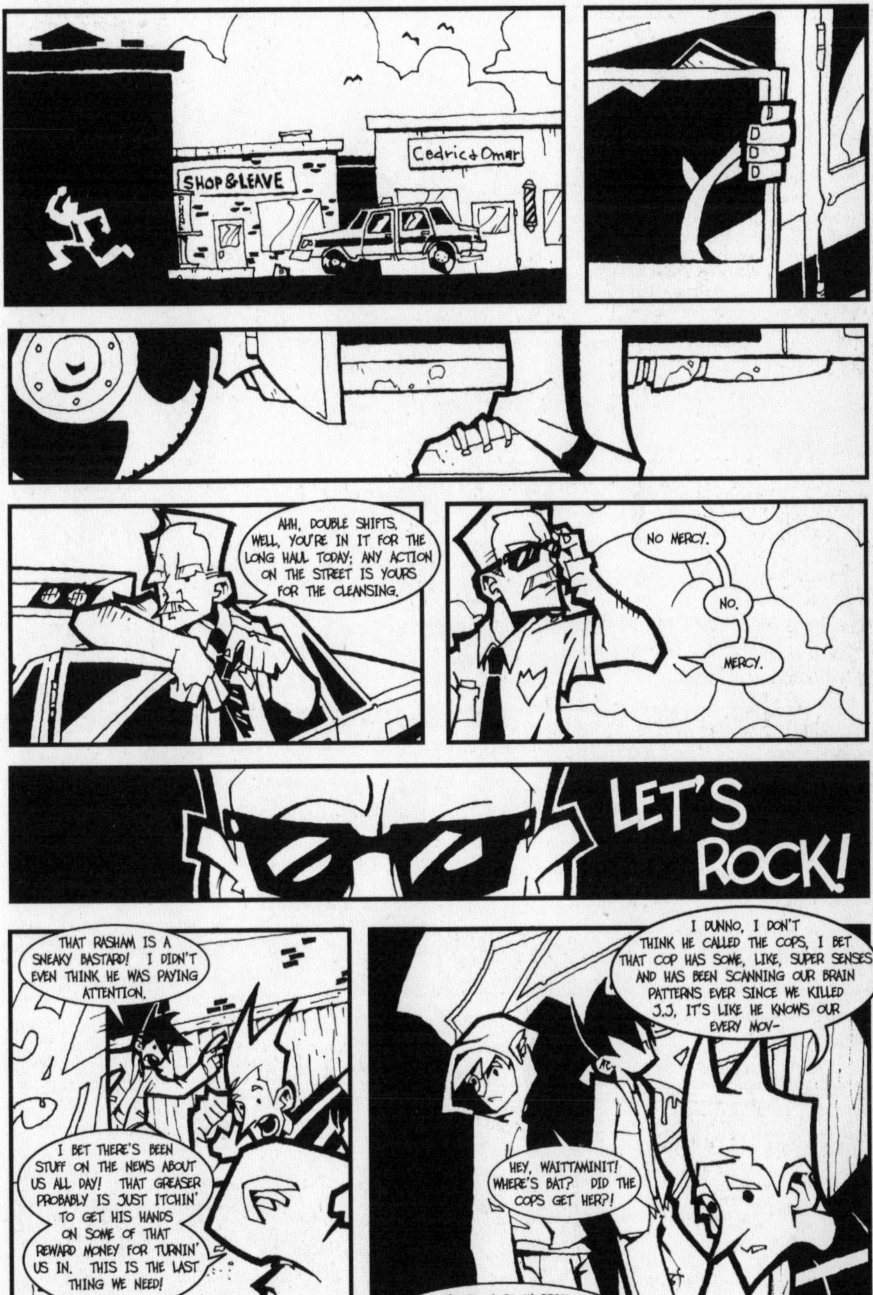
Cedric & Omar
SHOP & LEAVE
PHONE
AHH, DOUBLE SHIFTS. WELL, YOU'RE IN IT FOR THE LONG HAUL TODAY; ANY ACTION ON THE STREET IS YOURS FOR THE CLEANSING.
NO MERCY.
NO.
MERCY.
LET'S ROCK!
THAT RASHAM IS A SNEAKY BASTARD! I DIDN'T EVEN THINK HE WAS PAYING ATTENTION.
I BET THERE'S BEEN STUFF ON THE NEWS ABOUT US ALL DAY! THAT GREASER PROBABLY IS JUST ITCHIN' TO GET HIS HANDS ON SOME OF THAT REWARD MONEY FOR TURNIN' US IN. THIS IS THE LAST THING WE NEED!
I DUNNO, I DON'T THINK HE CALLED THE COPS, I BET THAT COP HAS SOME, LIKE, SUPER SENSES AND HAS BEEN SCANNING OUR BRAIN PATTERNS EVER SINCE WE KILLED J.J, IT'S LIKE HE KNOWS OUR EVERY MOV-
HEY, WAITTAMINIT! WHERE'S BAT? DID THE COPS GET HER?!
I'D BE MORE WORRIED ABOUT WHO MAY BE EAVESDROPPING ON YOUR CONVERSATION, MY FRIEND.

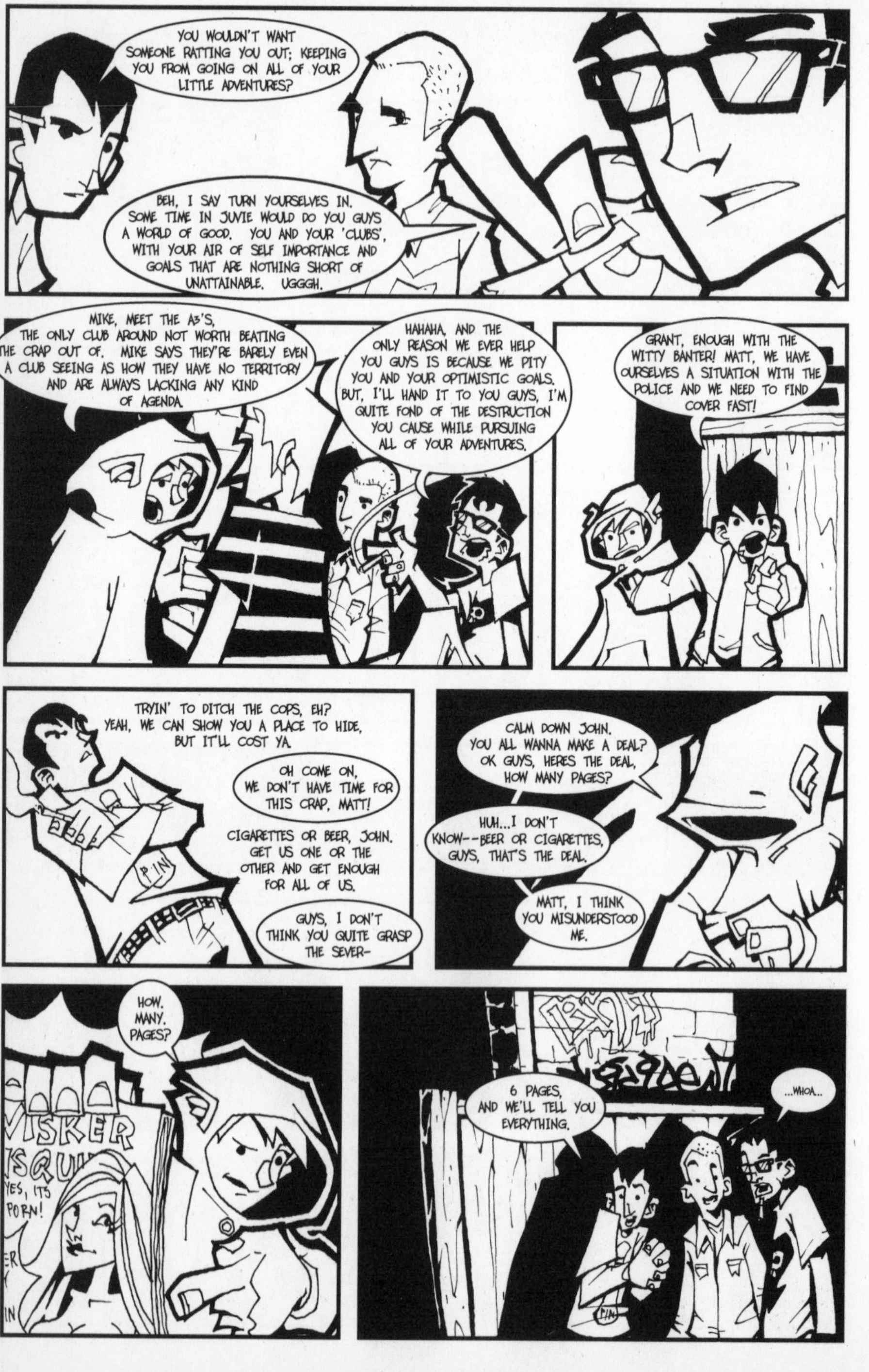

YOU WOULDN'T WANT SOMEONE RATTING YOU OUT; KEEPING YOU FROM GOING ON ALL OF YOUR LITTLE ADVENTURES?
BEH, I SAY TURN YOURSELVES IN. SOME TIME IN JUVIE WOULD DO YOU GUYS A WORLD OF GOOD. YOU AND YOUR 'CLUBS', WITH YOUR AIR OF SELF IMPORTANCE AND GOALS THAT ARE NOTHING SHORT OF UNATTAINABLE. UGGGH.
MIKE, MEET THE A3'S, THE ONLY CLUB AROUND NOT WORTH BEATING THE CRAP OUT OF. MIKE SAYS THEY'RE BARELY EVEN A CLUB SEEING AS HOW THEY HAVE NO TERRITORY AND ARE ALWAYS LACKING ANY KIND OF AGENDA.
HAHAHA, AND THE ONLY REASON WE EVER HELP YOU GUYS IS BECAUSE WE PITY YOU AND YOUR OPTIMISTIC GOALS. BUT, I'LL HAND IT TO YOU GUYS, I'M QUITE FOND OF THE DESTRUCTION YOU CAUSE WHILE PURSUING ALL OF YOUR ADVENTURES.
GRANT, ENOUGH WITH THE WITTY BANTER! MATT, WE HAVE OURSELVES A SITUATION WITH THE POLICE AND WE NEED TO FIND COVER FAST!
TRYIN' TO DITCH THE COPS, EH? YEAH, WE CAN SHOW YOU A PLACE TO HIDE, BUT IT'LL COST YA.
OH COME ON, WE DON'T HAVE TIME FOR THIS CRAP, MATT!
CIGARETTES OR BEER, JOHN. GET US ONE OR THE OTHER AND GET ENOUGH FOR ALL OF US.
GUYS, I DON'T THINK YOU QUITE GRASP THE SEVER-
CALM DOWN JOHN. YOU ALL WANNA MAKE A DEAL? OK GUYS, HERES THE DEAL, HOW MANY PAGES?
HUH...I DON'T KNOW--BEER OR CIGARETTES, GUYS, THAT'S THE DEAL.
MATT, I THINK YOU MISUNDERSTOOD ME.
HOW. MANY. PAGES?
WISKER
YES, ITS PORN!
6 PAGES, AND WE'LL TELL YOU EVERYTHING.
...WHOA...

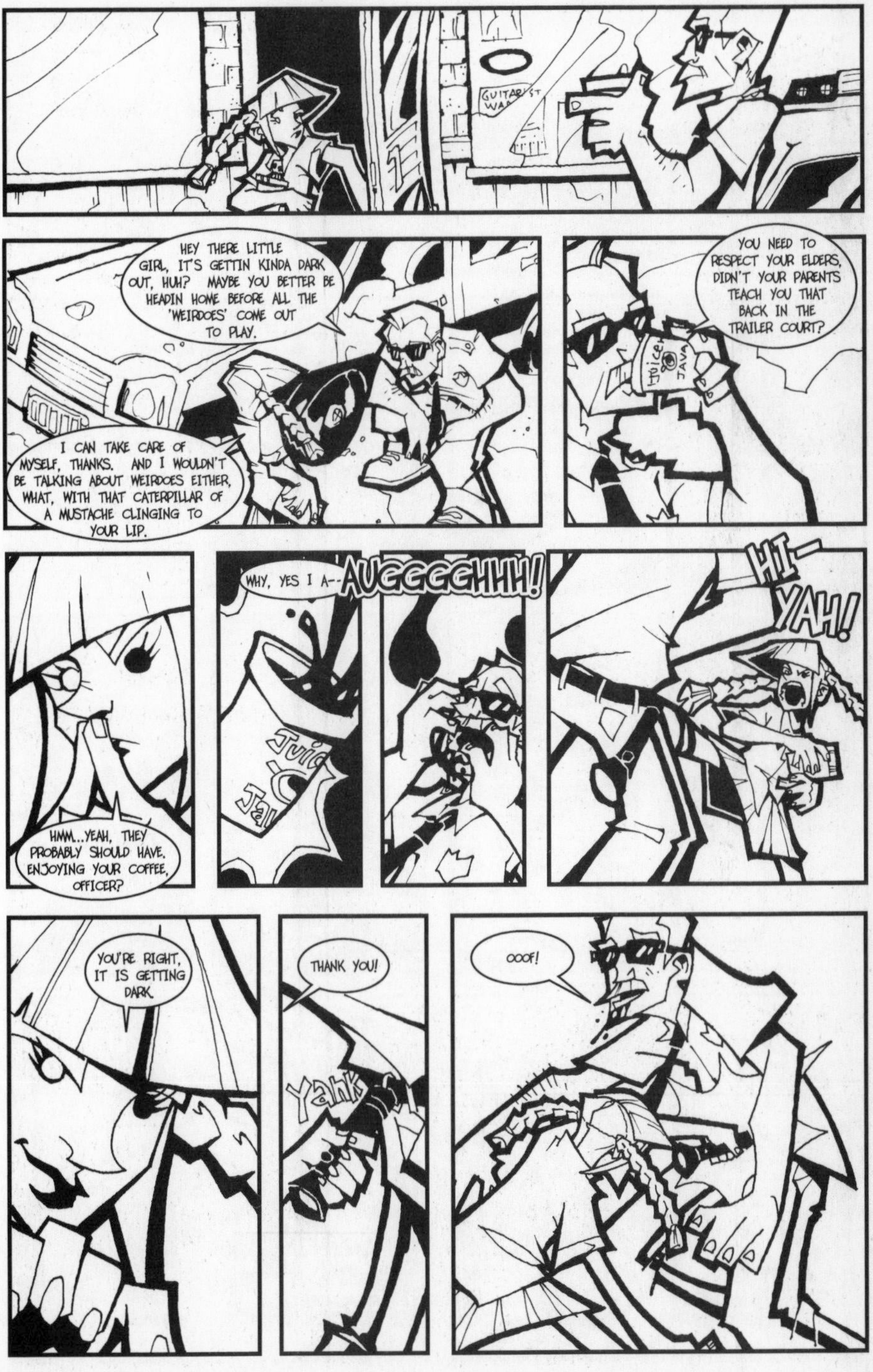
GUITARIST WA
HEY THERE LITTLE GIRL, IT'S GETTIN KINDA DARK OUT, HUH? MAYBE YOU BETTER BE HEADIN HOME BEFORE ALL THE 'WEIRDOES' COME OUT TO PLAY.
I CAN TAKE CARE OF MYSELF, THANKS. AND I WOULDN'T BE TALKING ABOUT WEIRDOES EITHER, WHAT, WITH THAT CATERPILLAR OF A MUSTACHE CLINGING TO YOUR LIP.
YOU NEED TO RESPECT YOUR ELDERS, DIDN'T YOUR PARENTS TEACH YOU THAT BACK IN THE TRAILER COURT?
Juicer JAVA
HMM...YEAH, THEY PROBABLY SHOULD HAVE. ENJOYING YOUR COFFEE, OFFICER?
WHY, YES I A--
AUGGGGHHH!
HI-YAH!
YOU'RE RIGHT, IT IS GETTING DARK.
THANK YOU!
Yank
OOOF!

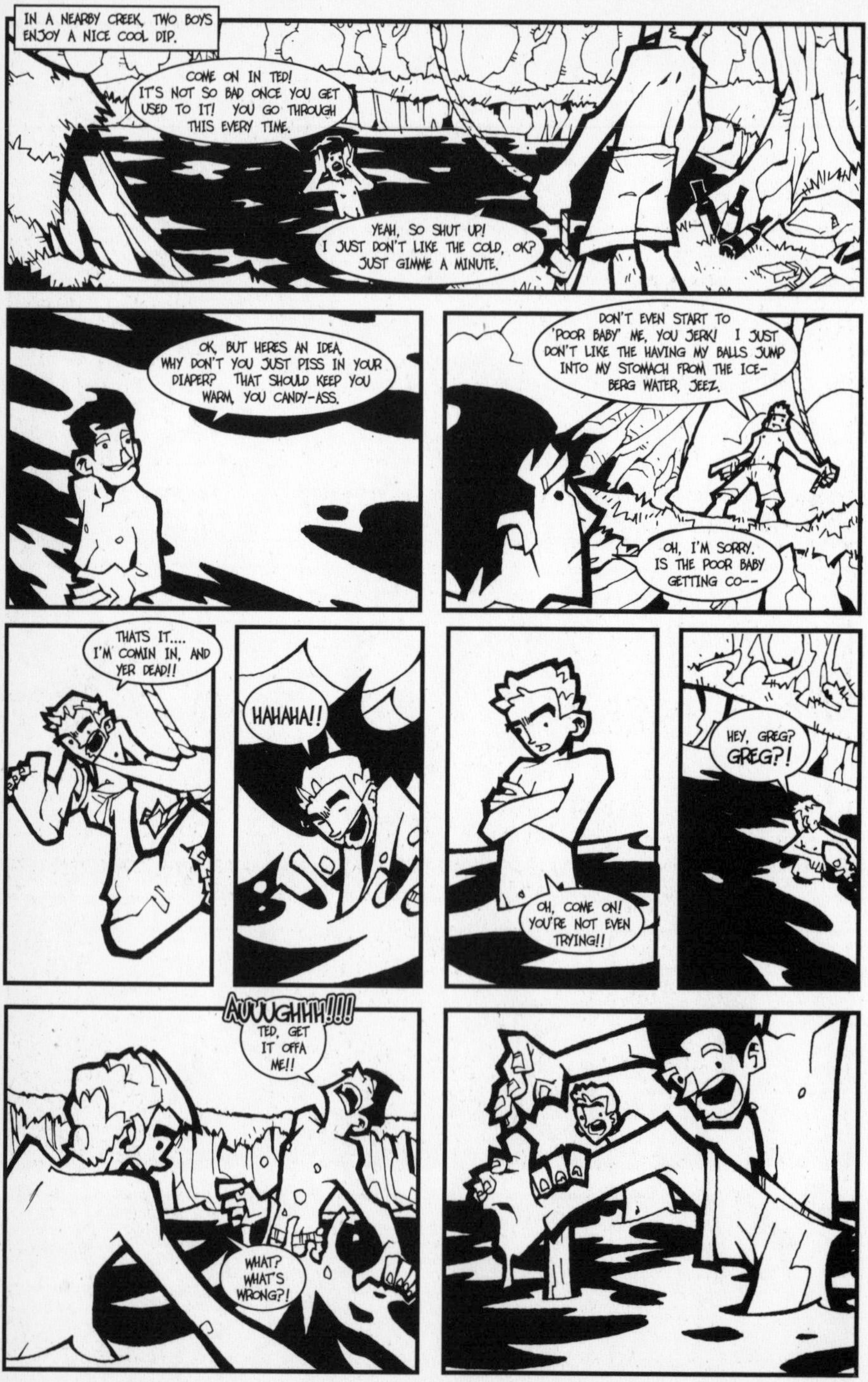
IN A NEARBY CREEK, TWO BOYS ENJOY A NICE COOL DIP.
COME ON IN TED! IT'S NOT SO BAD ONCE YOU GET USED TO IT! YOU GO THROUGH THIS EVERY TIME.
YEAH, SO SHUT UP! I JUST DON'T LIKE THE COLD, OK? JUST GIMME A MINUTE.
OK, BUT HERES AN IDEA, WHY DON'T YOU JUST PISS IN YOUR DIAPER? THAT SHOULD KEEP YOU WARM, YOU CANDY-ASS.
OH, I'M SORRY. IS THE POOR BABY GETTING CO--
DON'T EVEN START TO 'POOR BABY' ME, YOU JERK! I JUST DON'T LIKE THE HAVING MY BALLS JUMP INTO MY STOMACH FROM THE ICE-BERG WATER, JEEZ.
THATS IT.... I'M COMIN IN, AND YER DEAD!!
HAHAHA!!
OH, COME ON! YOU'RE NOT EVEN TRYING!!
HEY, GREG? GREG?!
AUUUGHHH!!!
TED, GET IT OFFA ME!!
WHAT? WHAT'S WRONG?!

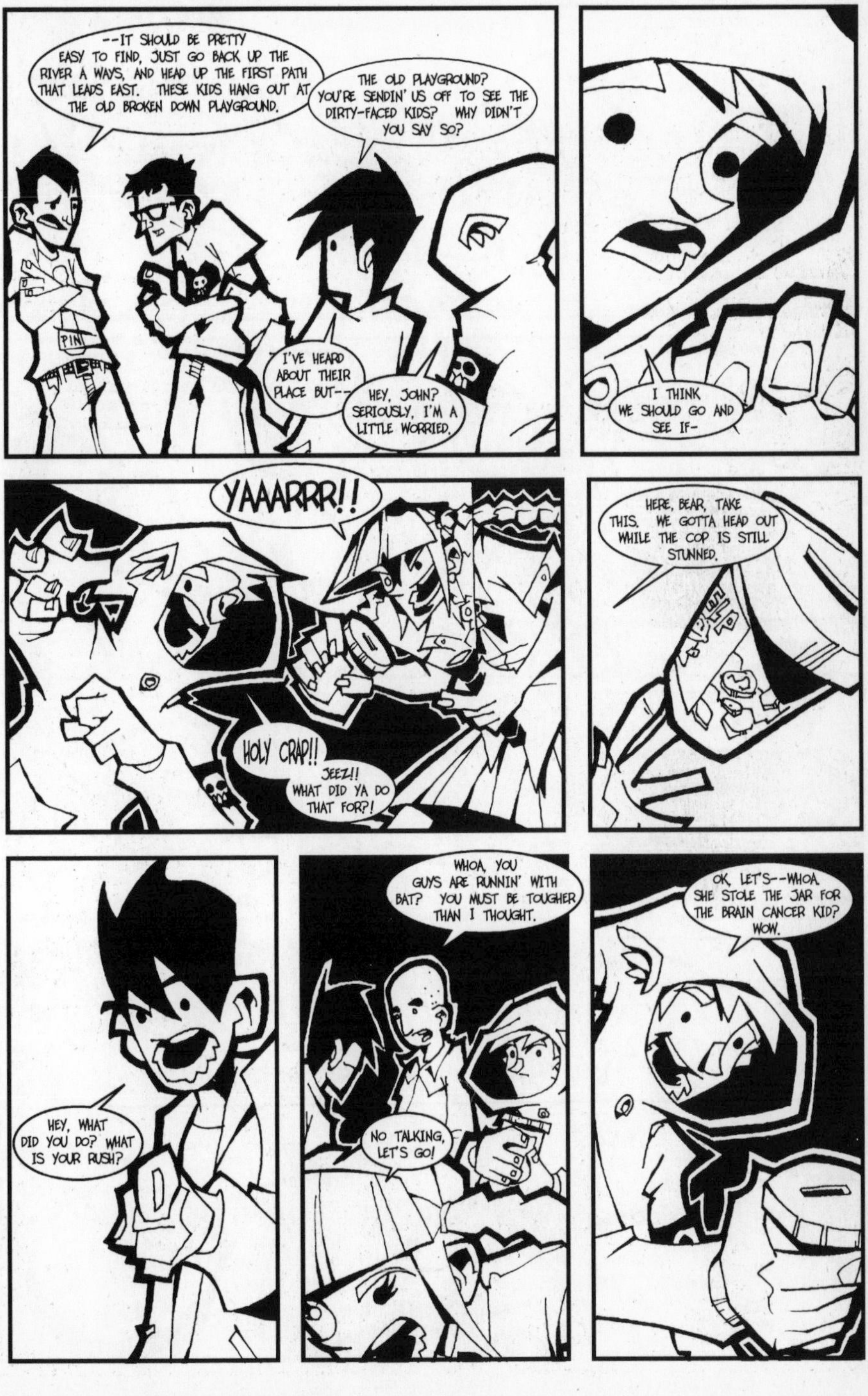
--IT SHOULD BE PRETTY EASY TO FIND, JUST GO BACK UP THE RIVER A WAYS, AND HEAD UP THE FIRST PATH THAT LEADS EAST. THESE KIDS HANG OUT AT THE OLD BROKEN DOWN PLAYGROUND.
THE OLD PLAYGROUND? YOU'RE SENDIN' US OFF TO SEE THE DIRTY-FACED KIDS? WHY DIDN'T YOU SAY SO?
PIN
I'VE HEARD ABOUT THEIR PLACE BUT--
HEY, JOHN? SERIOUSLY, I'M A LITTLE WORRIED.
I THINK WE SHOULD GO AND SEE IF-
YAAARRR!!
HOLY CRAP!!
JEEZ!! WHAT DID YA DO THAT FOR?!
HERE, BEAR, TAKE THIS. WE GOTTA HEAD OUT WHILE THE COP IS STILL STUNNED.
HEY, WHAT DID YOU DO? WHAT IS YOUR RUSH?
WHOA, YOU GUYS ARE RUNNIN' WITH BAT? YOU MUST BE TOUGHER THAN I THOUGHT.
NO TALKING, LET'S GO!
OK, LET'S--WHOA. SHE STOLE THE JAR FOR THE BRAIN CANCER KID? WOW.

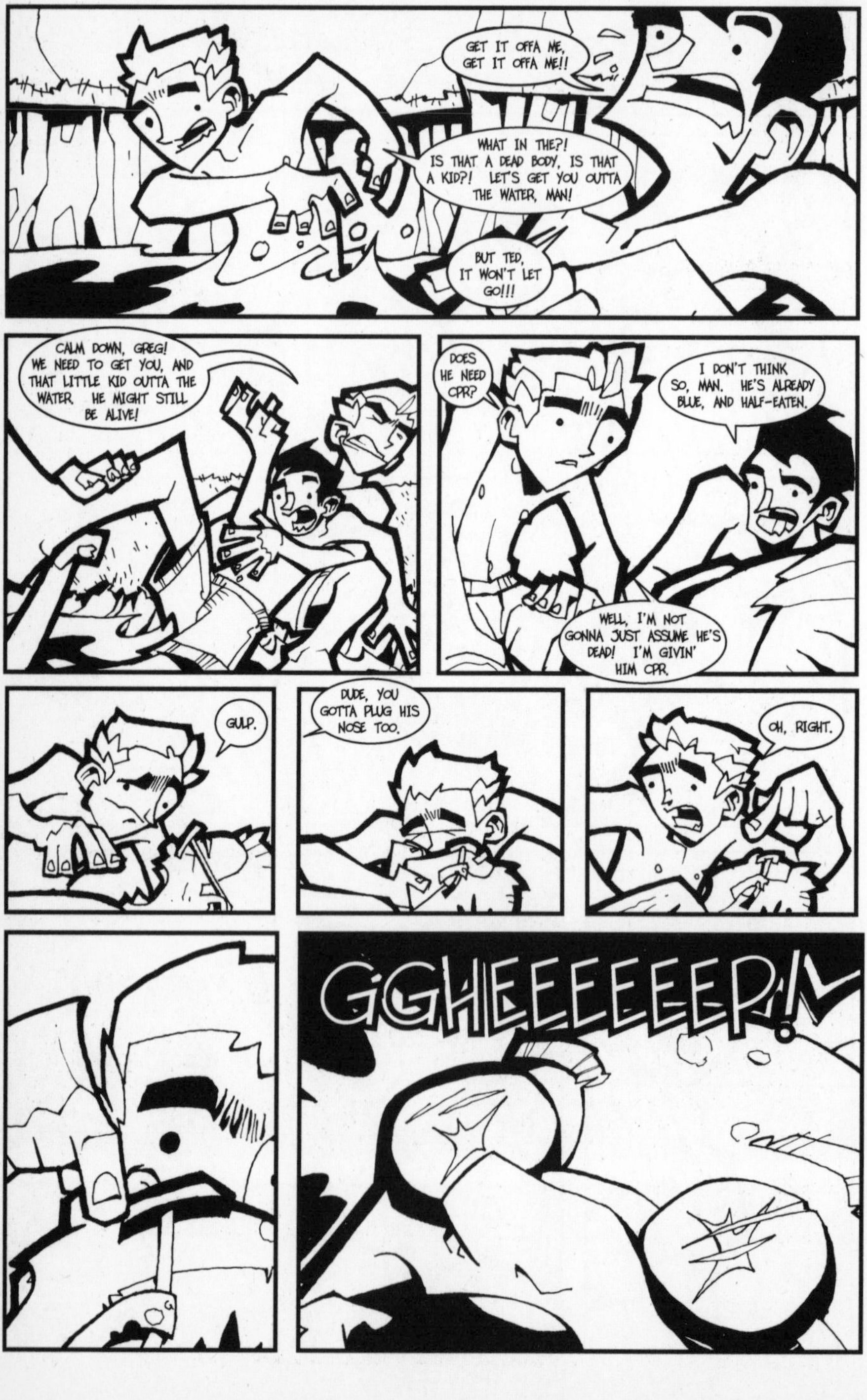
GET IT OFFA ME, GET IT OFFA ME!!
WHAT IN THE?! IS THAT A DEAD BODY, IS THAT A KID?! LET'S GET YOU OUTTA THE WATER, MAN!
BUT TED, IT WON'T LET GO!!!
CALM DOWN, GREG! WE NEED TO GET YOU, AND THAT LITTLE KID OUTTA THE WATER. HE MIGHT STILL BE ALIVE!
DOES HE NEED CPR?
I DON'T THINK SO, MAN. HE'S ALREADY BLUE, AND HALF-EATEN.
WELL, I'M NOT GONNA JUST ASSUME HE'S DEAD! I'M GIVIN' HIM CPR.
GULP.
DUDE, YOU GOTTA PLUG HIS NOSE TOO.
OH, RIGHT.
GGHEEEEEEEP!

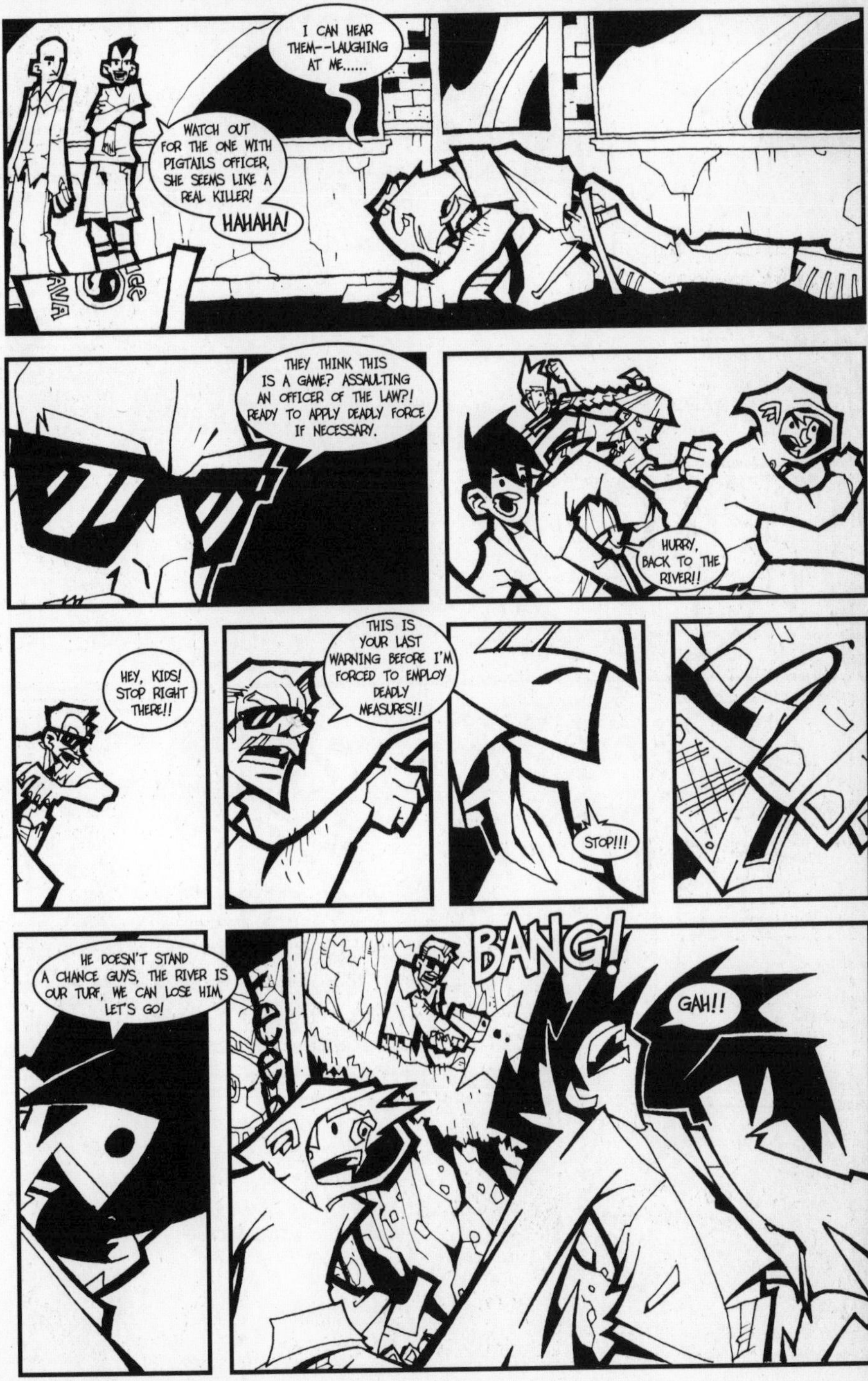
I CAN HEAR THEM--LAUGHING AT ME......
WATCH OUT FOR THE ONE WITH PIGTAILS OFFICER, SHE SEEMS LIKE A REAL KILLER!
HAHAHA!
THEY THINK THIS IS A GAME? ASSAULTING AN OFFICER OF THE LAW?! READY TO APPLY DEADLY FORCE IF NECESSARY.
HURRY, BACK TO THE RIVER!!
HEY, KIDS! STOP RIGHT THERE!!
THIS IS YOUR LAST WARNING BEFORE I'M FORCED TO EMPLOY DEADLY MEASURES!!
STOP!!!
HE DOESN'T STAND A CHANCE GUYS, THE RIVER IS OUR TURF, WE CAN LOSE HIM, LET'S GO!
BANG!
GAH!!

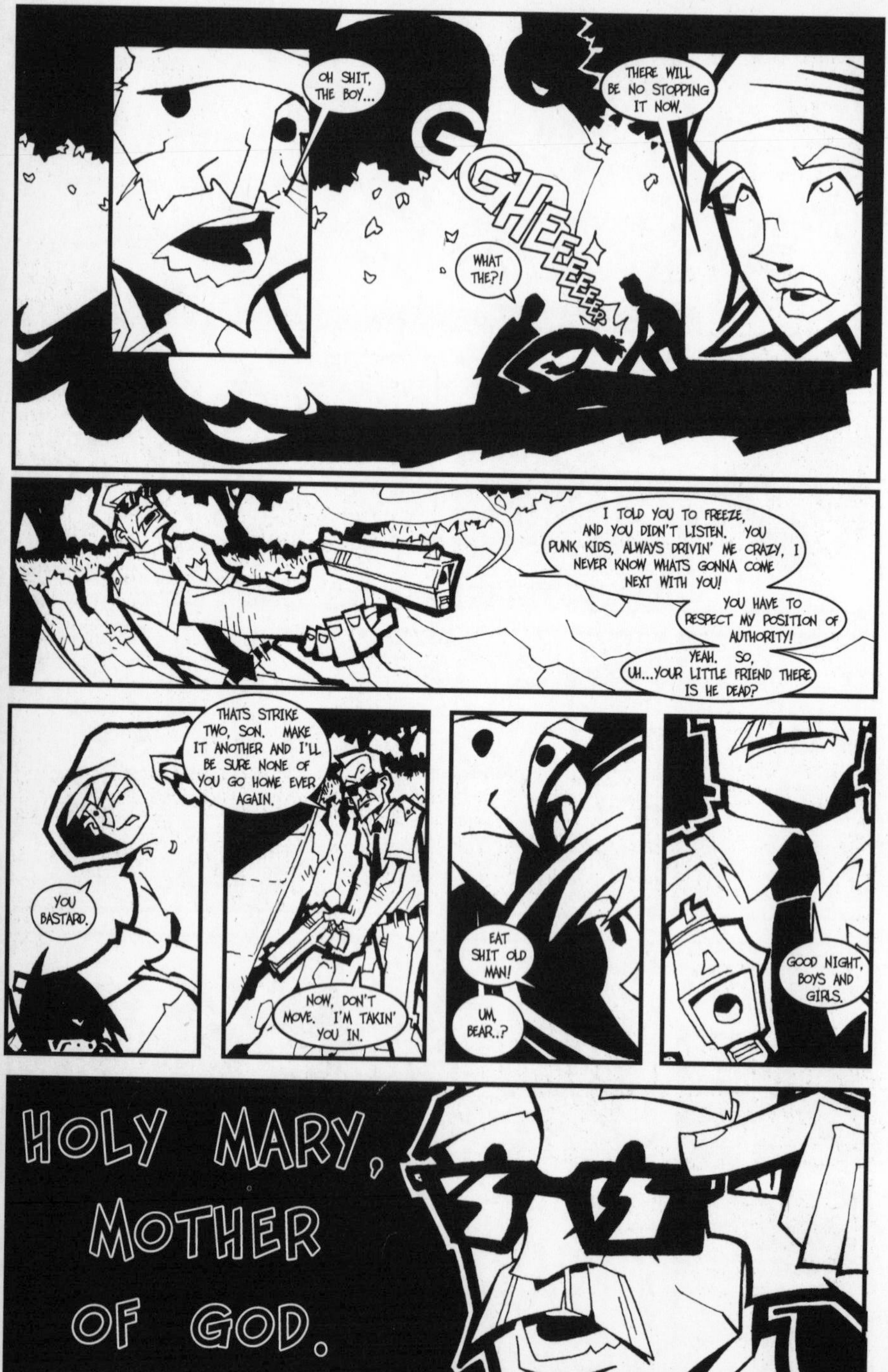
OH SHIT, THE BOY...
GGHEEEEEEP
THERE WILL BE NO STOPPING IT NOW.
WHAT THE?!
I TOLD YOU TO FREEZE, AND YOU DIDN'T LISTEN. YOU PUNK KIDS, ALWAYS DRIVIN' ME CRAZY, I NEVER KNOW WHATS GONNA COME NEXT WITH YOU!
YOU HAVE TO RESPECT MY POSITION OF AUTHORITY!
YEAH. SO, UH...YOUR LITTLE FRIEND THERE IS HE DEAD?
YOU BASTARD.
THATS STRIKE TWO, SON. MAKE IT ANOTHER AND I'LL BE SURE NONE OF YOU GO HOME EVER AGAIN.
NOW, DON'T MOVE. I'M TAKIN' YOU IN.
EAT SHIT OLD MAN!
UM, BEAR..?
GOOD NIGHT, BOYS AND GIRLS.
HOLY MARY, MOTHER OF GOD.

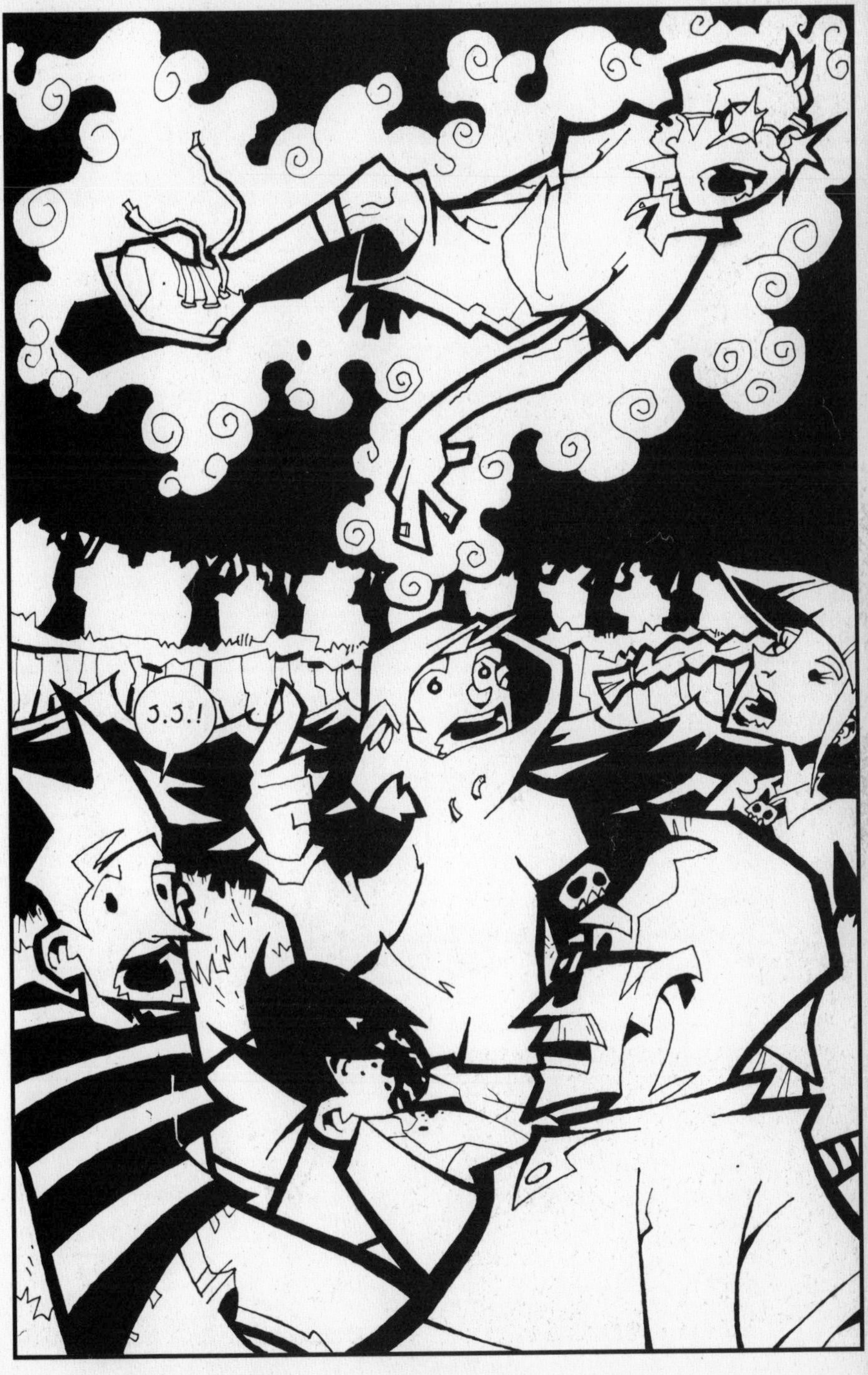
J.J.!

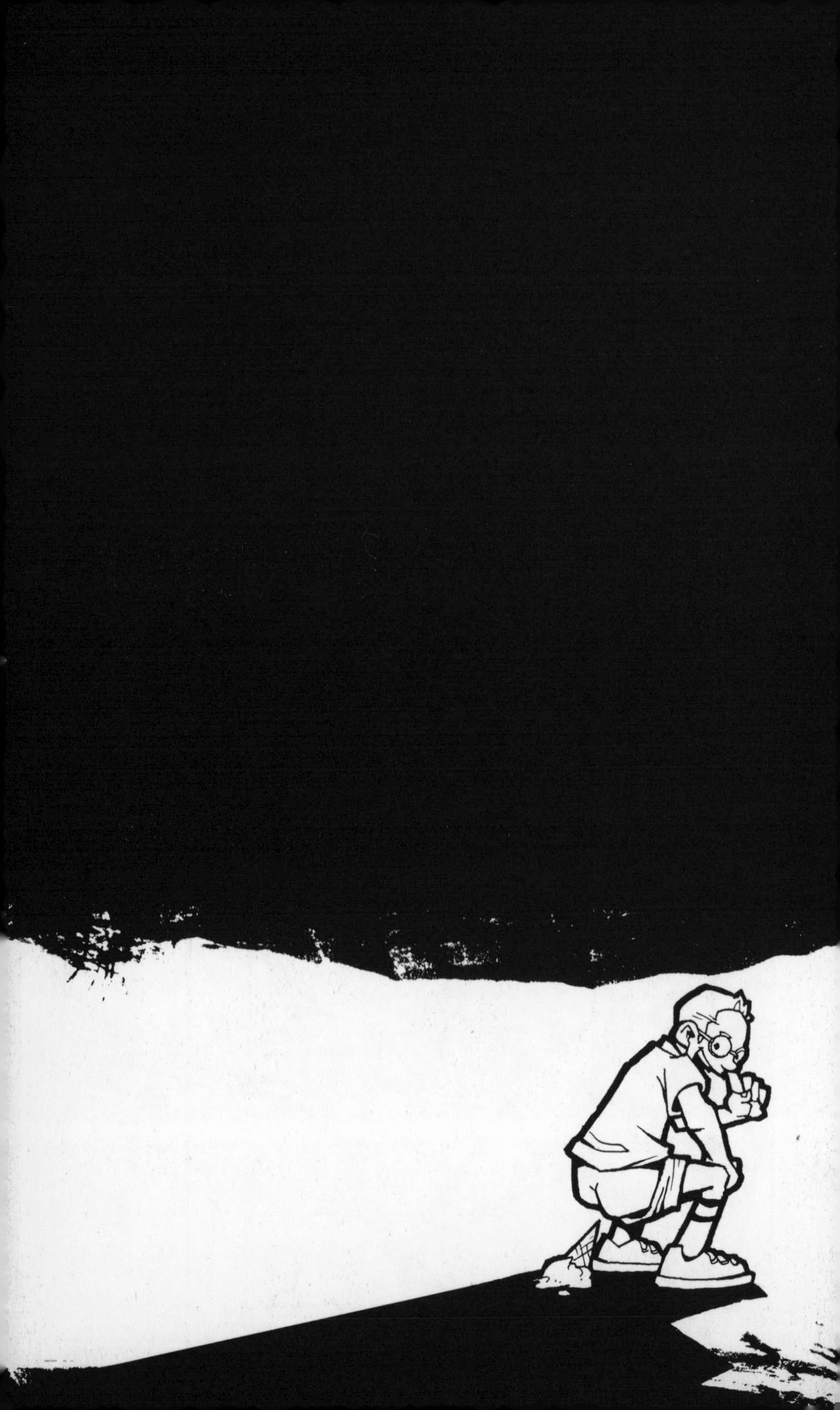

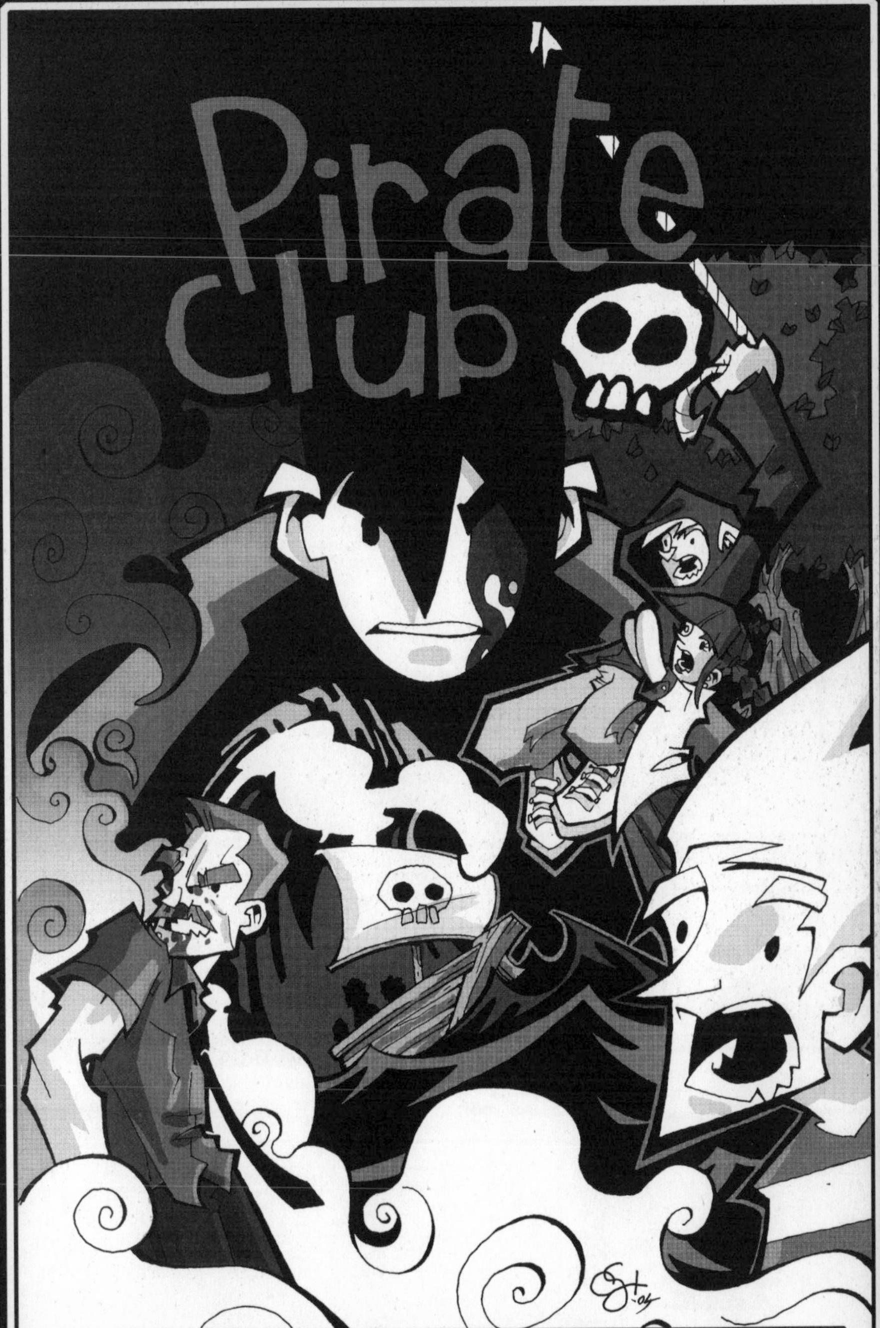
Pirate club

CHAPTER 4

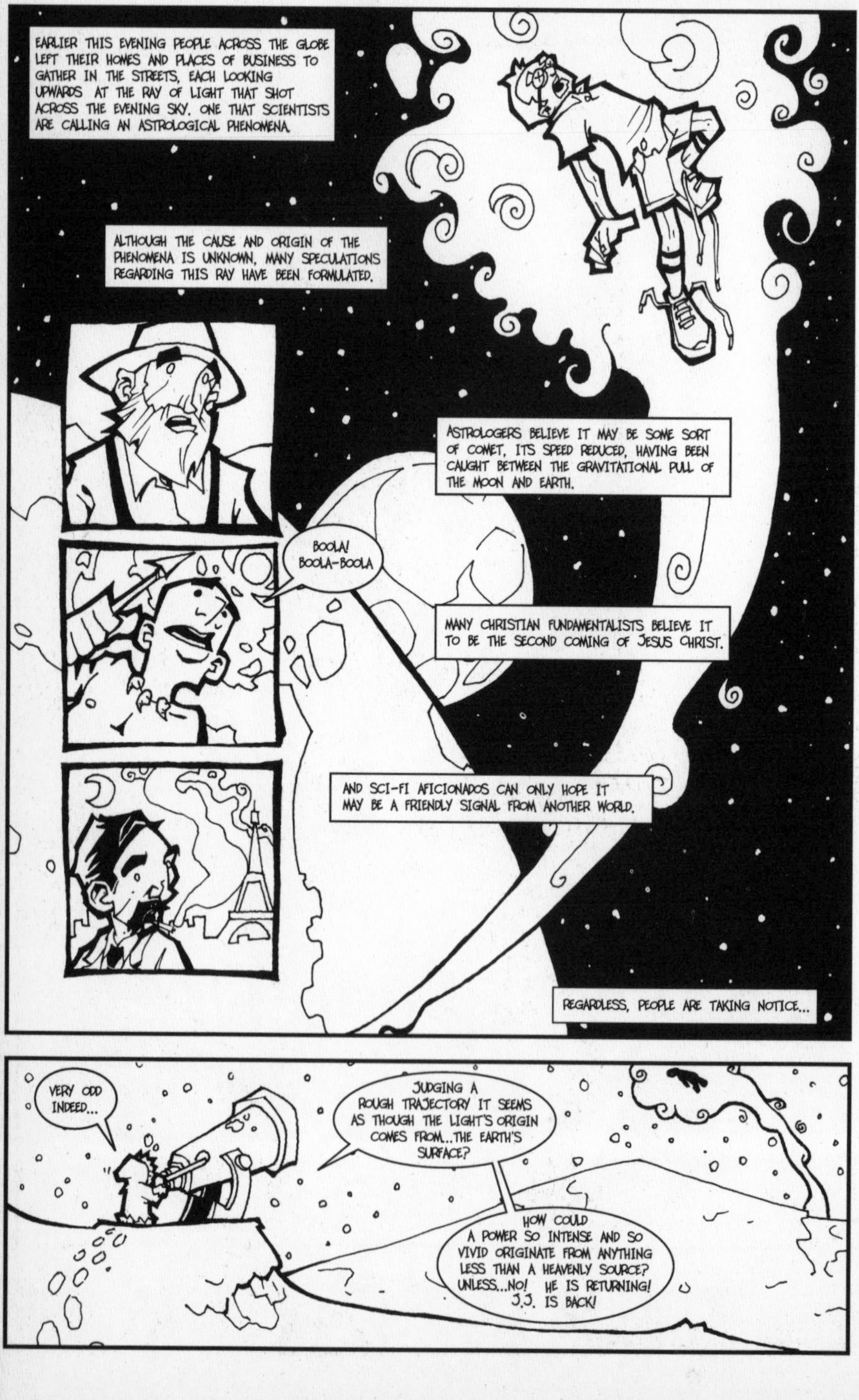
EARLIER THIS EVENING PEOPLE ACROSS THE GLOBE LEFT THEIR HOMES AND PLACES OF BUSINESS TO GATHER IN THE STREETS, EACH LOOKING UPWARDS AT THE RAY OF LIGHT THAT SHOT ACROSS THE EVENING SKY. ONE THAT SCIENTISTS ARE CALLING AN ASTROLOGICAL PHENOMENA.
ALTHOUGH THE CAUSE AND ORIGIN OF THE PHENOMENA IS UNKNOWN, MANY SPECULATIONS REGARDING THIS RAY HAVE BEEN FORMULATED.
ASTROLOGERS BELIEVE IT MAY BE SOME SORT OF COMET, ITS SPEED REDUCED, HAVING BEEN CAUGHT BETWEEN THE GRAVITATIONAL PULL OF THE MOON AND EARTH.
BOOLA! BOOLA-BOOLA
MANY CHRISTIAN FUNDAMENTALISTS BELIEVE IT TO BE THE SECOND COMING OF JESUS CHRIST.
AND SCI-FI AFICIONADOS CAN ONLY HOPE IT MAY BE A FRIENDLY SIGNAL FROM ANOTHER WORLD.
REGARDLESS, PEOPLE ARE TAKING NOTICE...
VERY ODD INDEED...
JUDGING A ROUGH TRAJECTORY IT SEEMS AS THOUGH THE LIGHT'S ORIGIN COMES FROM...THE EARTH'S SURFACE?
HOW COULD A POWER SO INTENSE AND SO VIVID ORIGINATE FROM ANYTHING LESS THAN A HEAVENLY SOURCE? UNLESS...NO! HE IS RETURNING! J.J. IS BACK!

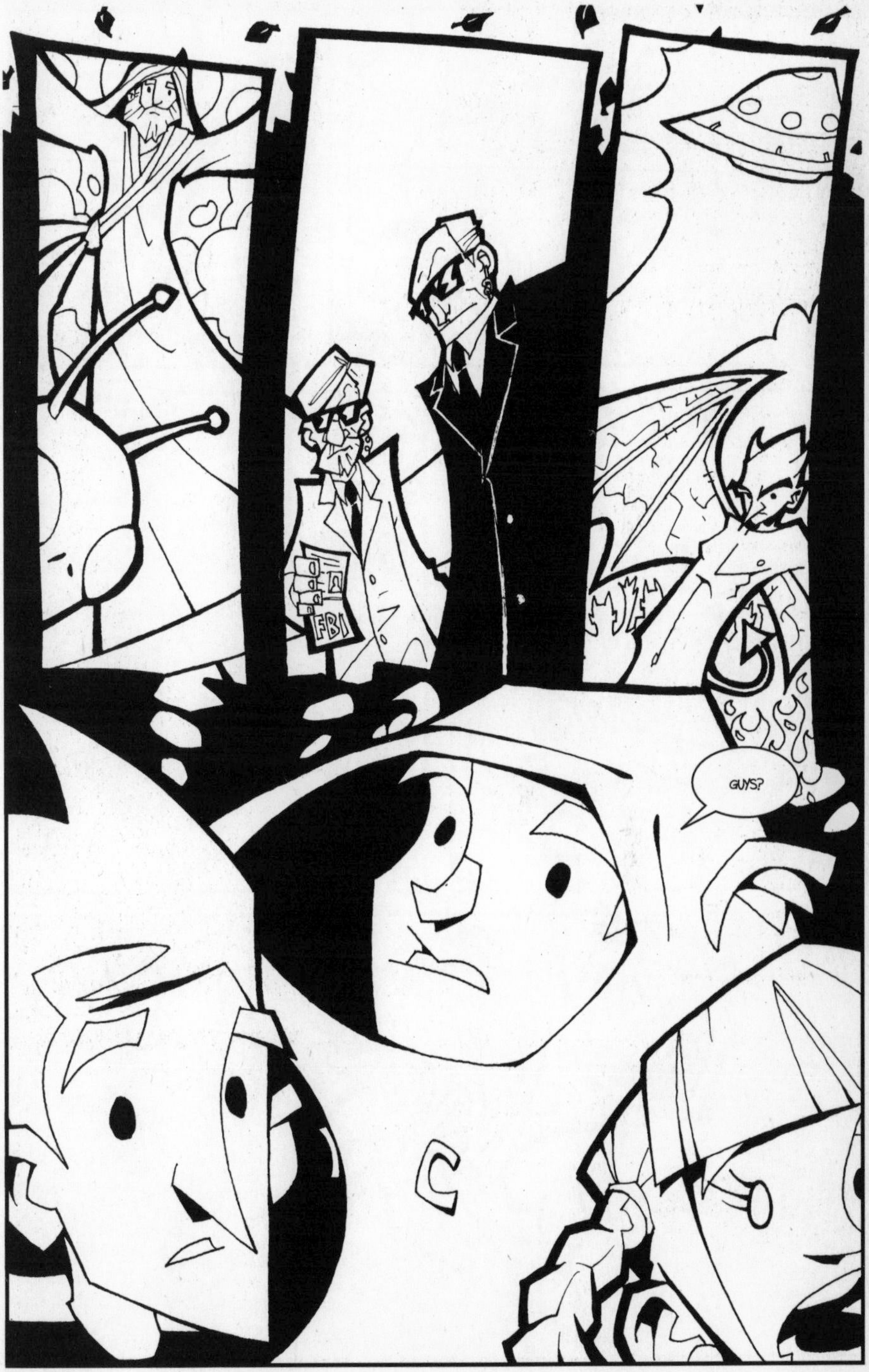
GUYS?

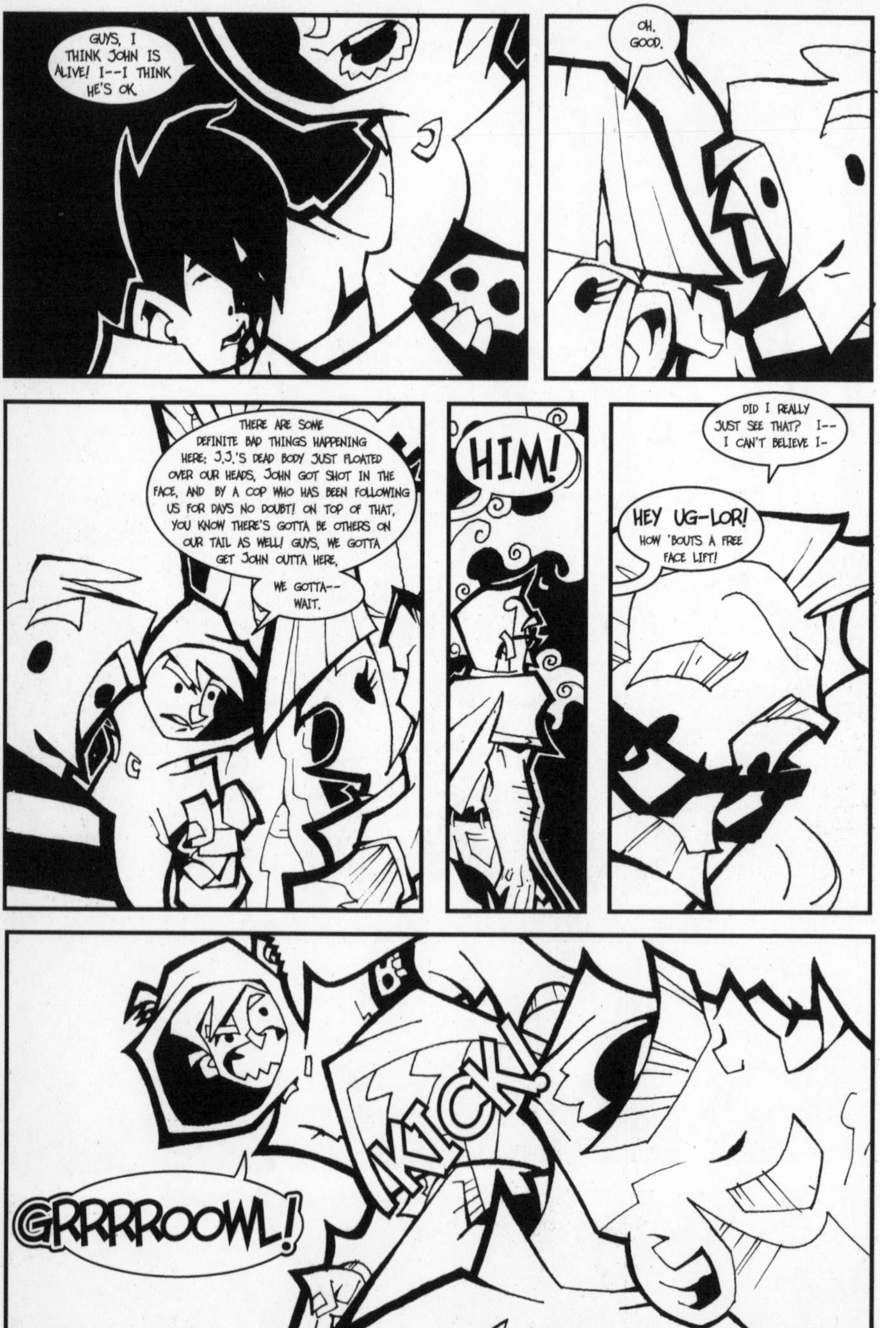
GUYS, I THINK JOHN IS ALIVE! I--I THINK HE'S OK.
OH. GOOD.
THERE ARE SOME DEFINITE BAD THINGS HAPPENING HERE: J.J.'S DEAD BODY JUST FLOATED OVER OUR HEADS, JOHN GOT SHOT IN THE FACE, AND BY A COP WHO HAS BEEN FOLLOWING US FOR DAYS NO DOUBT! ON TOP OF THAT, YOU KNOW THERE'S GOTTA BE OTHERS ON OUR TAIL AS WELL! GUYS, WE GOTTA GET JOHN OUTTA HERE.
WE GOTTA-- WAIT.
HIM!
DID I REALLY JUST SEE THAT? I-- I CAN'T BELIEVE I-
HEY UG-LOR! HOW 'BOUTS A FREE FACE LIFT!
KICK
GRRRROOWL!

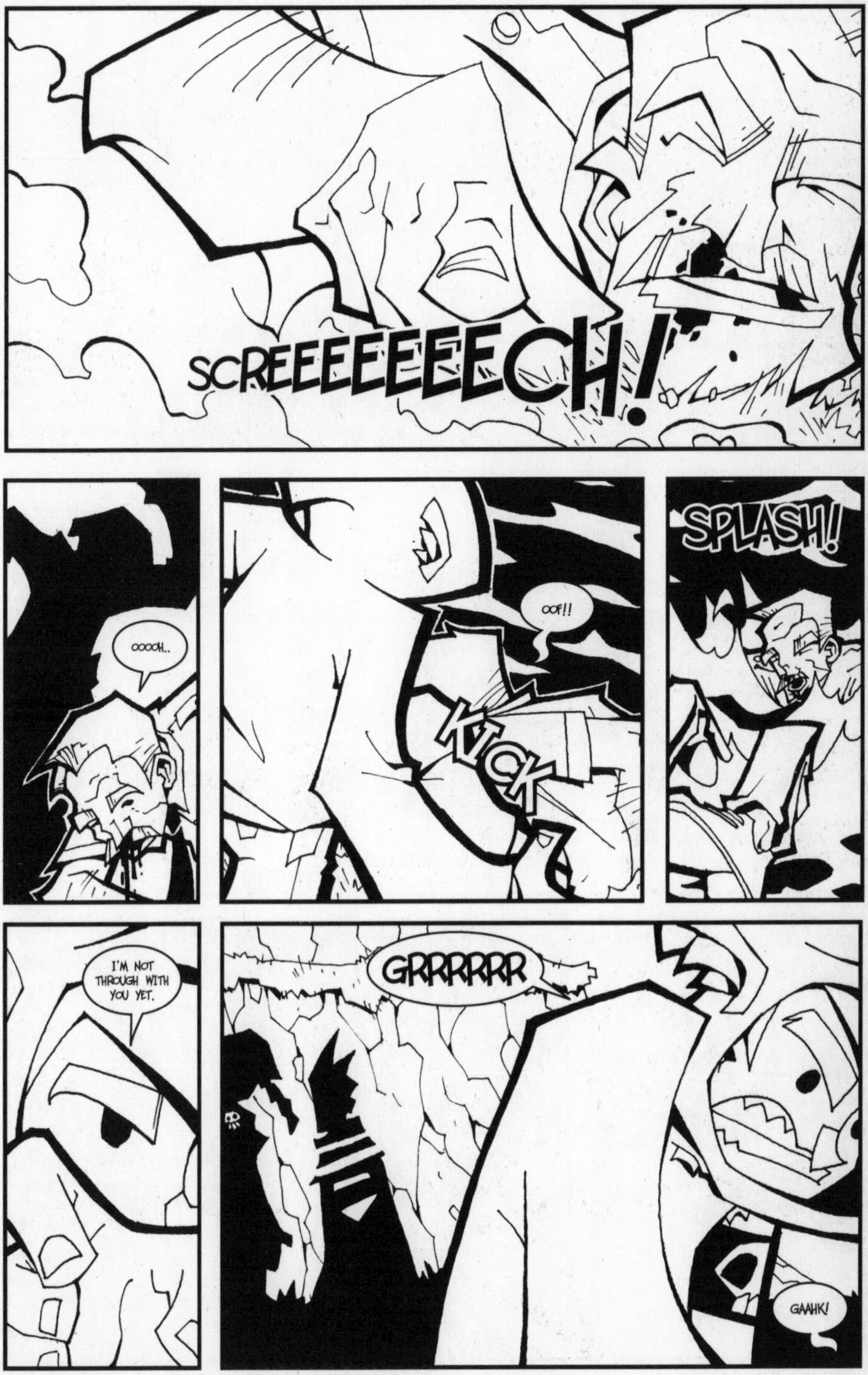

SCREEEEEEEECH!
OOOOH..
OOF!!
KICK
SPLASH!
I'M NOT THROUGH WITH YOU YET.
GRRRRRR
GAAHK!

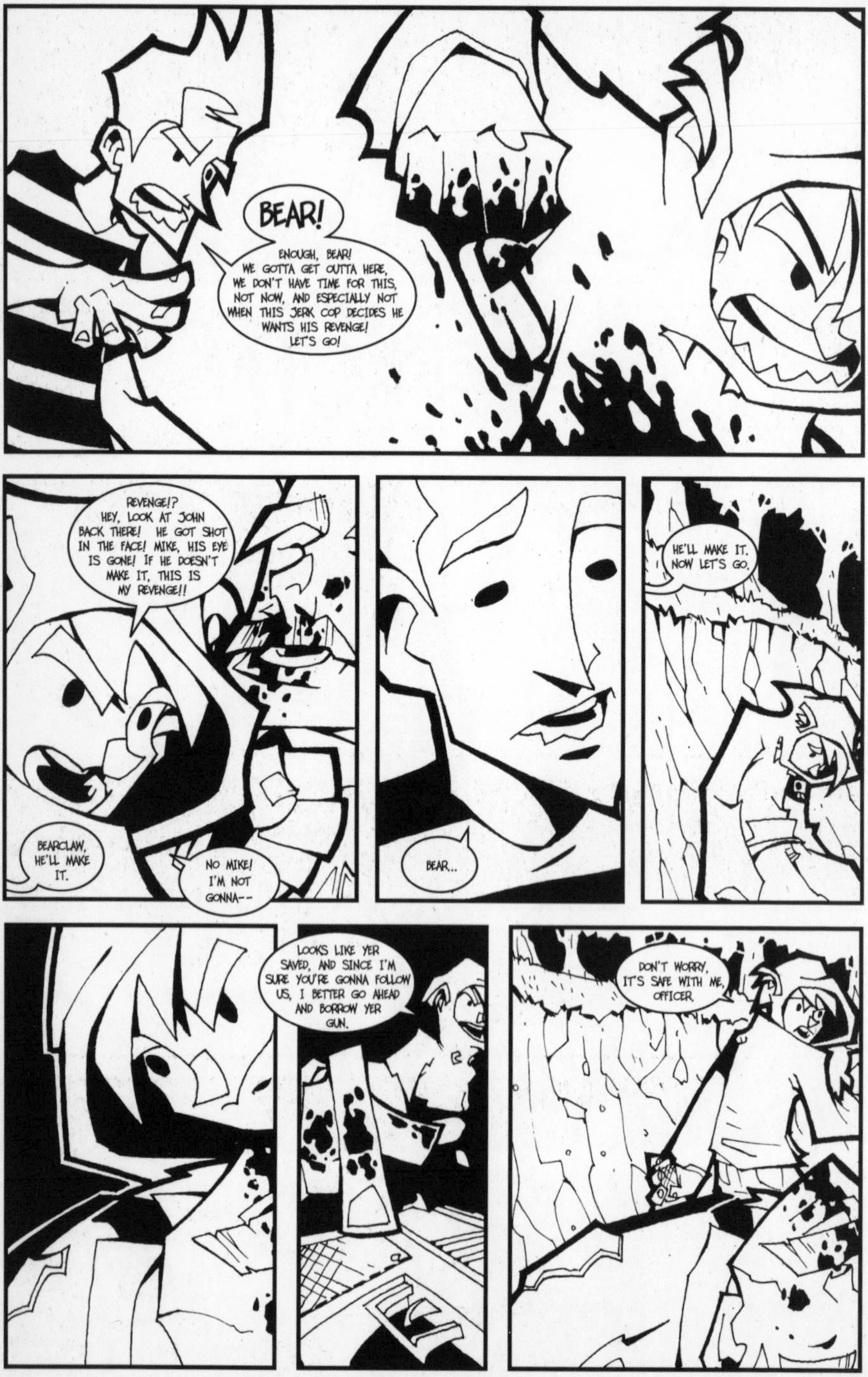

BEAR!
ENOUGH, BEAR! WE GOTTA GET OUTTA HERE, WE DON'T HAVE TIME FOR THIS, NOT NOW, AND ESPECIALLY NOT WHEN THIS JERK COP DECIDES HE WANTS HIS REVENGE! LET'S GO!
REVENGE!? HEY, LOOK AT JOHN BACK THERE! HE GOT SHOT IN THE FACE! MIKE, HIS EYE IS GONE! IF HE DOESN'T MAKE IT, THIS IS MY REVENGE!!
BEARCLAW, HE'LL MAKE IT.
NO MIKE! I'M NOT GONNA--
BEAR...
HE'LL MAKE IT. NOW LET'S GO.
LOOKS LIKE YER SAVED, AND SINCE I'M SURE YOU'RE GONNA FOLLOW US, I BETTER GO AHEAD AND BORROW YER GUN.
DON'T WORRY, IT'S SAFE WITH ME, OFFICER.

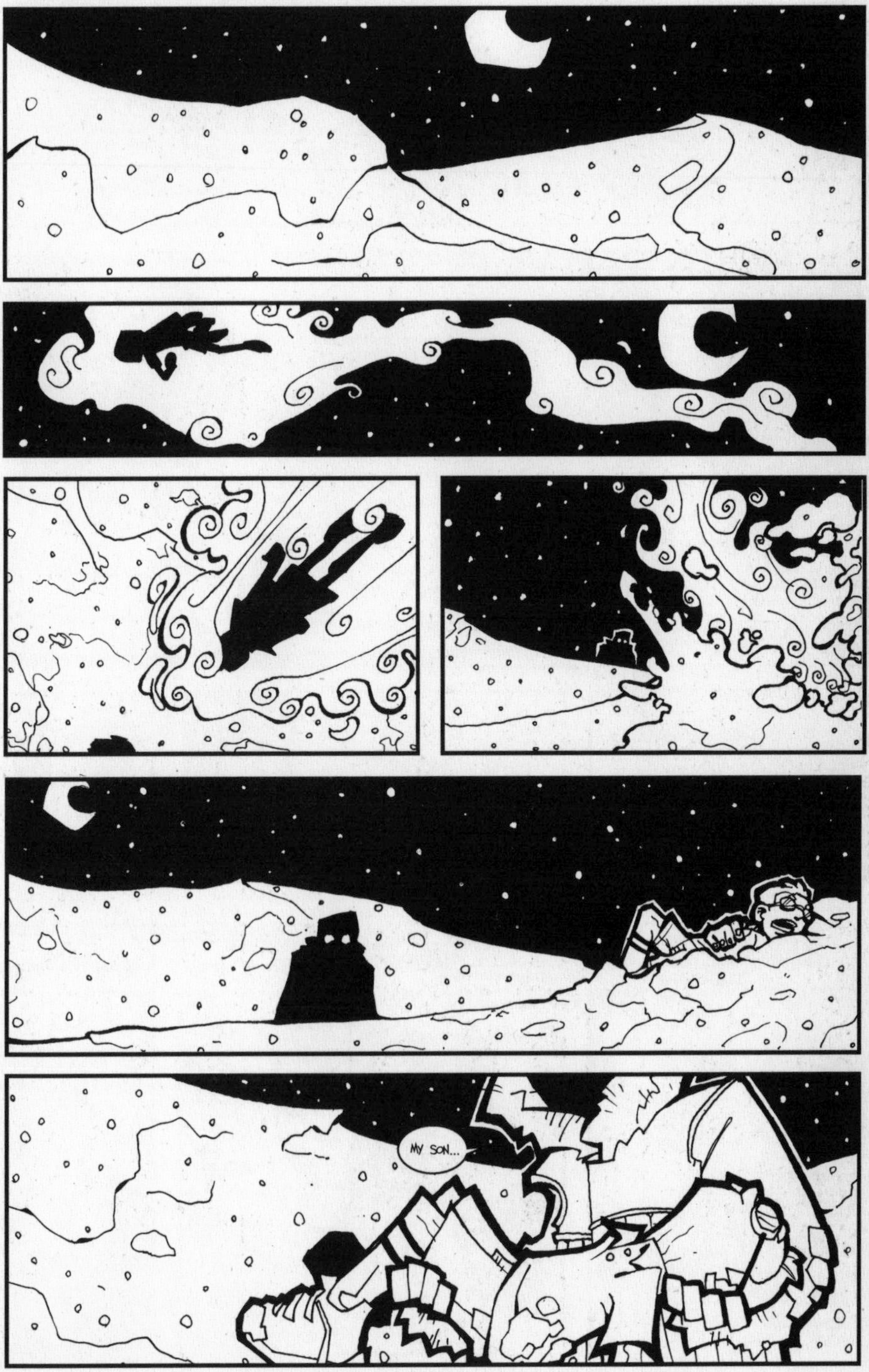
MY SON...

JOHN, YOU THERE, BUDDY? HEY, YOU OK?

LEAMME ALONE, MAN...I JUST-- I JUST WANNA...WHY ARE WE WALKING? LET'S SI'DOWN...

WE GOTTA KEEP HIM AWAKE. HEY, HEY JOHN? TELL US THAT ONE STORY MAN, BAT AND MIKE HAVEN'T HEARD IT YET.

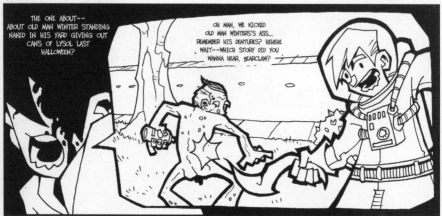

THE ONE ABOUT-- ABOUT OLD MAN WINTER STANDING NAKED IN HIS YARD GIVING OUT CANS OF LYSOL LAST HALLOWEEN?

OH MAN, WE KICKED OLD MAN WINTERS'S ASS... REMEMBER HIS DENTURES? HEHEHE WAIT--WHICH STORY DID YOU WANNA HEAR, BEARCLAW?

UM... NO, THE ONE ABOUT MS. HARRIS, WHEN YOU TRIED TO--

GUYS... WAI-WAI-WAIT! LOOK.....

r at your own ri...

is path belongs to

e dirty faced kids.

THIS LOOKS LIKE BAD NEWS. BOOBY TRAPS...

I'M GUESSIN' THESE KIDS MEAN BUSINESS.

WE'LL BE DEAD IF WE TRY TO MAKE IT THROUGH WITH JOHN THE WAY HE IS... BEAR, YOU SHOULD STAY HERE WITH JOHN. ME AN BAT ARE GONNA TRY AND GET SOME OF THESE TRAPS DISARMED.

HEY, WHY ARE YOU GOIN WITH BAT? I MEAN, I CAN GO....I DON'T HAVE TO STAY HERE.

BEAR, LOOK AT JOHN, YOU HAVE TO KEEP HIM AWAKE. WE'LL BE RIGHT BACK ANYWAYS.

WHAT, HIM?! HE'LL BE FINE! HEY! UH... MIKE...I NEED TO GO WITH BAT, UH...THE DIRTHEAD KIDS DON'T KNOW YOU GUYS.

FINE.

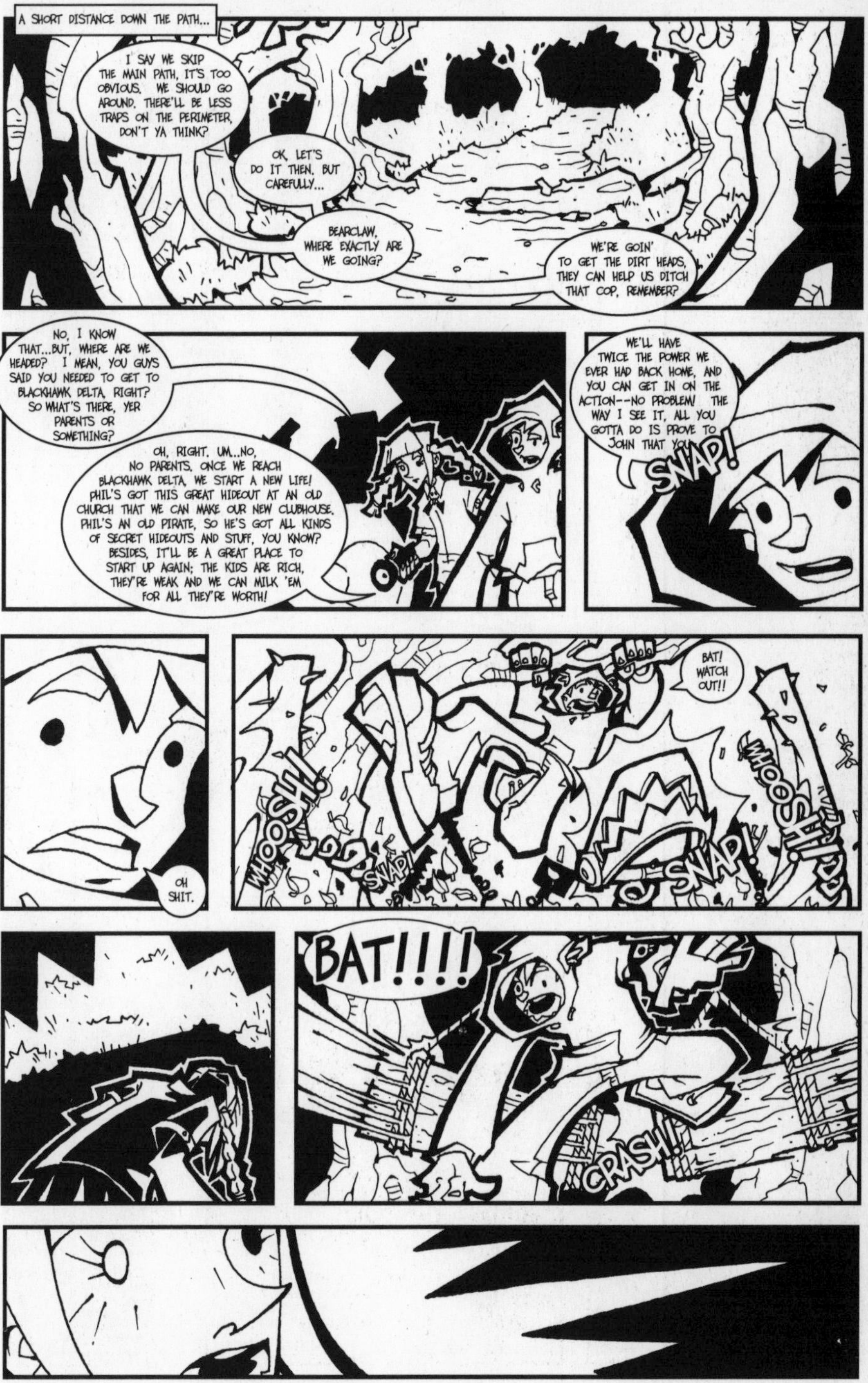
A SHORT DISTANCE DOWN THE PATH...
I SAY WE SKIP THE MAIN PATH, IT'S TOO OBVIOUS. WE SHOULD GO AROUND. THERE'LL BE LESS TRAPS ON THE PERIMETER, DON'T YA THINK?
OK, LET'S DO IT THEN. BUT CAREFULLY...
BEARCLAW, WHERE EXACTLY ARE WE GOING?
WE'RE GOIN' TO GET THE DIRT HEADS, THEY CAN HELP US DITCH THAT COP, REMEMBER?
NO, I KNOW THAT...BUT, WHERE ARE WE HEADED? I MEAN, YOU GUYS SAID YOU NEEDED TO GET TO BLACKHAWK DELTA, RIGHT? SO WHAT'S THERE, YER PARENTS OR SOMETHING?
OH, RIGHT. UM...NO, NO PARENTS. ONCE WE REACH BLACKHAWK DELTA, WE START A NEW LIFE! PHIL'S GOT THIS GREAT HIDEOUT AT AN OLD CHURCH THAT WE CAN MAKE OUR NEW CLUBHOUSE. PHIL'S AN OLD PIRATE, SO HE'S GOT ALL KINDS OF SECRET HIDEOUTS AND STUFF, YOU KNOW? BESIDES, IT'LL BE A GREAT PLACE TO START UP AGAIN; THE KIDS ARE RICH, THEY'RE WEAK AND WE CAN MILK 'EM FOR ALL THEY'RE WORTH!
WE'LL HAVE TWICE THE POWER WE EVER HAD BACK HOME, AND YOU CAN GET IN ON THE ACTION--NO PROBLEM! THE WAY I SEE IT, ALL YOU GOTTA DO IS PROVE TO JOHN THAT YOU
SNAP!
OH SHIT.
BAT! WATCH OUT!!
WHOOSH!
SNAP!
SNAP!
WHOOSH!
BAT!!!!
CRASH!

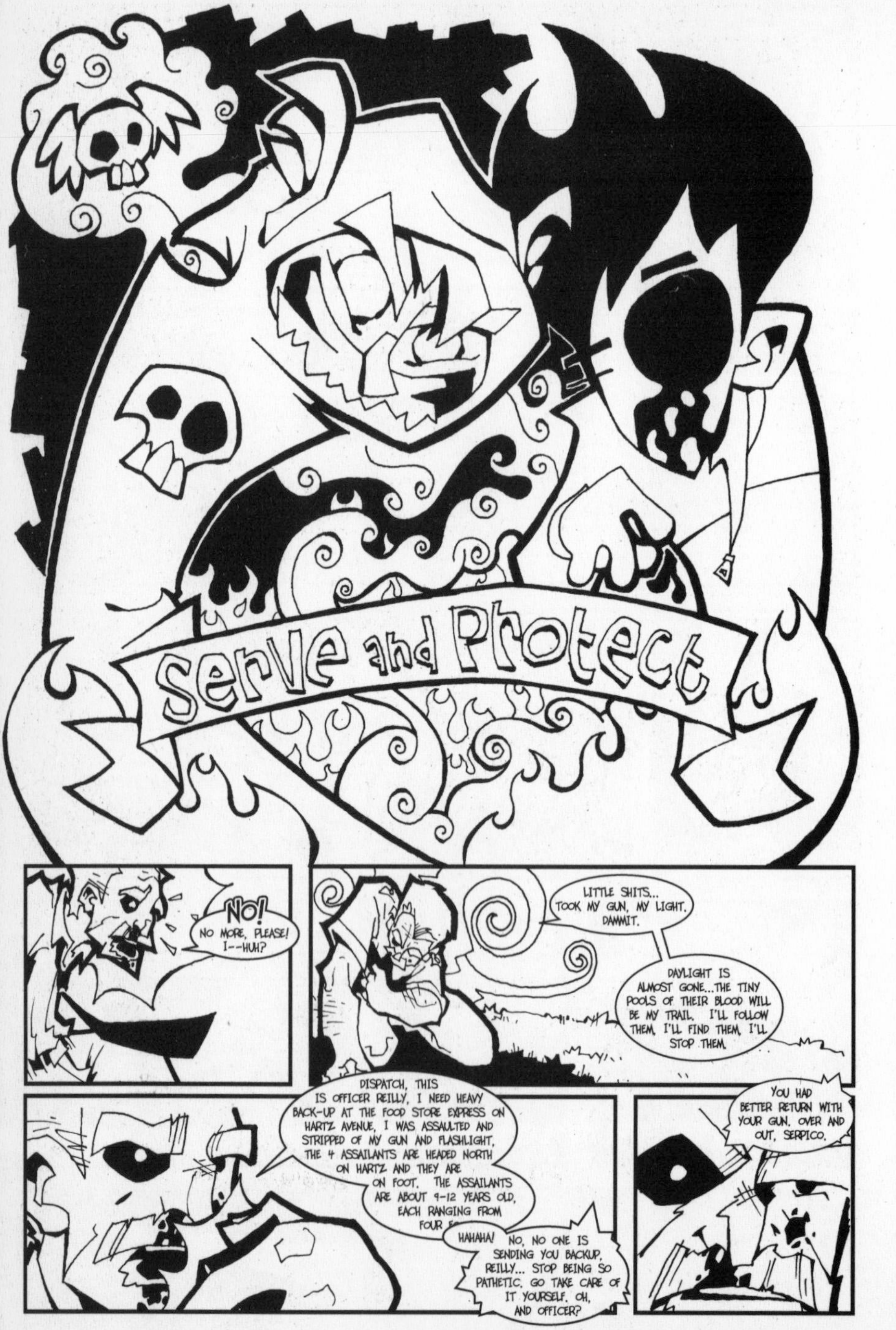
Serve and Protect
NO! NO MORE, PLEASE! I--HUH?
LITTLE SHITS... TOOK MY GUN, MY LIGHT. DAMMIT.
DAYLIGHT IS ALMOST GONE...THE TINY POOLS OF THEIR BLOOD WILL BE MY TRAIL. I'LL FOLLOW THEM, I'LL FIND THEM, I'LL STOP THEM.
DISPATCH, THIS IS OFFICER REILLY, I NEED HEAVY BACK-UP AT THE FOOD STORE EXPRESS ON HARTZ AVENUE, I WAS ASSAULTED AND STRIPPED OF MY GUN AND FLASHLIGHT, THE 4 ASSAILANTS ARE HEADED NORTH ON HARTZ AND THEY ARE ON FOOT. THE ASSAILANTS ARE ABOUT 9-12 YEARS OLD, EACH RANGING FROM FOUR
HAHAHA! NO, NO ONE IS SENDING YOU BACKUP, REILLY... STOP BEING SO PATHETIC. GO TAKE CARE OF IT YOURSELF. OH, AND OFFICER?
YOU HAD BETTER RETURN WITH YOUR GUN. OVER AND OUT, SERPICO.

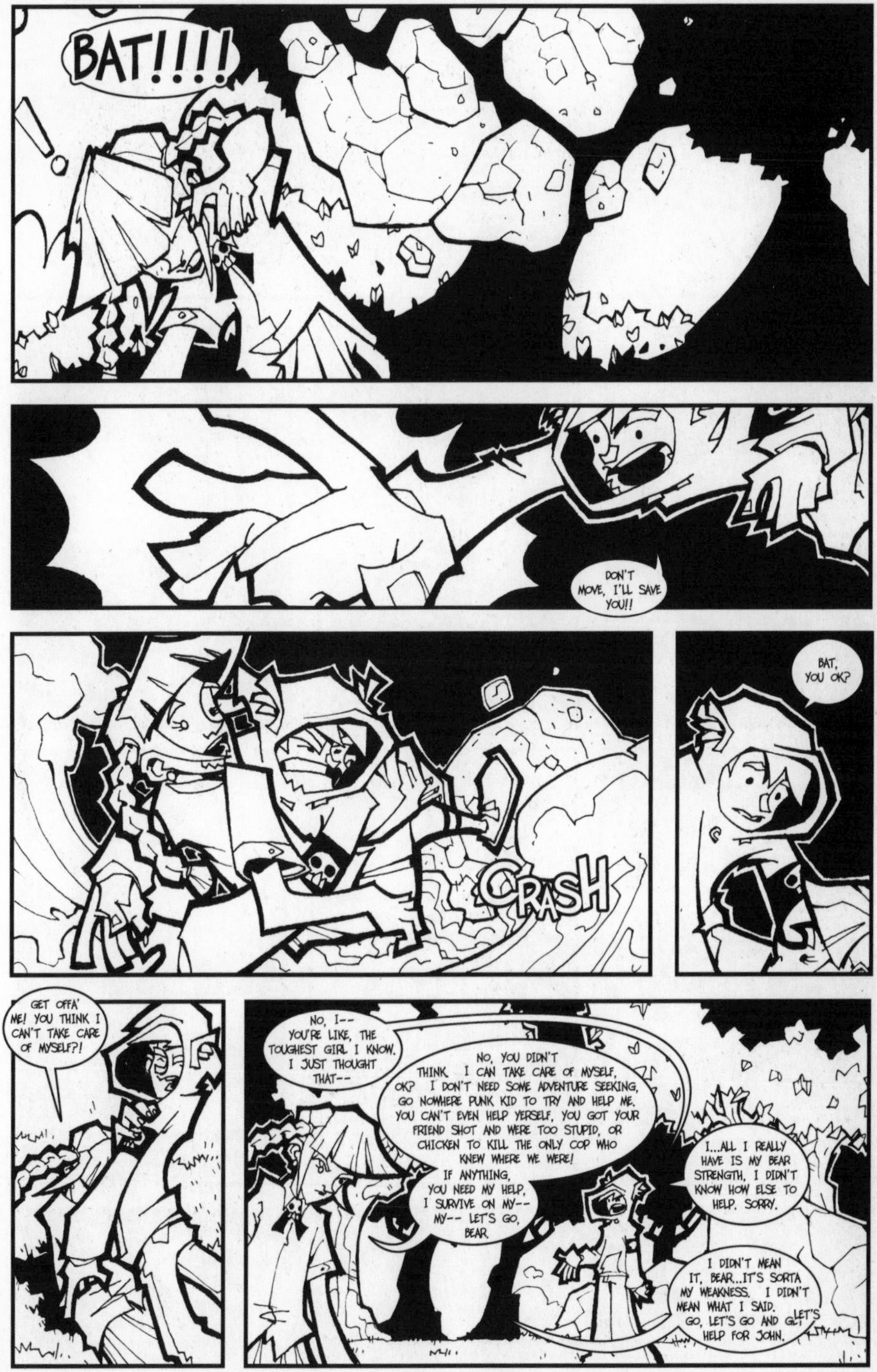
BAT!!!!
!
DON'T MOVE, I'LL SAVE YOU!!
CRASH
BAT, YOU OK?
GET OFFA' ME! YOU THINK I CAN'T TAKE CARE OF MYSELF?!
NO, I-- YOU'RE LIKE, THE TOUGHEST GIRL I KNOW. I JUST THOUGHT THAT--
NO, YOU DIDN'T THINK. I CAN TAKE CARE OF MYSELF, OK? I DON'T NEED SOME ADVENTURE SEEKING, GO NOWHERE PUNK KID TO TRY AND HELP ME. YOU CAN'T EVEN HELP YERSELF, YOU GOT YOUR FRIEND SHOT AND WERE TOO STUPID, OR CHICKEN TO KILL THE ONLY COP WHO KNEW WHERE WE WERE!
IF ANYTHING, YOU NEED MY HELP. I SURVIVE ON MY-- MY-- LET'S GO, BEAR.
I...ALL I REALLY HAVE IS MY BEAR STRENGTH, I DIDN'T KNOW HOW ELSE TO HELP. SORRY.
I DIDN'T MEAN IT, BEAR...IT'S SORTA MY WEAKNESS. I DIDN'T MEAN WHAT I SAID. GO, LET'S GO AND G LET'S HELP FOR JOHN.

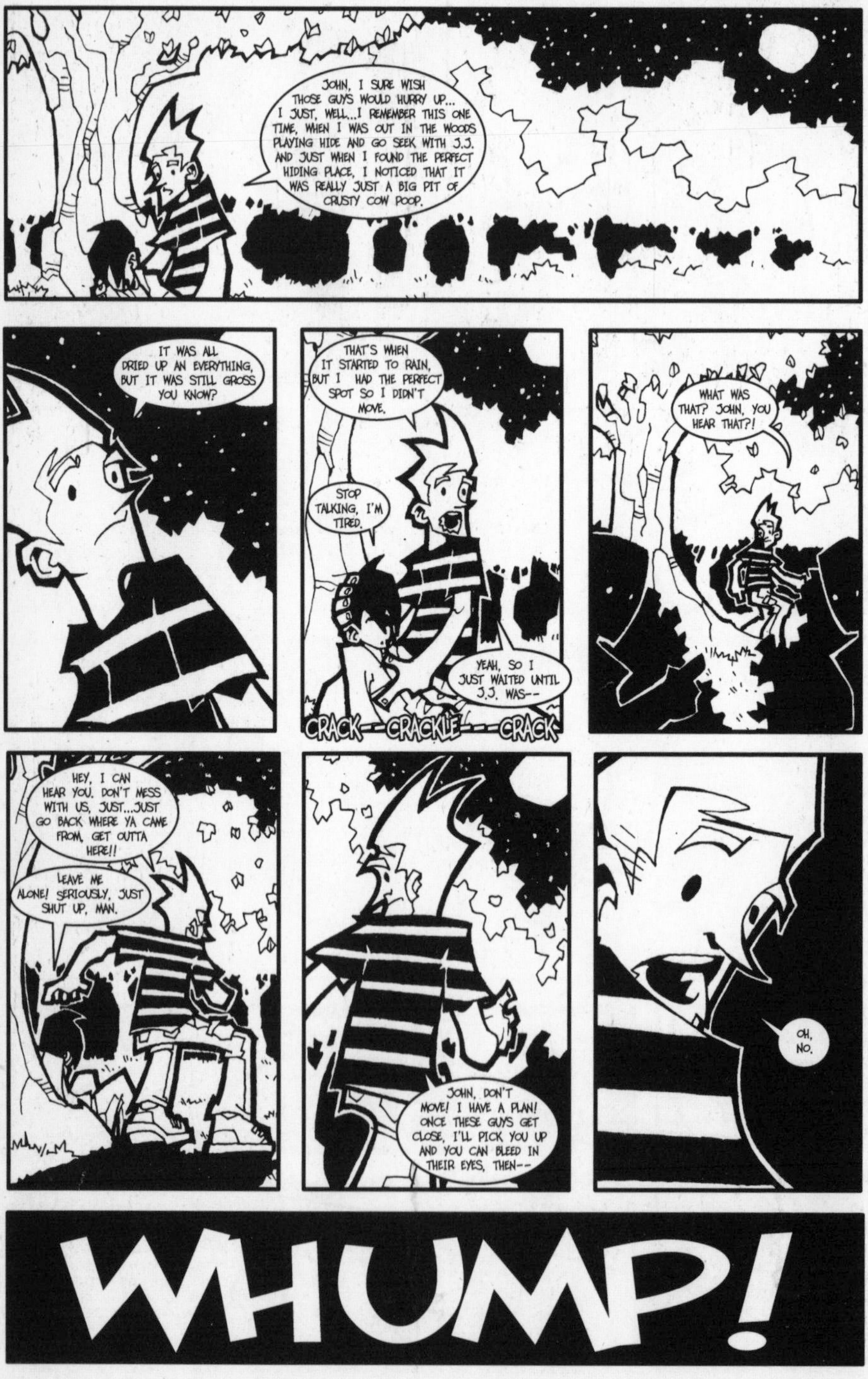

JOHN, I SURE WISH THOSE GUYS WOULD HURRY UP... I JUST, WELL...I REMEMBER THIS ONE TIME, WHEN I WAS OUT IN THE WOODS PLAYING HIDE AND GO SEEK WITH J.J. AND JUST WHEN I FOUND THE PERFECT HIDING PLACE, I NOTICED THAT IT WAS REALLY JUST A BIG PIT OF CRUSTY COW POOP.
IT WAS ALL DRIED UP AN EVERYTHING, BUT IT WAS STILL GROSS YOU KNOW?
THAT'S WHEN IT STARTED TO RAIN, BUT I HAD THE PERFECT SPOT SO I DIDN'T MOVE.
STOP TALKING, I'M TIRED.
YEAH, SO I JUST WAITED UNTIL J.J. WAS--
CRACK--CRACKLE--CRACK
WHAT WAS THAT? JOHN, YOU HEAR THAT?!
HEY, I CAN HEAR YOU. DON'T MESS WITH US, JUST...JUST GO BACK WHERE YA CAME FROM, GET OUTTA HERE!!
LEAVE ME ALONE! SERIOUSLY, JUST SHUT UP, MAN.
JOHN, DON'T MOVE! I HAVE A PLAN! ONCE THESE GUYS GET CLOSE, I'LL PICK YOU UP AND YOU CAN BLEED IN THEIR EYES, THEN--
OH, NO.
WHUMP!

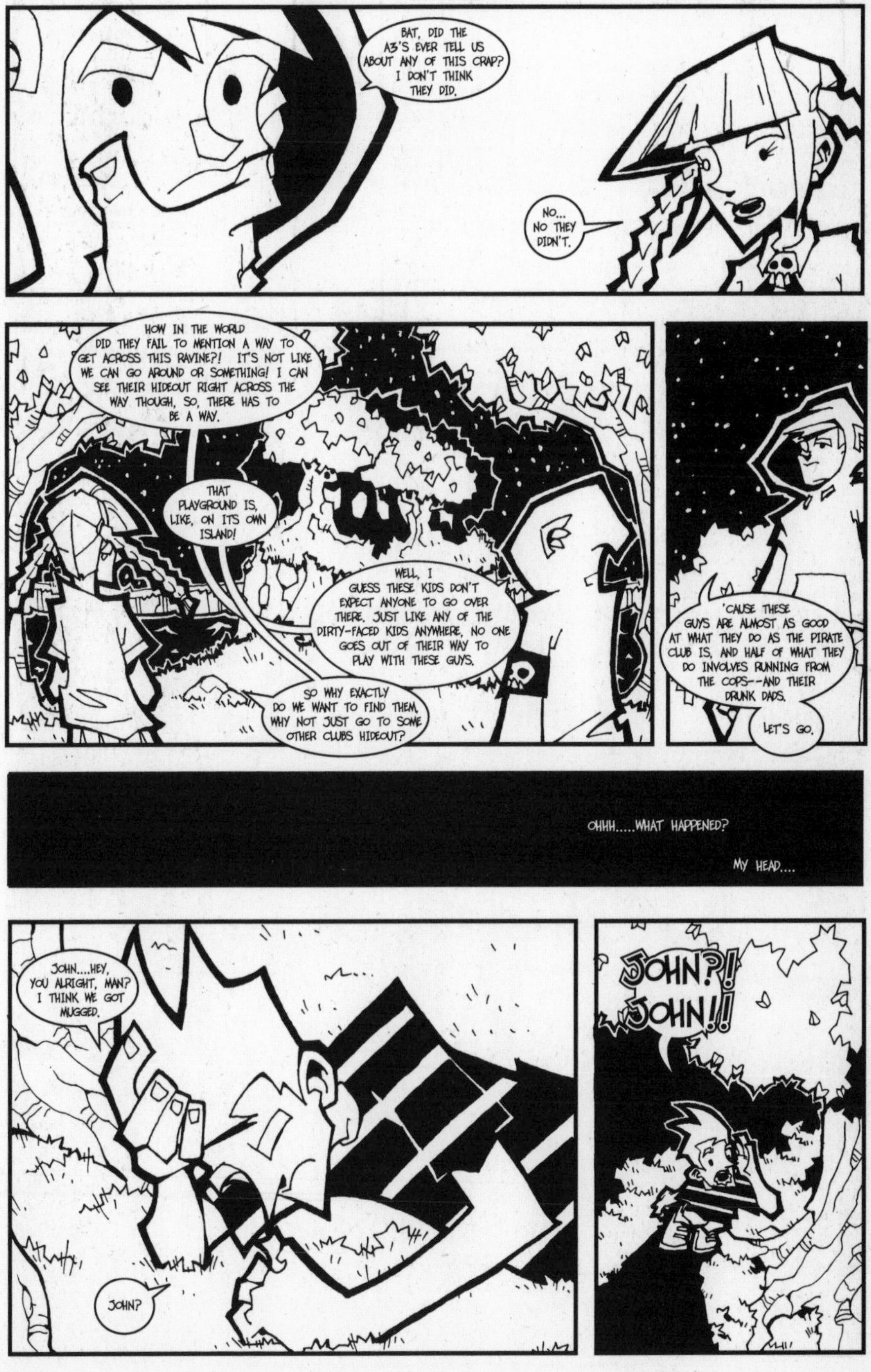
BAT, DID THE A3'S EVER TELL US ABOUT ANY OF THIS CRAP? I DON'T THINK THEY DID.
NO... NO THEY DIDN'T.
HOW IN THE WORLD DID THEY FAIL TO MENTION A WAY TO GET ACROSS THIS RAVINE?! IT'S NOT LIKE WE CAN GO AROUND OR SOMETHING! I CAN SEE THEIR HIDEOUT RIGHT ACROSS THE WAY THOUGH, SO, THERE HAS TO BE A WAY.
THAT PLAYGROUND IS, LIKE, ON ITS OWN ISLAND!
WELL, I GUESS THESE KIDS DON'T EXPECT ANYONE TO GO OVER THERE. JUST LIKE ANY OF THE DIRTY-FACED KIDS ANYWHERE, NO ONE GOES OUT OF THEIR WAY TO PLAY WITH THESE GUYS.
SO WHY EXACTLY DO WE WANT TO FIND THEM, WHY NOT JUST GO TO SOME OTHER CLUBS HIDEOUT?
'CAUSE THESE GUYS ARE ALMOST AS GOOD AT WHAT THEY DO AS THE PIRATE CLUB IS, AND HALF OF WHAT THEY DO INVOLVES RUNNING FROM THE COPS--AND THEIR DRUNK DADS.
LET'S GO.
OHHH.....WHAT HAPPENED?
MY HEAD....
JOHN....HEY, YOU ALRIGHT, MAN? I THINK WE GOT MUGGED.
JOHN?
JOHN?! JOHN!!

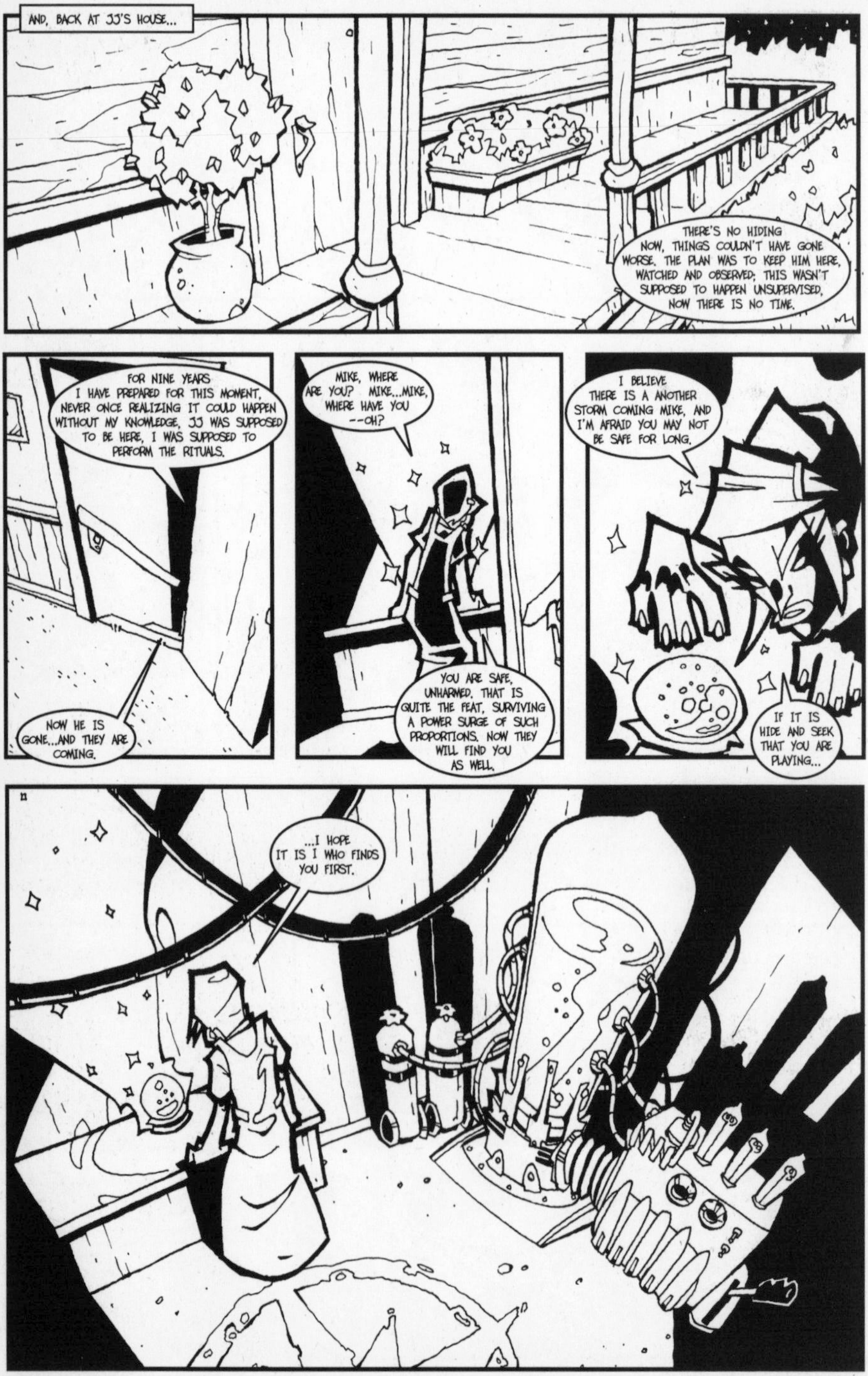
AND, BACK AT JJ'S HOUSE...
THERE'S NO HIDING NOW, THINGS COULDN'T HAVE GONE WORSE. THE PLAN WAS TO KEEP HIM HERE, WATCHED AND OBSERVED; THIS WASN'T SUPPOSED TO HAPPEN UNSUPERVISED, NOW THERE IS NO TIME.
FOR NINE YEARS I HAVE PREPARED FOR THIS MOMENT, NEVER ONCE REALIZING IT COULD HAPPEN WITHOUT MY KNOWLEDGE. JJ WAS SUPPOSED TO BE HERE, I WAS SUPPOSED TO PERFORM THE RITUALS.
NOW HE IS GONE...AND THEY ARE COMING.
MIKE, WHERE ARE YOU? MIKE...MIKE, WHERE HAVE YOU --OH?
YOU ARE SAFE, UNHARMED. THAT IS QUITE THE FEAT, SURVIVING A POWER SURGE OF SUCH PROPORTIONS. NOW THEY WILL FIND YOU AS WELL.
I BELIEVE THERE IS A ANOTHER STORM COMING MIKE, AND I'M AFRAID YOU MAY NOT BE SAFE FOR LONG.
IF IT IS HIDE AND SEEK THAT YOU ARE PLAYING...
...I HOPE IT IS I WHO FINDS YOU FIRST.

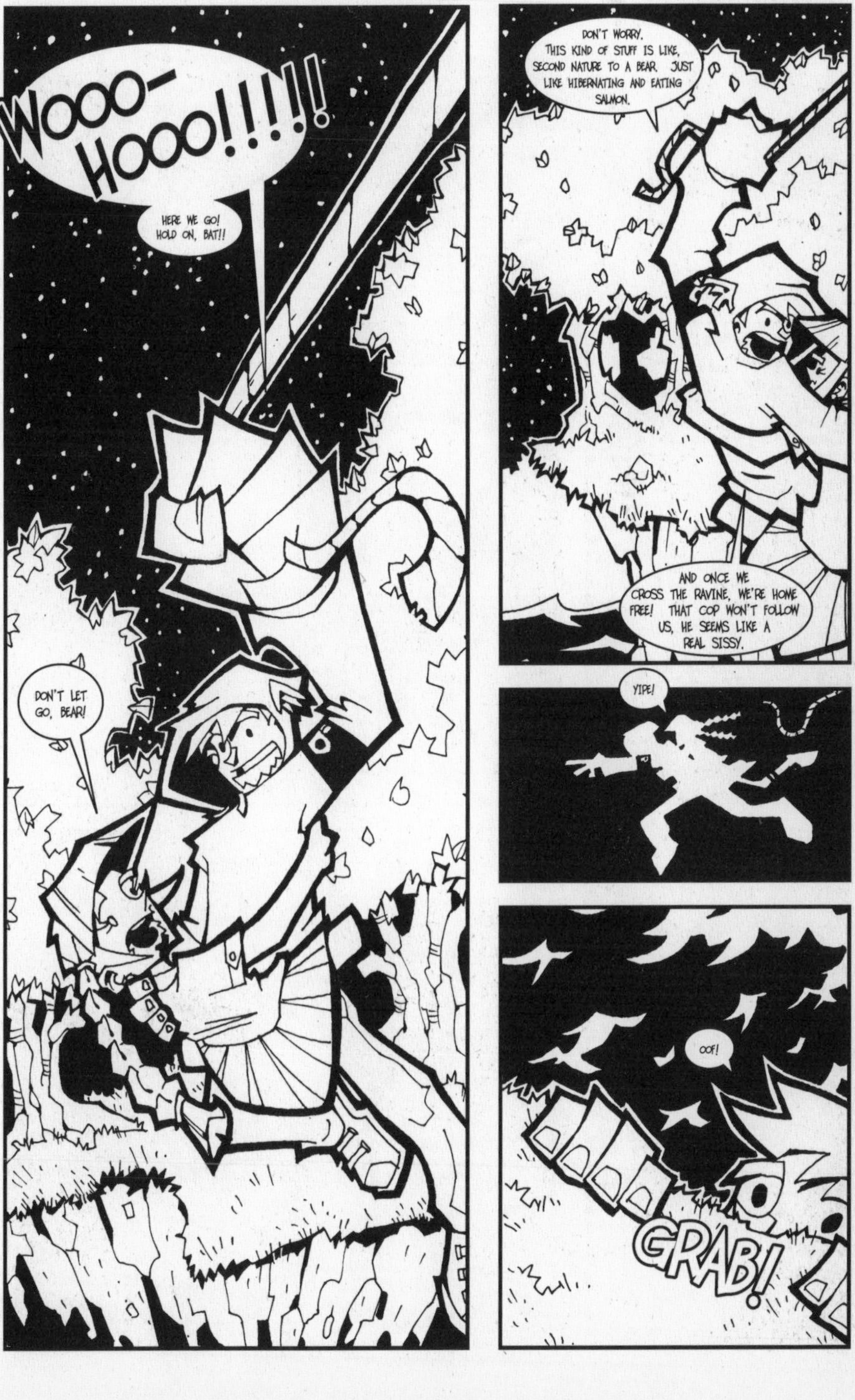
WOOO-HOOO!!!!!
HERE WE GO! HOLD ON, BAT!!
DON'T LET GO, BEAR!
DON'T WORRY. THIS KIND OF STUFF IS LIKE, SECOND NATURE TO A BEAR. JUST LIKE HIBERNATING AND EATING SALMON.
AND ONCE WE CROSS THE RAVINE, WE'RE HOME FREE! THAT COP WON'T FOLLOW US, HE SEEMS LIKE A REAL SISSY.
YIPE!
OOF!
GRAB!

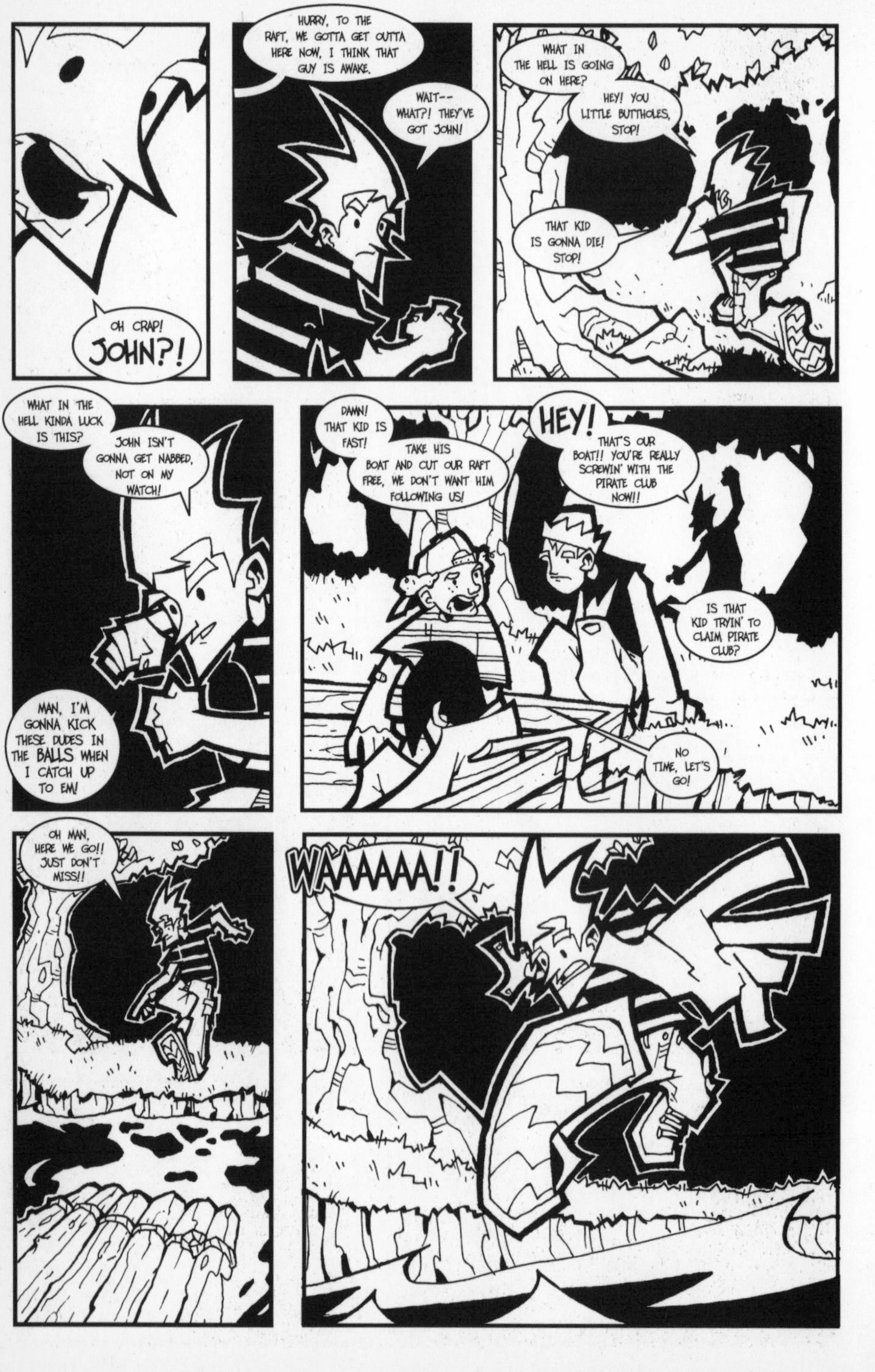
OH CRAP! JOHN?!
HURRY, TO THE RAFT, WE GOTTA GET OUTTA HERE NOW, I THINK THAT GUY IS AWAKE.
WAIT-- WHAT?! THEY'VE GOT JOHN!
WHAT IN THE HELL IS GOING ON HERE?
HEY! YOU LITTLE BUTTHOLES, STOP!
THAT KID IS GONNA DIE! STOP!
WHAT IN THE HELL KINDA LUCK IS THIS?
JOHN ISN'T GONNA GET NABBED, NOT ON MY WATCH!
MAN, I'M GONNA KICK THESE DUDES IN THE BALLS WHEN I CATCH UP TO EM!
DAMN! THAT KID IS FAST!
TAKE HIS BOAT AND CUT OUR RAFT FREE, WE DON'T WANT HIM FOLLOWING US!
HEY!
THAT'S OUR BOAT!! YOU'RE REALLY SCREWIN' WITH THE PIRATE CLUB NOW!!
IS THAT KID TRYIN' TO CLAIM PIRATE CLUB?
NO TIME, LET'S GO!
OH MAN, HERE WE GO!! JUST DON'T MISS!!
WAAAAAA!!

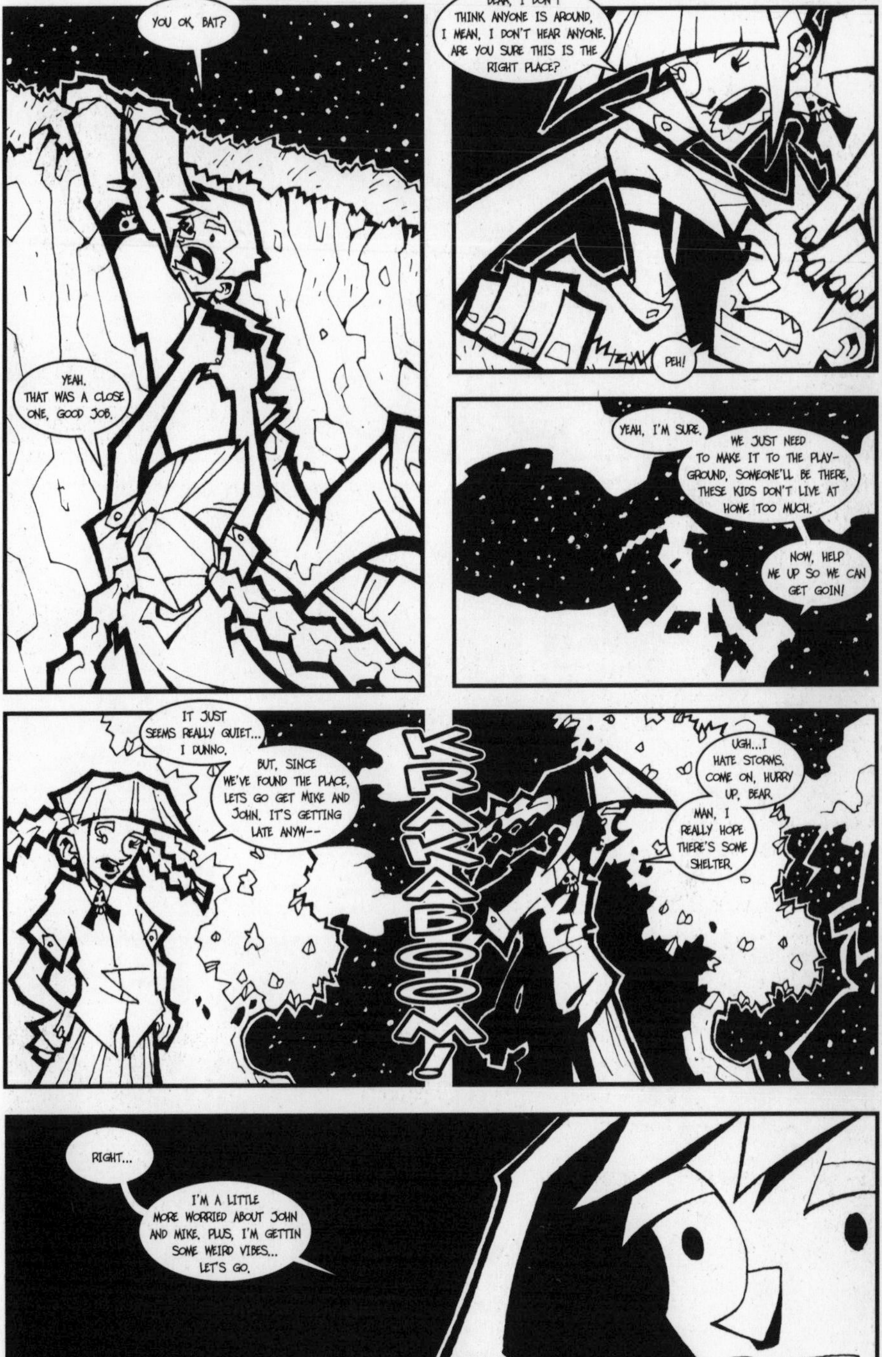

YOU OK, BAT?
YEAH. THAT WAS A CLOSE ONE, GOOD JOB.
BEAR, I DON'T THINK ANYONE IS AROUND, I MEAN, I DON'T HEAR ANYONE. ARE YOU SURE THIS IS THE RIGHT PLACE?
PEH!
YEAH, I'M SURE.
WE JUST NEED TO MAKE IT TO THE PLAY-GROUND, SOMEONE'LL BE THERE, THESE KIDS DON'T LIVE AT HOME TOO MUCH.
NOW, HELP ME UP SO WE CAN GET GOIN!
IT JUST SEEMS REALLY QUIET... I DUNNO.
BUT, SINCE WE'VE FOUND THE PLACE, LETS GO GET MIKE AND JOHN. IT'S GETTING LATE ANYW--
KRAKABOOM!
UGH...I HATE STORMS. COME ON, HURRY UP, BEAR.
MAN, I REALLY HOPE THERE'S SOME SHELTER.
RIGHT...
I'M A LITTLE MORE WORRIED ABOUT JOHN AND MIKE. PLUS, I'M GETTIN SOME WEIRD VIBES... LET'S GO.

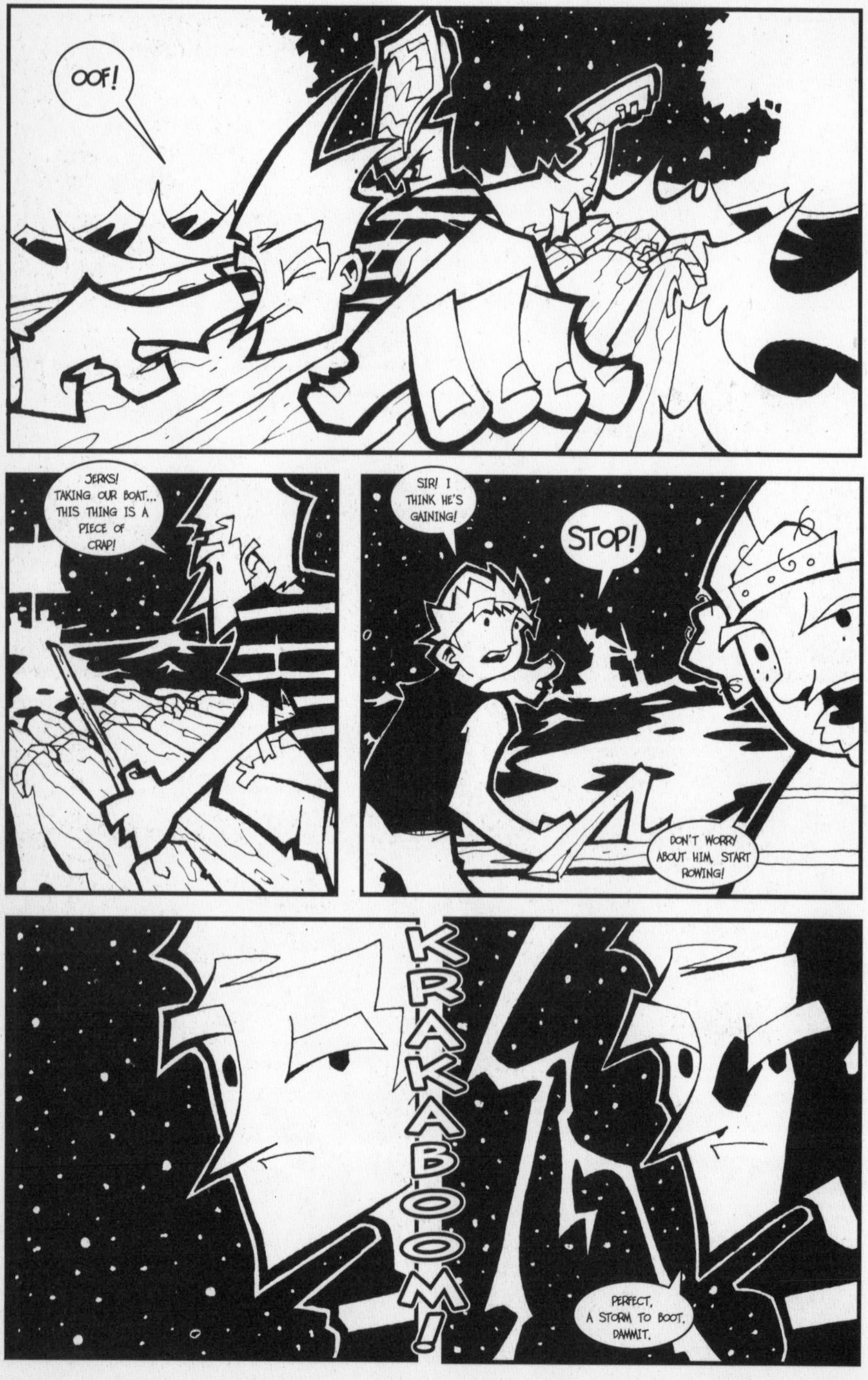
OOF!
JERKS! TAKING OUR BOAT... THIS THING IS A PIECE OF CRAP!
SIR! I THINK HE'S GAINING!
STOP!
DON'T WORRY ABOUT HIM, START ROWING!
KRAKABOOM!
PERFECT, A STORM TO BOOT. DAMMIT.

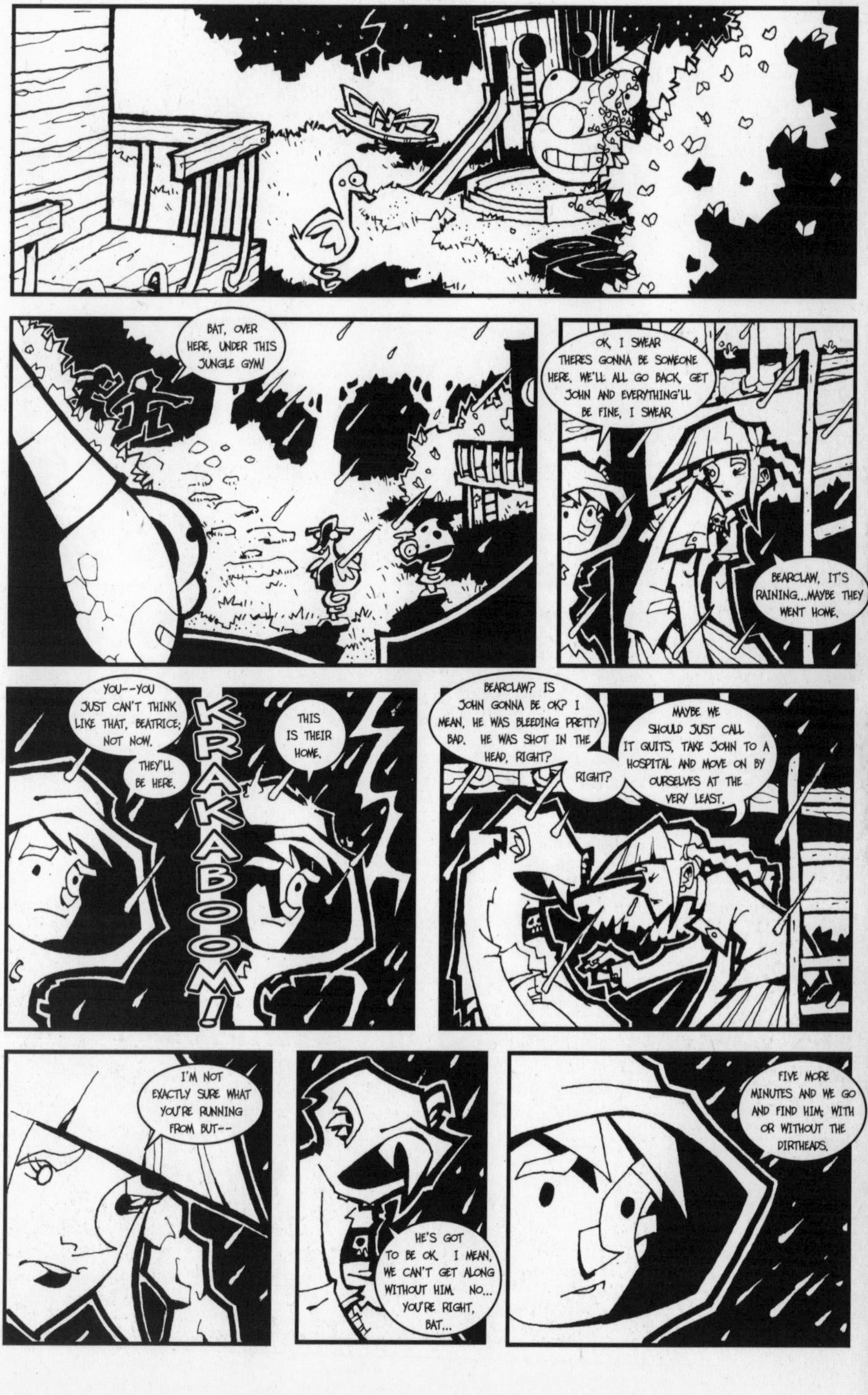
BAT, OVER HERE, UNDER THIS JUNGLE GYM!
OK, I SWEAR THERES GONNA BE SOMEONE HERE. WE'LL ALL GO BACK, GET JOHN AND EVERYTHING'LL BE FINE, I SWEAR.
BEARCLAW, IT'S RAINING...MAYBE THEY WENT HOME.
YOU--YOU JUST CAN'T THINK LIKE THAT, BEATRICE; NOT NOW.
THEY'LL BE HERE.
KRAKABOOM!
THIS IS THEIR HOME.
BEARCLAW? IS JOHN GONNA BE OK? I MEAN, HE WAS BLEEDING PRETTY BAD. HE WAS SHOT IN THE HEAD, RIGHT?
RIGHT?
MAYBE WE SHOULD JUST CALL IT QUITS, TAKE JOHN TO A HOSPITAL AND MOVE ON BY OURSELVES AT THE VERY LEAST.
I'M NOT EXACTLY SURE WHAT YOU'RE RUNNING FROM BUT--
HE'S GOT TO BE OK. I MEAN, WE CAN'T GET ALONG WITHOUT HIM. NO... YOU'RE RIGHT, BAT...
FIVE MORE MINUTES AND WE GO AND FIND HIM; WITH OR WITHOUT THE DIRTHEADS.

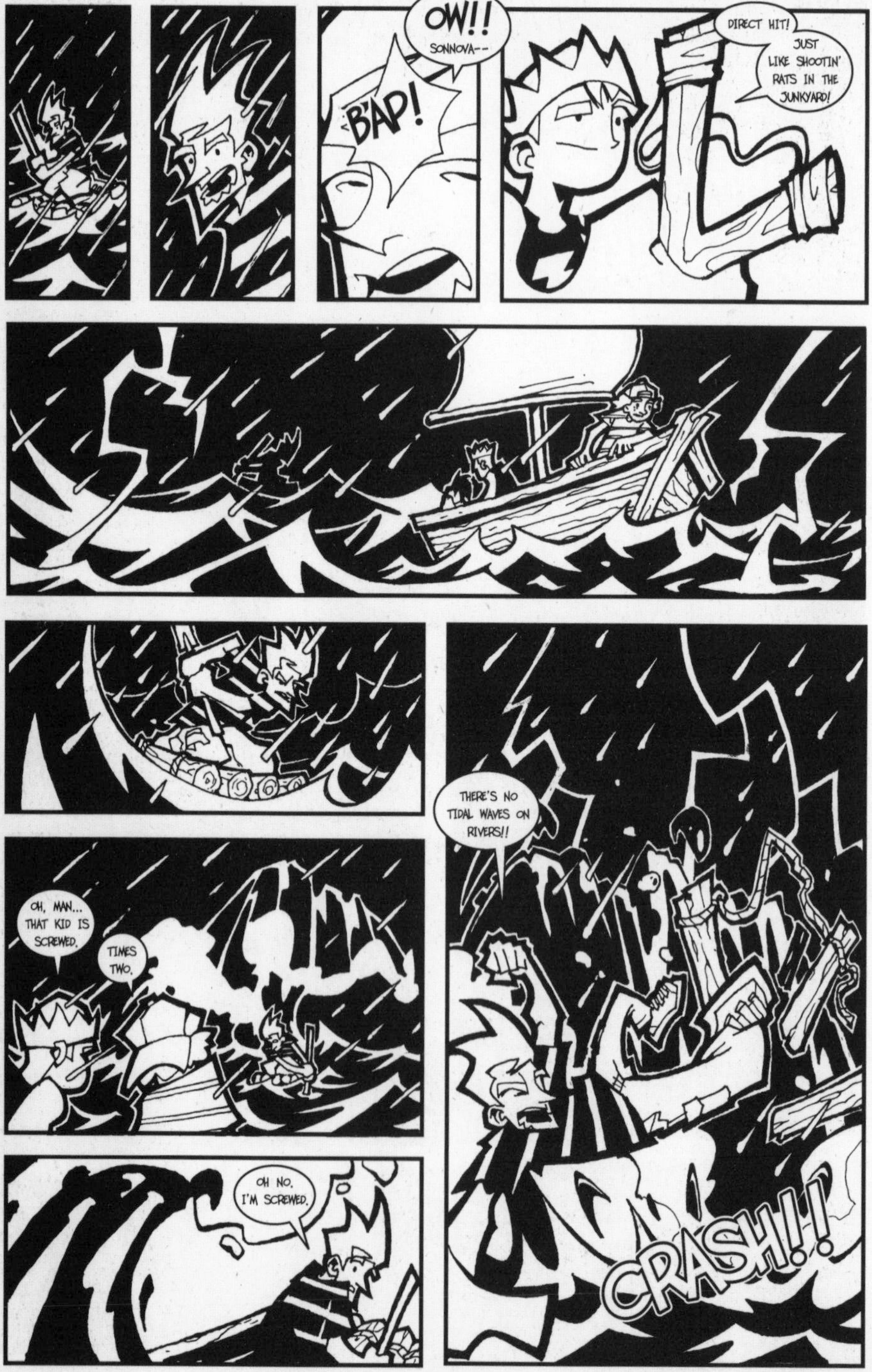
OW!!
SONNOVA--
BAP!
DIRECT HIT!
JUST LIKE SHOOTIN' RATS IN THE JUNKYARD!
THERE'S NO TIDAL WAVES ON RIVERS!!
OH, MAN... THAT KID IS SCREWED.
TIMES TWO.
OH NO. I'M SCREWED.
CRASH!!

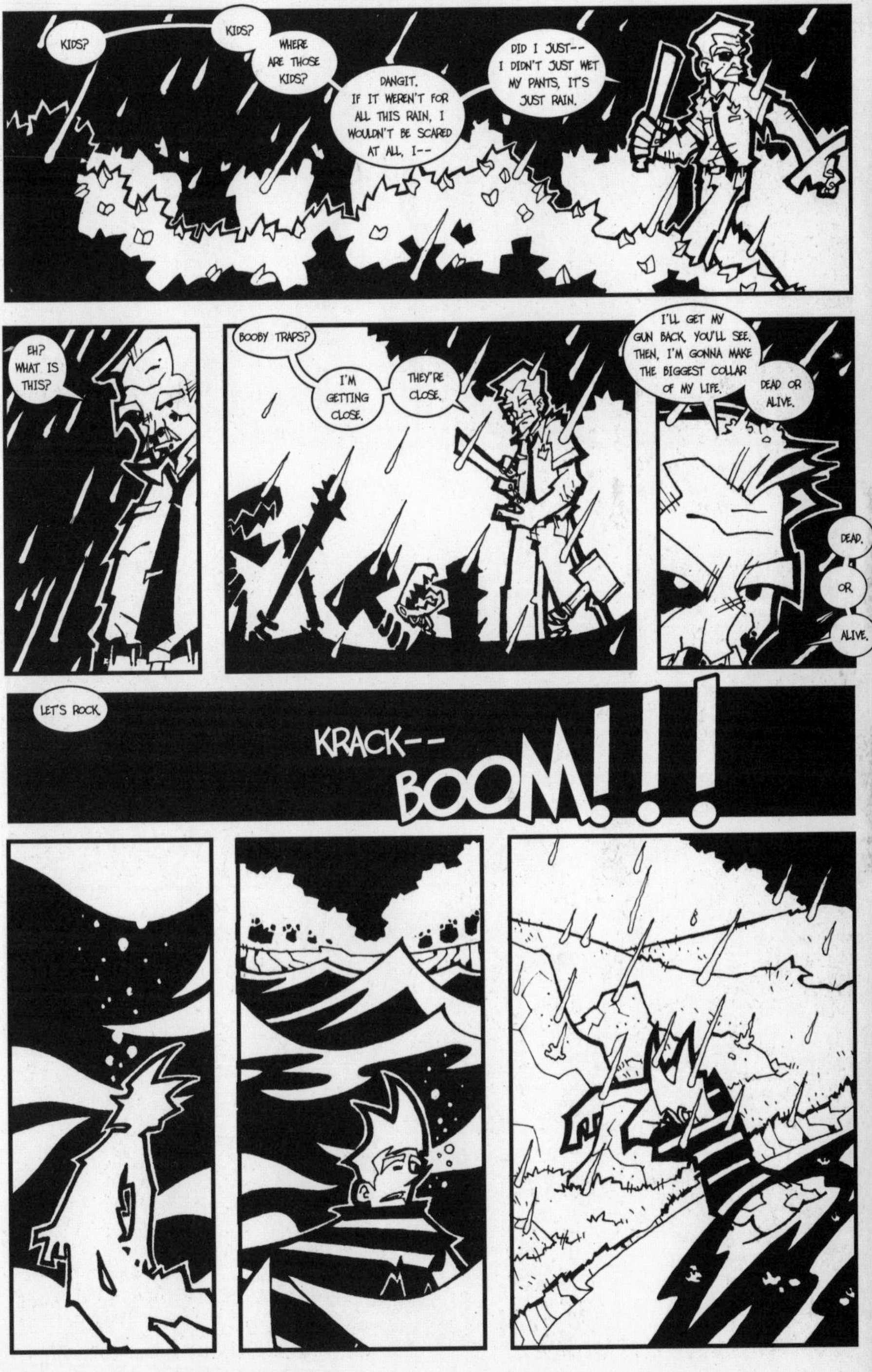
KIDS?
KIDS?
WHERE ARE THOSE KIDS?
DANGIT. IF IT WEREN'T FOR ALL THIS RAIN, I WOULDN'T BE SCARED AT ALL, I--
DID I JUST-- I DIDN'T JUST WET MY PANTS, IT'S JUST RAIN.
EH? WHAT IS THIS?
BOOBY TRAPS?
I'M GETTING CLOSE.
THEY'RE CLOSE.
I'LL GET MY GUN BACK, YOU'LL SEE. THEN, I'M GONNA MAKE THE BIGGEST COLLAR OF MY LIFE.
DEAD OR ALIVE.
DEAD.
OR
ALIVE.
LET'S ROCK.
KRACK--
BOOM!!!

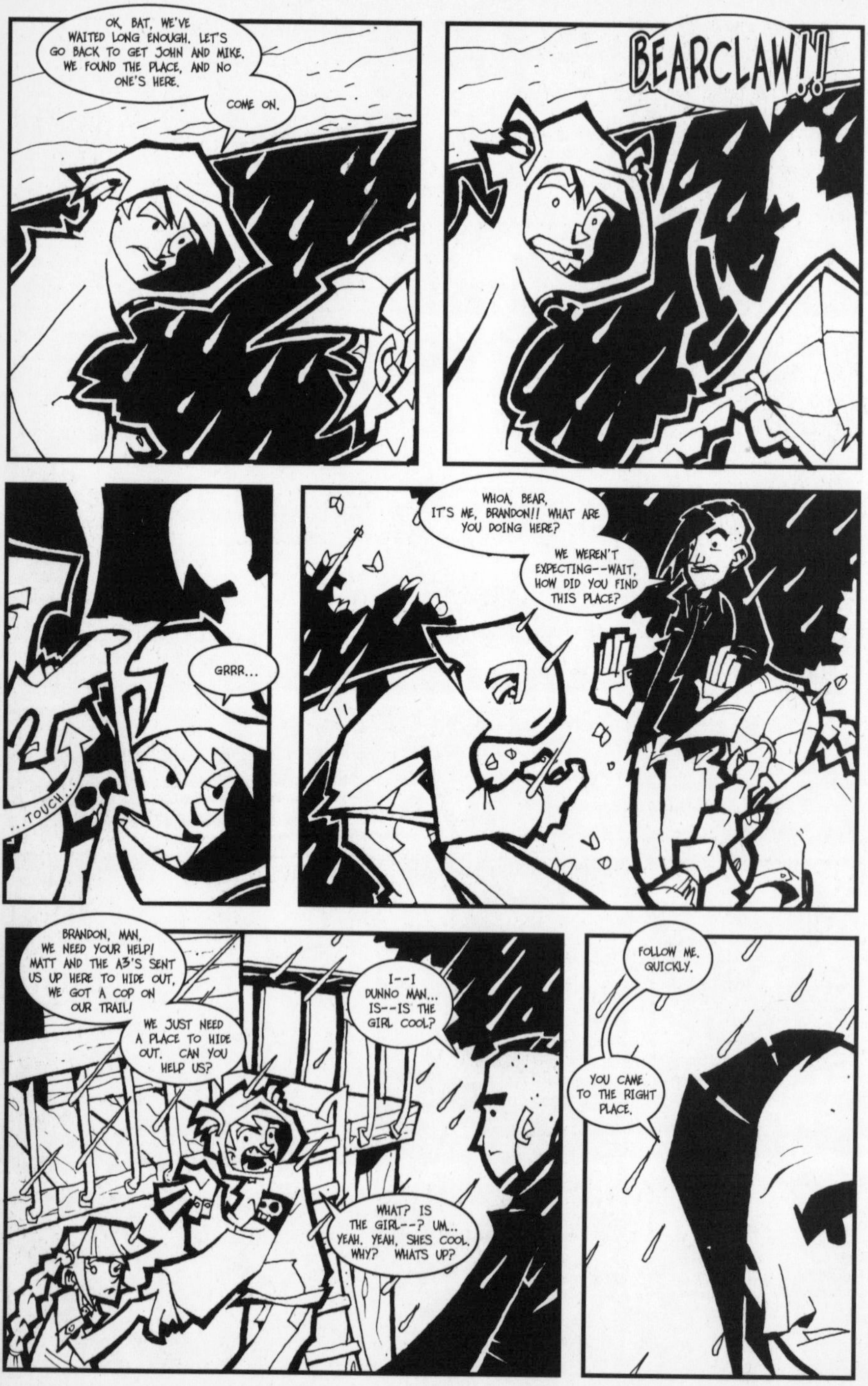

OK, BAT, WE'VE WAITED LONG ENOUGH. LET'S GO BACK TO GET JOHN AND MIKE. WE FOUND THE PLACE, AND NO ONE'S HERE.
COME ON.
BEARCLAW!!
GRRR...
...TOUCH...
WHOA, BEAR, IT'S ME, BRANDON!! WHAT ARE YOU DOING HERE?
WE WEREN'T EXPECTING--WAIT, HOW DID YOU FIND THIS PLACE?
BRANDON, MAN, WE NEED YOUR HELP! MATT AND THE A3'S SENT US UP HERE TO HIDE OUT, WE GOT A COP ON OUR TRAIL!
WE JUST NEED A PLACE TO HIDE OUT. CAN YOU HELP US?
I--I DUNNO MAN... IS--IS THE GIRL COOL?
WHAT? IS THE GIRL--? UM... YEAH. YEAH, SHES COOL. WHY? WHATS UP?
FOLLOW ME. QUICKLY.
YOU CAME TO THE RIGHT PLACE.

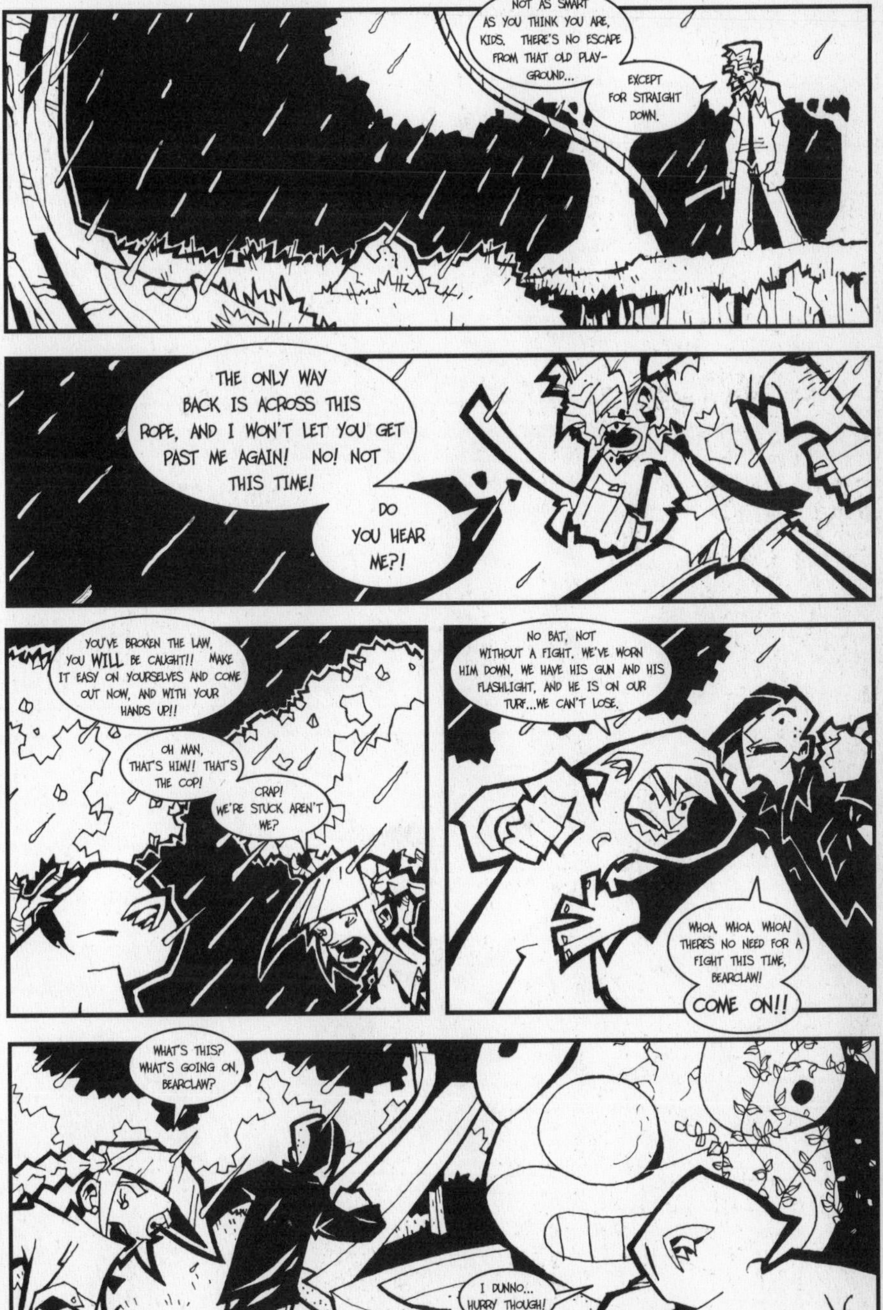
NOT AS SMART AS YOU THINK YOU ARE, KIDS. THERE'S NO ESCAPE FROM THAT OLD PLAY-GROUND...
EXCEPT FOR STRAIGHT DOWN.
THE ONLY WAY BACK IS ACROSS THIS ROPE, AND I WON'T LET YOU GET PAST ME AGAIN! NO! NOT THIS TIME!
DO YOU HEAR ME?!
YOU'VE BROKEN THE LAW, YOU WILL BE CAUGHT!! MAKE IT EASY ON YOURSELVES AND COME OUT NOW, AND WITH YOUR HANDS UP!!
OH MAN, THAT'S HIM!! THAT'S THE COP!
CRAP! WE'RE STUCK AREN'T WE?
NO BAT, NOT WITHOUT A FIGHT. WE'VE WORN HIM DOWN, WE HAVE HIS GUN AND HIS FLASHLIGHT, AND HE IS ON OUR TURF...WE CAN'T LOSE.
WHOA, WHOA, WHOA! THERES NO NEED FOR A FIGHT THIS TIME, BEARCLAW!
COME ON!!
WHAT'S THIS? WHAT'S GOING ON, BEARCLAW?
I DUNNO... HURRY THOUGH!

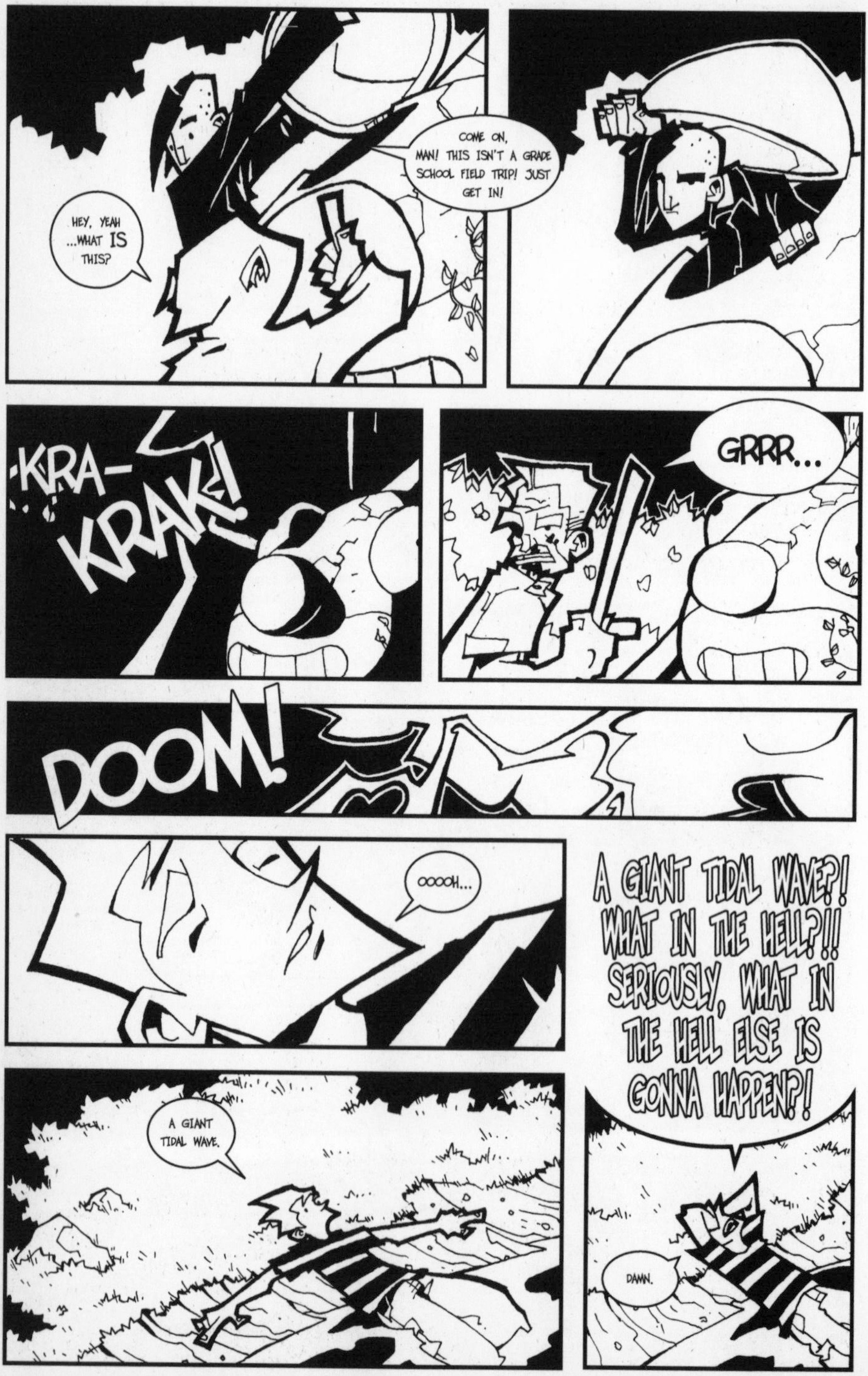
HEY, YEAH ...WHAT IS THIS?
COME ON, MAN! THIS ISN'T A GRADE SCHOOL FIELD TRIP! JUST GET IN!
-KRA-KRAK!
GRRR...
DOOM!
OOOOH...
A GIANT TIDAL WAVE?! WHAT IN THE HELL?!! SERIOUSLY, WHAT IN THE HELL ELSE IS GONNA HAPPEN?!
A GIANT TIDAL WAVE.
DAMN.

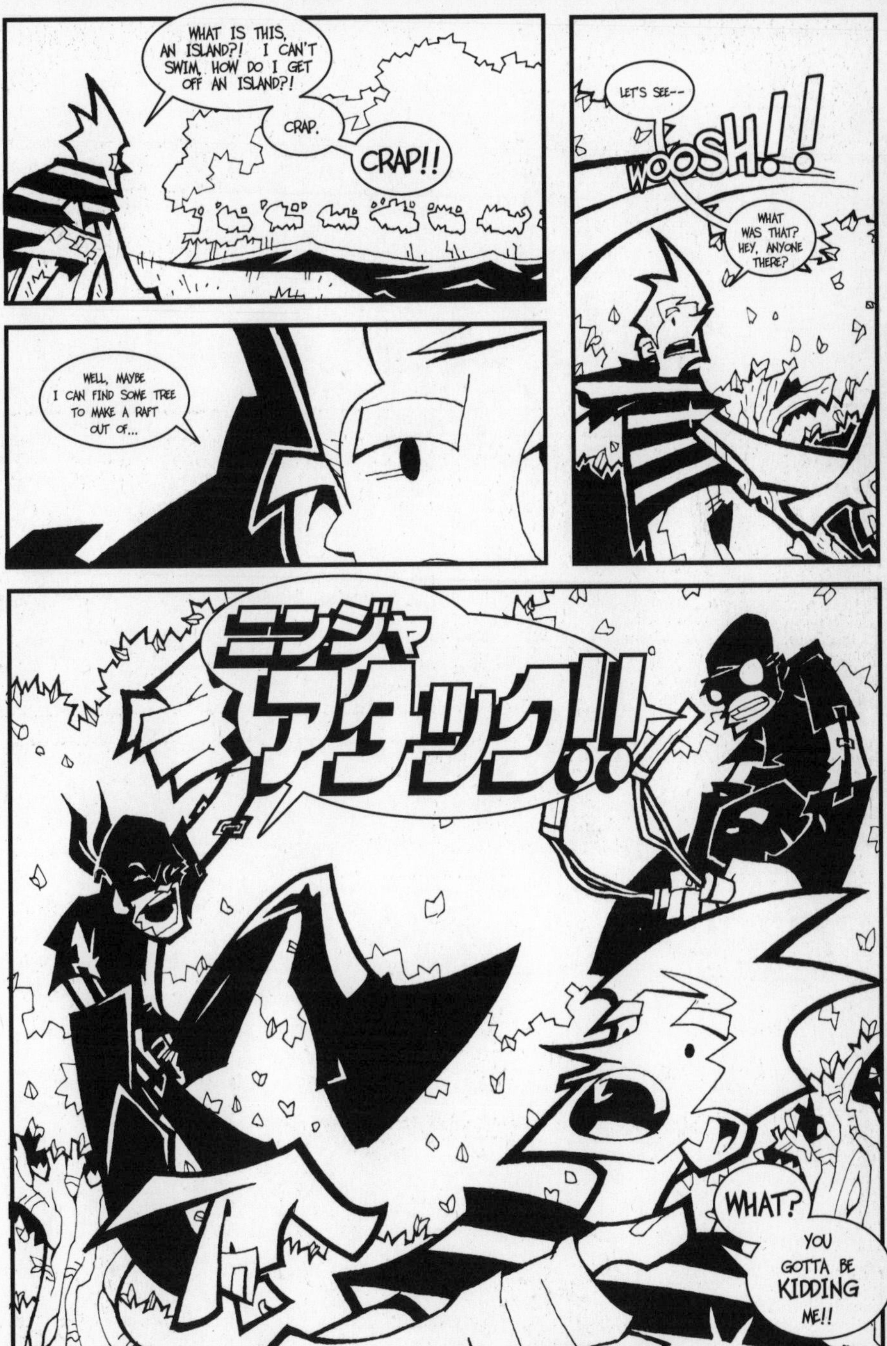
WHAT IS THIS, AN ISLAND?! I CAN'T SWIM, HOW DO I GET OFF AN ISLAND?!
CRAP.
CRAP!!
LET'S SEE--
WOOSH!!
WHAT WAS THAT? HEY, ANYONE THERE?
WELL, MAYBE I CAN FIND SOME TREE TO MAKE A RAFT OUT OF...
ニンジャアタック!!
WHAT?
YOU GOTTA BE KIDDING ME!!

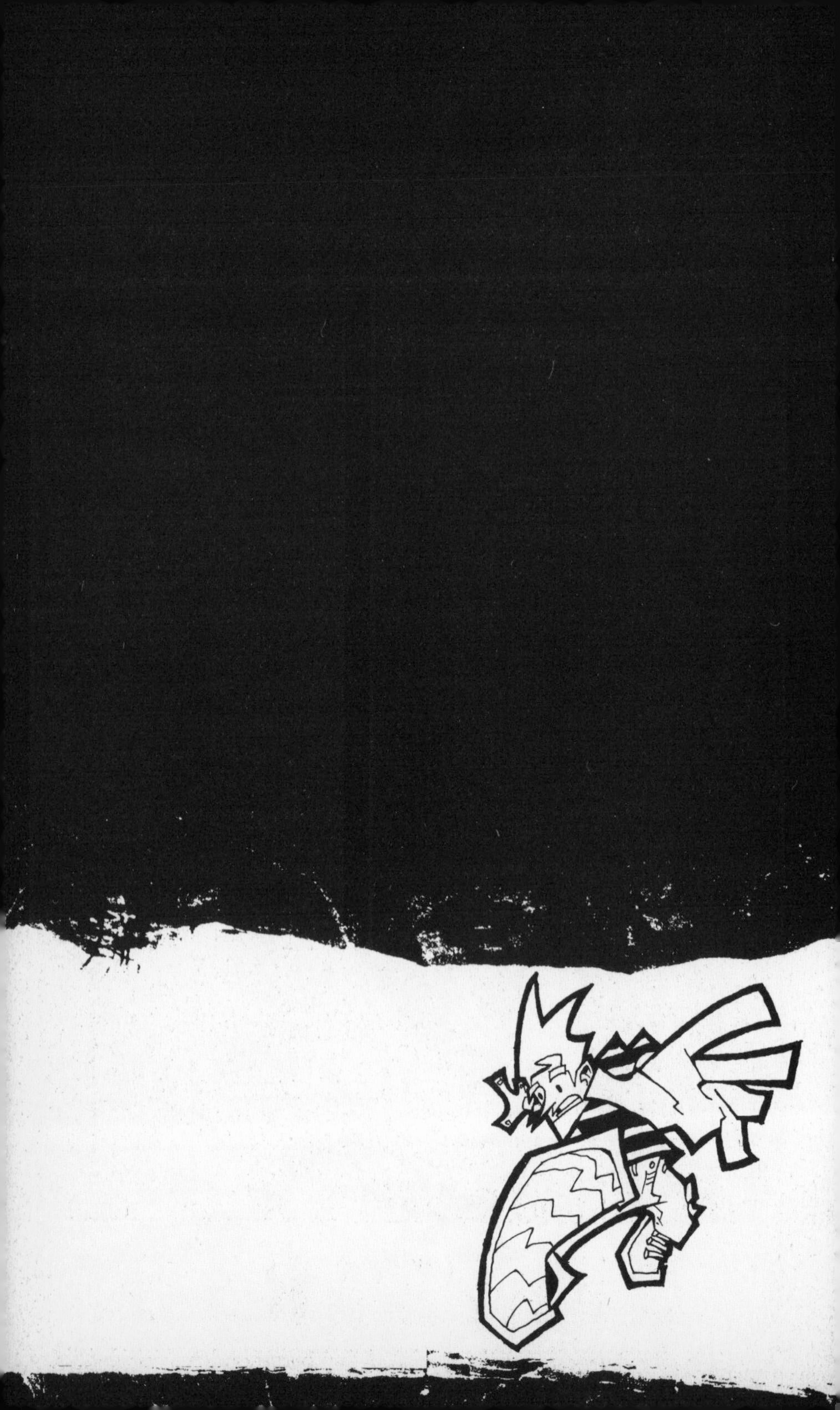

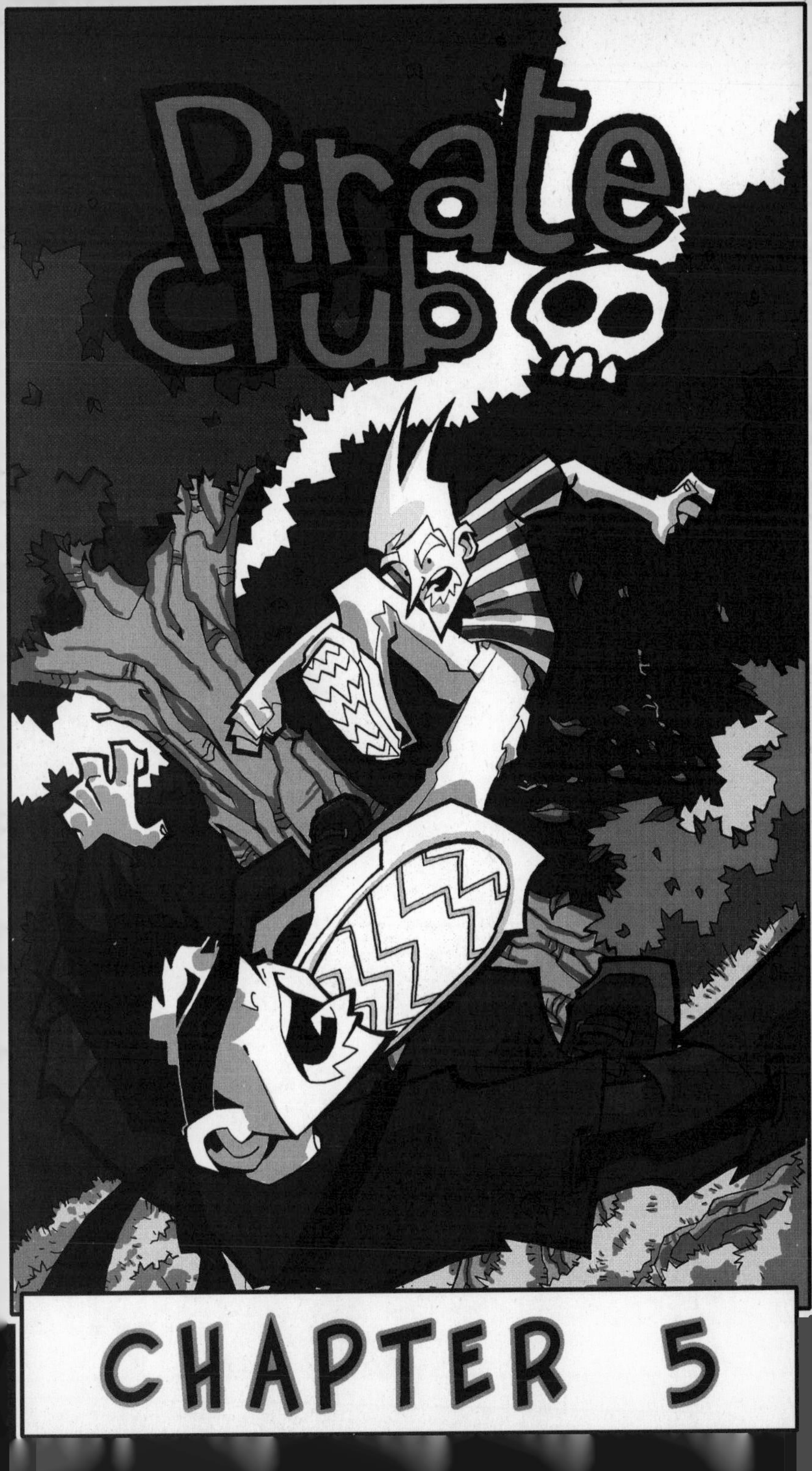
Pirate club
CHAPTER 5

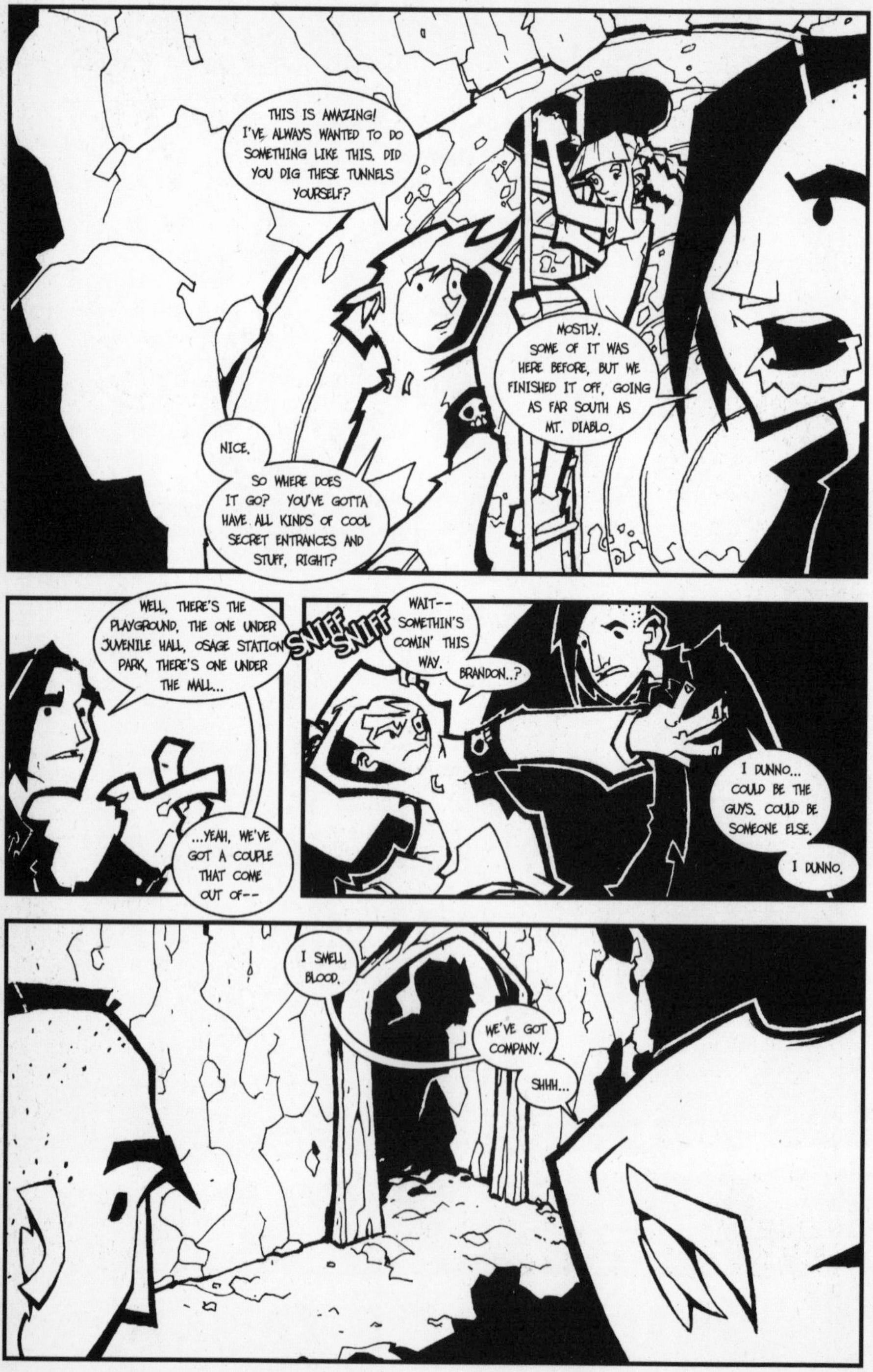
THIS IS AMAZING! I'VE ALWAYS WANTED TO DO SOMETHING LIKE THIS. DID YOU DIG THESE TUNNELS YOURSELF?
MOSTLY. SOME OF IT WAS HERE BEFORE, BUT WE FINISHED IT OFF, GOING AS FAR SOUTH AS MT. DIABLO.
NICE.
SO WHERE DOES IT GO? YOU'VE GOTTA HAVE ALL KINDS OF COOL SECRET ENTRANCES AND STUFF, RIGHT?
WELL, THERE'S THE PLAYGROUND, THE ONE UNDER JUVENILE HALL, OSAGE STATION PARK, THERE'S ONE UNDER THE MALL...
...YEAH, WE'VE GOT A COUPLE THAT COME OUT OF--
SNIFF SNIFF
WAIT-- SOMETHIN'S COMIN' THIS WAY.
BRANDON..?
I DUNNO... COULD BE THE GUYS. COULD BE SOMEONE ELSE.
I DUNNO.
I SMELL BLOOD.
WE'VE GOT COMPANY.
SHHH...

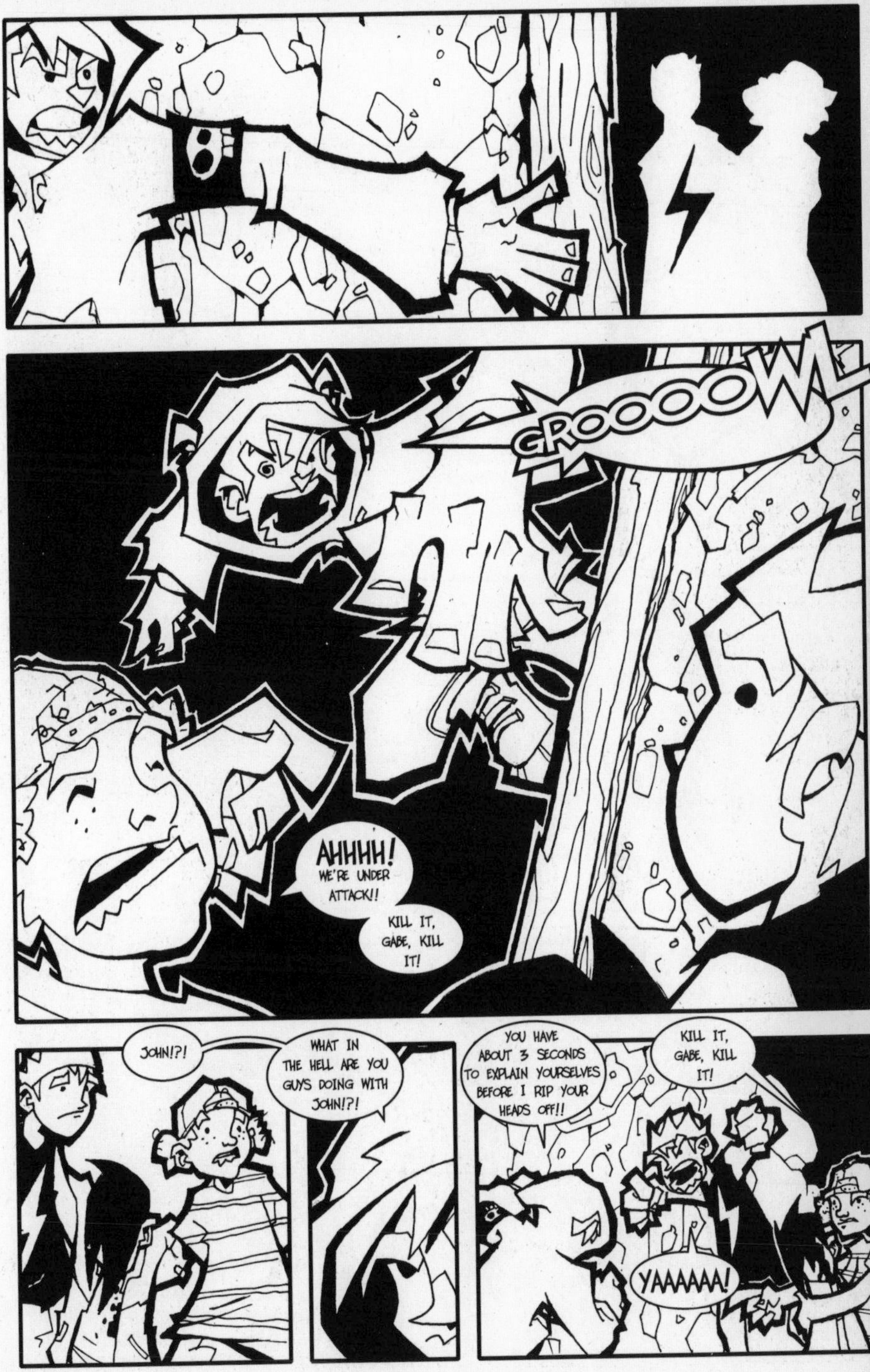

GROOOOOWL
AHHHH! WE'RE UNDER ATTACK!!
KILL IT, GABE, KILL IT!
JOHN!?!
WHAT IN THE HELL ARE YOU GUYS DOING WITH JOHN!?!
YOU HAVE ABOUT 3 SECONDS TO EXPLAIN YOURSELVES BEFORE I RIP YOUR HEADS OFF!!
KILL IT, GABE, KILL IT!
YAAAAAA!

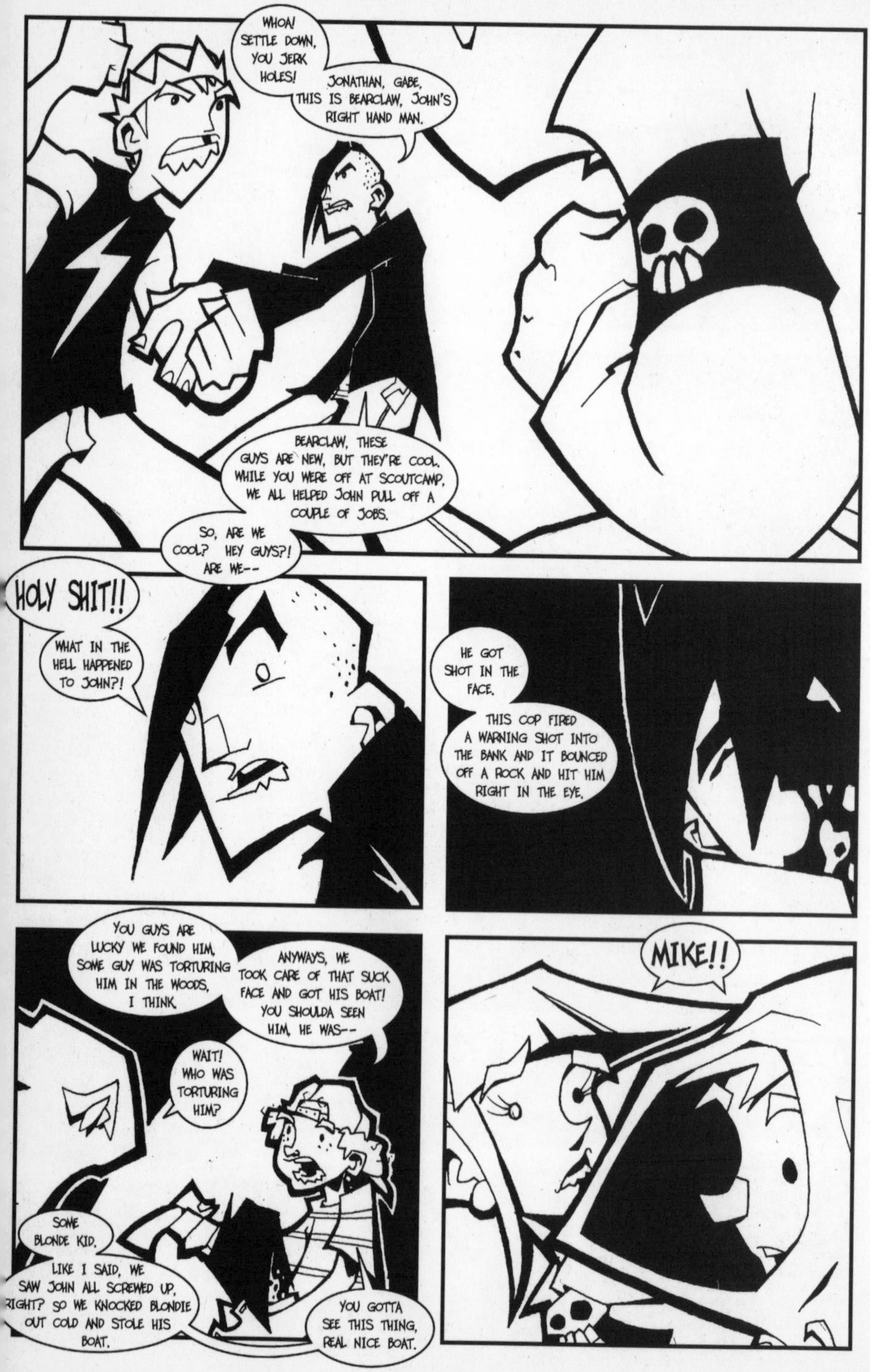
WHOA! SETTLE DOWN, YOU JERK HOLES!
JONATHAN, GABE, THIS IS BEARCLAW, JOHN'S RIGHT HAND MAN.
BEARCLAW, THESE GUYS ARE NEW, BUT THEY'RE COOL. WHILE YOU WERE OFF AT SCOUTCAMP, WE ALL HELPED JOHN PULL OFF A COUPLE OF JOBS.
SO, ARE WE COOL? HEY GUYS?! ARE WE--
HOLY SHIT!!
WHAT IN THE HELL HAPPENED TO JOHN?!
HE GOT SHOT IN THE FACE.
THIS COP FIRED A WARNING SHOT INTO THE BANK AND IT BOUNCED OFF A ROCK AND HIT HIM RIGHT IN THE EYE.
YOU GUYS ARE LUCKY WE FOUND HIM. SOME GUY WAS TORTURING HIM IN THE WOODS, I THINK.
ANYWAYS, WE TOOK CARE OF THAT SUCK FACE AND GOT HIS BOAT! YOU SHOULDA SEEN HIM, HE WAS--
WAIT! WHO WAS TORTURING HIM?
SOME BLONDE KID.
LIKE I SAID, WE SAW JOHN ALL SCREWED UP, RIGHT? SO WE KNOCKED BLONDIE OUT COLD AND STOLE HIS BOAT.
YOU GOTTA SEE THIS THING, REAL NICE BOAT.
MIKE!!

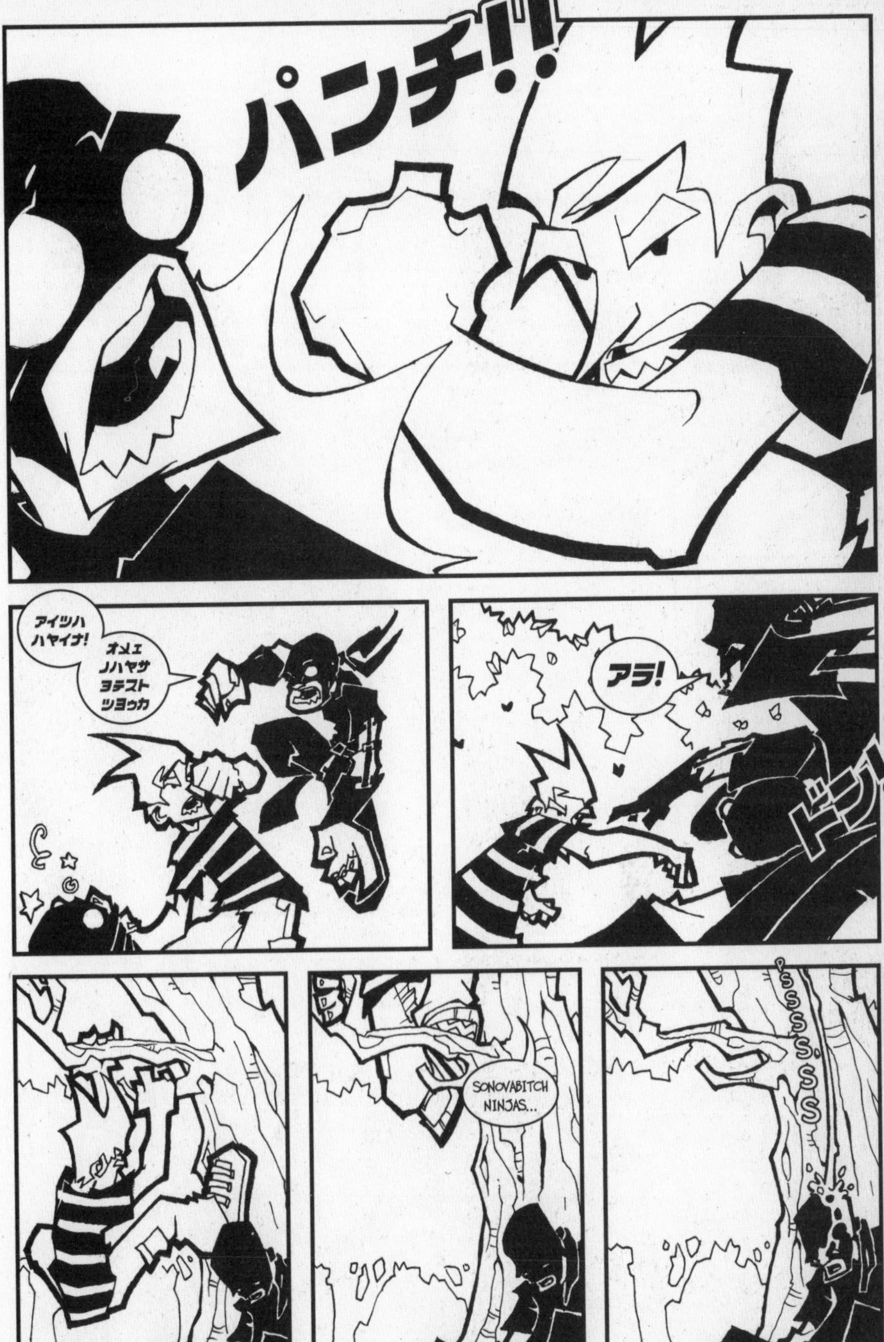
パンチ!!
アイツハ ハヤイナ!
オメエ ノハヤサ ヨテスト ツヨッカ
アラ!
ドン!
SONOVABITCH NINJAS...
PSSSSSS

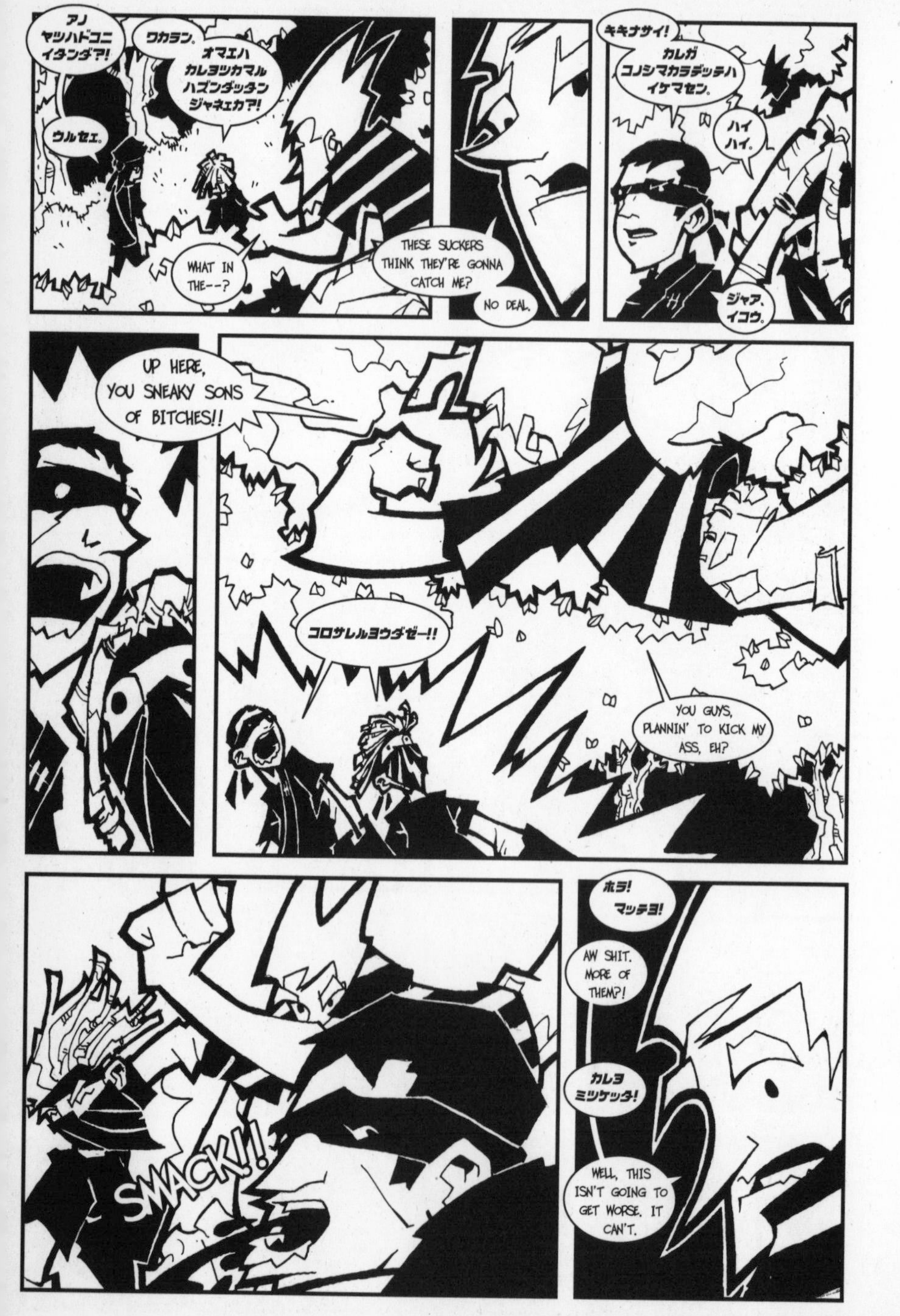
アノ ヤツハドコニ イタンダ?!
ワカラン。
オマエハ カレヲツカマル ハズンダッタン ジャネェカ?!
ウルセェ。
WHAT IN THE--?
THESE SUCKERS THINK THEY'RE GONNA CATCH ME?
NO DEAL.
キキナサイ!
カレガ コノシマカラデッテハ イケマセン。
ハイ ハイ。
ジャア、イコウ。
UP HERE, YOU SNEAKY SONS OF BITCHES!!
コロサレルヨウダゼー!!
YOU GUYS, PLANNIN' TO KICK MY ASS, EH?
SMACK!!
ホラ! マッテヨ!
AW SHIT. MORE OF THEM?!
カレヲ ミツケッタ!
WELL, THIS ISN'T GOING TO GET WORSE. IT CAN'T.

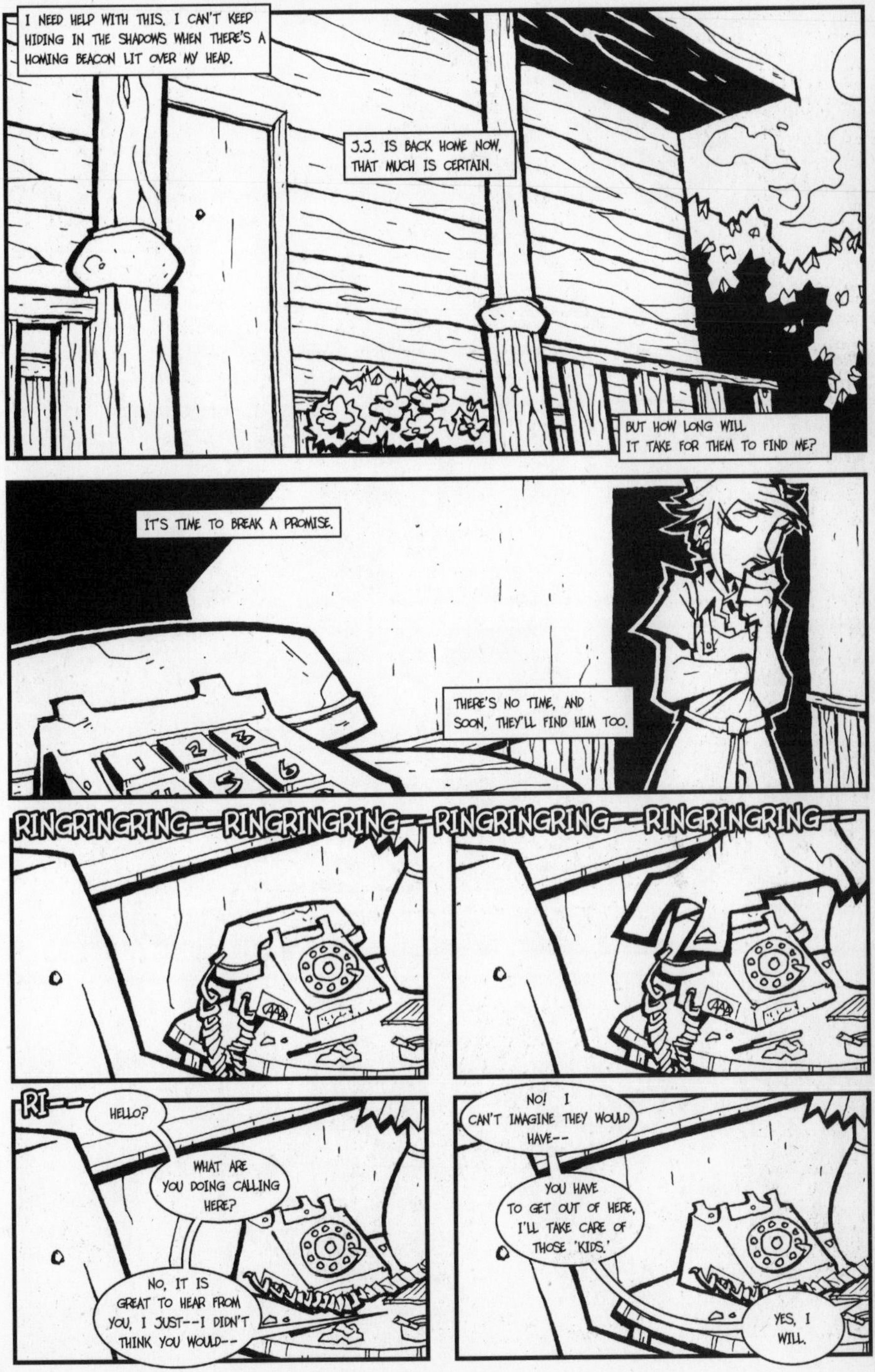
I NEED HELP WITH THIS. I CAN'T KEEP HIDING IN THE SHADOWS WHEN THERE'S A HOMING BEACON LIT OVER MY HEAD.
J.J. IS BACK HOME NOW, THAT MUCH IS CERTAIN.
BUT HOW LONG WILL IT TAKE FOR THEM TO FIND ME?
IT'S TIME TO BREAK A PROMISE.
THERE'S NO TIME, AND SOON, THEY'LL FIND HIM TOO.
RINGRINGRING--RINGRINGRING--RINGRINGRING--RINGRINGRING--
RI--
HELLO?
WHAT ARE YOU DOING CALLING HERE?
NO, IT IS GREAT TO HEAR FROM YOU, I JUST--I DIDN'T THINK YOU WOULD--
NO! I CAN'T IMAGINE THEY WOULD HAVE--
YOU HAVE TO GET OUT OF HERE, I'LL TAKE CARE OF THOSE 'KIDS.'
YES, I WILL.

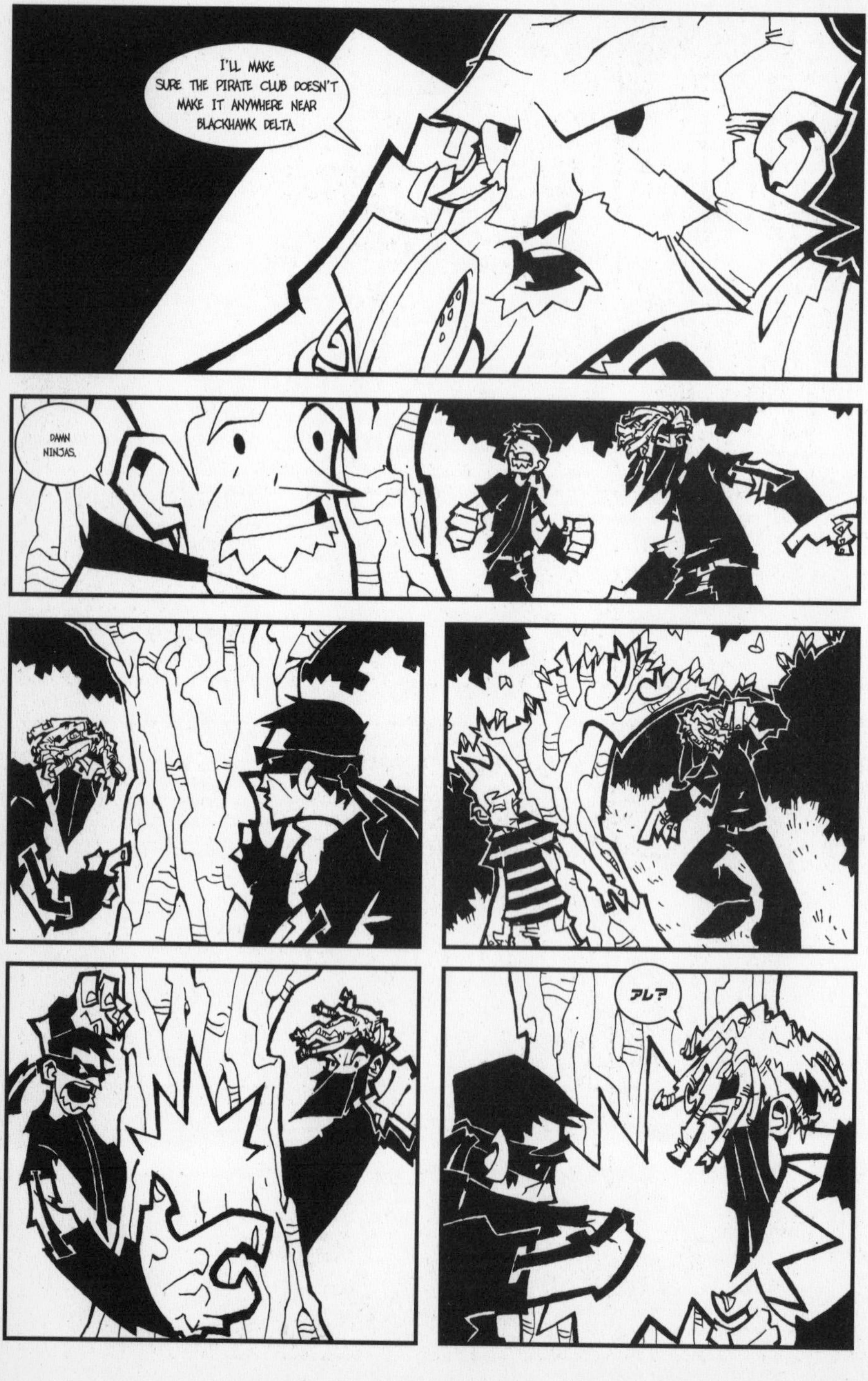
I'LL MAKE SURE THE PIRATE CLUB DOESN'T MAKE IT ANYWHERE NEAR BLACKHAWK DELTA.
DAMN NINJAS.
アレ?

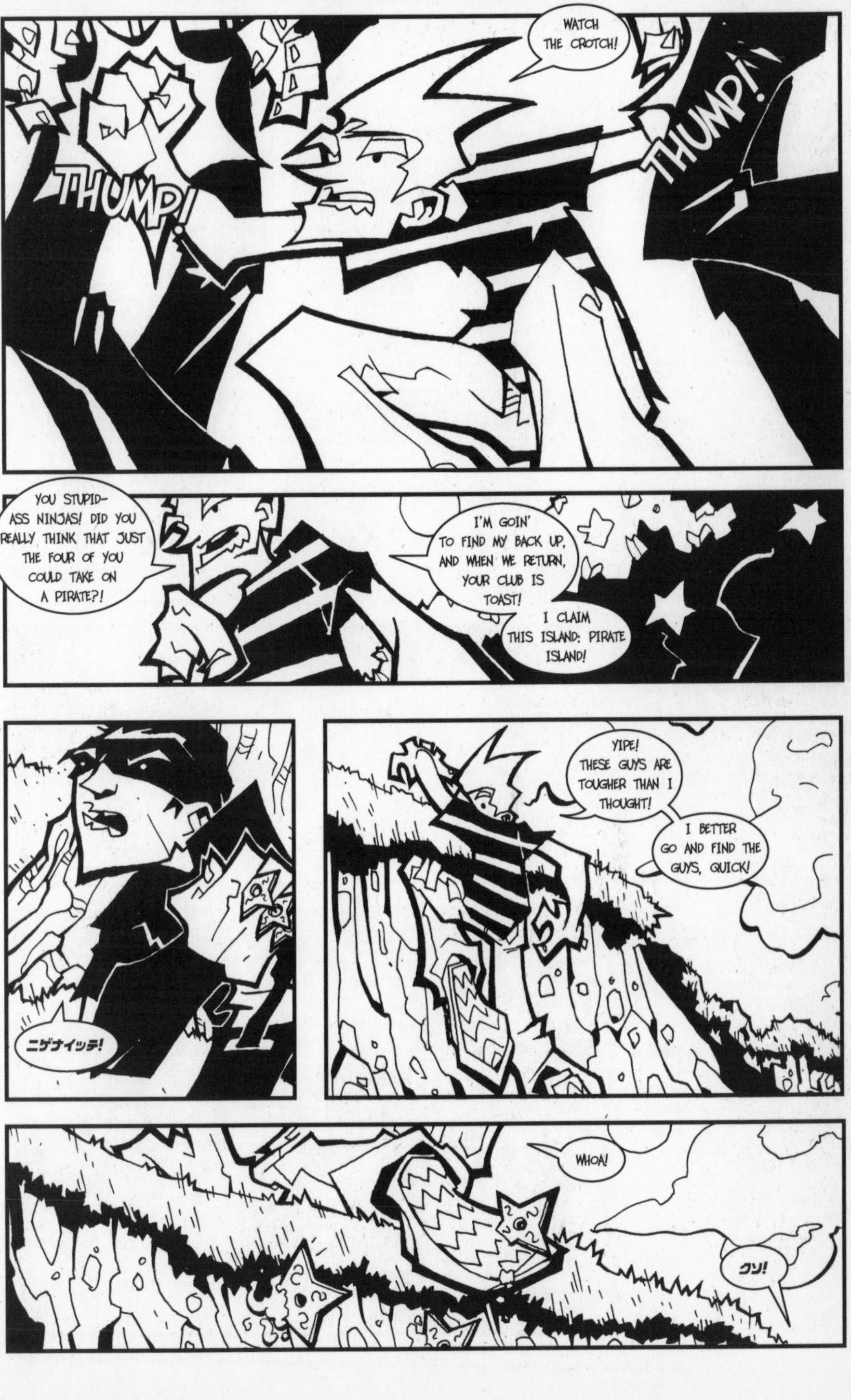
WATCH THE CROTCH!
THUMP!
THUMP!
YOU STUPID-ASS NINJAS! DID YOU REALLY THINK THAT JUST THE FOUR OF YOU COULD TAKE ON A PIRATE?!
I'M GOIN' TO FIND MY BACK UP, AND WHEN WE RETURN, YOUR CLUB IS TOAST!
I CLAIM THIS ISLAND: PIRATE ISLAND!
ニゲナイッテ!
YIPE! THESE GUYS ARE TOUGHER THAN I THOUGHT!
I BETTER GO AND FIND THE GUYS, QUICK!
WHOA!
クソ!

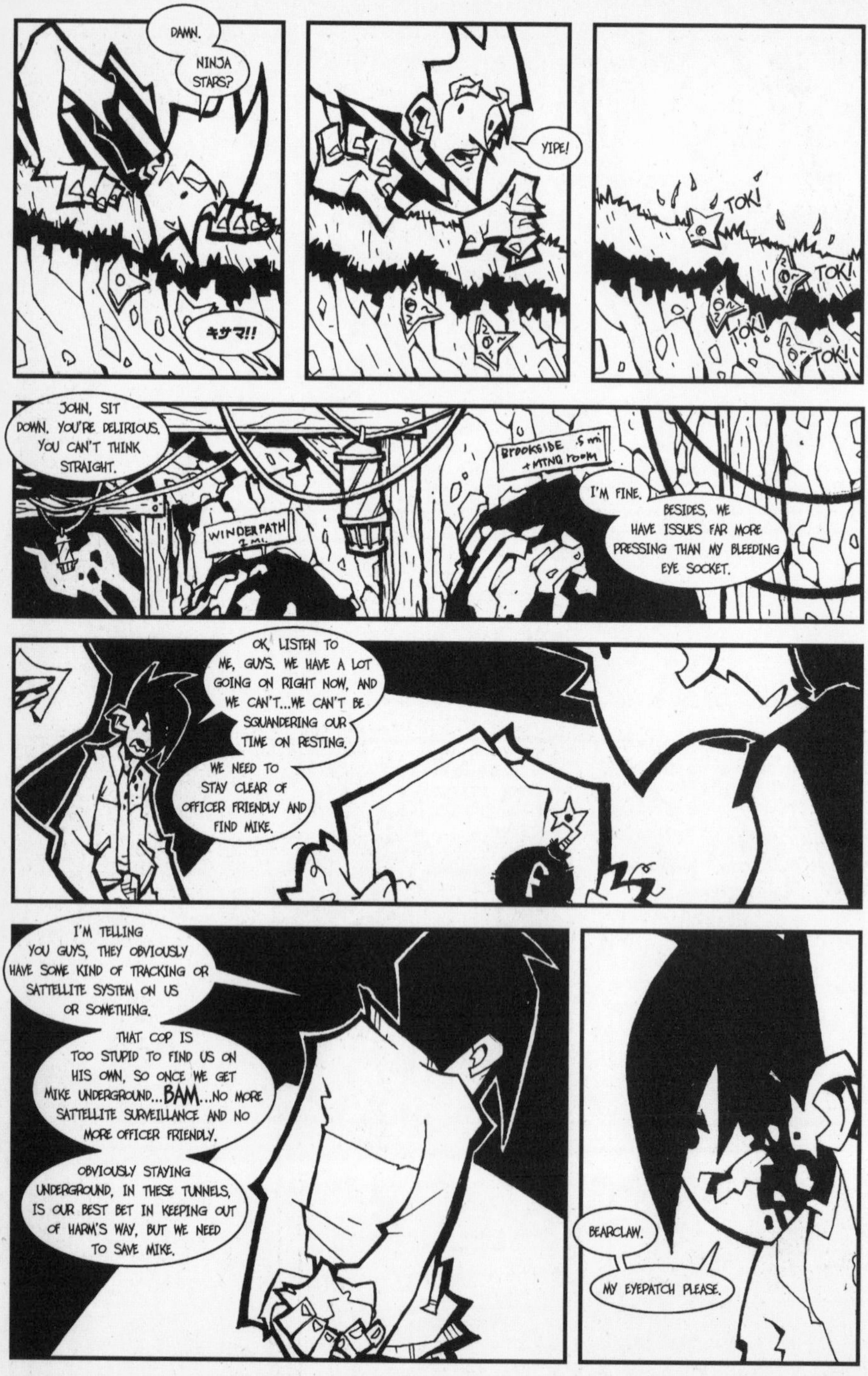

DAMN.
NINJA STARS?
キサマ!!
YIPE!
TOK!
TOK!
TOK!
TOK!
JOHN, SIT DOWN. YOU'RE DELIRIOUS. YOU CAN'T THINK STRAIGHT.
BROOKSIDE .5 mi +MTNG room
WINDERPATH 2 mi.
I'M FINE.
BESIDES, WE HAVE ISSUES FAR MORE PRESSING THAN MY BLEEDING EYE SOCKET.
OK, LISTEN TO ME, GUYS. WE HAVE A LOT GOING ON RIGHT NOW, AND WE CAN'T...WE CAN'T BE SQUANDERING OUR TIME ON RESTING.
WE NEED TO STAY CLEAR OF OFFICER FRIENDLY AND FIND MIKE.
I'M TELLING YOU GUYS, THEY OBVIOUSLY HAVE SOME KIND OF TRACKING OR SATTELLITE SYSTEM ON US OR SOMETHING.
THAT COP IS TOO STUPID TO FIND US ON HIS OWN, SO ONCE WE GET MIKE UNDERGROUND...BAM...NO MORE SATTELLITE SURVEILLANCE AND NO MORE OFFICER FRIENDLY.
OBVIOUSLY STAYING UNDERGROUND, IN THESE TUNNELS, IS OUR BEST BET IN KEEPING OUT OF HARM'S WAY, BUT WE NEED TO SAVE MIKE.
BEARCLAW.
MY EYEPATCH PLEASE.

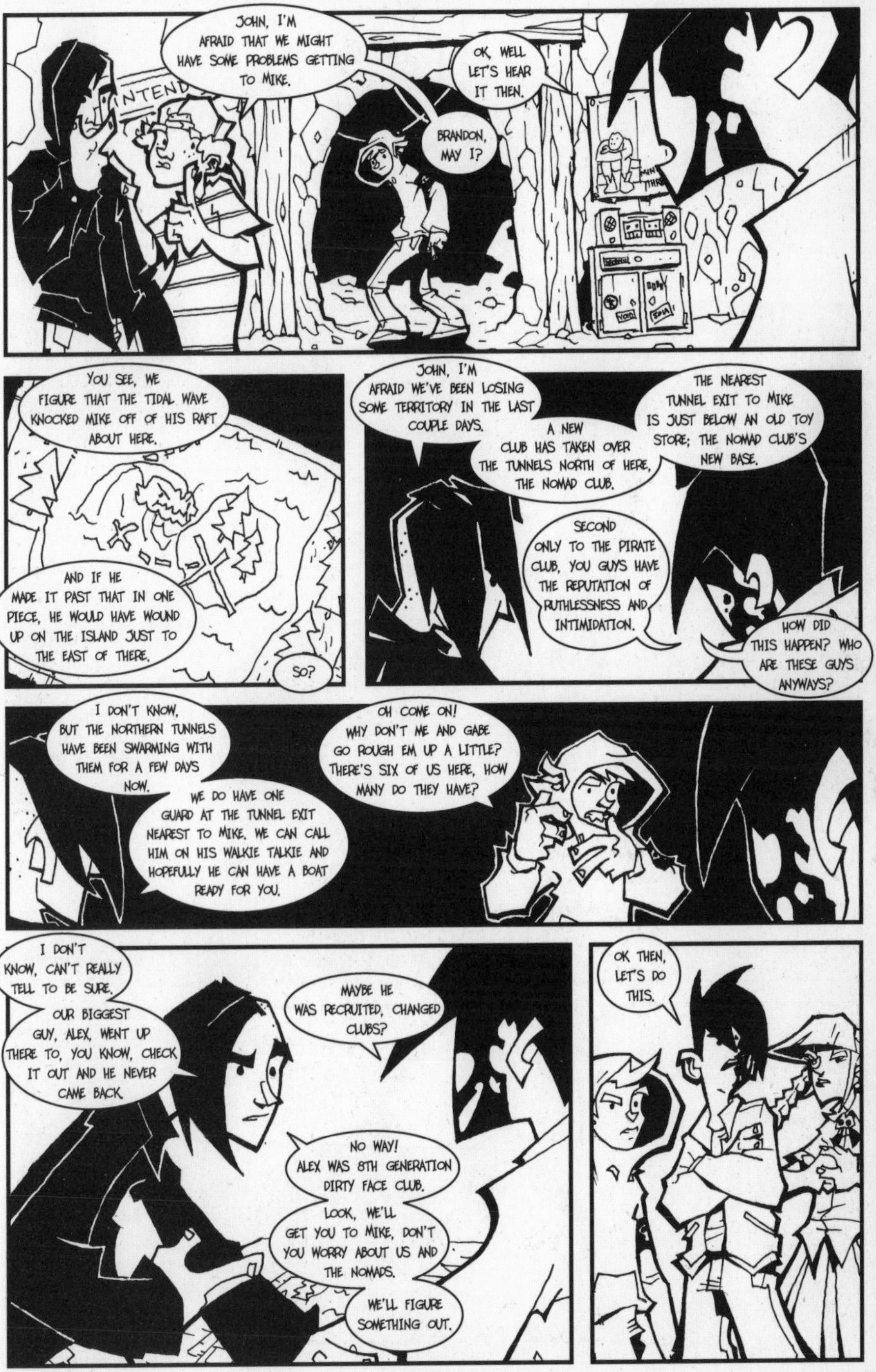
JOHN, I'M AFRAID THAT WE MIGHT HAVE SOME PROBLEMS GETTING TO MIKE.
OK, WELL LET'S HEAR IT THEN.
BRANDON, MAY I?
INTEND
YOU SEE, WE FIGURE THAT THE TIDAL WAVE KNOCKED MIKE OFF OF HIS RAFT ABOUT HERE.
AND IF HE MADE IT PAST THAT IN ONE PIECE, HE WOULD HAVE WOUND UP ON THE ISLAND JUST TO THE EAST OF THERE.
SO?
JOHN, I'M AFRAID WE'VE BEEN LOSING SOME TERRITORY IN THE LAST COUPLE DAYS.
A NEW CLUB HAS TAKEN OVER THE TUNNELS NORTH OF HERE, THE NOMAD CLUB.
THE NEAREST TUNNEL EXIT TO MIKE IS JUST BELOW AN OLD TOY STORE; THE NOMAD CLUB'S NEW BASE.
SECOND ONLY TO THE PIRATE CLUB, YOU GUYS HAVE THE REPUTATION OF RUTHLESSNESS AND INTIMIDATION.
HOW DID THIS HAPPEN? WHO ARE THESE GUYS ANYWAYS?
I DON'T KNOW, BUT THE NORTHERN TUNNELS HAVE BEEN SWARMING WITH THEM FOR A FEW DAYS NOW.
WE DO HAVE ONE GUARD AT THE TUNNEL EXIT NEAREST TO MIKE. WE CAN CALL HIM ON HIS WALKIE TALKIE AND HOPEFULLY HE CAN HAVE A BOAT READY FOR YOU.
OH COME ON! WHY DON'T ME AND GABE GO ROUGH EM UP A LITTLE? THERE'S SIX OF US HERE, HOW MANY DO THEY HAVE?
I DON'T KNOW, CAN'T REALLY TELL TO BE SURE.
OUR BIGGEST GUY, ALEX, WENT UP THERE TO, YOU KNOW, CHECK IT OUT AND HE NEVER CAME BACK.
MAYBE HE WAS RECRUITED, CHANGED CLUBS?
NO WAY! ALEX WAS 8TH GENERATION DIRTY FACE CLUB.
LOOK, WE'LL GET YOU TO MIKE, DON'T YOU WORRY ABOUT US AND THE NOMADS.
WE'LL FIGURE SOMETHING OUT.
OK THEN, LET'S DO THIS.

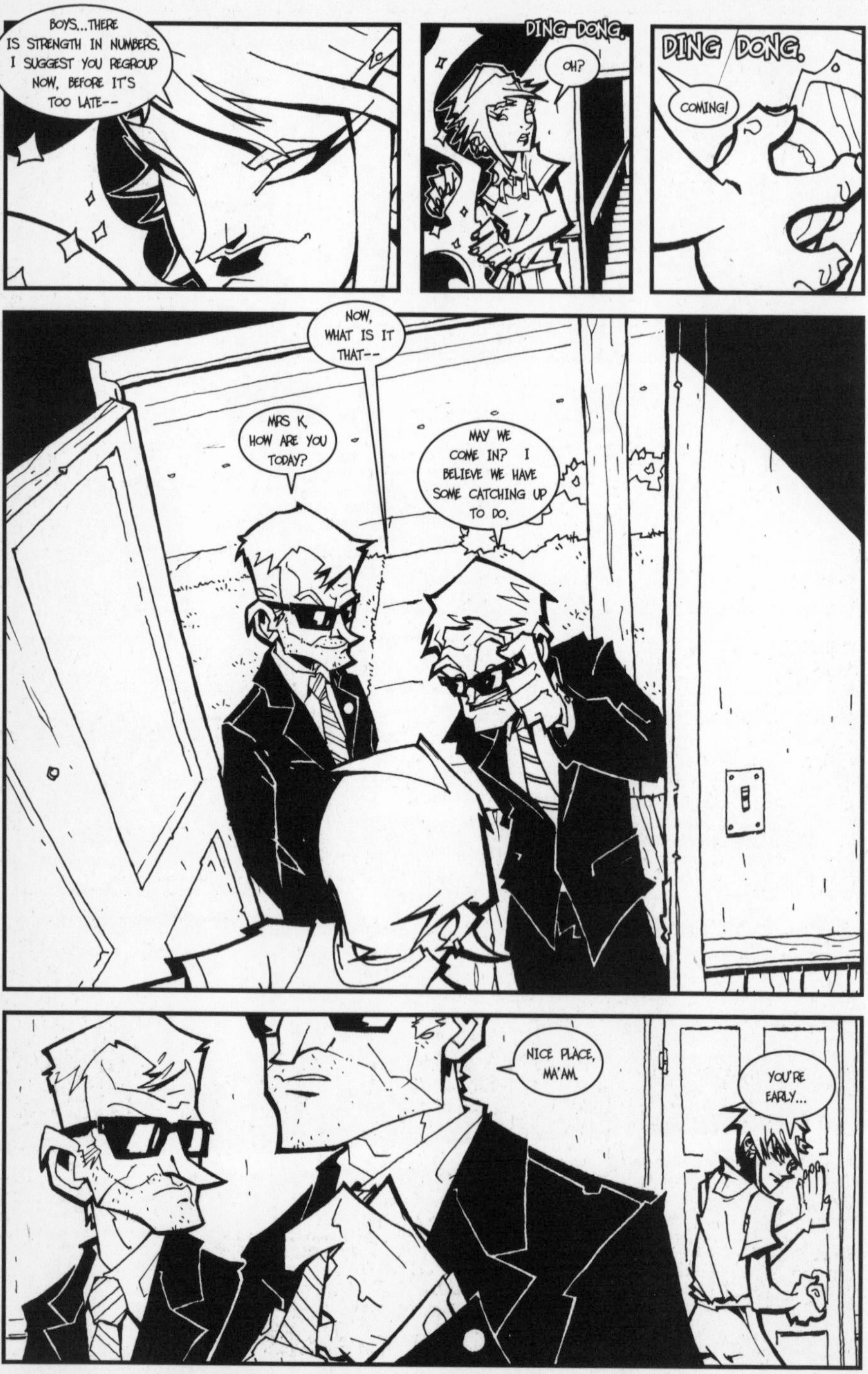
BOYS...THERE IS STRENGTH IN NUMBERS. I SUGGEST YOU REGROUP NOW, BEFORE IT'S TOO LATE--
DING DONG.
OH?
DING DONG.
COMING!
NOW, WHAT IS IT THAT--
MRS K, HOW ARE YOU TODAY?
MAY WE COME IN? I BELIEVE WE HAVE SOME CATCHING UP TO DO.
NICE PLACE, MA'AM.
YOU'RE EARLY...

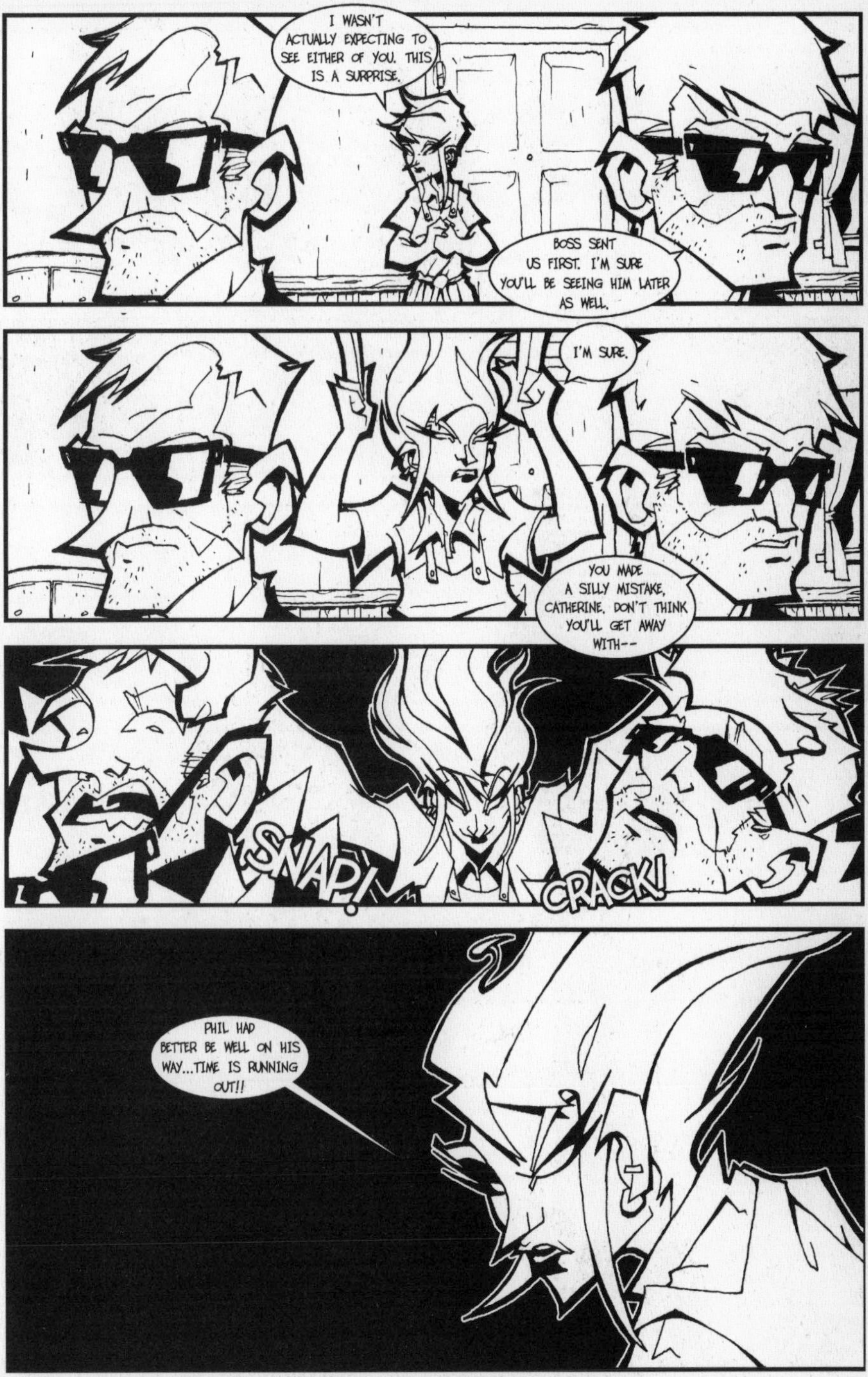
I WASN'T ACTUALLY EXPECTING TO SEE EITHER OF YOU. THIS IS A SURPRISE.
BOSS SENT US FIRST. I'M SURE YOU'LL BE SEEING HIM LATER AS WELL.
I'M SURE.
YOU MADE A SILLY MISTAKE, CATHERINE. DON'T THINK YOU'LL GET AWAY WITH--
SNAP!
CRACK!
PHIL HAD BETTER BE WELL ON HIS WAY...TIME IS RUNNING OUT!!

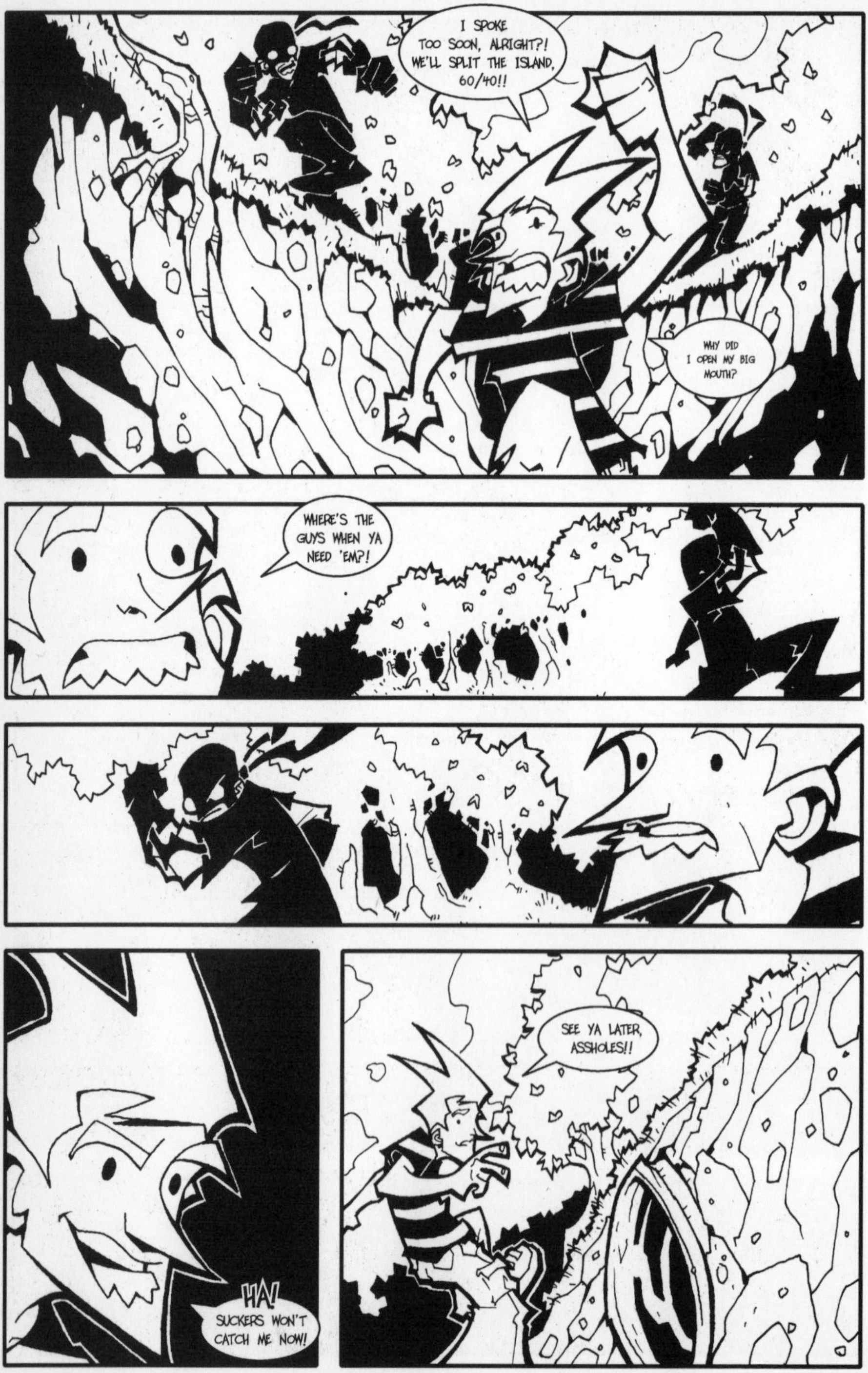
I SPOKE TOO SOON, ALRIGHT?! WE'LL SPLIT THE ISLAND, 60/40!!
WHY DID I OPEN MY BIG MOUTH?
WHERE'S THE GUYS WHEN YA NEED 'EM?!
HA! SUCKERS WON'T CATCH ME NOW!
SEE YA LATER, ASSHOLES!!

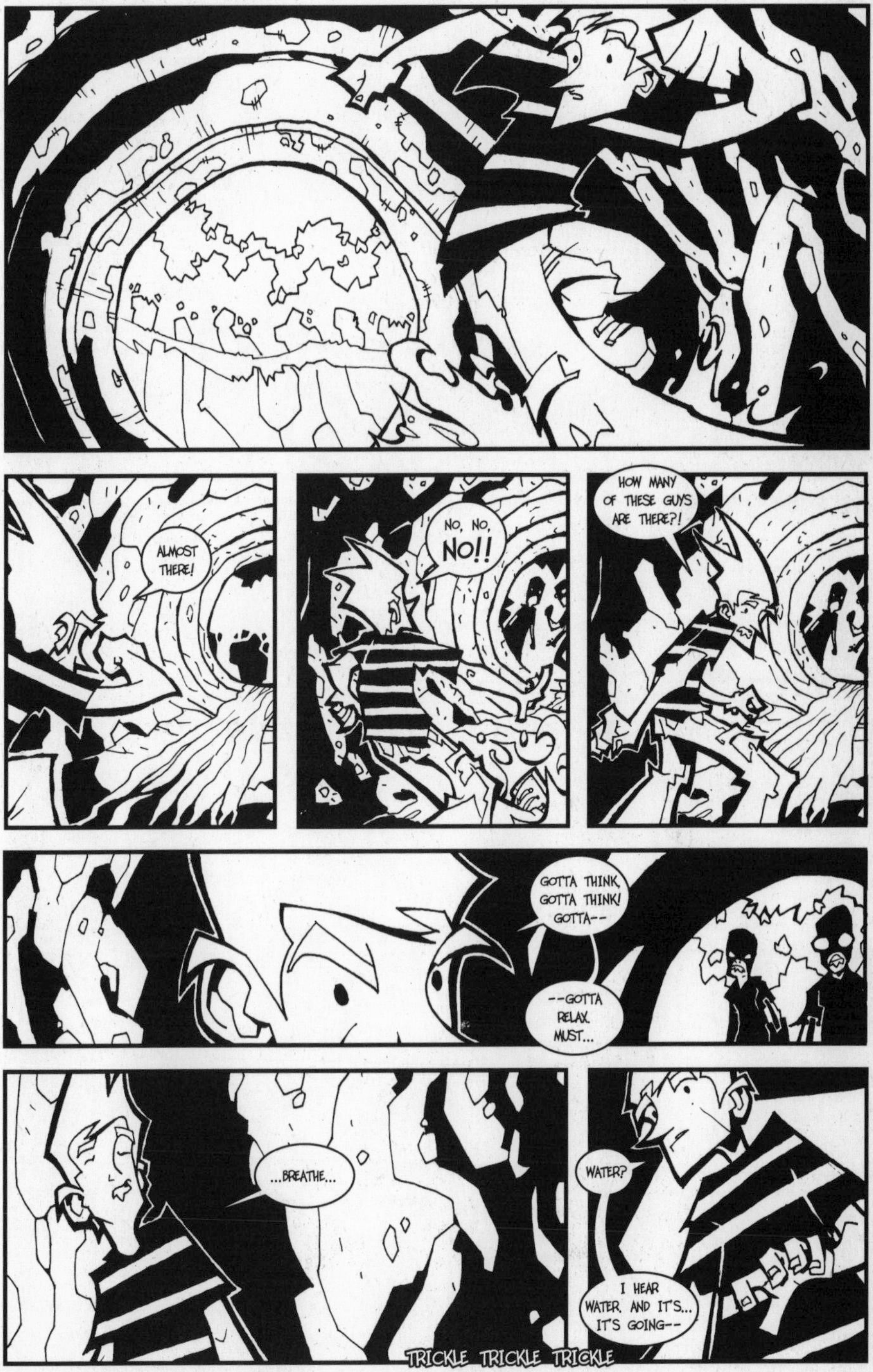
ALMOST THERE!
NO, NO, NO!!
HOW MANY OF THESE GUYS ARE THERE?!
GOTTA THINK, GOTTA THINK! GOTTA--
--GOTTA RELAX. MUST...
...BREATHE...
WATER?
I HEAR WATER. AND IT'S... IT'S GOING--
TRICKLE TRICKLE TRICKLE

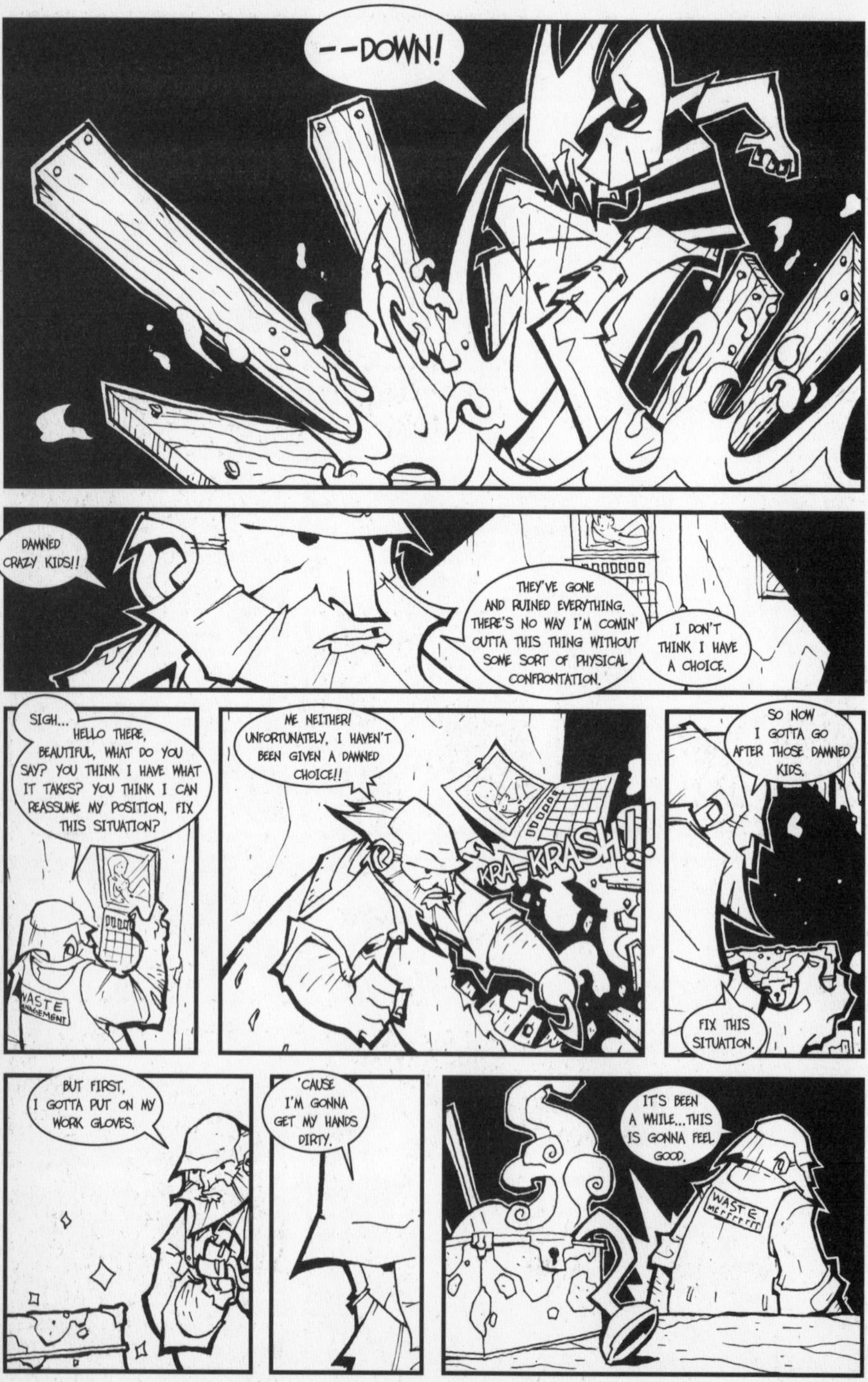
--DOWN!
DAMNED CRAZY KIDS!!
THEY'VE GONE AND RUINED EVERYTHING. THERE'S NO WAY I'M COMIN' OUTTA THIS THING WITHOUT SOME SORT OF PHYSICAL CONFRONTATION.
I DON'T THINK I HAVE A CHOICE.
SIGH... HELLO THERE, BEAUTIFUL. WHAT DO YOU SAY? YOU THINK I HAVE WHAT IT TAKES? YOU THINK I CAN REASSUME MY POSITION, FIX THIS SITUATION?
WASTE MANAGEMENT
ME NEITHER! UNFORTUNATELY, I HAVEN'T BEEN GIVEN A DAMNED CHOICE!!
KRA-KRASH!!!
SO NOW I GOTTA GO AFTER THOSE DAMNED KIDS.
FIX THIS SITUATION.
BUT FIRST, I GOTTA PUT ON MY WORK GLOVES.
'CAUSE I'M GONNA GET MY HANDS DIRTY.
IT'S BEEN A WHILE...THIS IS GONNA FEEL GOOD.
WASTE

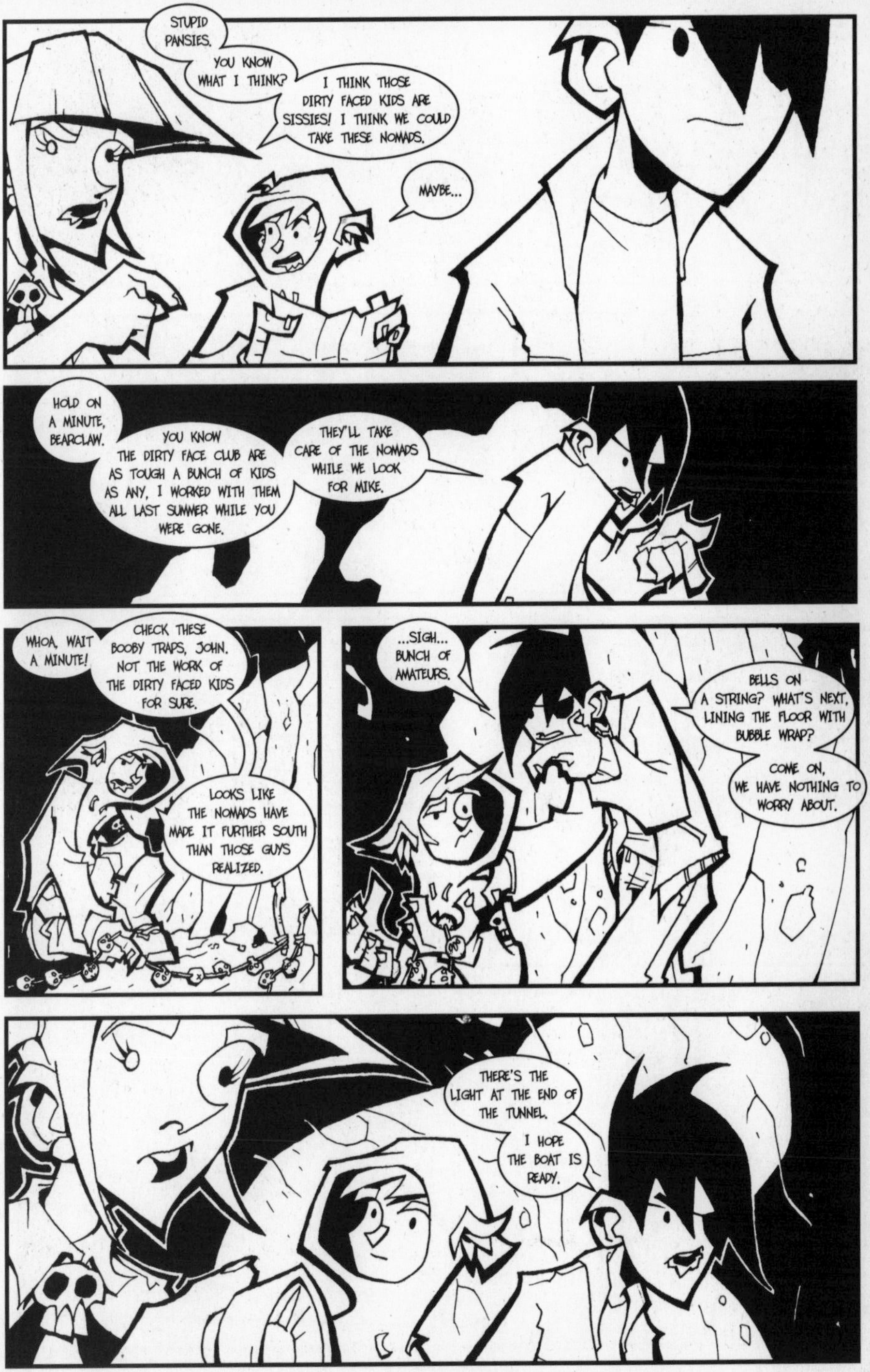
STUPID PANSIES.
YOU KNOW WHAT I THINK?
I THINK THOSE DIRTY FACED KIDS ARE SISSIES! I THINK WE COULD TAKE THESE NOMADS.
MAYBE...
HOLD ON A MINUTE, BEARCLAW.
YOU KNOW THE DIRTY FACE CLUB ARE AS TOUGH A BUNCH OF KIDS AS ANY, I WORKED WITH THEM ALL LAST SUMMER WHILE YOU WERE GONE.
THEY'LL TAKE CARE OF THE NOMADS WHILE WE LOOK FOR MIKE.
WHOA, WAIT A MINUTE!
CHECK THESE BOOBY TRAPS, JOHN. NOT THE WORK OF THE DIRTY FACED KIDS FOR SURE.
LOOKS LIKE THE NOMADS HAVE MADE IT FURTHER SOUTH THAN THOSE GUYS REALIZED.
...SIGH... BUNCH OF AMATEURS.
BELLS ON A STRING? WHAT'S NEXT, LINING THE FLOOR WITH BUBBLE WRAP?
COME ON, WE HAVE NOTHING TO WORRY ABOUT.
THERE'S THE LIGHT AT THE END OF THE TUNNEL.
I HOPE THE BOAT IS READY.

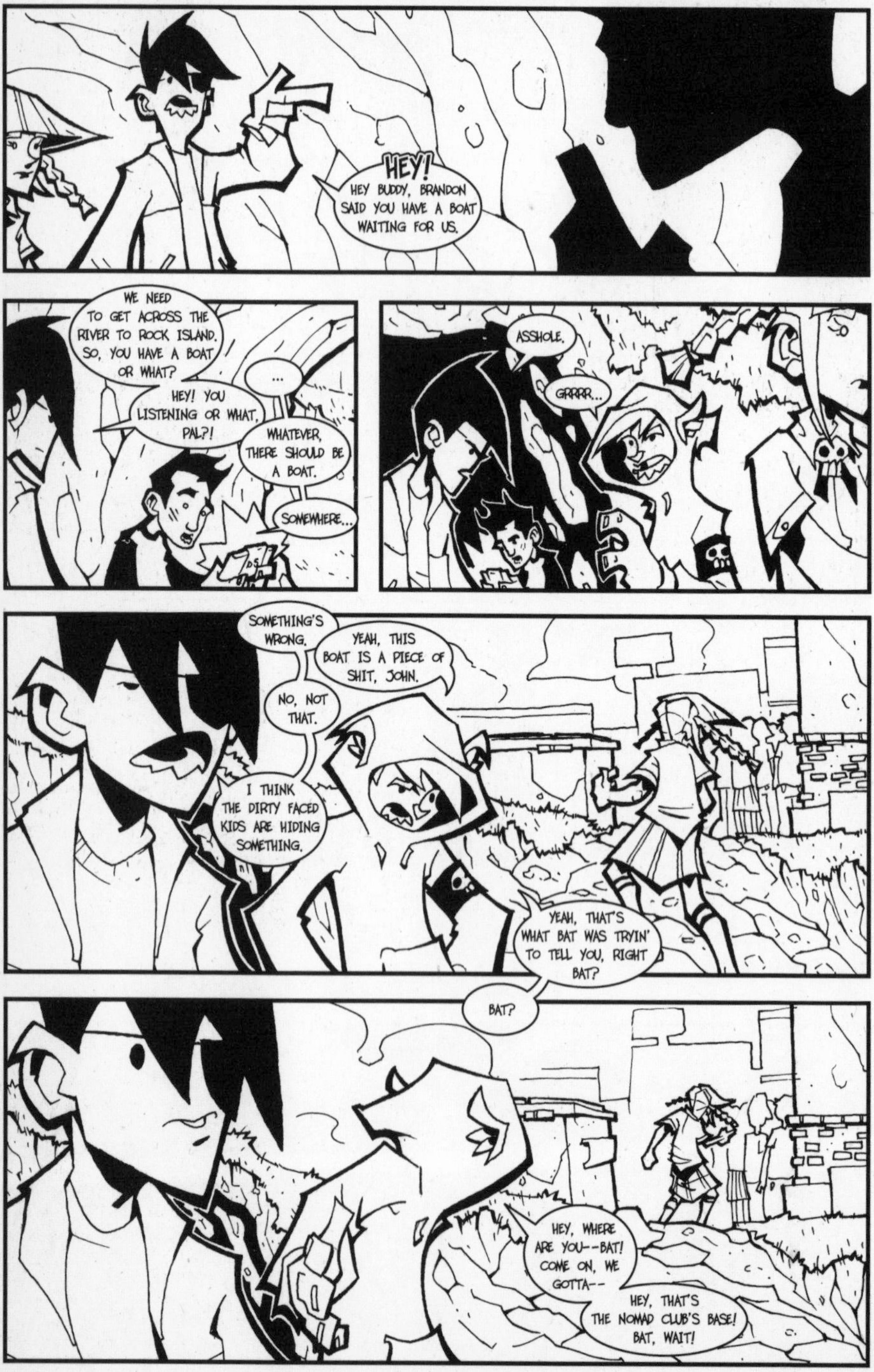
HEY!
HEY BUDDY, BRANDON SAID YOU HAVE A BOAT WAITING FOR US.
WE NEED TO GET ACROSS THE RIVER TO ROCK ISLAND. SO, YOU HAVE A BOAT OR WHAT?
...
HEY! YOU LISTENING OR WHAT, PAL?!
WHATEVER, THERE SHOULD BE A BOAT.
SOMEWHERE...
ASSHOLE.
GRRRR...
SOMETHING'S WRONG.
YEAH, THIS BOAT IS A PIECE OF SHIT, JOHN.
NO, NOT THAT.
I THINK THE DIRTY FACED KIDS ARE HIDING SOMETHING.
YEAH, THAT'S WHAT BAT WAS TRYIN' TO TELL YOU, RIGHT BAT?
BAT?
HEY, WHERE ARE YOU--BAT! COME ON, WE GOTTA--
HEY, THAT'S THE NOMAD CLUB'S BASE! BAT, WAIT!

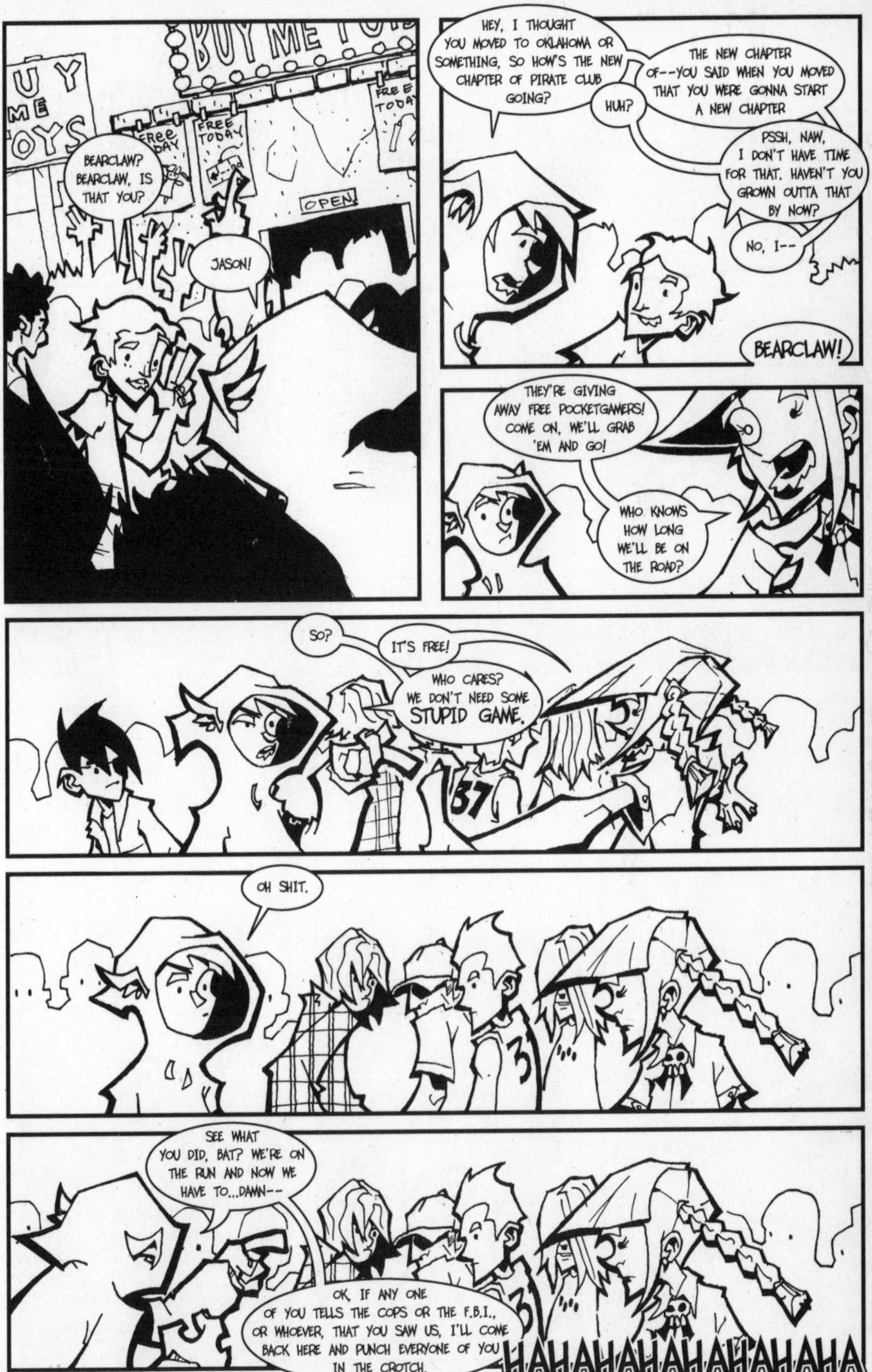
BUY ME TOYS
U Y ME OYS
FREE TODAY
FREE TODAY
FREE TODAY
BEARCLAW? BEARCLAW, IS THAT YOU?
OPEN
JASON!
HEY, I THOUGHT YOU MOVED TO OKLAHOMA OR SOMETHING, SO HOW'S THE NEW CHAPTER OF PIRATE CLUB GOING?
HUH?
THE NEW CHAPTER OF--YOU SAID WHEN YOU MOVED THAT YOU WERE GONNA START A NEW CHAPTER
PSSH, NAW, I DON'T HAVE TIME FOR THAT. HAVEN'T YOU GROWN OUTTA THAT BY NOW?
NO, I--
BEARCLAW!
THEY'RE GIVING AWAY FREE POCKETGAMERS! COME ON, WE'LL GRAB 'EM AND GO!
WHO KNOWS HOW LONG WE'LL BE ON THE ROAD?
SO?
IT'S FREE!
WHO CARES? WE DON'T NEED SOME STUPID GAME.
37
OH SHIT.
SEE WHAT YOU DID, BAT? WE'RE ON THE RUN AND NOW WE HAVE TO...DAMN--
OK, IF ANY ONE OF YOU TELLS THE COPS OR THE F.B.I., OR WHOEVER, THAT YOU SAW US, I'LL COME BACK HERE AND PUNCH EVERYONE OF YOU IN THE CROTCH.
HAHAHAHAHAHAHAHAHA

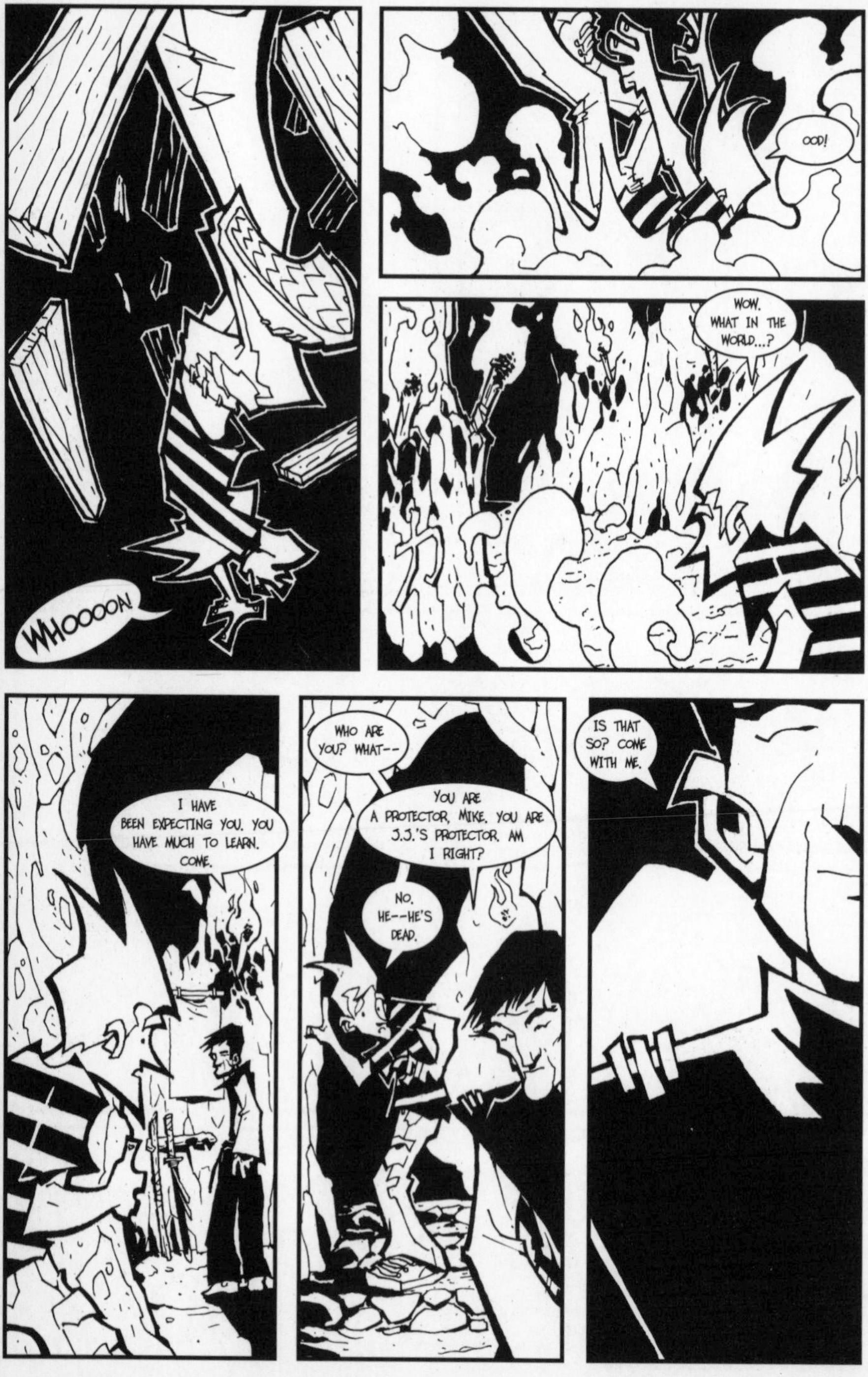
WHOOOOA!
OOF!
WOW. WHAT IN THE WORLD...?
I HAVE BEEN EXPECTING YOU. YOU HAVE MUCH TO LEARN. COME.
WHO ARE YOU? WHAT--
YOU ARE A PROTECTOR, MIKE. YOU ARE J.J.'S PROTECTOR. AM I RIGHT?
NO. HE--HE'S DEAD.
IS THAT SO? COME WITH ME.

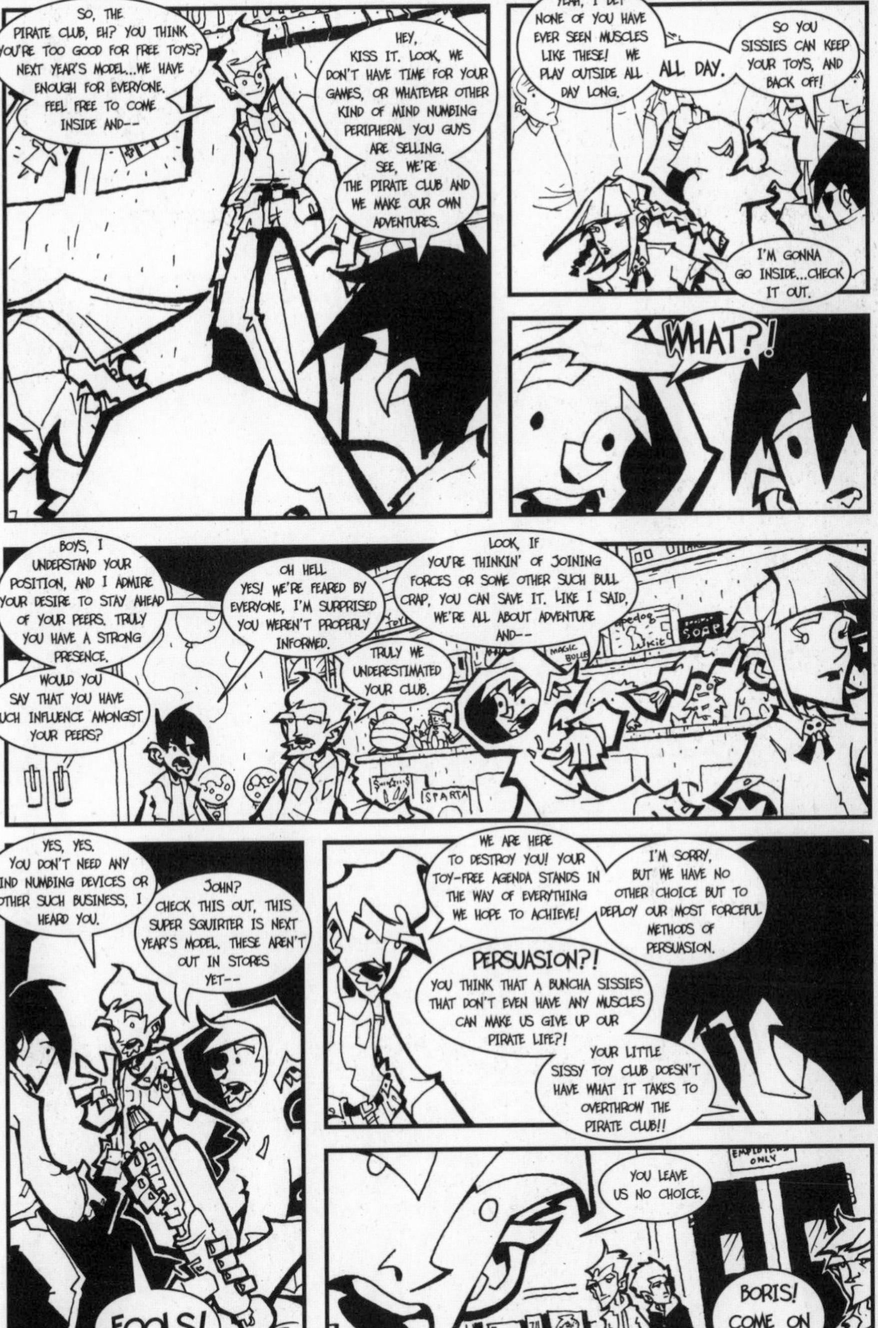
SO, THE PIRATE CLUB, EH? YOU THINK YOU'RE TOO GOOD FOR FREE TOYS? NEXT YEAR'S MODEL...WE HAVE ENOUGH FOR EVERYONE. FEEL FREE TO COME INSIDE AND--
HEY, KISS IT. LOOK, WE DON'T HAVE TIME FOR YOUR GAMES, OR WHATEVER OTHER KIND OF MIND NUMBING PERIPHERAL YOU GUYS ARE SELLING. SEE, WE'RE THE PIRATE CLUB AND WE MAKE OUR OWN ADVENTURES.
YEAH, I BET NONE OF YOU HAVE EVER SEEN MUSCLES LIKE THESE! WE PLAY OUTSIDE ALL DAY LONG.
ALL DAY.
SO YOU SISSIES CAN KEEP YOUR TOYS, AND BACK OFF!
I'M GONNA GO INSIDE...CHECK IT OUT.
WHAT?!
BOYS, I UNDERSTAND YOUR POSITION, AND I ADMIRE YOUR DESIRE TO STAY AHEAD OF YOUR PEERS. TRULY YOU HAVE A STRONG PRESENCE.
WOULD YOU SAY THAT YOU HAVE MUCH INFLUENCE AMONGST YOUR PEERS?
OH HELL YES! WE'RE FEARED BY EVERYONE, I'M SURPRISED YOU WEREN'T PROPERLY INFORMED.
TRULY WE UNDERESTIMATED YOUR CLUB.
LOOK, IF YOU'RE THINKIN' OF JOINING FORCES OR SOME OTHER SUCH BULL CRAP, YOU CAN SAVE IT. LIKE I SAID, WE'RE ALL ABOUT ADVENTURE AND--
MAGIC
SOAP
SPARTA
YES, YES. YOU DON'T NEED ANY MIND NUMBING DEVICES OR OTHER SUCH BUSINESS, I HEARD YOU.
JOHN? CHECK THIS OUT, THIS SUPER SQUIRTER IS NEXT YEAR'S MODEL. THESE AREN'T OUT IN STORES YET--
FOOLS!
WE ARE HERE TO DESTROY YOU! YOUR TOY-FREE AGENDA STANDS IN THE WAY OF EVERYTHING WE HOPE TO ACHIEVE!
I'M SORRY, BUT WE HAVE NO OTHER CHOICE BUT TO DEPLOY OUR MOST FORCEFUL METHODS OF PERSUASION.
PERSUASION?! YOU THINK THAT A BUNCHA SISSIES THAT DON'T EVEN HAVE ANY MUSCLES CAN MAKE US GIVE UP OUR PIRATE LIFE?!
YOUR LITTLE SISSY TOY CLUB DOESN'T HAVE WHAT IT TAKES TO OVERTHROW THE PIRATE CLUB!!
YOU LEAVE US NO CHOICE.
BORIS! COME ON OUT!

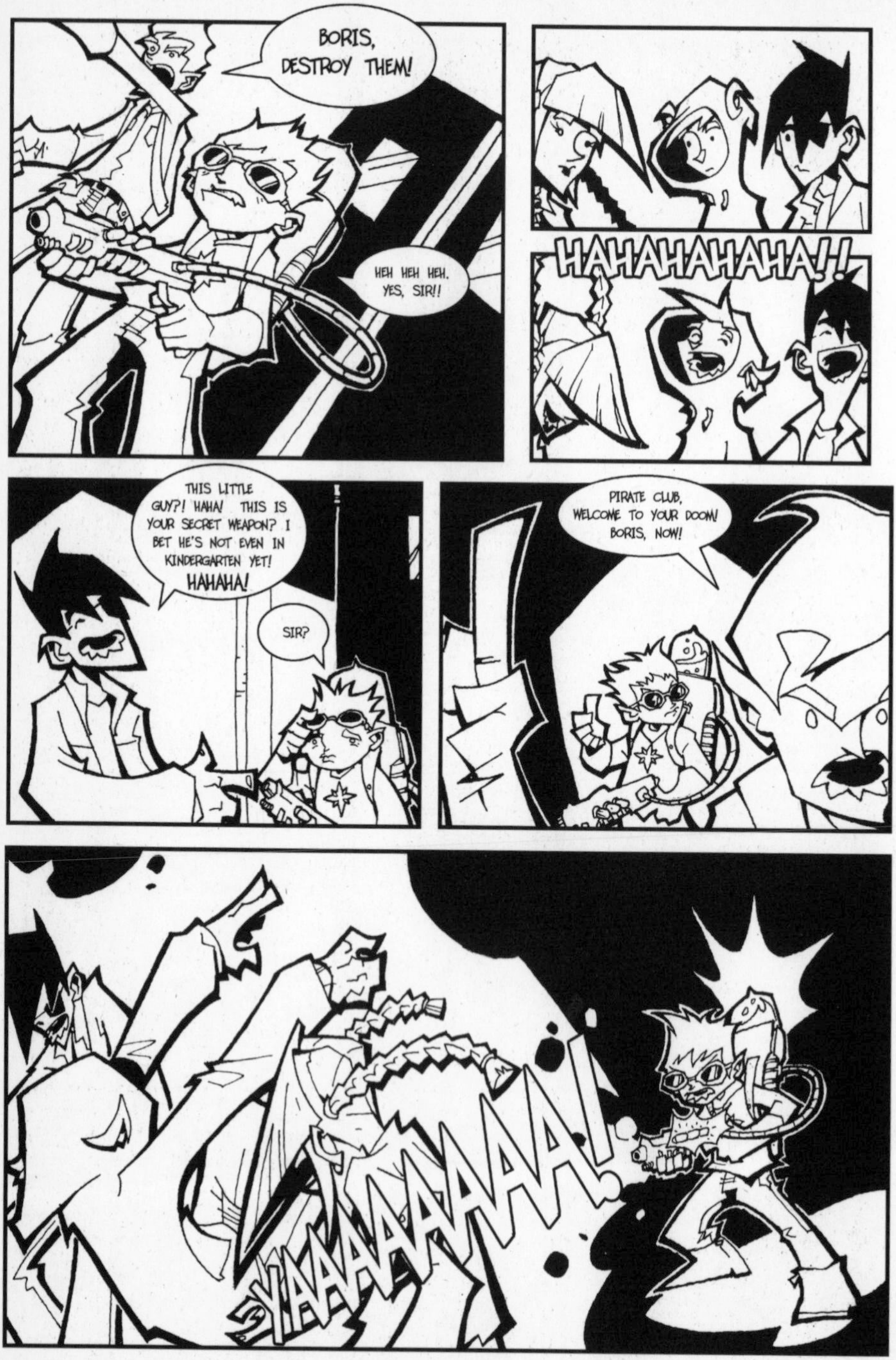
BORIS, DESTROY THEM!
HEH HEH HEH. YES, SIR!!
HAHAHAHAHA!!
THIS LITTLE GUY?! HAHA! THIS IS YOUR SECRET WEAPON? I BET HE'S NOT EVEN IN KINDERGARTEN YET! HAHAHA!
SIR?
PIRATE CLUB, WELCOME TO YOUR DOOM! BORIS, NOW!
YAAAAAAAAA!

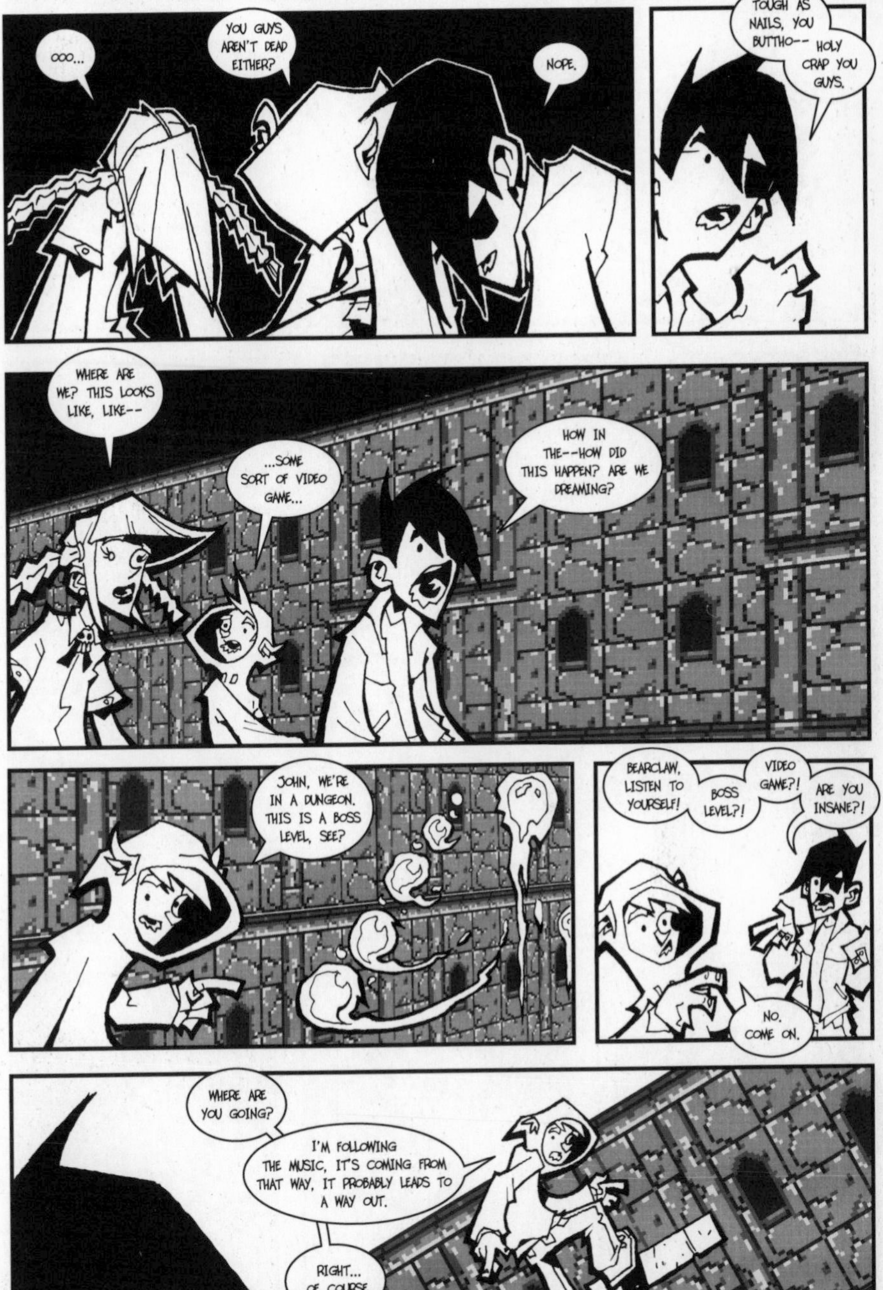
OOO...
YOU GUYS AREN'T DEAD EITHER?
NOPE.
TOUGH AS NAILS, YOU BUTTHO--
HOLY CRAP YOU GUYS.
WHERE ARE WE? THIS LOOKS LIKE, LIKE--
...SOME SORT OF VIDEO GAME...
HOW IN THE--HOW DID THIS HAPPEN? ARE WE DREAMING?
JOHN, WE'RE IN A DUNGEON. THIS IS A BOSS LEVEL, SEE?
BEARCLAW, LISTEN TO YOURSELF!
BOSS LEVEL?!
VIDEO GAME?!
ARE YOU INSANE?!
NO. COME ON.
WHERE ARE YOU GOING?
I'M FOLLOWING THE MUSIC, IT'S COMING FROM THAT WAY, IT PROBABLY LEADS TO A WAY OUT.
RIGHT... OF COURSE.

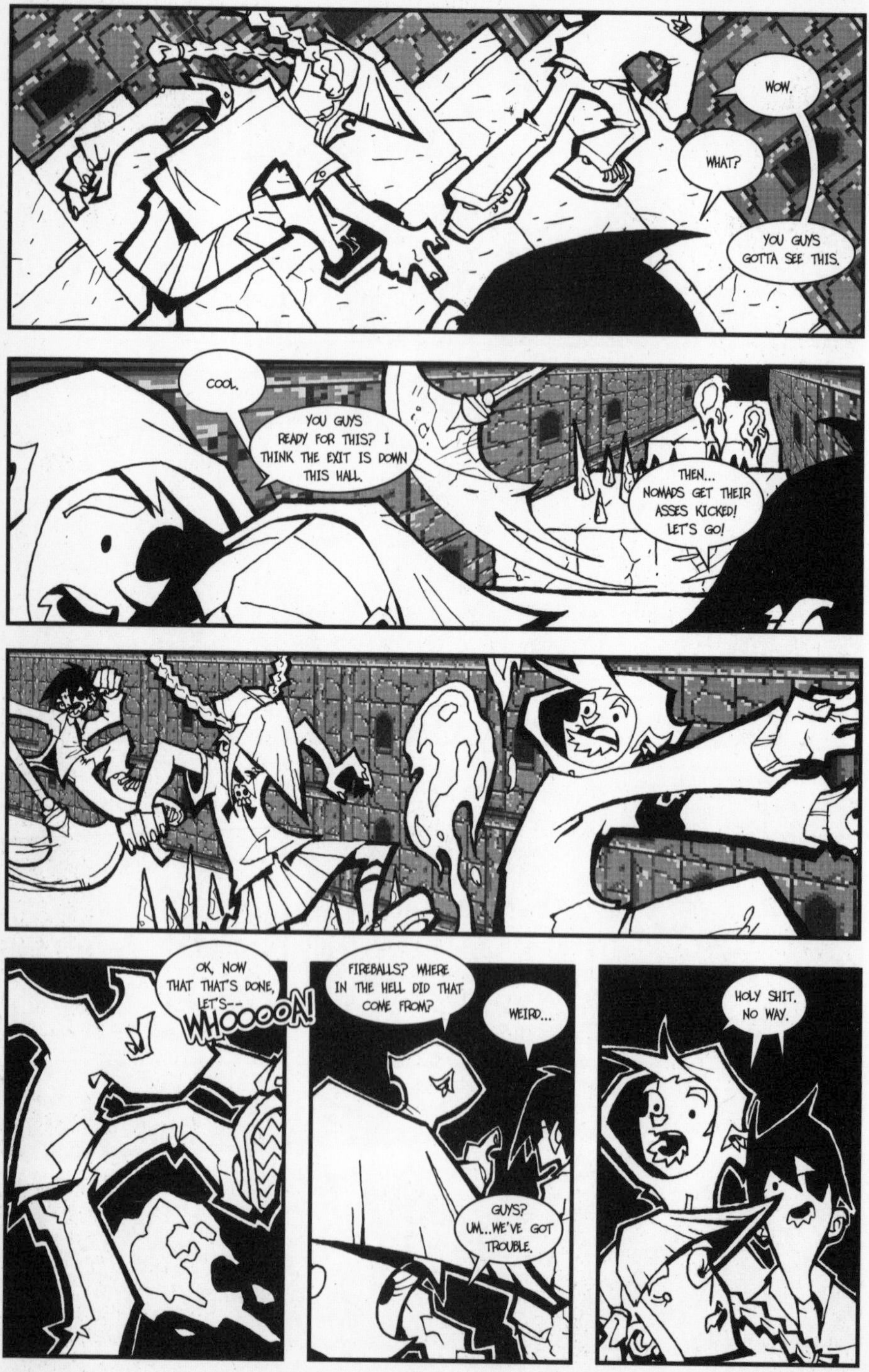
WOW.
WHAT?
YOU GUYS GOTTA SEE THIS.
COOL.
YOU GUYS READY FOR THIS? I THINK THE EXIT IS DOWN THIS HALL.
THEN... NOMADS GET THEIR ASSES KICKED! LET'S GO!
OK, NOW THAT THAT'S DONE, LET'S--
WHOOOOA!
FIREBALLS? WHERE IN THE HELL DID THAT COME FROM?
WEIRD...
GUYS? UM...WE'VE GOT TROUBLE.
HOLY SHIT. NO WAY.

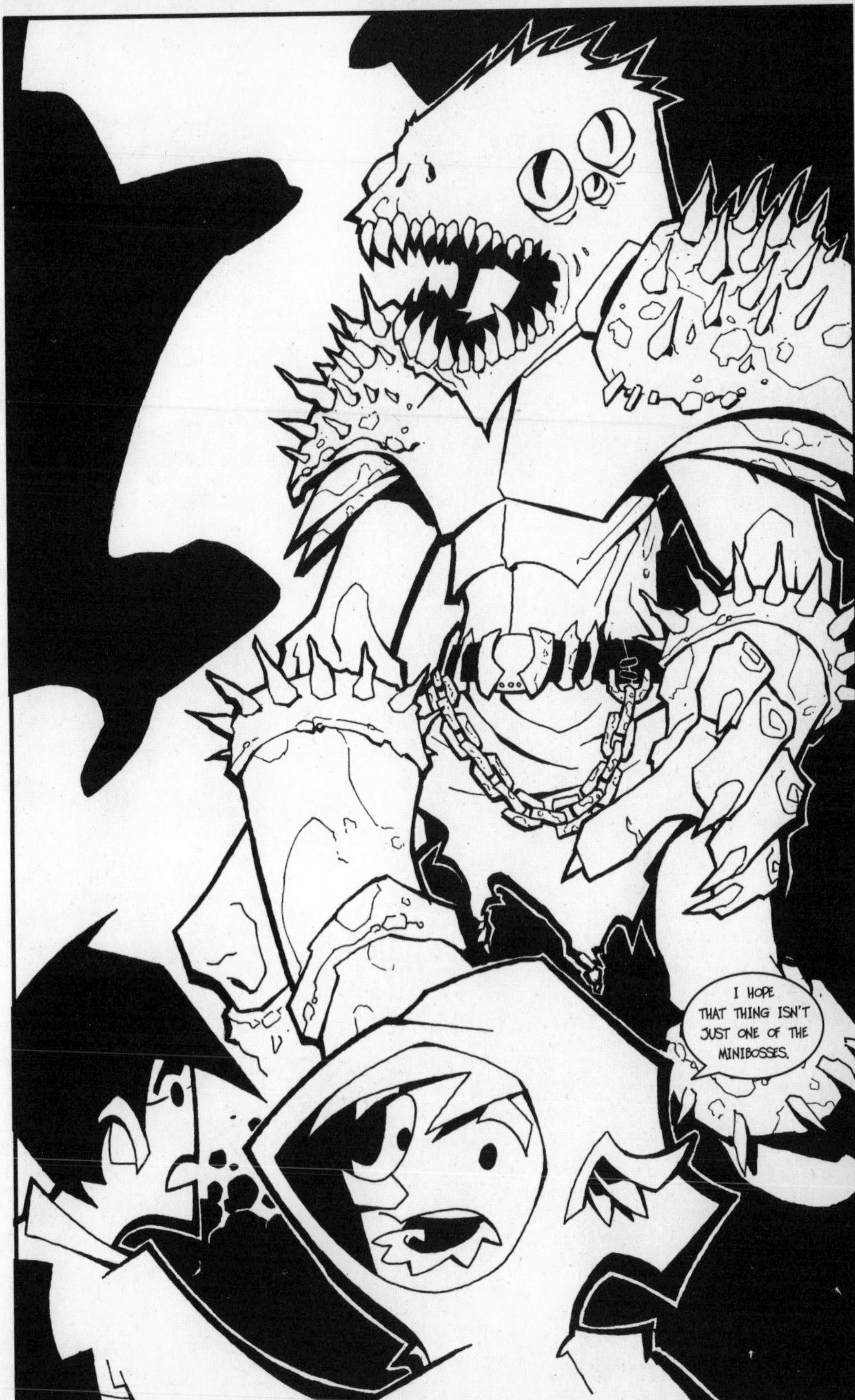
I HOPE THAT THING ISN'T JUST ONE OF THE MINIBOSSES.

END
part one

The Making of
PIRATE CLUB.

Summer 2001.

Although too old to really start a club, that's what my friends and I did. That summer was to be the last hurrah before we entered the reality of adulthood. To make sure we had the most awesome summer since those when we were kids, we started the Pirate Club. We went camping a few times a week, ate burgers at the Santa Queen (at which I bounced a check that ended up costing me $200), watched movies and drew pictures. It was an awesome summer and we were proud of the club, as well as our apparent lack of maturity; so proud, in fact that we wanted to make some T-shirts. Pirate Club t-shirts.

A few weeks after summer ended, I was on the phone at work, doodling on a sketch pad and I wrote out the Pirate Club logo that I wanted to put onto shirts. As soon as I saw that logo on paper, it threw my brain into a creative frenzy, I sketched out a few characters, some story ideas and before I knew it, I had all I needed to start a Pirate Club comic book. This was even better than t-shirts, I could capture the spirit of that summer in comic form. I set out to make a comic about kids. Kids having fun and kids screwing around, just like we always did. Every spare moment afterwards was spent on making the comic and after 3 months of planning, writing, drawing, and avoiding a social life, I held the first issue of Pirate Club in my hands. What a great feeling it was. To celebrate the achievement, my friends and I took a road trip to California, we were to attend Wondercon and try to sell the book to the masses. The convention was a blast, we met a lot of cool people and Pirate Club was met with great response, the most exciting was the attention that came my direction from Dan Vado, head honcho at Slave Labor Graphics. He dug the comic, and after a few sweaty handshakes and nervous mumbles I had somehow managed to get Pirate Club on the Slave Labor Graphics roster, huzzah!

Now that Pirate Club had a proper home, and I could ditch printing the book myself at Kinko's, I knew it was time to really kick the book into high gear. I spent the next few weeks developing the story I had intended to tell a bit further, and I knew I needed to spend a lot more time on the art chores of the book as well. What you hold in your hands is my first published work. What started out as a fun joke between friends, and a story to be enjoyed by few has turned into a work that I am very proud of. These first five issues really chronicle the first major growth I've had as an artist, and although it may seem rough around the edges, this book comes straight from the heart. I hope you enjoyed it, and that you will join me for volume two.

Thanks, friends!

Derek Hunter.

Pirate Club

First Logo Design. Dec. '02

I drew this while I was on the phone with the Provo City Police Department after my car was broken into. They caught the girl who did it, but she'd already sold most of my crap. At least I got my art supplies back.

First Designs of Phil and John. Dec. '02

Right from the first I knew this story would have a mentor to the club, and what better mentor for a pirate than one who has a hook-hand. I thought this design for Phil was a bit too gruff so I changed Phils design to what he is now...a cartoon version of my Dad. As for the Pirate Club members themselves, I needed them to look like normal kids with a little bit of flare.

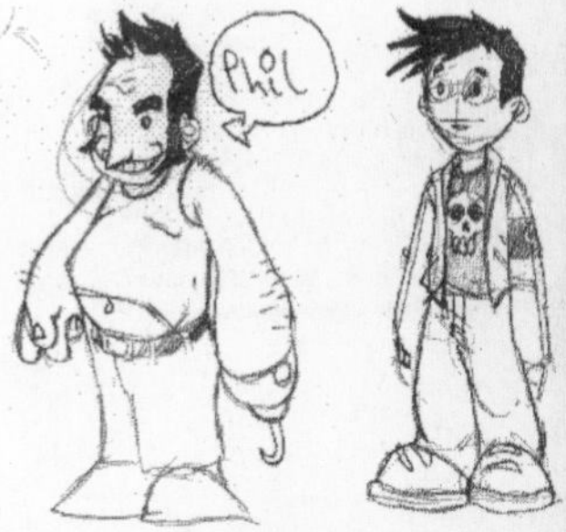
Phil

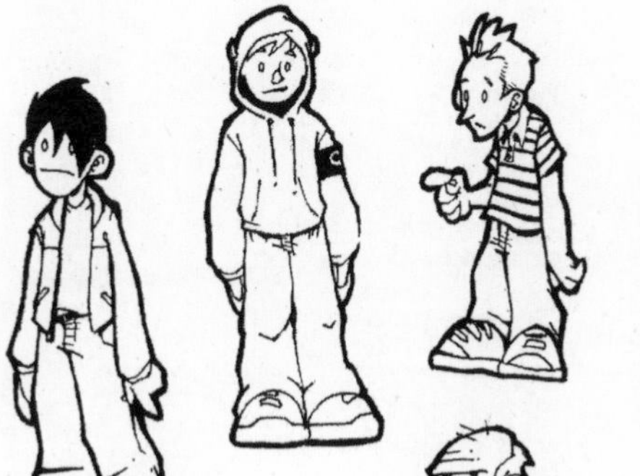
CITY WASTE

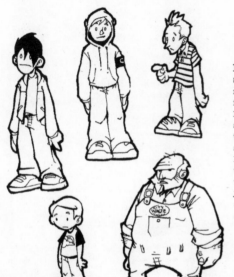

First "Final" Designs for the club and friends.

Since I figured I'd be drawing John and Bearclaw the most, I wanted to make them easier to draw. Johns hair is all black and Bearclaw wears a hood. The wings on Bearclaws hoodie are a nod to my friend Joe, who has similar wings on his hoodie. Mike has a striped shirt that he was to turn into a Pirate Headband later in the series. JJ changed a lot from this drawing cause he looked less like a nerd and more like a toddler. Adding the coke bottle glasses and knee high socks was all it took to transform him. As stated before, Phil is basically just my Dad. As for why I made him a garbage man...as a kid, I used to wish my Dad was a Garbage man instead of a Dentist. Dentistry is boring.

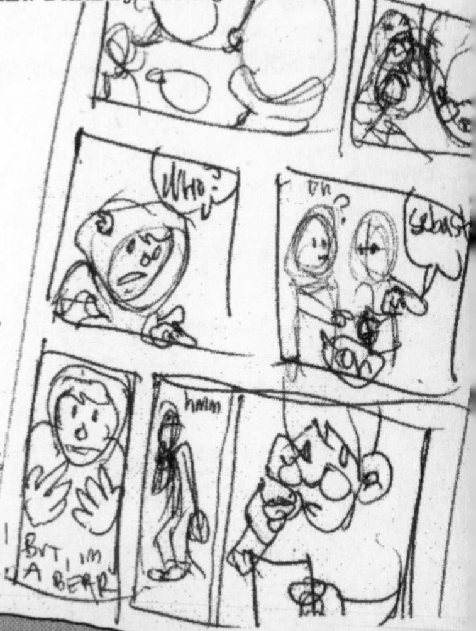
WHO?
hmm
BUT, IM A BEAR

Thumbnails from Issue 1

These are just some of the quick sketches I do to get a feel for the design of any given page. I didn't do these too much at the start of the series, but now I do 2 or 3 of them per page, a nice thumbnail helps to limit the amount of suckage per page.

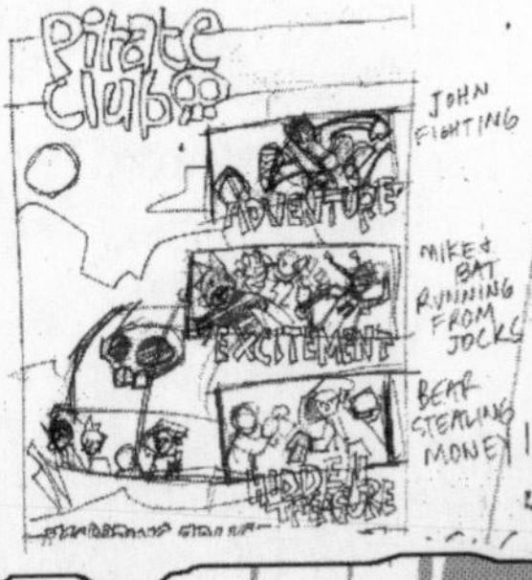
Pirate Club
JOHN FIGHTING
ADVENTURE
MIKE & BAT RUNNING FROM JOCKS
EXCITEMENT
BEAR STEALING MONEY

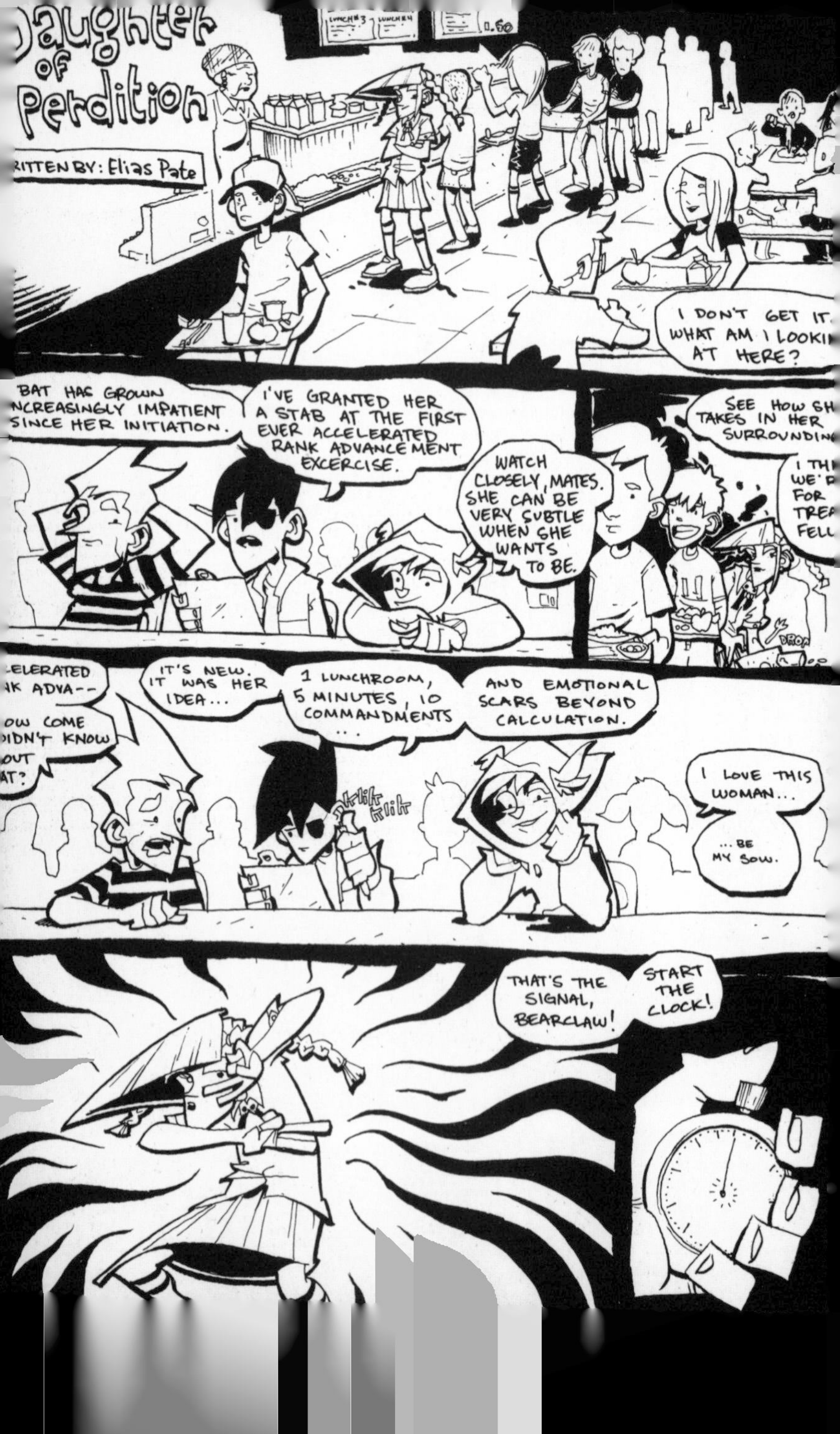
Daughter of Perdition
WRITTEN BY: Elias Pate
LUNCH #3
LUNCH #4
1.50
I DON'T GET IT. WHAT AM I LOOKIN AT HERE?
BAT HAS GROWN INCREASINGLY IMPATIENT SINCE HER INITIATION.
I'VE GRANTED HER A STAB AT THE FIRST EVER ACCELERATED RANK ADVANCEMENT EXCERCISE.
WATCH CLOSELY, MATES. SHE CAN BE VERY SUBTLE WHEN SHE WANTS TO BE.
SEE HOW SH TAKES IN HER SURROUNDIN
I TH WE'R FOR TREA FELL
CELERATED NK ADVA--
OW COME DIDN'T KNOW OUT AT?
IT'S NEW. IT WAS HER IDEA...
1 LUNCHROOM, 5 MINUTES, 10 COMMANDMENTS ...
AND EMOTIONAL SCARS BEYOND CALCULATION.
klik klik
I LOVE THIS WOMAN...
... BE MY SOW.
THAT'S THE SIGNAL, BEARCLAW!
START THE CLOCK!

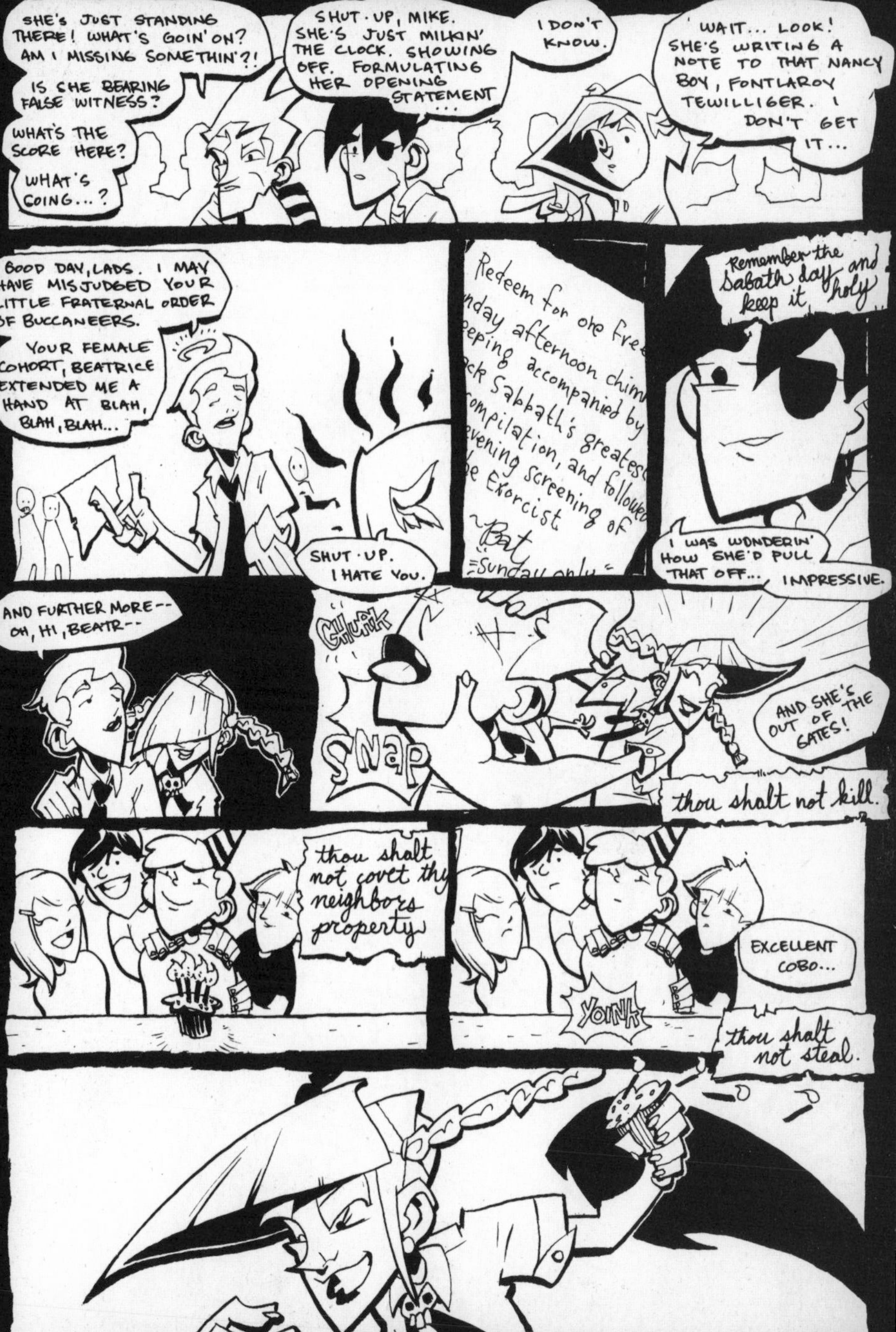
SHE'S JUST STANDING THERE! WHAT'S GOIN' ON? AM I MISSING SOMETHIN'?!
IS SHE BEARING FALSE WITNESS?
WHAT'S THE SCORE HERE?
WHAT'S GOING...?
SHUT·UP, MIKE. SHE'S JUST MILKIN' THE CLOCK. SHOWING OFF. FORMULATING HER OPENING STATEMENT...
I DON'T KNOW.
WAIT... LOOK! SHE'S WRITING A NOTE TO THAT NANCY BOY, FONTLAROY TEWILLIGER. I DON'T GET IT...
GOOD DAY, LADS. I MAY HAVE MISJUDGED YOUR LITTLE FRATERNAL ORDER OF BUCCANEERS.
YOUR FEMALE COHORT, BEATRICE EXTENDED ME A HAND AT BLAH, BLAH, BLAH...
SHUT·UP. I HATE YOU.
Redeem for one free Sunday afternoon chiming keeping accompanied by Black Sabbath's greatest compilation, and followed evening screening of The Exorcist ~Bat =Sunday only=
Remember the Sabath day and keep it holy
I WAS WONDERIN' HOW SHE'D PULL THAT OFF...
IMPRESSIVE.
AND FURTHER MORE-- OH, HI, BEATR--
CHUNK
SNAP
AND SHE'S OUT OF THE GATES!
thou shalt not kill.
thou shalt not covet thy neighbors property
YOINK
EXCELLENT COBO...
thou shalt not steal.

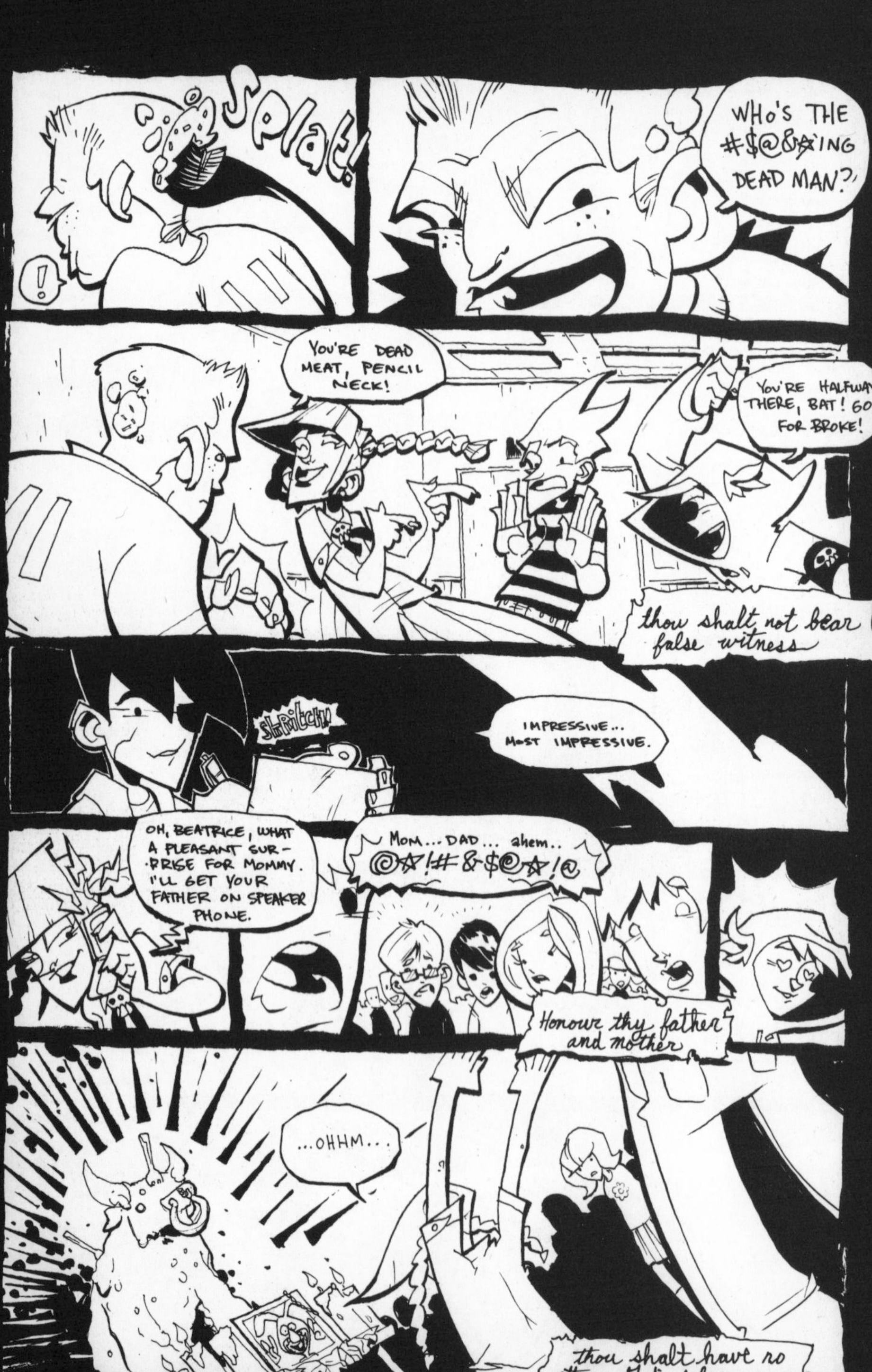
Splat!
!
WHO'S THE #$@&☆ING DEAD MAN?
YOU'RE DEAD MEAT, PENCIL NECK!
YOU'RE HALFWAY THERE, BAT! GO FOR BROKE!
thou shalt not bear false witness
IMPRESSIVE... MOST IMPRESSIVE.
OH, BEATRICE, WHAT A PLEASANT SUR-PRISE FOR MOMMY. I'LL GET YOUR FATHER ON SPEAKER PHONE.
MOM... DAD... ahem.. @☆!#&$@☆!@
Honour thy father and mother
...OHHM...
thou shalt have no other Gods before me.

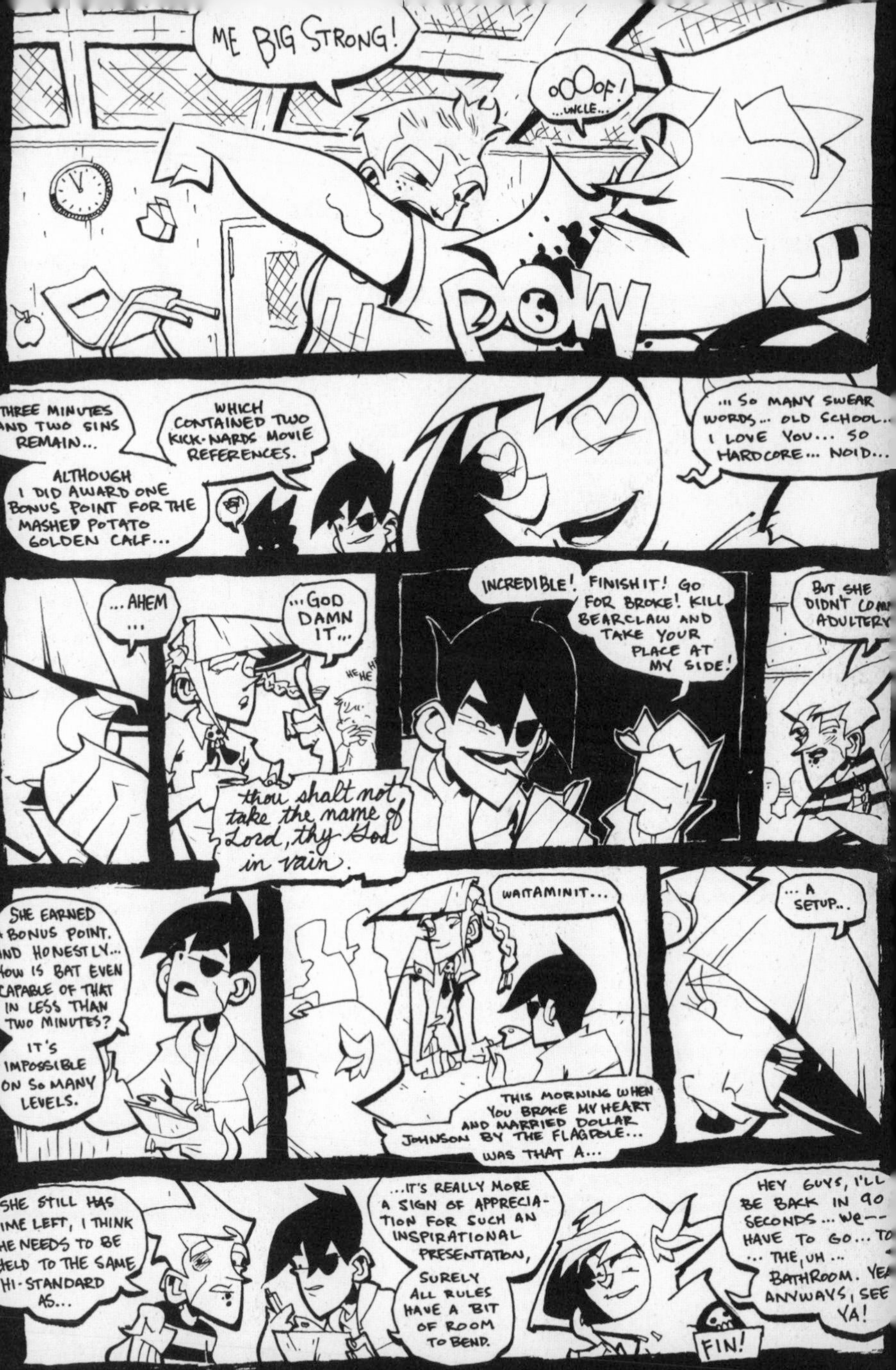

ME BIG STRONG!
oOOoF! ...UNCLE...
POW
THREE MINUTES AND TWO SINS REMAIN...
WHICH CONTAINED TWO KICK-NARDS MOVIE REFERENCES.
ALTHOUGH I DID AWARD ONE BONUS POINT FOR THE MASHED POTATO GOLDEN CALF...
... SO MANY SWEAR WORDS... OLD SCHOOL... I LOVE YOU... SO HARDCORE... NOID...
... AHEM ...
... GOD DAMN IT...
HE HE HE
thou shalt not take the name of Lord, thy God in vain.
INCREDIBLE! FINISH IT! GO FOR BROKE! KILL BEARCLAW AND TAKE YOUR PLACE AT MY SIDE!
BUT SHE DIDN'T COMM ADULTERY
SHE EARNED A BONUS POINT. AND HONESTLY... HOW IS BAT EVEN CAPABLE OF THAT IN LESS THAN TWO MINUTES?
IT'S IMPOSSIBLE ON SO MANY LEVELS.
WAITAMINIT...
THIS MORNING WHEN YOU BROKE MY HEART AND MARRIED DOLLAR JOHNSON BY THE FLAGPOLE... WAS THAT A...
... A SETUP...
SHE STILL HAS TIME LEFT, I THINK SHE NEEDS TO BE HELD TO THE SAME HI-STANDARD AS...
...IT'S REALLY MORE A SIGN OF APPRECIATION FOR SUCH AN INSPIRATIONAL PRESENTATION,
SURELY ALL RULES HAVE A BIT OF ROOM TO BEND.
HEY GUYS, I'LL BE BACK IN 90 SECONDS... WE-- HAVE TO GO... TO ... THE, UH ... BATHROOM. YEA ANYWAYS, SEE YA!
FIN!

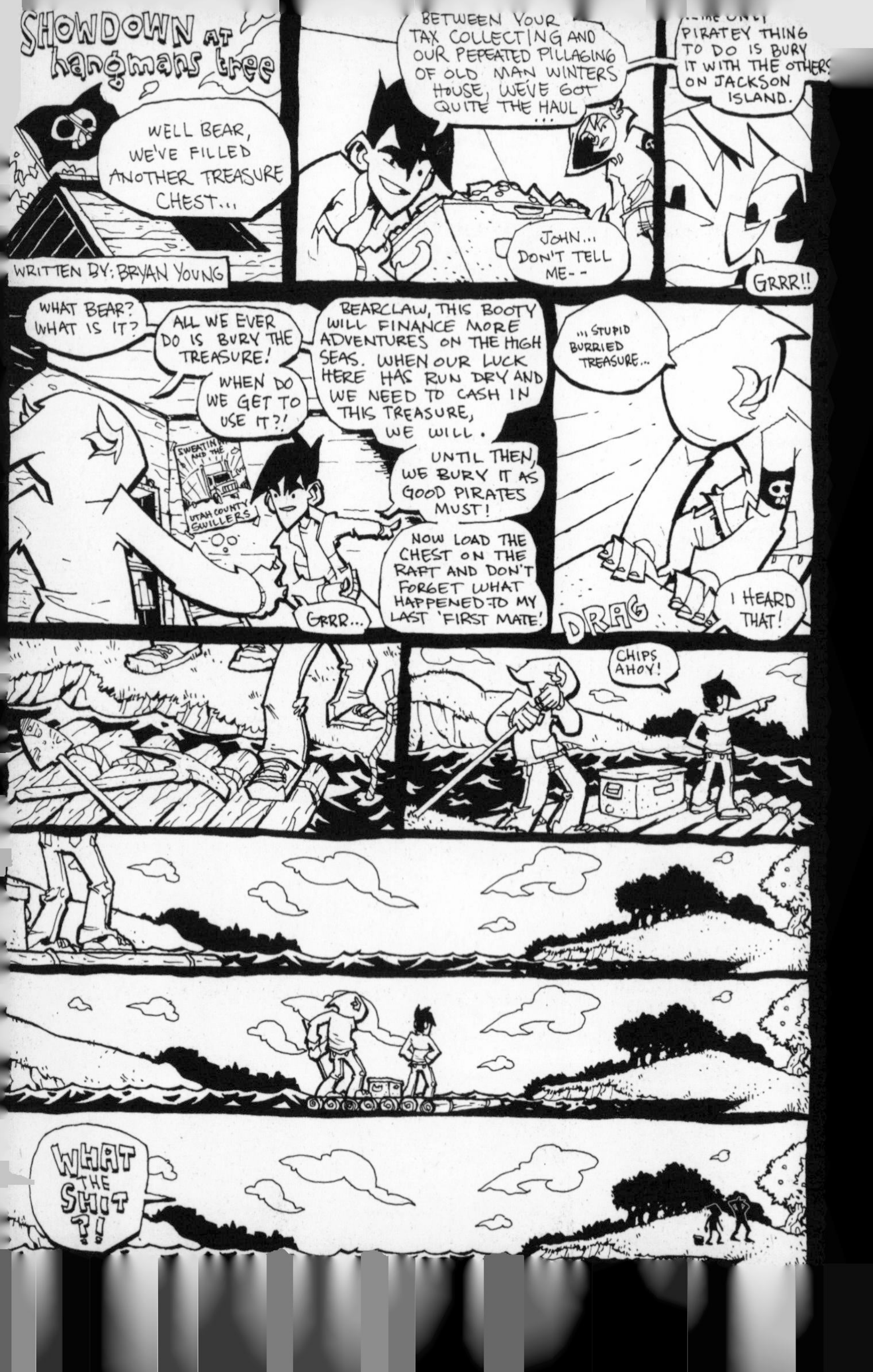
SHOWDOWN AT hangmans tree
WELL BEAR, WE'VE FILLED ANOTHER TREASURE CHEST...
WRITTEN BY: BRYAN YOUNG
BETWEEN YOUR TAX COLLECTING AND OUR PEPEATED PILLAGING OF OLD MAN WINTERS HOUSE, WE'VE GOT QUITE THE HAUL ...
JOHN... DON'T TELL ME--
PIRATEY THING TO DO IS BURY IT WITH THE OTHERS ON JACKSON ISLAND.
GRRR!!
WHAT BEAR? WHAT IS IT?
ALL WE EVER DO IS BURY THE TREASURE!
WHEN DO WE GET TO USE IT?!
BEARCLAW, THIS BOOTY WILL FINANCE MORE ADVENTURES ON THE HIGH SEAS. WHEN OUR LUCK HERE HAS RUN DRY AND WE NEED TO CASH IN THIS TREASURE, WE WILL.
UNTIL THEN, WE BURY IT AS GOOD PIRATES MUST!
NOW LOAD THE CHEST ON THE RAFT AND DON'T FORGET WHAT HAPPENED TO MY LAST 'FIRST MATE'!
GRRR...
UTAH COUNTY SWILLERS
...STUPID BURRIED TREASURE...
DRAG
I HEARD THAT!
CHIPS AHOY!
WHAT THE SHIT ?!

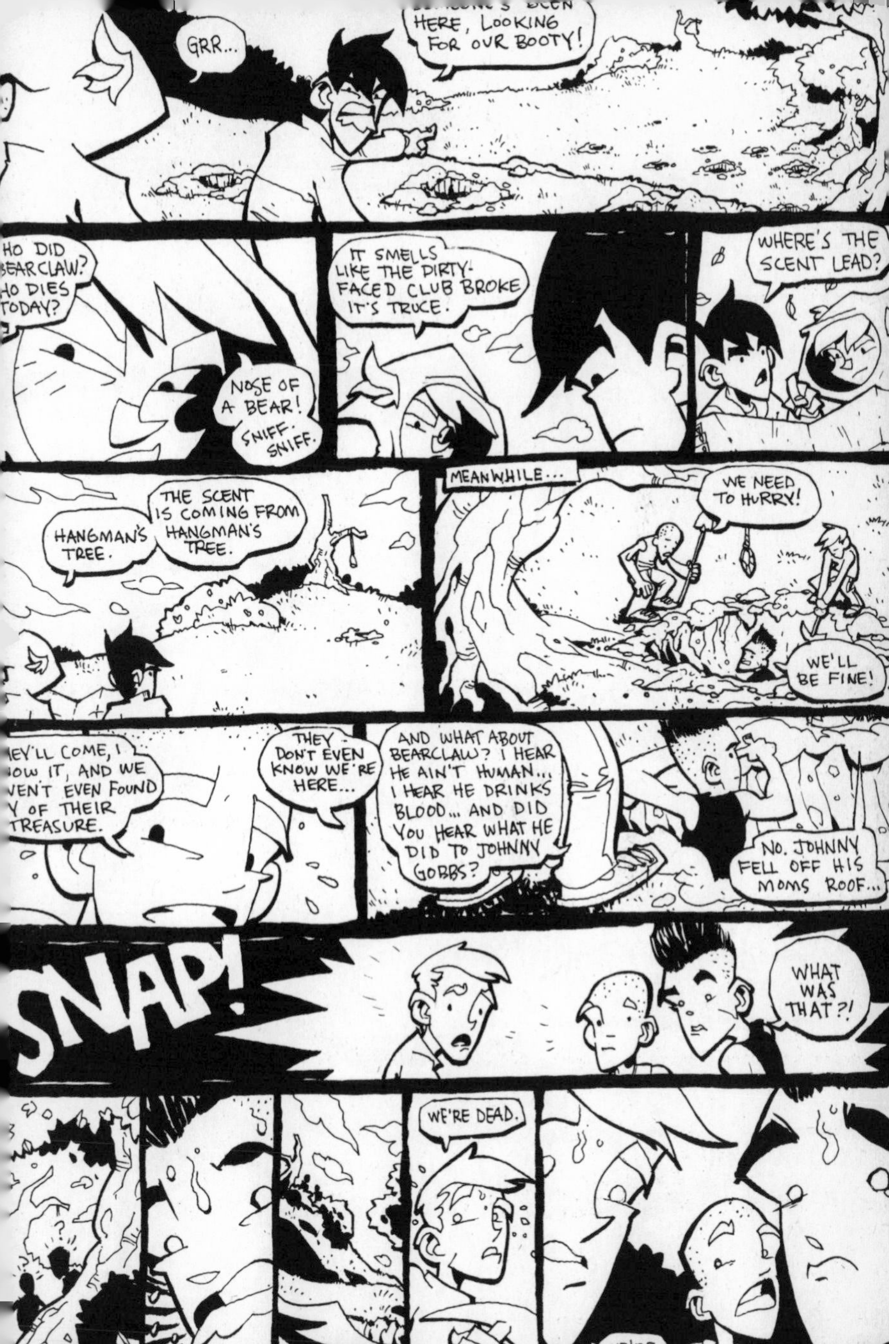

GRR...
HERE, LOOKING FOR OUR BOOTY!
HO DID BEARCLAW? HO DIES TODAY?
NOSE OF A BEAR! SNIFF. SNIFF.
IT SMELLS LIKE THE DIRTY-FACED CLUB BROKE IT'S TRUCE.
WHERE'S THE SCENT LEAD?
THE SCENT IS COMING FROM HANGMAN'S TREE.
HANGMAN'S TREE.
MEANWHILE...
WE NEED TO HURRY!
WE'LL BE FINE!
HEY'LL COME, I NOW IT, AND WE VEN'T EVEN FOUND Y OF THEIR TREASURE.
THEY DON'T EVEN KNOW WE'RE HERE...
AND WHAT ABOUT BEARCLAW? I HEAR HE AIN'T HUMAN... I HEAR HE DRINKS BLOOD... AND DID YOU HEAR WHAT HE DID TO JOHNNY GOBBS?
NO. JOHNNY FELL OFF HIS MOMS ROOF...
SNAP!
WHAT WAS THAT?!
WE'RE DEAD.
WE'RE DEAD MEN...

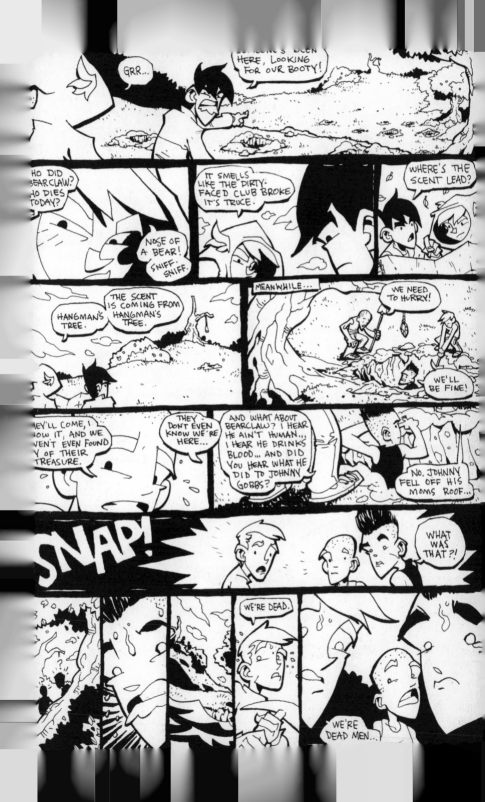

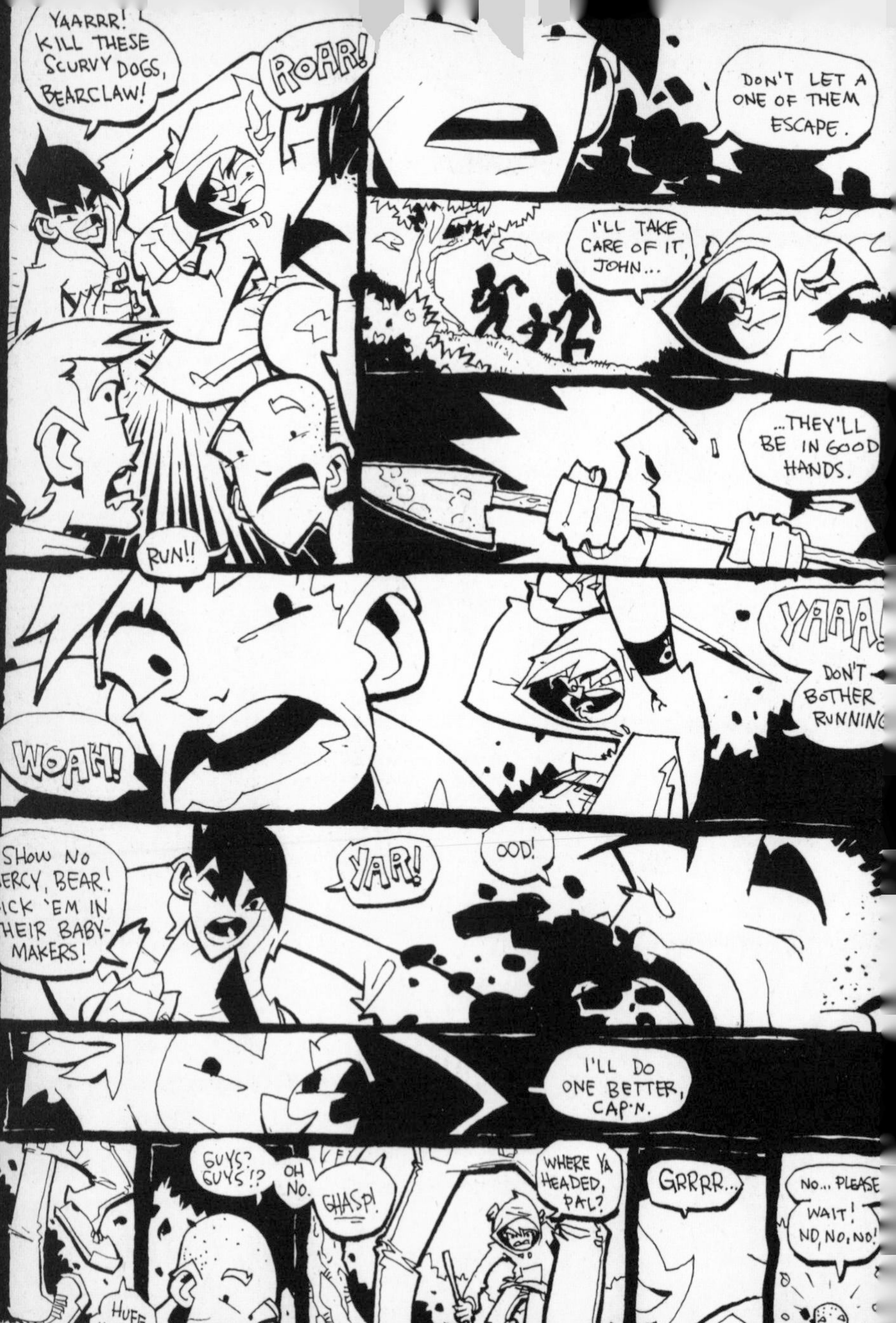
YAARRR! KILL THESE SCURVY DOGS, BEARCLAW!
ROAR!
DON'T LET A ONE OF THEM ESCAPE.
I'LL TAKE CARE OF IT, JOHN...
...THEY'LL BE IN GOOD HANDS.
RUN!!
YAAA!
DON'T BOTHER RUNNING
WOAH!
SHOW NO MERCY, BEAR! KICK 'EM IN THEIR BABY-MAKERS!
YAR!
OOD!
I'LL DO ONE BETTER, CAP'N.
GUYS? GUYS!?
OH NO.
GHASP!
HUFF HUFF.
WHERE YA HEADED, PAL?
GRRRR...
NO... PLEASE WAIT! NO, NO, NO!

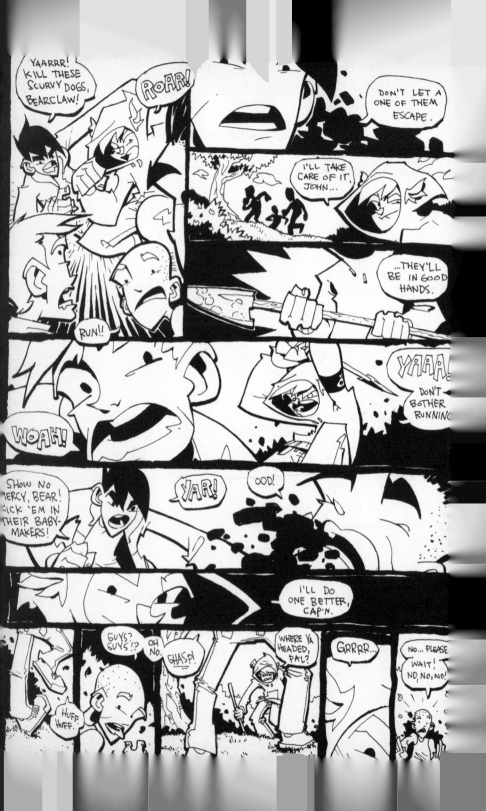

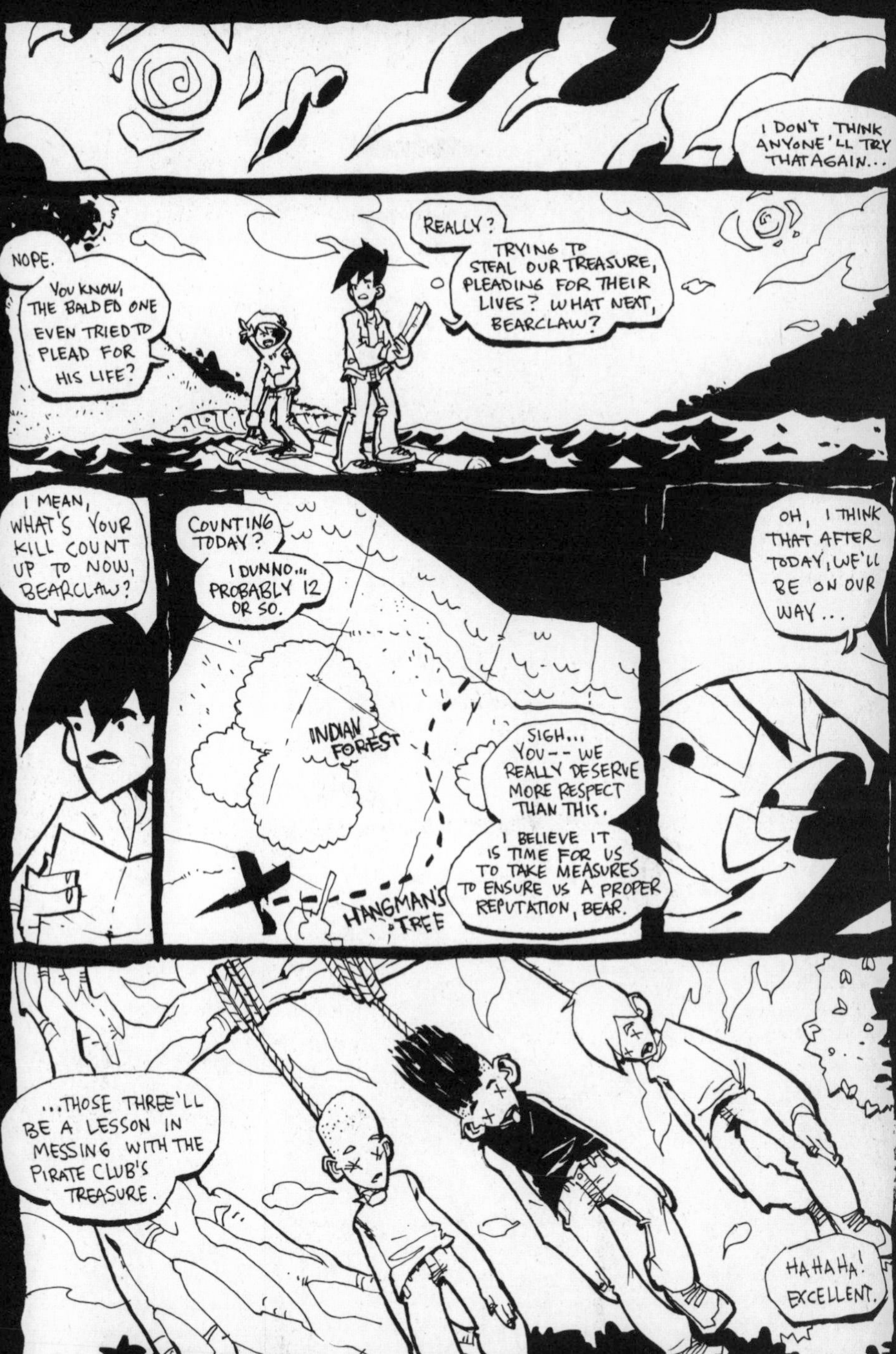
I DON'T THINK ANYONE'LL TRY THAT AGAIN...
NOPE.
YOU KNOW, THE BALDED ONE EVEN TRIED TO PLEAD FOR HIS LIFE?
REALLY?
TRYING TO STEAL OUR TREASURE, PLEADING FOR THEIR LIVES? WHAT NEXT, BEARCLAW?
I MEAN, WHAT'S YOUR KILL COUNT UP TO NOW, BEARCLAW?
COUNTING TODAY?
I DUNNO... PROBABLY 12 OR SO.
INDIAN FOREST
HANGMAN'S TREE
SIGH... YOU-- WE REALLY DESERVE MORE RESPECT THAN THIS.
I BELIEVE IT IS TIME FOR US TO TAKE MEASURES TO ENSURE US A PROPER REPUTATION, BEAR.
OH, I THINK THAT AFTER TODAY, WE'LL BE ON OUR WAY...
...THOSE THREE'LL BE A LESSON IN MESSING WITH THE PIRATE CLUB'S TREASURE.
HAHAHA! EXCELLENT.
THE END.

PIRATE CLUB: BRAINWASH ESCAPE VICTIMS. VOLUME ONE
CREATED BY: DEREK HUNTER
WRITTEN AND DRAWN BY: DEREK HUNTER
SUPPLEMENTARY COMIC MATERIAL WRITTEN BY: ELIAS PATE AND BRYAN YOUNG
SCRIPT ASSISTANCE: ELIAS PATE AND BRYAN YOUNG
BOOK DESIGN AND LAYOUT: DEREK HUNTER, RACHEL HUNTER AND BRYAN YOUNG

SLAVE LABOR GRAPHICS

DAN VADO: PRESIDENT
JENNIFER DE GUZMAN: EDITOR-IN-CHIEF
DEB MOSKYOK: DIRECTOR OF SALES

A VERY SPECIAL THANKS GOES OUT TO:
RACHEL KAY HUNTER
MY PARENTS AND SIX OLDER SISTERS, DAN VADO AND THE SLG CREW, ELIAS AND MICHELLE PATE, BRYAN YOUNG, SHANE
HILLMAN, SCOTT MORSE, KERRY JACKSON AND THE X96 GEEK SHOW, DAN JAMES, RYAN AND ERIN OTTLEY, JEREMY TREECE,
CHAD HURD, THE LAS VEGAS CHAPTER, MIMI AND NIGHT FLIGHT COMICS, ALL THE ARTISTS AT EATPOO.COM, LED HEAVY
FORUMS, BRYAN DOBROW, JOHN BUSH, JAKE BELL AND THE ARIZONA BOYS, DRESSED TO KILL SKATE CREW, JOE OLSON,
CHAD BOTT, THE SUCHC, ALAN TEW, MIKE MAY, MANFRED NEBER, GREG CORSO, JUICE AND JAVA OREM, RAVI SINGH, TODD
MEISTER AND JEN FEINBERG, KEVIN WATKINS, RYAN HOUCK, JEFF TORQUEMADA, ALL OF THE MEMBERS OF THE PIRATE CLUB,
AUTUMN SIMS, ADAM AND PAT, MARK ANDREW SMITH, FANBOY RADIO, THE GREAT RETAILERS THAT SUPPORT INDY BOOKS,
EVERYONE ELSE WHO GAVE THIS BOOK A CHANCE, AND YOU.

WWW.PIRATECLUB.COM   WWW.SLAVELABOR.COM

IRATE CLUB T-SHIRT!

A TERRIBLY AWESOME IMAGE PERSONA
SCREENPRINTED, BY YOUR CAPTAIN, ON
A BASEBALL JERSEY MAKES FOR A COO
SLICE OF CHILDHOOD MEMORIES.

NAVY BLUE PRINT ON A
NAVY BLUE/WHITE
3/4 SLEEVE JERSEY.

AVAILABLE SIZES:
YOUTH MED. - ADULT
(ADULT SMALL SOLD O

$15 (S&H INCLUDED)

Issues #1-5

Missed out on some of the action? don't worry! You can order all of the past issues right here!

$3.00 ppd ea.

Skid Marks #1

Collections of awesome short stories you can't live without. Including a new pirate club short.

$2.00 ppd ea.

Button Set

everyone will know you mean business when you show up with the pirate club on your lapel!

$3.00 ppd

HEY KIDS, ARE YOU READY TO JOIN UP WITH THE TOUGHEST GROUP OF HOOLIGANS THIS SIDE OF BLACKHAWK DELTA? NOW IS YOUR CHANCE TO BECOME A MEMBER OF THE PIRATE CLUB AND LIVE LIFE IN THE TRUE PIRATE STYLE!

Pirate Club Membership

$10 gets you...

- OFFICIAL PIRATE CLUB HANDBOOK
- PIRATE ARMBAND
  (send measurements)
- MEMBERSHIP CARD
- PIRATE CLUB PIN
- PIRATE CLUB STICKERS